SEASONS OF LIFE
TELECOURSE
STUDY GUIDE
FIFTH EDITION

by

Richard O. Straub
University of Michigan-Dearborn

Worth Publishers

Seasons of Life Telecourse Study Guide, Fifth Edition
by Richard O. Straub

This *Study Guide* is part of a full college course, which also includes five one-hour television programs; 26 half-hour audio programs; and **The Developing Person Through the Life Span**, Sixth Edition, by Kathleen Stassen Berger (Worth Publishers). For information about licensing the course, purchasing video and audiocassettes, or course print components, call 1-800-LEARNER, or write Annenberg/CPB Multimedia Collection, P.O. Box 2345, South Burlington, VT 05407.

Funding for **Seasons of Life** is provided by the Annenberg/CPB Project.

ISBN: 0-7167-6230-7 (EAN: 978971676300)

First printing 2004

Worth Publishers
41 Madison Avenue
New York, NY 10010

Contents

Preface

Seasons of Life is an introductory telecourse in life-span development—an exploration of the fascinating biological, social, and psychological changes that occur from the beginning of life to its end. In *Seasons of Life* you'll meet dozens of people in all stages of life and hear the views of nearly 50 leading social scientists.

Each of the twenty-six lessons of the telecourse consists of a thirty-minute audio program hosted by psychologist John Kotre; a chapter from *The Developing Person Through the Life Span*, Sixth Edition, by Kathleen Stassen Berger; and an assignment in this *Study Guide*.

Seasons of Life also features five one-hour television programs hosted by David Hartman, formerly of ABC's "Good Morning, America." Each program looks at a particular stage, or "season" of life. Program One introduces the "clocks" that influence biological, social, and psychological development throughout life and explores development during the first six years. Program Two covers development during childhood and adolescence (ages 6–20), and Program Three looks at early adulthood (ages 20–24). Program Four focuses on middle adulthood (ages 40–60) and Program Five concludes with late adulthood (ages 60+).

This *Study Guide* is designed to help you evaluate and enhance your understanding of the telecourse material. Your instructor will inform you of the lessons and assignments to be completed. At the end of the course you will be asked to complete a Television Term Project. The purpose of the project is to help you to integrate the material presented in the audio, video, and textbook components of the telecourse and to interpret your own experiences in view of what you have learned.

This *Study Guide* also includes a section, "How to Manage Your Time Efficiently and Study More Effectively" (page xi), which provides information on how to use the *Study Guide* for maximum benefit. It also offers additional study suggestions for time management, effective note-taking, evaluation of exam performance, and ways to improve your reading comprehension.

We are grateful to everyone who has contributed to this project. Special thanks go to our core group of advisors: Urie Bronfenbrenner of Cornell University, David Gutmann of Northwestern University, Bernice Neugarten of the University of Chicago, Anne Petersen of Penn State University, Alice Rossi of the University of Massachusetts–Amherst, and Sheldon White of Harvard University. Jack Mitchell of WHA at the University of Wisconsin provided much wise counsel regarding audio programming. Janet Whitaker of Rio Salado Community College was especially helpful in the design of our supplementary materials. Margie Moeller of WQED wrote excellent descriptions of the people in the television programs. Wilbert McKeachie and Elizabeth Douvan of the University of Michigan offered help close to home, and the staff of Worth Publishers supplied patience and professionalism. Major funding for *Seasons of Life* was provided by the Annenberg/CPB Project.

In preparing the materials that make up the *Seasons of Life* project, we were guided by a simple idea: that by examining the stories people tell about their lives, we can come to an understanding not only of these lives but of the life cycle itself, and of its "seasons." We hope your journey through the telecourse experience will be an enjoyable one and will provide you with information that enhances your insight into your own life story and those of others.

Richard O. Straub, Ph.D.
Professor of Psychology
University of Michigan–Dearborn

The Seasons of Life Study Guide

This study guide has many features that will help you study more effectively. Part I of this introduction describes these features. Part II provides suggestions that can help you to use your study time more effectively.

Part I FEATURES OF THIS STUDY GUIDE

THE LESSONS

Each Study Guide lesson consists of nine sections designed to help direct your study activities. After a while, you will discover which sections are the most helpful for you, and you can concentrate on them.

Orientation This section provides an overview of the lesson, highlighting important themes, placing facts in context, and integrating the audio program with the textbook. It also introduces the experts and stories that appear in each audio program and helps you relate its content to important ideas covered in other lessons.

Lesson Goals These goals—typically four or five for each lesson—identify the major themes of each lesson. They are drawn from both the textbook and the audio program.

Audio Assignment This section contains several specific questions drawn from the important facts and concepts covered in the lesson's audio program. Once you have finished listening to the program, try to answer the questions in your own words. Completing this section will help you to identify concepts you may need to review by replaying portions of the program.

Textbook Assignment This section contains a series of fill-in-the-blank questions drawn from important facts and concepts presented in the textbook chapter. Once you have finished reading the chapter, try to answer all the questions. Completing the questions will help you to identify those points you may need to review.

Testing Yourself This section consists of between 15 and 20 multiple-choice questions drawn from both the audio program and the textbook chapter. They should be answered only after you have listened to the program, read the chapter, and completed the audio and textbook assignments. Correct answers, along with explanations and text-book page references (as appropriate), are provid-ed at the end of the chapter. If you miss a question, read the explanation and, if you need to, review the appropriate text pages or portion of the audio program.

Exercise This section contains a short assignment that you are to complete and hand in to your instructor. The exercise will help you make mean-ingful connections between the lesson content and your own life story. In some cases the exercise involves gathering information from a relative or friend. In others, it is based on applying important lesson concepts to your own experiences.

Lesson Guidelines Organized into separate sec-tions for the audio program and the textbook, this section will help you to evaluate your answers to question in the "Audio Assignment" and "Textbook Assignment" sections of the Study Guide. Taken together, the items provide a sum-mary of the main points covered in the lesson.

Answers to Testing Yourself This section can be used to evaluate your performance on the ques-tions in the "Testing Yourself" section of the Study Guide. For each question, the correct answer is given, along with the question's source—whether material in the audio program or the text. For questions based on the text, page references are given where the answer can be found.

THE TELEVISION TERM PROJECT

The Television Term Project consists of 25 essay ques-tions designed to integrate the audio, video, and print components of the telecourse. The questions are divided into two categories. For each television pro-gram, there are four questions which should be answered soon after the program is viewed. For the entire series, there are five additional questions that cover major themes and help you to make meaningful connections between the telecourse and your own life experiences.

KEEPING TRACK

The following grid will help you keep track of your progress through the *Seasons of Life* telecourse. Your actual assignments, of course, will depend on your instructor.

Lesson	Exercise Score	Quiz Score
1		
2		
3		
4		
5		
6	————	————
7	————	————
8	————	————
9	————	————
10	————	————
11	————	————
12	————	————
13	————	————
14	————	————
15	————	————
16	————	————
17	————	————
18	————	————
19	————	————
20	————	————
21	————	————
22	————	————
23	————	————
24	————	————
25	————	————
26	————	————
Total	————	————
Average	————	————
Exercise average	————	————
Quiz average	————	————
Mid-term exam	————	————
Final exam	————	
Television term project	————	
Overall Average	————	
Final Grade	————	

Part II HOW TO MANAGE YOUR TIME EFFICIENTLY AND STUDY MORE EFFECTIVELY

Students who are new to college life or who are returning after a long absence may be unsure of their study skills. Suggestions for making the best use of your time and improving your skills may be found in the following section of the Study Guide. These suggestions will help you not only with *Seasons of Life*, but also with many of your other college courses.

How effectively do you study? Good study habits make the job of being a college student much easier. Many students, who could succeed in college, fail or drop out because they have never learned to manage their time efficiently. Even the best students can usually benefit from an in-depth evaluation of their current study habits.

There are many ways to achieve academic success, of course, but your approach may not be the most effective or efficient. Are you sacrificing your social life or your physical or mental health in order to get A's on your exams? Good study habits result in better grades *and* more time for other activities.

EVALUATE YOUR CURRENT STUDY HABITS

To improve your study habits, you must first have an accurate picture of how you currently spend your time. Begin by putting together a profile of your present living and studying habits. Answer the following questions by writing "yes" or "no" on each line.

_____ 1. Do you usually set up a schedule to budget your time for studying, recreation, and other activities?

_____ 2. Do you often put off studying until time pressures force you to cram?

_____ 3. Do other students seem to study less than you do, but get better grades?

_____ 4. Do you usually spend hours at a time studying one subject, rather than dividing that time between several subjects?

_____ 5. Do you often have trouble remembering what you have just read in a textbook?

_____ 6. Before reading a chapter in a textbook, do you skim through it and read the section headings?

_____ 7. Do you try to predict exam questions from your lecture notes and reading?

_____ 8. Do you usually attempt to paraphrase or summarize what you have just finished reading?

_____ 9. Do you find it difficult to concentrate very long when you study?

_____ 10. Do you often feel that you studied the wrong material for an exam?

Thousands of college students have participated in similar surveys. Students who are fully realizing their academic potential usually respond as follows: (1) yes, (2) no, (3) no, (4) no, (5) no, (6) yes, (7) yes, (8) yes, (9) no, (10) no.

Compare your responses with those of successful students. The greater the discrepancy, the more you could benefit from a program to improve your study habits. The questions are designed to identify areas of weakness. Once you have identified your weaknesses, you will be able to set specific goals for improvement and implement a program for reaching them.

MANAGE YOUR TIME

Do you often feel frustrated because there isn't enough time to do all the things you must and want to do? Take heart. Even the most productive and successful people feel this way at times. But they establish priorities for their activities and they learn to budget time for each of them. There's much in the saying, "If you want something done, ask a busy person to do it." A busy person knows how to get things done.

If you don't now have a system for budgeting your time, develop one. Not only will your academic accomplishments increase, but you will actually find more time in your schedule for other activities. And you won't have to feel guilty about "taking time off," because all your obligations will be covered.

Establish a Baseline

As a first step in preparing to budget your time, keep a diary for a few days to establish a summary, or baseline, of the time you spend in studying, socializing, working, and so on. If you are like many students, much of your "study" time is nonproductive; you may sit at your desk and leaf through a book, but the time is actually wasted. Or you may procrastinate. You are always getting ready to study, but you rarely do.

Table 1   Sample Time-Management Diary

Monday		
Activity	Time Completed	Duration Hours: Minutes
Sleep	7:00	7:30
Dressing	7:25	:25
Breakfast	7:45	:20
Commute	8:20	:35
Coffee	9:00	:40
French	10:00	1:00
Socialize	10:15	:15
Videogame	10:35	:20
Coffee	11:00	:25
Psychology	12:00	1:00
Lunch	12:25	:25
Study Lab	1:00	:35
Psych. Lab	4:00	3:00
Work	5:30	1:30
Commute	6:10	:40
Dinner	6:45	:35
TV	7:30	:45
Study Psych.	10:00	2:30
Socialize	11:30	1:30
Sleep		

Prepare a similar chart for each day of the week. When you finish an activity, note it on the chart and write down the time it was completed. Then determine its duration by subtracting the time the previous activity was finished from the newly entered time.

Besides revealing where you waste time, your diary will give you a realistic picture of how much time you need to allot for meals, commuting, and other fixed activities. In addition, careful rec-ords should indicate the times of the day when you are consistently most productive. A sample time-management diary is shown in Table 1.

Plan the Term

Having established and evaluated your baseline, you are ready to devise a more efficient schedule. Buy a calendar that covers the entire school term and has ample space for each day. Using the course outlines provided by your instructors, enter the dates of all exams, term paper deadlines, and other important academic obligations. If you have any long-range personal plans (concerts, weekend trips, etc.), enter the dates on the calendar as well. Keep your calendar up to date and refer to it often. I recommend carrying it with you at all times.

Develop a Weekly Calendar

Now that you have a general picture of the school term, develop a weekly schedule that includes all of your activities. Aim for a schedule that you can live with for the entire school term. A sample weekly schedule, incorporating the following guidelines, is shown in Table 2.

1. Enter your class times, work hours, and any other fixed obligations first. *Be thorough.* Using information from your time-management diary, allow plenty of time for such things as commuting, meals, laundry, and the like.

2. Set up a study schedule for each of your courses. The study habits survey and your time-management diary will direct you. The following guidelines should also be useful.

   a. Establish regular study times for each course. The 4 hours needed to study one subject, for example, are most profitable when divided into shorter periods spaced over several days. If you cram your studying into one 4-hour block, what you attempt to learn in the third or fourth hour will interfere with what you studied in the first 2 hours. Newly acquired knowledge is like wet cement. It needs some time to "harden" to become fixed in your memory.

   b. Alternate subjects. The type of interference just mentioned is greatest between similar topics. Set up a schedule in which you spend time on several *different* courses during each study session. Besides reducing the potential for interference, alternating subjects will help to prevent mental fatigue with one topic.

   c. Set weekly goals to determine the amount of study time you need to do well in each course. This will depend on, among other things, the difficulty of your courses and the effectiveness of your methods. Many professors recommend studying at least 1 to 2 hours for each hour in class. If your time-management diary indicates that you presently study less time than that, do not plan to jump immediately to a much higher level. Increase study time from your baseline by setting weekly goals [see (4)] that will gradually bring you up to the desired level. As an initial schedule, for example, you might set aside an amount of study time for each course that matches class time.

Table 2   Sample Weekly Schedule

Time	Mon.	Tues.	Wed.	Thurs.	Fri.	Sat.
7–8	Dress Eat	Dress Eat	Dress Eat	Dress Eat	Dress Eat	
8–9	Psych.	Study Psych.	Psych.	Study Psych.	Psych.	Dress Eat
9–10	Eng.	Study Eng.	Eng.	Study Eng.	Eng.	Study Eng.
10–11	Study French	Free	Study French	Open Study	Study French	Study Stats.
11–12	French	Study Psych. Lab	French	Open Study	French	Study Stats.
12–1	Lunch	Lunch	Lunch	Lunch	Lunch	Lunch
1–2	Stats.	Psych. Lab	Stats.	Study or Free	Stats.	Free
2–3	Bio.	Psych. Lab	Bio.	Free	Bio.	Free
3–4	Free	Psych.	Free	Free	Free	Free
4–5	Job	Job	Job	Job	Job	Free
5–6	Job	Job	Job	Job	Job	Free
6–7	Dinner	Dinner	Dinner	Dinner	Dinner	Dinner
7–8	Study Bio.	Study Bio.	Study Bio.	Study Bio.	Free	Free
8–9	Study Eng.	Study Stats.	Study Psych.	Open Study	Open Study	Free
9–10	Open Study	Open Study	Open Study	Open Study	Free	Free

This is a sample schedule for a student with a 16-credit load and a 10-hour-per-week part-time job. Using this chart as an illustration, make up a weekly schedule, following the guidelines outlined here.

d. Schedule for maximum effectiveness. Tailor your schedule to meet the demands of each course. For the course that emphasizes lecture notes, schedule time for a daily review soon after the class. This will give you a chance to revise your notes and clean up any hard-to-decipher shorthand while the material is still fresh in your mind. If you are evaluated for class participation (for example, in a language course), allow time for a review just *before* the class meets. Schedule study time for your most difficult (or least motivating) courses during hours when you are the most alert and distractions are fewest.

e. Schedule open study time. Emergencies, additional obligations, and the like could throw off your schedule. And you may simply need some extra time periodically for a project or for review in one of your courses. Schedule several hours each week for such purposes.

3. After you have budgeted time for studying, fill in slots for recreation, hobbies, relaxation, household errands, and the like.

4. Set specific goals. Before each study session, make a list of specific goals. The simple note "7–8 PM.: study psychology" is too broad to ensure the most effective use of the time. Formulate your daily goals according to what you know you must accomplish during the term. If you have course outlines with advance assignments, set systematic daily goals that will allow you, for example, to cover fifteen chapters before the exam. And be realistic: Can you actually expect to cover a 78-page chapter in one session? Divide large tasks into smaller units; stop at the most logical resting points. When you complete a specific goal, take a 5- or 10-minute break before tackling the next goal.

5. Evaluate how successful or unsuccessful your studying has been on a daily or weekly basis. Did you reach most of your goals? If so, reward yourself immediately. You might even make a list of five to ten rewards to choose from. If you have trouble studying regularly, you may be able to motivate yourself by making such rewards contingent on completing specific goals.

6. Finally, until you have lived with your schedule for several weeks, don't hesitate to revise it. You may need to allow more time for chemistry, for example, and less for some other course. If you are trying to study regularly for the first time and are feeling burned-out, you probably have set your initial goals too high. Don't let failure cause you to despair and abandon the program. Accept your limitations and revise your schedule so that you are studying only 15 to 20 minutes more each evening than you are used to. The point is to *identify a regular schedule with which you can achieve some success.* Time management, like any skill, must be practiced to become effective.

TECHNIQUES FOR EFFECTIVE STUDY

Knowing how to put study time to best use is, of course, as important as finding a place for it in your schedule. Here are some suggestions that should enable you to increase your reading comprehension and improve your note-taking. A few study tips are included as well.

Using SQ3R to Increase Reading Comprehension

How do you study from a textbook? If you are like many students, you simply read and reread in a passive manner. Studies have shown, however, that most students who simply read a textbook cannot remember more than half the material ten minutes after they have finished. Often, what is retained is the unessential material rather than the important points upon which exam questions will be based.

This Study Guide employs a program known as SQ3R (Survey, Question, Read, Recite, and Review) to facilitate, and allow you to assess, your comprehension of the important facts and concepts in the *Seasons of Life* telecourse. It will help you to integrate material from the audio and television programs with that in Kathleen Stassen Berger's text, *The Developing Person Through the Life Span*, 6/e.

Research has shown that students using SQ3R achieve significantly greater comprehension of textbooks than students reading in the more traditional passive manner. Once you have learned this program, you can improve your comprehension of any textbook.

Survey   Before reading a chapter, determine whether the text or the Study Guide has an outline or list of objectives. Read this material and the summary at the end of the chapter. Next, read the textbook chapter fairly quickly, paying special attention to the major headings and subheadings. This survey will give you an idea of the chapter's content and organization. You will then be able to divide the chapter into logical sections in order to formulate specific goals for a more careful reading of the chapter.

In this Study Guide, the "Orientation" summarizes the major topics of the audio program and the textbook chapter. This section also provides a few suggestions for approaching topics you may find difficult.

Question   You will retain material longer when you have a use for it. If you look up a word's definition in order to solve a crossword puzzle, for example, you will remember it longer than if you merely fill in the letters as a result of putting other words in. Surveying the chapter will allow you to generate important questions that the chapter will proceed to answer. These questions correspond to "mental files" into which knowledge will be sorted for easy access.

As you survey, jot down several questions for each chapter section. One simple technique is to generate questions by rephrasing a section heading. For example, the "Preoperational Thought" head could be turned into "What is preoperational thought?" Good questions will allow you to focus on the important points in the text. Examples of good questions are those that begin as follows: "List two examples of" "What is the function of?" "What is the significance of?" Such questions give a purpose to your reading. The audio assignment questions in this Study Guide can be used for this purpose. Similarly, you can formulate questions based on the chapter outline.

Read   When you have established "files" for each section of the chapter, review your first question, begin reading, and continue until you have discovered its answer. If you come to material that seems to answer an important question you don't have a file for, stop and write down the question.

Be sure to read everything. Don't skip photo or art captions, graphs, or marginal notes. In some cases, what may seem vague in reading will be made clear by a simple graph. Keep in mind that test questions are sometimes drawn from illustrations and charts.

Recite When you have found the answer to a question, close your eyes and mentally recite the question and its answer. Then *write* the answer next to the question. It is important that you recite an answer in your own words rather than the author's. Don't rely on your short-term memory to repeat the author's words verbatim.

In responding to the questions, pay close attention to what is called for. If you are asked to identify or list, do just that. If asked to compare, contrast, or do both, you should focus on the similarities (compare) and differences (contrast) between the concepts or theories. Answering the questions carefully will not only help you to focus your attention on the important concepts of the audio program, but it will also provide excellent practice for essay exams. For the textbook assignment, after completing all the questions on a topic you should try to summarize the material in your own words.

Recitation is an extremely effective study technique, recommended by many learning experts. In addition to increasing reading comprehension, it is useful for review. Trying to explain something in your own words clarifies your knowledge, often by revealing aspects of your answer that are vague or incomplete. If you repeatedly rely upon "I know" in recitation, you really *may not know.*

Recitation has the additional advantage of simulating an exam, especially an essay exam; the same skills are required in both cases. Too often students study without ever putting the book and notes aside, which makes it easy for them to develop false confidence in their knowledge. When the material is in front of you, you may be able to *recognize* an answer, but will you be able to *recall* it later, when you take an exam that does not provide these retrieval cues?

After you have recited and written your answer, continue with your next question. Read, recite, and so on.

Review When you have answered the last question on the material you have designated as a study goal, go back and review. Read over each question and your written answer to it. Your review might also include a brief written summary that integrates all of your questions and answers. This review need not take longer than a few minutes, but it is important. It will help you retain the material longer and will greatly facilitate a final review of each chapter before the exam.

An excellent way to review your understanding of the chapters of *The Developing Person Through the Life Span, 5/e*, is to complete the "Key Questions" at the end of each textbook chapter. Then go through the "Lesson Guidelines" section of this Study Guide. You may be surprised to discover that you didn't know the chapter as well as you thought you did!

Also provided to facilitate your review are multiple-choice questions in the "Testing Yourself" section of the Study Guide. These questions cover both audio program and textbook content and should *not* be answered until you have listened to the program, read the chapter, and completed the audio and textbook assignments in the Study Guide. Correct answers, along with explanations of why each alternative is correct or incorrect, are provided at the end of the chapter. The relevant text page numbers for each question are also given. If you miss a question, read these explanations and, if you need to, review the text pages to further understand why. The questions do not test every aspect of a concept, so you should treat an incorrect answer as an indication that you need to review the concept.

One final suggestion: Incorporate SQ3R into your time-management calendar. Set specific goals for completing SQ3R with each assigned chapter. Keep a record of chapters completed, and reward yourself for being conscientious. Initially, it takes more time and effort to "read" using SQ3R, but with practice, the steps will become automatic. More important, you will comprehend significantly more material and retain what you have learned longer than passive readers do.

Listening to the Audio Programs

Using audio tapes and television programs for learning requires much more active attention to their content than when these media are used simply for entertainment.

In following the steps outlined in each Study Guide lesson, you will gain the most from each program by applying the SQ3R method to your audio tape listening. You will find it helpful to read the lesson orientation, lesson goals, and audio review questions before listening to the program. You may choose to listen to the entire program first and then answer the questions, replaying portions of the program as necessary. Or you may find it works better for you to answer the questions as you go along, stopping the tape as necessary. Soon after listening to the program, you should compare your answers with material in the "Lesson Guidelines" section of the Study Guide. Make sure that you have a good grasp of the answer to each audio question before you continue with the lesson.

Watching the Television Programs

The five television programs illustrate many of the facts and concepts of the course. They may be viewed any time during the semester and perhaps more than once. Before watching each program, you will find it helpful to read the program synopsis and story descriptions which appear in the Television Term Project chapter at the end of the Study Guide. To help focus your viewing on important series and program themes, you also should review the four essay questions that follow the story descriptions for each program.

Evaluating Your Exam Performance

How often have you received a grade on an exam that did not do justice to the effort you spent preparing for the exam? This is a common experience that can leave one feeling bewildered and abused. "What do I have to do to get an A?" "The test was unfair!" "I studied the wrong material!"

The chances of this happening are greatly reduced if you have an effective time-management schedule and use the study techniques described here. But it can happen, even to the best-prepared student. It is most likely to occur on your first exam in a new course.

Remember that there are two main reasons for studying. One is to learn for your own general academic development. Many people believe that such knowledge is all that really matters. Of course it is possible, though unlikely, to be an expert on a topic without achieving commensurate grades, just as one can, occasionally, earn an excellent grade without truly mastering the course material. During a job interview or in the workplace, however, your A in Java won't mean much if you can't actually program a computer.

In order to keep career options open after you graduate, you must both know the material *and* maintain competitive grades. In the short run, this means performing well on exams, which is the second main objective in studying.

Probably the single best piece of advice to keep in mind when studying for exams is to *try to predict exam questions*. This means ignoring the trivia and focusing on the important questions and their answers (with your instructor's emphasis in mind).

A second point is obvious. How well you do on exams is determined by your mastery of *both* lecture (or, in this case, audio tape) and textbook material. Many students (partly because of poor time management) concentrate too much on one at the expense of the other.

To evaluate how well you are learning the audio tape and textbook material, analyze the questions you missed on the first exam. Divide the questions into two categories, those drawn primarily from the audio tapes and those drawn primarily from the textbook. Determine the percentage of questions you missed in each category. If your errors are evenly distributed and you are satisfied with your grade, you have no problem. If you are weaker in one area, you will need to set goals for increasing and/or improving your study of that area.

Similarly, note the percentage of test questions drawn from each category. While your instructor may not be entirely consistent in making up future exams, you may be able to tailor your studying by placing *additional* emphasis on the appropriate area.

Exam evaluation will also point out the types of questions your instructor prefers. Does the exam consist primarily of
multiple-choice or essay questions? You may also discover that an instructor is fond of wording questions in certain ways. For example, an instructor may rely heavily on questions that require you to draw an analogy between a theory or concept and a real-world example. Evaluate both your instructor's style and how well you do with each format. Use this information to guide your future exam preparation.

Important aids, not only in studying for exams but also in determining how well prepared you are, are the "Testing Yourself" sections of the Study Guide. If these tests don't include all of the types of questions your instructor typically writes, make up your own practice exam questions. Spend extra time testing yourself with question formats that are most difficult for you. There is no better way to evaluate your preparatin for an upcoming exam than by testing yourself under the conditions most likely to be in effect during the actual test.

A FEW PRACTICAL TIPS

Even the best intentions for studying sometimes fail. Some of these failures occur because students attempt to work under conditions that are simply not conducive to concentrated study. To help ensure the success of your time-management program, here are a few suggestions that should assist you in reducing the possibility of procrastination or distraction.

1. If you have set up a schedule for studying, make your roommate, family, and friends aware of this commitment, and ask them to honor your quiet study time. Close your door and post a "Do Not Disturb" sign.

2. Set up a place to study that minimizes potential distractions. Use a desk or table, not your bed or

an extremely comfortable chair. Keep your desk and the walls around it free from clutter. If you need a place other than your room, find one that meets as many of the above requirements as possible—for example, in the library stacks.

3. Do nothing but study in this place. It should become associated with studying so that it "triggers" this activity, just as a mouth-watering aroma elicits an appetite.

4. Never study with the television on or with other distracting noises present. If you must have music in the background in order to mask outside noise, for example, play soft instrumental music. Don't pick vocal selections; your mind will be drawn to the lyrics.

5. Study by yourself. Other students can be distracting or can break the pace at which *your* learning is most efficient. In addition, there is always the possibility that group studying will become a social gathering. Reserve that for its own place in your schedule.

If you continue to have difficulty concentrating for very long, try the following suggestions.

6. Study your most difficult or most challenging subjects first, when you are most alert.

7. Start with relatively short periods of concentrated study, with breaks in between. If your attention starts to wander, get up immediately and take a break. It is better to study effectively for 15 minutes and then take a break than to fritter away 45 minutes out of an hour. Gradually increase the length of study periods, using your attention span as an indicator of successful pacing.

SOME CLOSING THOUGHTS

I hope that these suggestions help make you more successful academically, and that they enhance the quality of your college life in general. Having the necessary skills makes any job a lot easier and more pleasant. Let me repeat my warning not to attempt to make too drastic a change in your lifestyle immediately. Good habits require time and self-discipline to develop. Once established they can last a lifetime.

Introduction

ORIENTATION

Developmental psychology is concerned with how people change as they grow older and how they remain the same. According to the **life-span perspective**, development is a lifelong process. Far from believing that our fates are sealed by the end of childhood, as some earlier theorists proposed, experts today believe that development continues throughout the life span and is unpredictable. The message is simple: you cannot tell how a life story will end just by knowing how it began.

Lesson 1 of the *Seasons of Life* series introduces the three **developmental clocks** that govern our progress through the seasons of life. The **biological clock** is a metaphor for the body's way of timing its physical development. The **social clock** reflects society's age norms for when certain life events should occur. The **psychological clock** represents each person's inner timetable for development.

In Chapter 1 of *The Developing Person Through the Life Span,* 6/e, Kathleen Berger defines development, introduces the life-span perspective, identifies five characteristics of the scientific study of human development, and explains different aspects of the overlapping contexts in which people develop. The story of David illustrates the effects of these contexts.

The next two sections discuss the strategies developmentalists use in their research, beginning with the scientific method and including scientific observation, correlational research, experiments, surveys, and case studies. To study people over time, developmentalists have created several research designs: cross-sectional, longitudinal, and cross-sequential. The ecological-systems approach—Bronfenbrenner's description of how the individual is affected by, and affects, many other individuals, groups of individuals, and larger systems in the environment—can be used with any research strategy.

The final section discusses the ethics of research with humans. In addition to ensuring confidentiality and safety, developmentalists who study children are especially concerned that the benefits of research outweigh the risks.

Audio program 1, "Of Seasons, Stories, and Lives," describes a basic method of developmental research: the interpretation of **life stories**. We hear several people recall their earliest memories and their memories of **nuclear episodes**: the most significant moments in their life stories. Through the expert commentary of psychologist Dan McAdams, we learn what such **autobiographical memories** tell researchers about a person's life story. With the help of commentary by psychologist Richard Lerner, we come to a fuller appreciation of the life-span perspective.

As the program opens, we hear a woman recounting her earliest memory—the opening scene of her life story.

LESSON GOALS

By the end of this lesson you should be prepared to:

1. Define developmental psychology, and explain the life-span and ecological-systems perspectives.

2. Identify five characteristics of development identified by the life-span perspective, and discuss the three broad, overlapping contexts that affect development throughout the life span, noting the threee domains into which development is divided.

3. List and describe the basic steps of the scientific method.

4. Discuss the significance of the three developmental clocks through the life span.

5. Describe the components of an experiment and three basic research designs used by developmental psychologists.

6. Explain how the interpretation of life stories and autobiographical memories helps psychologists to understand development through the life span.

Audio Assignment

Listen to the audio tape that accompanies Lesson 1: "Of Seasons, Stories, and Lives." Write answers to the following questions. You may replay portions of the program if you need to refresh your memory. Answer guidelines may be found in the Lesson Guidelines section at the end of this chapter.

1. Explain the "life-span perspective" in developmental psychology and the concept that there are "seasons" of life.

2. Compare and contrast the three developmental clocks.

3. Explain the significance of first memories and nuclear episodes in the interpretation of life stories.

Textbook Assignment

Read Chapter 1: "Introduction," pages 3–31 in *The Developing Person Through the Life Span*, 6/e, then work through the material that follows to review it. Complete the sentences and answer the questions. As you proceed, evaluate your performance for each section by consulting the answers on page 11. Do not continue with the next section until you understand each answer. If you need to, review or reread the appropriate section in the textbook before continuing.

Studying the Life Span: Five Characteristics (pp. 3–18)

1. The scientific study of human development can be defined as the science that seeks to understand

   _____

   _____.

2. Central to the study of development is the

   _____-_____

   _____ , which recognizes the

   sources of continuity and discontinuity from the beginning of life to the end.

   The five developmental characteristics embodied within the life-span perspective are that development is

   a. _____

   b. _____

   c. _____

   d. _____

   e. _____

3. Three important insights of this perspective are the concepts of _____ _____ , which refers to the continual change that occurs within each person and each social group; the _____ _____ , in which even a tiny change in one system can have a profound effect on the other systems of development; and the power of _____ , in which even large changes seemingly have no effect.

4. A group of people born within a few years of each other is called a _____ . These people tend to be affected by history in _____ (the same way/different ways).

5. A widely shared idea that is built more on shared perceptions than on objective reality is a _____ _____ . An important point about such ideas is that they _____ (often change/are very stable) over time.

6. A contextual influence that is determined by a person's income, education, place of residence, and occupation is called _____

_____ , which is often abbreviated _____ . Although poverty is a useful signal for severe problems throughout life, other variables, such as the presence of _____ _____ within a family, play a crucial role in determining individual development. Another variable is _____ _____ , which refers to the degree to which neighbors create a functioning, informal network of people who show concern for each other.

7. The values, assumptions, and customs as well as the physical objects that a group of people have adopted as a design for living constitute a _____ .

8. The impact of cultural variations in _____ _____ can be seen in the fact that children who _____ (sleep alone/sleep with parents) are taught to be independent of their families, while those who _____ (sleep alone/sleep with parents) are taught to depend on them for warmth and protection. A _____ is a kind of farming commune developed in _____ , whose members share _____ _____ .

9. A collection of people who share certain attributes, such as ancestry, national origin, religion, and language and, as a result, tend to have similar beliefs, values, and cultural experiences is called a(n) _____ . Biological traits used to differentiate people whose ancestors come from different regions is the definition of _____ .

10. The study of human development can be divided into three domains: _____ , _____ , and _____ .

11. One of the most encouraging aspects of the life-span perspective is that development is characterized by _____ , or the capability of change.

12. (In Person) Because his mother contracted the disease _____ during her pregnancy, David was born with a heart defect and cataracts over both eyes. Thus, his immediate problems centered on _____ problems. However, because he was born at a particular time, he was already influenced by the larger _____ context. Particularly in the church community, the _____-_____ context benefitted him. David's continuing development of his skills is a testimony for _____ .

Developmental Study as a Science (pp. 18–23)

13. In order, the basic steps of the scientific method are

a. _____

b. _____

c. _____

d. _____

e. _____

14. A specific, testable prediction that forms the basis of a research project is called a _____ .

15. To repeat an experimental test procedure and obtain the same results is to _____ the test of the hypothesis.

16. In designing research studies, scientists are concerned with four issues: _____ , or whether a study measures what it purports to measure; _____ , or whether its measurements are correct; _____ , or whether the study applies to other populations and situations; and _____ , or whether it solves real-life problems.

17. When researchers observe and record, in a systematic and unbiased manner, what research subjects do, they are using _____ _____ .

18. People may be observed in a _____ setting or in a _____ .

19. A chief limitation of observation is that it does not indicate the _____ of the behavior being observed.

20. A number that indicates the degree of relation-ship between two variables is a

_____ . To say that two variables are related in this way _____ (does/does not) necessarily imply that one caused the other.

21. The method that allows a scientist to determine cause and effect is the _____ . In this method, researchers manipulate a(n) _____ variable to determine its effect on a(n) _____ variable.

22. In an experiment, the subjects who receive a par-ticular treatment constitute the _____

_____ ; the subjects who do not receive the treatment constitute the

_____ _____ .

23. To determine whether a difference between two groups occurred purely by coincidence, or chance, researchers apply a mathematical test of statistical _____ .

24. Experiments are sometimes criticized for study-ing behavior in a situation that is

_____ .

25. Another limitation is that participants in this research technique (except very young children) who know they are research subjects may attempt to _____

_____ . The most accurate and ethical way to conduct devel-opmental research on children is the

_____ _____ .

26. In a(n) _____ , scientists collect information from a large group of people by per-sonal interview, written questionnaire, or some other means.

27. Potential problems with this research method are that the questions may be _____ and respondents may give answers they think the researcher _____ .

28. An intensive study of one individual is called a(n) _____ _____ . An advantage of this method is that it provides a rich _____ description of development, rather than relying only on _____

data. Another important use is that it provides a good _____ _____ for other research.

Studying Changes Over Time (pp. 23–28)

29. Research that involves the comparison of people of different ages is called a _____-_____ research design.

30. With cross-sectional research it is very difficult to ensure that the various groups differ only in their _____ . In addition, every cross-sectional study will, to some degree, reflect

_____ _____ .

31. Research that follows the same people over a rel-atively long period of time is called a _____ research design.

State three drawbacks of this type of research design.

32. The research method that combines the longitudi-nal and cross-sectional methods is the

_____-_____

research method.

33. The approach that emphasizes the influence of the systems that support the developing person is called the _____-_____ approach. This approach was emphasized by

_____ .

34. According to this model, the family, the peer group, and other aspects of the immediate social setting constitute the _____ .

35. Systems that link one microsystem to another constitute the _____ .

36. Community institutions such as school and church make up the _____ .

37. Cultural values, political philosophies, economic patterns, and social systems make up the

_____ .

38. The final system in this model is the

_____ , which emphasizes the

importance of historical time on development.

Ethics and Science (pp. 29–30)

39. Developmental researchers work from a set of

moral principles that constitute their

_____ _____

_____ . Researchers who study

humans must obtain _____

_____ , which refers to written per-

mission, ensure that their subjects are not

_____ and that they are allowed to

stop at any time.

40. A research study that is a compilation of data

from many other sources is called a

_____-_____ .

Testing Yourself

After you have completed the audio and text review
questions, see how well you do on the following quiz.
Correct answers, with text and audio references, may
be found at the end of this chapter.

1. Which of the following statements most accurately expresses the life-span perspective on development?
   a. Human development reflects the interaction
   of three developmental clocks.
   b. Human development is a continuous process
   rather than a series of stages.
   c. Human development occurs in discontinuous
   stages.
   d. Human development is a lifelong process of
   change.

2. The research method in which the same group of
people is studied over a long period of time is
called the:
   a. cross-sectional method.
   b. longitudinal method.
   c. survey method.
   d. naturalistic method.

3. Culturally determined age norms for when to
enter school, when to start a family, and when to
retire, are set according to:
   a. the biological clock.

   b. the social clock.
   c. the psychological clock.
   d. all three developmental clocks.

4. Memories of especially significant events in a life
story are called:
   a. flashbulb memories.
   b. iconic memories.
   c. nuclear episodes.
   d. eidetic images.

5. Dan McAdams studies autobiographical memories by:
   a. coding them for the presence of certain
   motives.
   b. interviewing relatives of the subject of a case
   study.
   c. using the cross-sectional method.
   d. interpreting art produced by subjects at different stages in their life span.

6. The scientific study of human development is
defined as the study of:
   a. how and why people change or remain the
   same over time.
   b. psychosocial influences on aging.
   c. individual differences in learning over the life
   span.
   d. all of the above.

7. Developmental psychologists explore three areas
of development:
   a. physical, cognitive, psychosocial.
   b. physical, biosocial, cognitive.
   c. biosocial, cognitive, psychosocial.
   d. biosocial, cognitive, emotional.

8. In differentiating ethnicity and culture, we note
that:
   a. ethnicity is an exclusively biological phenomenon.
   b. an ethnic group is a group of people who
   were born within a few years of each other.
   c. people of many ethnic groups can share one
   culture, yet maintain their ethnic identities.
   d. racial identity is always an element of culture.

9. If developmentalists discovered that poor people
are happier than wealthy people are, this would
indicate that wealth and happiness are:
   a. unrelated.
   b. correlated.
   c. examples of nature and nurture, respectively.
   d. causally related.

10. The ecological-systems model of developmental psychology focuses on the:
    a. biochemistry of the body systems.
    b. macrosystems only.
    c. internal thinking processes.
    d. overall environment of development.

11. Researchers who take a life-span perspective on development focus on:
    a. the sources of continuity from the beginning of life to the end.
    b. the sources of discontinuity throughout life.
    c. the "nonlinear" character of human development.
    d. all of the above.

12. That fluctuations in body weight are affected by genes, appetite, caregiving, culture, and food supply indicates that body weight:
    a. is characterized by linear change.
    b. is a dynamic system.
    c. often has a butterfly effect.
    d. is characterized by all of the above.

13. A hypothesis is a:
    a. conclusion.
    b. prediction to be tested.
    c. statistical test.
    d. correlation.

14. A developmentalist who is interested in studying the influences of a person's immediate environment on his or her behavior is focusing on which system?
    a. mesosystem
    b. macrosystem
    c. microsystem
    d. exosystem

15. Socioeconomic status is determined by a combination of variables, including:
    a. age, education, and income.
    b. income, ethnicity, and occupation.
    c. income, education, and occupation.
    d. age, ethnicity, and occupation.

16. A disadvantage of experiments is that:
    a. people may behave differently in the artificial environment of the laboratory.
    b. control groups are too large to be accommodated in most laboratories.
    c. they are the method most vulnerable to bias on the part of the researcher.
    d. proponents of the ecological-systems approach overuse them.

17. In an experiment testing the effects of group size on individual effort in a tug-of-war task, the number of people in each group is the:
    a. hypothesis.
    b. independent variable
    c. dependent variable.
    d. level of significance.

18. Which research method would be most appropriate for investigating the relationship between parents' religious beliefs and their attitudes toward middle school sex education?
    a. experimentation
    b. longitudinal research
    c. naturalistic observation
    d. the survey

19. Dr. Weston is comparing research findings for a group of 30-year-olds with findings for the same individuals at age 20, as well as with findings for groups who were 30 in 1990. Which research method is she using?
    a. longitudinal research
    b. cross-sectional research
    c. case study
    d. cross-sequential research

20. Developmentalists who carefully observe the behavior of schoolchildren during recess are using a research method known as:
    a. the case study.
    b. cross-sectional research.
    c. naturalistic observation.
    d. cross-sequential research.

21. Which of the following describes a neighborhood in which people pitch in to keep children safe, keep trash off the streets, and generally show concern for one another?
    a. cohort effect
    b. collective efficacy
    c. meta-analysis
    d. butterfly effect

22. When we say that the idea of old age as we know it is a "social construction," we are saying that:
    a. the idea is built on the shared perceptions of members of society.
    b. old age has only recently been regarded as a distinct period of life.
    c. old age cannot be defined.
    d. the idea is based on a well-tested hypothesis.

23. Professor Jorgenson believes development is plastic. By this she means that:

    a. change in development occurs in every direction, not always in a straight line.
    b. human lives are embedded in many different contexts.
    c. there are many cultures that influence development.
    d. every individual, and every trait within each individual, can be altered at any point in the life span.

NAME _____   INSTRUCTOR _____

LESSON 1: FIRST MEMORIES

Exercise

The audio program notes that one way of understanding an individual's life is by listening to his or her life story. In order to make sense of **life stories**, psychologists are beginning to probe **autobiographical memory**. This kind of memory begins with each individual's very first memory of life. Although first memories are often a mixture of fact and fiction, they are especially revealing glimpses into each person's current identity.

To further your understanding of the material presented in this lesson, the Exercise asks you to reflect on the first memories of characters heard in the audio program. Answer the following questions and hand the completed exercise in to your instructor.

1. How did Mary's first memory relate to the rest of her life story? How did it express her identity?

2. How did Arnelle Douglas's first memory relate to the rest of his life story? How did it express his identity?

3. Of course, not all first memories relate to the rest of a person's story. Ask someone you know about his or her earliest memory (or try to remember your own). Do you see any connection between the memory and the rest of the person's life story? between the memory and your subject's sense of who he or she is?

LESSON GUIDELINES

Audio Question Guidelines

1. The life-span perspective states that development is not fixed early in the life span, as earlier theorists had proposed, but continues throughout the seasons of life.

   Developmental psychologists recognize separate life-span seasons of infancy, childhood, adolescence, early adulthood, middle adulthood, and late adulthood.

   The life-span perspective emphasizes that people become more diverse as they age, that they are capable of controlling their development, that is, of being the authors of their own life stories.

   The life-span perspective has also made experts aware of the three developmental clocks—the biological, social, and psychological clocks—that interact to pace human development.

2. The developmental clocks are metaphors for the three ways in which people change during the seasons of life. To begin with, people change because their bodies change. The **biological clock** represents the body's mechanisms for timing physical development. It times birth, growth, the reproductive cycle, and aging.

   People also change because the world around them changes. The **social clock** represents each society's age norms for when certain life events should occur—for example, when people should enter school, start a family, and retire.

   Finally, people change because their own inner needs change. The **psychological clock** represents a person's inner timetable for development, that is, his or her own way of determining the right time for certain life events.

3. One way of understanding life-span development is to listen to a specific person's **life story**. The story, although continually evolving and being rewritten, may be what gives each life continuity and purpose. It may represent each individual's sense of who he or she is.

   The interpretation of **autobiographical memory**, including nuclear episodes and first memories, is especially interesting. Cognitive psychologists suggest that what we remember from the past is reconstructed over time so that such memories are generally combinations of fact and fantasy.

   Early memories, whether true or not, say something about a person's current identity and highlight significant themes in his or her entire life story.

Nuclear episodes are personal memories that are very significant to the individual. How people describe nuclear episodes often reveals important personality traits—for example, a desire for intimacy.

Textbook Question Answers

1. how and why people change, and how they do not change, from conception until death
2. life-span perspective
   a. multidirectional
   b. multicontextual
   c. multicultural
   d. multidisciplinary
   e. plastic
3. dynamic systems; butterfly effect; continuity
4. cohort; the same way
5. social construction; often change
6. socioeconomic status; SES; supportive relationships; collective efficacy
7. culture
8. sleeping places; sleep alone; sleep with parents; kibbutz; Israel; work, meals, income, and child care
9. ethnic group; race
10. biosocial; cognitive; psychosocial
11. plasticity
12. rubella; physical; historical; cultural-ethnic; plasticity
13. a. formulate a research question;
    b. develop a hypothesis;
    c. test the hypothesis;
    d. draw conclusions;
    e. make the findings available.
14. hypothesis
15. replicate
16. validity; accuracy; generalizability; usefulness
17. scientific observation
18. naturalistic; laboratory
19. cause
20. correlation; does not
21. experiment; independent; dependent
22. experimental group; comparison group
23. significance
24. artificial
25. produce the results they believe the experimenter is looking for; natural experiment
26. survey

27. biased; expects (wants)

28. case study; qualitative; quantitative; starting point

29. cross-sectional

30. ages; cohort differences

31. longitudinal

Over time, some subjects may leave the study. Some people may change simply because they are part of the study. Longitudinal studies are time-consuming and expensive.

32. cross-sequential

33. ecological-systems; Urie Bronfenbrenner

34. microsystem

35. mesosystem

36. exosystem

37. macrosystem

38. chronosystem

39. code of ethics; informed consent; harmed

40. meta-analysis

Answers to Testing Yourself

1. **d.** In contrast to earlier views that development was largely fixed early in life, the life-span perspective views development as continuing throughout the seasons of life. (audio program; textbook, p. 4)

2. **b.** The *long*itudinal method studies development over a *long* period of time. (audio program; textbook, p. 25)

3. **b.** The social clock represents society's way of telling us to "act our age." (audio program)

4. **c.** The nucleus is "at the center." Nuclear episodes are central to our sense of who we are. (audio program)

5. **a.** In McAdams's view, autobiographical memories reflect each person's sense of identity. (audio program)

6. **a.** is the answer. (textbook, p. 3)

   b. & c. The study of development is concerned with a broader range of phenomena, including biosocial aspects of development, than these answers specify.

7. **c.** is the answer. (textbook, p. 3)

8. **c.** is the answer. (textbook, p. 13)

   a. & d. Ethnicity refers to shared attributes, such as ancestry, national origin, religion, and language.

   b. This describes a cohort.

9. **b.** is the answer. (textbook, p. 20)

   a. Wealth and happiness clearly *are* related.

   c. For one thing, poverty is clearly an example of nurture, not nature.

   d. Correlation does not imply causation.

10. **d.** is the answer. This approach sees development as occurring within five interacting levels, or environments. (textbook, p. 27)

11. **d.** is the answer. (textbook, p. 4)

12. **b.** is the answer. (textbook, p. 5)

    a. Body weight does not always increase in a linear fashion.

    c. Although it is possible that a small change in a person's body weight could set off a series of changes that culminate in a major event, the question is concerned with the interconnectedness of body weight, nutrition, and other dynamic developmental systems.

13. **b.** is the answer. (textbook, p. 19)

14. **c.** is the answer. (textbook, p. 27)

    a. This refers to systems that link one microsystem to another.

    b. This refers to cultural values, political philosophies, economic patterns, and social conditions.

    d. This includes the community structures that affect the functioning of smaller systems.

15. **c.** is the answer. (textbook, p. 9)

16. **a.** is the answer. (textbook, p. 22)

17. **b.** is the answer. (textbook, p. 20)

    a. A possible hypothesis for this experiment would be that the larger the group, the less hard a given individual will pull.

    c. The dependent variable is the measure of individual effort.

    d. Significance level refers to the numerical value specifying the possibility that the results of an experiment could have occurred by chance.

18. **d.** is the answer. (textbook, p. 22)

    a. Experimentation is appropriate when one is seeking to uncover cause-and-effect relationships; in this example the researcher is only interested in determining whether the parents' beliefs *predict* their attitudes.

    b. Longitudinal research would be appropriate if the researcher sought to examine the development of these attitudes over a long period of time.

    c. Mere observation would not allow the researcher to determine the attitudes of the participants.

19. **d.** is the answer. (textbook, p. 27)

    a. & c. In these research methods, only one group of people is studied.

    b. Dr. Weston's design includes comparison of groups of people of different ages *over time.*

20. **c.** is the answer. (textbook, p. 19)

    a. In this method, *one* person is studied over a period of time.

    b. & d. In these research methods, two or more *groups* of participants are studied and compared.

21. **b.** is the answer. (textbook, p. 9)

22. **a.** is the answer. (textbook, p. 7)

23. **d.** is the answer. (textbook, p. 15)

    a. This describes the multidirectional nature of development.

    b. This describes the multicontextual nature of development.

    c. This describes the multicultural nature of development.

Theories of Development

AUDIO PROGRAM: The Story of Erik Erikson

ORIENTATION

Lesson 1 introduced the subject matter of developmental psychology, described the three clocks that govern development, and introduced the many contexts of development. Lesson 2 deals with theories of human development, including that of Erik Erikson, who is the subject of the audio program.

Theories provide a useful way of organizing ideas about behavior into testable hypotheses. In Chapter 2 of *The Developing Person Through the Life Span,* 6/e, five theories that have significantly influenced life-span psychology are described, evaluated, and compared. The theories complement one another: each emphasizes different aspects of development and is too restricted to be used on its own to explain the diverse ways in which development occurs. **Psychoanalytic theory** focuses on early experiences and distinguishable stages of growth, and **behaviorism** emphasizes environmental influences. **Cognitive theory** emphasizes the influence of thinking on behavior, and **sociocultural theory** explains human development in terms of the support provided by one's culture. **Epigenetic systems theory** emphasizes the genetic origins of behavior but also stresses that genes, over time, are directly and systematically affected by environmental forces.

Most developmental psychologists today take an *eclectic perspective*, applying insights from various theories rather than limiting themselves to only one school of thought. The final test of a theory is its usefulness in clarifying observations and suggesting new hypotheses.

One theory that has withstood this test is that of Erik Erikson. A student of Freud, Erikson was one of the first psychologists to devote attention to the entire life cycle—to adulthood as well as to childhood. Erikson spent his childhood in Germany and came to America when Adolf Hitler became Chancellor and

Freud's writings were publicly burned in Berlin. In America, Erikson practiced as one of the first psychoanalysts for children, studying people as diverse as the Native American Sioux and soldiers who suffered emotional trauma during World War II. Erikson's experiences led him to the conclusion that Freud's **psychosexual stages** were too limited. In Erikson's view there were eight important challenges, or *crises*, in life and, hence, eight (rather than five) stages of development. Unlike Freud's stages, Erikson's reflect social and cultural influences; as a result, they are called **psychosocial stages**. In the program, these stages are outlined and contrasted with those embodied in Freud's theory.

The program begins with Erikson himself describing how he came to create one of psychology's most influential theories of the life cycle.

LESSON GOALS

By the end of this lesson you should be prepared to:

1. Explain the role theories play in developmental psychology, and differentiate grand theories, minitheories, and emergent theories.

2. Outline the basic terms and themes of the five major theories of human development: psychoanalytic theory, behaviorism, cognitive theory, sociocultural theory, and epigenetic systems theory.

3. Discuss Harlow's research with infant monkeys and the ethology of infant social instincts and adult caregiving impulses.

4. Summarize the contributions and criticisms of the major developmental theories, and explain the eclectic perspective in developmental psychology.

5. Describe Erikson's eight stages of psychosocial development, and discuss the significance of Erikson's theory in life-span psychology.

Audio Assignment

Listen to the audio tape that accompanies Lesson 2: "The Story of Erik Erikson."

Write answers to the following questions. You may replay portions of the program if you need to refresh your memory. Answer guidelines may be found in the Lesson Guidelines section at the end of this chapter.

1. Outline Freud's five stages of psychosexual development.

2. Outline Erikson's eight stages of psychosocial development.

3. Describe how Erikson's psychosocial theory has contributed to the study of development, noting how it diverges from that of Freud; then, cite criticisms of it.

Textbook Assignment

Read Chapter 2: "Theories of Development," pages 33–57 in *The Developing Person Through the Life Span*, 6/e, then work through the material that follows to review it. Complete the sentences and answer the

questions. As you proceed, evaluate your performance for each section by consulting the answers on page 23. Do not continue with the next section until you understand each answer. If you need to, review or reread the appropriate section in the textbook before continuing.

What Theories Do (pp. 33–34)

1. A systematic set of principles and generalizations that provides a coherent framework for studying and explaining development is called a(n)

_____ _____ .

2. Developmental theories form the basis for educated guesses, or _____ , about behavior; they generate _____ , and they offer insight and guidance for everyday concerns by providing a _____ view of human development.

3. Developmental theories fall into three categories: _____ theories, which traditionally offer a comprehensive view of development; _____ theories, which explain a specific area of development; and _____ theories, which may be the comprehensive theories of the future.

Grand Theories (pp. 34–45)

4. Psychoanalytic theories interpret human development in terms of intrinsic _____ and _____ , many of which are _____ (conscious/ unconscious) and _____ .

5. According to Freud's _____ theory, children experience sexual pleasures and desires during the first six years as they pass through three _____ _____ . From infancy to early childhood to the preschool years, these stages are the _____ stage, the _____ stage, and the _____ stage. One of Freud's most influential ideas was that each stage includes its own potential _____ between child and parent.

Specify the focus of sexual pleasure and the major developmental need associated with each of Freud's stages.

oral _____

_____

anal _____

_____

phallic _____

_____

genital _____

_____

6. Erik Erikson's theory of development, which focuses on social and cultural influences, is called a(n) _____ theory. In this theory, there are _____ (number) developmental stages, each characterized by a particular developmental _____ related to the person's relationship to the social environment. Unlike Freud, Erikson proposed stages of development that _____ (span/do not span) a person's lifetime.

Complete the following chart regarding Erikson's stages of psychosocial development.

Age Period	Stage
Birth to 1 yr.	trust vs. _____
1–3 yrs.	autonomy vs. _____
3–6 yrs.	initiative vs. _____
7–11 yrs.	_____ vs. inferiority
Adolescence	identity vs. _____
Young adulthood	_____ vs. isolation
Middle adulthood	_____ vs. stagnation
Older adulthood	_____ vs. despair

7. A major theory in American psychology, which directly opposed psychoanalytic theory, was _____ . This theory, which emerged early in the twentieth century under the influence of _____ , is also called _____ theory because of its emphasis on how we learn specific behaviors.

8. Behaviorists have formulated laws of behavior that are believed to apply _____ (only at certain ages/at all ages). The learning process, which is called _____ , takes two forms: _____ _____ and _____ _____ .

9. In classical conditioning, which was discovered by the Russian scientist _____ and is also called _____ conditioning, a person or an animal learns to associate a(n) _____ stimulus with a meaningful one.

10. According to _____ , the learning of more complex responses is the result of _____ conditioning, in which a person learns that a particular behavior produces a particular _____ , such as a reward. This type of learning is also called _____ conditioning.

11. The process of repeating a consequence to make it more likely that the behavior in question will recur is called _____ . The consequence that increases the likelihood that a behavior will be repeated is called the _____ .

12. (Thinking Like a Scientist) The behavior of infant monkeys separated from their mothers led researcher _____ to investigate the origins of _____ in infant monkeys. These studies, which demonstrated that infant monkeys clung more often to "surrogate" mothers that provided _____ (food/contact comfort), disproved _____ theory's idea that infants seek to satisfy oral needs and _____ view that reinforcement directs behavior.

13. The application of behaviorism that emphasizes the ways that people learn new behaviors by observing others is called _____ . The process whereby a child patterns his or her behavior after a parent or

teacher, for example, is called

_____ .

14. This process is most likely to occur when an observer is _____ or _____ and when the model is

_____ .

This type of learning is also affected by the individual's _____ . Human social learning is related to _____ ,

_____ , _____

_____ , and feelings of

_____ .

15. The structure and development of the individual's thought processes and the way those thought processes affect the person's understanding of the world are the focus of

_____ theory. A major pioneer of this theory is _____ .

16. In Piaget's first stage of development, the

_____ stage, children experience the world through their senses and motor abilities. This stage occurs between birth and age

_____ .

17. According to Piaget, during the preschool years (up to age _____), children are in the _____ stage. A hallmark of this stage is that children begin to think

_____ . Another hallmark is that sometimes the child's thinking is

_____ , or focused on seeing the world solely from his or her own perspective.

18. Piaget believed that children begin to think logically in a consistent way at about

_____ years of age. At this time, they enter the _____

_____ stage.

19. In Piaget's final stage, the _____

_____ stage, reasoning expands from the purely concrete to encompass

_____ thinking. Piaget believed

most children enter this stage by age

_____ .

20. According to Piaget, cognitive development is guided by the need to maintain a state of mental balance, called _____

_____ .

21. When new experiences challenge existing understanding, creating a kind of imbalance, the individual experiences _____

_____ , which eventually leads to mental growth.

22. According to Piaget, people adapt to new experiences either by reinterpreting them to fit into, or _____ with, old ideas. Some new experiences force people to revamp old ideas so that they can _____ new experiences.

Emergent Theories (pp. 45–52)

23. In contrast to the grand theories, the two emergent theories draw from the findings of

_____ (one/many) discipline(s).

24. Sociocultural theory sees human development as the result of _____

_____ between developing persons and their surrounding society and

_____ .

25. A major pioneer of this perspective was

_____ , who was primarily interested in the development of

_____ competencies.

26. Vygotsky believed that these competencies result from the interaction between _____ and more mature members of the society, acting as _____ , in a process that has been called an _____ _____

_____ .

27. In Vygotsky's view, the best way to accomplish the goals of apprenticeship is through

_____ _____ , in

which the tutor engages the learner in joint activities.

28. According to Vygotsky, a mentor draws a child into the _____

_____ _____

_____ , which is defined as the range of skills that a person can exercise and master with _____ but cannot perform independently.

Cite a contribution and a criticism of sociocultural theory.

29. The newest of the emergent theories, _____ theory, emphasizes the interaction between

_____ and the _____ . This idea contrasts sharply with the idea of _____ , according to which everything is set in advance by genes.

30. In using the word *genetic*, this theory emphasizes that we have powerful _____ and abilities that arise from our _____ heritage.

31. The prefix "epi" refers to the various _____ factors that affect the expression of _____

_____ . These include _____ factors such as injury, temperature, and crowding. Others are _____ factors such as nourishing food and freedom to play.

32. Some epigenetic factors are the result of the evolutionary process called _____

_____ , in which, over generations, genes for useful traits that promote survival of the species become more prevalent.

33. "Everything that seems to be genetic is actually epigenetic." This statement highlights the fact that _____ (some/most/all) genetic instructions are affected by the environment.

34. (In Person) The study of animal behavior as it is related to the evolution and survival of a species is called _____ . Newborn animals and human infants are genetically programmed for _____ _____ as a means of survival. Similarly, adult animals and humans are genetically programmed for

_____ _____ .

What Theories Can Contribute (pp. 52–56)

35. Which major theory of development emphasizes:

    a. the importance of culture in fostering development? _____

    b. the ways in which thought processes affect actions? _____

    c. environmental influences? _____

    d. the impact of "hidden dramas" on development? _____

    _____

    e. the interaction of genes and environment?_____

    _____

36. Which major theory of development has been criticized for:

    a. being too mechanistic?

    _____

    b. undervaluing genetic differences?

    _____

    c. being too subjective?

    _____

    d. neglecting society?

    _____

    e. neglecting individuals?

    _____

37. Because no one theory can encompass all of human behavior, most developmentalists have a(n) _____ perspective, which capitalizes on the strengths of all the theories.

38. The debate over the relative influence of heredity and environment in shaping personal traits and characteristics is called the

_____–_____ controversy. Traits inherited at the moment of conception give evidence of the influence of

_____ ; those that emerge in response to learning and environmental influences give evidence of the effect of

_____ .

39. Developmentalists agree that, at every point, the _____ between nature and nurture is the crucial influence on any particular aspect of development.

40. Children who are especially impulsive, restless, and unable to attend to anything for more than a moment may be suffering from

_____ . This disorder is more common in _____ (girls/boys).

State several pieces of evidence that genetic inheritance is responsible for AD/HD

41. All the grand theories tended to explain homosexuality in terms of _____ (nature/nurture). However, new research suggests that it is at least partly due to _____ (nature/nurture).

Testing Yourself

After you have completed the audio and text review questions, see how well you do on the following quiz. Correct answers, with text and audio references, may be found at the end of this chapter.

1. Erik Erikson's theory of development:
   a. is based on eight crises all people are thought to face.
   b. emphasizes cultural and social influences on development.
   c. was one of the first to emphasize that development is lifelong.
   d. includes all of the factors listed above.

2. Freud's stages of development are called _____ stages; Erikson's are called _____ stages.
   a. psychosexual; psychosocial
   b. psychosocial; psychosexual
   c. psychosexual; social learning
   d. psychoanalytic; neo-Freudian

3. According to Freud's theory, the correct sequence of stages of development is:
   a. oral, anal, genital, latent, phallic.
   b. anal, oral, phallic, latent, genital.
   c. genital, oral, anal, latent, phallic.
   d. oral, anal, phallic, latent, genital.

4. The zone of proximal development refers to:
   a. a stage during which the child exhibits preoperational thinking.
   b. the influence of a pleasurable stimulus on behavior.
   c. the range of skills a child can exercise with assistance but cannot perform independently.
   d. the tendency of a child to model an admired adult's behavior.

5. Freud believed that sexual forces become dormant between ages 7 and 11; Erikson, on the other hand, saw this age period as a critical time of conflict between:
   a. autonomy and shame.
   b. trust and mistrust.
   c. industry and inferiority.
   d. identity and role confusion.

6. The purpose of a developmental theory is to:
   a. provide a broad and coherent view of the complex influences on human development.
   b. offer guidance for practical issues encountered by parents, teachers, and therapists.
   c. generate testable hypotheses about development.
   d. do all of the above.

7. Which developmental theory emphasizes the influence of unconscious drives and motives on behavior?
   a. psychoanalytic   c. cognitive
   b. behaviorism   d. sociocultural

8. Erikson's psychosocial theory of human development describes:
   a. eight crises all people are thought to face.
   b. four psychosocial stages and a latency period.
   c. the same number of stages as Freud's, but with different names.
   d. a stage theory that is not psychoanalytic.

9. Which of the following theories does *not* belong with the others?
   a. psychoanalytic
   b. behaviorism
   c. sociocultural
   d. cognitive

10. An American psychologist who explained complex human behaviors in terms of operant conditioning was:
   a. Lev Vygotsky.
   b. Ivan Pavlov.
   c. B. F. Skinner.
   d. Jean Piaget.

11. Pavlov's dogs learned to salivate at the sound of a bell because they associated the bell with food. Pavlov's experiment with dogs was an early demonstration of:
   a. classical conditioning.
   b. operant conditioning.
   c. positive reinforcement.
   d. social learning.

12. The nature–nurture controversy considers the degree to which traits, characteristics, and behaviors are the result of:
   a. early or lifelong learning.
   b. genes or heredity.
   c. heredity or experience.
   d. different historical concepts of childhood.

13. Modeling, an integral part of social learning theory, is so called because it:
   a. follows the scientific model of learning.
   b. molds character.
   c. follows the immediate reinforcement model developed by Bandura.
   d. involves people's patterning their behavior after that of others.

14. Which developmental theory suggests that each person is born with genetic possibilities that must be nurtured in order to grow?
   a. sociocultural
   b. cognitive
   c. behaviorism
   d. epigenetic

15. Vygotsky's theory has been criticized for neglecting:
   a. the role of genes in guiding development.
   b. developmental processes that are not primarily biological.
   c. the importance of language in development.
   d. social factors in development.

16. Which is the correct sequence of stages in Piaget's theory of cognitive development?
   a. sensorimotor, preoperational, concrete operational, formal operational
   b. sensorimotor, preoperational, formal operational, concrete operational
   c. preoperational, sensorimotor, concrete operational, formal operational
   d. preoperational, sensorimotor, formal operational, concrete operational

17. When an individual's existing understanding no longer fits his or her present experiences, the result is called:
   a. a psychosocial crisis.
   b. equilibrium.
   c. disequilibrium.
   d. negative reinforcement.

18. In explaining the origins of homosexuality, the grand theories have traditionally emphasized:
   a. nature over nurture.
   b. nurture over nature.
   c. a warped mother–son or father–daughter relationship.
   d. the individual's voluntary choice.

19. Four-year-old Bjorn takes great pride in successfully undertaking new activities. Erikson would probably say that Bjorn is capably meeting the psychosocial challenge of:
   a. trust vs. mistrust.
   b. initiative vs. guilt.
   c. industry vs. inferiority.
   d. identity vs. role confusion.

20. Dr. Cleaver's developmental research draws upon insights from several theoretical perspectives. Evidently, Dr. Cleaver is working from a(n) _____ perspective.
   a. cognitive
   b. behaviorist
   c. eclectic
   d. sociocultural

NAME _____   INSTRUCTOR _____

LESSON 2: THEORIES OF HUMAN DEVELOPMENT

Exercise

Four major theories of human development are described, compared, and evaluated in Chapter 2. These are the **psychoanalytic theories** of Freud and neo-Freudians such as Erikson; the **learning** and **social learning theories** of Pavlov, Skinner, and Bandura; the **cognitive theories of** Piaget and the information-processing theorists; and the **sociocultural theory** of Vygotsky. Although each theory is too restricted to account solely for the tremendous diversity in human development, each has made an important contribution to life-span psychology.

To help clarify your understanding of the major **developmental theories**, this exercise asks you to focus on the similar, contradictory, and complementary aspects of the four theories. Answer the following questions and hand the completed exercise in to your instructor.

1. Which of the major developmental theories are stage theories? Which are not?

2. Which theories emphasize individual conscious organization of experience? unconscious urges? observable behavior? individuality? social and cultural influences?

3. Which theories emphasize the impact of early experience on development?

4. How does each theory view the child?

5. Do the theories use the same methodology? What is the relationship of the research strategies to the various theories?

6. How does each theory view adult development?

LESSON GUIDELINES

Audio Question Guidelines

1. According to Freud's **psychoanalytic theory** of **childhood sexuality**, children have sexual pleasures and fantasies long before adolescence.

   During the first five or six years, development progresses through three **psychosexual stages**, characterized by the focusing of sexual interest and pleasure, successively, on the mouth (**oral stage**), the anus (**anal stage**), and the sexual organs (**phallic stage**).

   Freud believed that personality was well established by the end of stage three, about the age of 6.

   Following a five- or six-year period of sexual **latency**, the individual enters the **genital stage**, which lasts throughout adulthood.

2. Erikson's **psychosocial theory** emphasizes each person's relationship to the social environment. Erikson proposed eight developmental stages, each characterized by a particular crisis that must be resolved in order for the individual to progress developmentally.

   During the first stage (*trust versus mistrust*), babies learn either to trust or to mistrust that others will meet their basic needs.

   During the second and third years of life (*autonomy versus shame and doubt*) children learn either to be self-sufficient in many activities or to doubt their own abilities.

   During the third stage (*initiative versus guilt*) children begin to envisage goals and to undertake many adultlike activities, sometimes experiencing guilt as they overstep the limits set by their parents.

   During the years from 6 to 12 (*industry versus inferiority*) children busily learn to feel useful and productive; failing that, they feel inferior and unable to do anything well.

   At adolescence (*identity versus role confusion*) individuals establish sexual, ethnic, and career identities or become confused about who they are.

   Young adults (*intimacy versus isolation*) seek companionship and love from another person or become isolated from others.

   Middle-aged adults (*generativity versus stagnation*) feel productive in their work and family or become stagnant and self-absorbed.

   Older adults (*integrity versus despair*) try to make sense of their lives; they either see life as meaningful or they feel despair in their failure to attain goals.

3. Erikson was one of the first psychologists to view development as a life-long process, not one largely fixed by the end of childhood, as Freud had proposed.

   Erikson also emphasized the importance of cultural and social influences on development.

   Some critics say that Erikson's theory is biased toward male development.

   The principal objection to Erikson's theory is its basic outline of life as a sequence of fixed stages. Critics argue that development is much more variable and flexible than this discontinuous, stage approach implies.

Textbook Question Answers

1. developmental theory
2. hypotheses; discoveries; coherent
3. grand; mini; emergent
4. motives; drives; unconscious; irrational
5. psychoanalytic; psychosexual stages; oral; anal; phallic; conflicts

Oral stage: The mouth is the focus of pleasurable sensations as the baby becomes emotionally attached to the person who provides the oral gratifications derived from sucking.

Anal stage: Pleasures related to control and self-control, initially in connection with defecation and toilet training, are paramount.

Phallic stage: Pleasure is derived from genital stimulation.

Genital stage: Mature sexual interests that last throughout adulthood emerge.

6. psychosocial; eight; crisis (challenge); span

Age Period	Stage
Birth to 1 yr.	trust vs. **mistrust**
1–3 yrs.	autonomy vs. **shame and doubt**
3–6 yrs.	initiative vs. **guilt**
7–11 yrs.	**industry** vs. inferiority
Adolescence	identity vs. **role confusion**
Young adulthood	**intimacy** vs. isolation
Middle adulthood	**generativity** vs. stagnation
Older adulthood	**integrity** vs. despair

7. behaviorism; John B. Watson; learning

8. at all ages; conditioning; classical conditioning; operant conditioning

9. Ivan Pavlov; respondent; neutral

10. B. F. Skinner; operant; consequence; instrumental

11. reinforcement; reinforcer

12. Harry Harlow; attachment; contact comfort; psychoanalytic; behaviorism's

13. social learning; modeling

14. uncertain; inexperienced; admirable and powerful, nurturing, or similar to the observer; self-understanding; self-confidence; social reflection; self-efficacy

15. cognitive; Jean Piaget

16. sensorimotor; 2

17. 6; preoperational; symbolically; egocentric

18. 7; concrete operational

19. formal operational; abstract (hypothetical); 12

20. cognitive equilibrium

21. cognitive disequilibrium

22. assimilate; accommodate

23. many

24. dynamic interaction; culture

25. Lev Vygotsky; cognitive

26. novices; mentors (or tutors); apprenticeship in thinking

27. guided participation

28. zone of proximal development; assistance

Sociocultural theory has emphasized the need to study development in the specific cultural context in which it occurs. The theory has been criticized for neglecting the importance of developmental processes that are not primarily social, such as the role of biological maturation in development.

29. epigenetic; genes; environment; preformism

30. instincts; biological

31. environmental; genetic instructions; stress; facilitating

32. selective adaptation

33. all

34. ethology; social contact; infant caregiving

35. a. sociocultural
    b. cognitive
    c. behaviorism
    d. psychoanalytic
    e. epigenetic

36. a. behaviorism
    b. cognitive
    c. psychoanalytic
    d. epigenetic
    e. sociocultural

37. eclectic

38. nature–nurture; genes (nature); nurture

39. interaction

40. attention-deficit/hyperactivity disorder (AD/HD); boys

    AD/HD children:
    • often have close male relatives with the same problem
    • are overactive in every context
    • calm down when they take stimulants

41. nurture; nature

Answers to Testing Yourself

1. **d.** is the answer. All of these are true of Erikson's theory. (audio program; textbook, pp. 35–37)

2. **a.** is the answer. Freud's psychosexual stages focus on gratification of sexual pleasure; Erikson's psychosocial stages focus on each person's relationship with the social environment. (audio program; textbook, p. 37)

3. **d.** is the answer. (audio program; textbook, pp. 35, 37)

4. **c.** is the answer. (textbook, p. 47)

   a. This is a stage of Piaget's cognitive theory.

   b. This describes positive reinforcement.

   d. This is an aspect of social learning theory.

5. **c.** During this stage, according to Erikson, children learn to be competent and productive or feel inferior and unable to do anything well. (audio program)

6. **d.** is the answer (textbook, pp. 33–34)

7. **a.** is the answer. (textbook, p. 34)

   b. Behaviorism emphasizes the influence of the immediate environment on behavior.

   c. Cognitive theory emphasizes the impact of *conscious* thought processes on behavior.

   d. Sociocultural theory emphasizes the influence on development of social interaction in a specific cultural context.

8. **a.** is the answer. (textbook, p. 36)

b. & c. Whereas Freud identified four stages of psychosexual development, Erikson proposed eight psychosocial stages.

d. Although his theory places greater emphasis on social and cultural forces than Freud's did, Erikson's theory is nevertheless classified as a psychoanalytic theory.

9. **c.** is the answer. Sociocultural theory is an emergent theory. (textbook, p. 34)

a., b., & d. Each of these is an example of a grand theory.

10. **c.** is the answer. (textbook, p. 38)

11. **a.** is the answer. In classical conditioning, a neutral stimulus—in this case, the bell—is associated with a meaningful stimulus—in this case, food. (textbook, p. 38)

b. In operant conditioning, the consequences of a voluntary response determine the likelihood of its being repeated. Salivation is an involuntary response.

c. & d. Positive reinforcement and social learning pertain to voluntary, or operant, responses.

12. **c.** is the answer. (textbook, p. 53)

a. These are both examples of nurture.

b. Both of these refer to nature.

d. The impact of changing historical concepts of childhood on development is an example of how environmental forces (nurture) shape development.

13. **d.** is the answer. (textbook, p. 42)

a. & c. These can be true in all types of learning.

b. This was not discussed as an aspect of developmental theory.

14. **d.** is the answer. (textbook, pp. 48–49)

a. & c. Sociocultural theory and behaviorism focus almost entirely on environmental factors (nurture) in development.

b. Cognitive theory emphasizes the developing person's own mental activity but ignores genetic differences in individuals.

15. **a.** is the answer. (textbook, p. 48)

b. Vygotsky's theory does not emphasize biological processes.

c. & d. Vygotsky's theory places considerable emphasis on language and social factors.

16. **a.** is the answer. (textbook, pp. 43, 44)

17. **c.** is the answer. (textbook, p. 43)

a. This refers to the core of Erikson's psychosocial stages, which deals with people's interactions with the environment.

b. Equilibrium occurs when existing schemes *do* fit a person's current experiences.

d. Negative reinforcement is the removal of a stimulus as a consequence of a desired behavior.

18. **b.** is the answer. (textbook, pp. 54–55)

c. This is only true of psychoanalytic theory.

d. Although the grand theories have emphasized nurture over nature in this matter, no theory suggests that sexual orientation is voluntarily chosen.

19. **b.** is the answer. (textbook, p. 37)

a. According to Erikson, this crisis concerns younger children.

c. & d. In Erikson's theory, these crises concern older children.

20. **c.** is the answer. (textbook, p. 53)

a., b., & d. These are three of the many theoretical perspectives upon which someone working from an eclectic perspective might draw.

Heredity and Environment

AUDIO PROGRAM: And Then We Knew: The Impact of Genetic Information

---

ORIENTATION

Lessons 1 and 2 of *Seasons of Life* examined the meaning of life stories and the methods and theories of lifespan development. Now we turn to the journey through life itself. Lesson 3 focuses on the mechanisms of biological inheritance and the interaction of those mechanisms with environmental influences. The audio program and text explain how physical characteristics are inherited from our parents through **genes**, **chromosomes**, and **DNA**. They also describe **genetic** and **chromosomal abnormalities**, which occur when a fertilized egg has destructive genes or too few or too many chromosomes, and the physical and mental disorders that may result.

As described in Chapter 3 of *The Developing Person Through the Life Span*, 6/e, and by the experts in the audio program, genetic testing can help to predict whether a couple will produce a child with a genetic problem. In addition, the emerging field of **genetic counseling** plays a vital role in helping people to understand and cope with genetic information. The audio program further notes that through the new experimental techniques of **gene mapping** and **gene replacement therapy**, researchers are gaining a deeper understanding of the causes of many genetic disorders and of how to prevent them.

As the audio program illustrates, the price of advances in genetic technology is increased knowledge, the implications of which many individuals would rather not confront. Knowing that the husband, Don, is a **carrier** of a deleterious gene, a young couple faces the difficult decision of whether or not to have children. In addition to its potentially devastating impact on Don's self-esteem, the genetic "news" deeply affects both his wife, Karen, and his mother. As the story unfolds, we learn from geneticist Dr. Donald Rucknagel and genetic counselor Diane Baker of the incredible technological advances that have made genetic counseling possible, and of the impact this technology has on a real couple and their extended families.

LESSON GOALS

By the end of this lesson, you should be prepared to:

1. Describe the process of conception and the first hours of development of the zygote.

2. Explain the basic mechanisms of heredity, including the significance of chromosomes and genes.

3. Describe common causes of genetic and chromosomal abnormalities and several techniques of genetic testing for the presence of such disorders.

4. Discuss the process and importance of genetic counseling.

Audio Assignment

Listen to the audio tape that accompanies Lesson 3: "And Then We Knew."

Write answers to the following questions. You may replay portions of the program if you need to refresh your memory. Answer guidelines may be found in the Lesson Guidelines section at the end of this chapter.

1. What is the difference between a person's genotype and phenotype?

2. In the audio program, how was amniocentesis used to determine that Karen and Don's first child would have been mentally retarded and physically deformed?

3. What is the baseline genetic risk factor that is present in any pregnancy?

4. How can genetic counseling help in each of the following areas?

   a. prenatal diagnosis

   b. pediatric genetics

   c. adult-onset conditions

5. Describe each of the following techniques for treating genetic abnormalities, and explain its significance.

   a. chorionic villi sampling

   b. gene mapping

   c. gene replacement therapy

Textbook Assignment

Read Chapter 3: "Heredity and Environment," pages 59–89 in *The Developing Person Through the Life Span*, 6/e, then work through the material that follows to review it. Complete the sentences and answer the questions. As you proceed, evaluate your performance for each section by consulting the answers on page 35. Do not continue with the next section until you understand each answer. If you need to, review or reread the appropriate section in the textbook before continuing.

The Genetic Code (pp. 59-70)

1. The work of body cells is done by _____ , under the direction of instructions stored in molecules of _____ , each of which is called a _____ . The sum total of these genetic instructions for a given species is called its _____ .

2. Each normal person inherits _____ chromosomes, _____ from each parent. The genetic instructions in chromosomes are organized into units called _____ , each of which contains instructions for a specific _____ , which in turn is composed of chemical building blocks called

   _____ _____ .

3. Genetic instructions are "written" in a chemical code, made up of four pairs of bases:
   _____ , _____ ,
   _____ , and_____ .
   These pairs are arranged in groups of _____ (how many?), which are called

   _____ .

4. The human reproductive cells, which are called _____ , include the male's _____ and the female's

   _____ .

5. When the gametes' nuclei fuse, a living cell called a _____ is formed.

6. This new cell receives _____ chromosomes from the father and _____ from the mother.

7. The sum total of all the genes a person inherits is called the _____ .

8. The chromosomes in a pair are generally identical or similar. Some genes come in several slight, normal variations called _____ .

9. The developing person's sex is determined by the _____ pair of chromosomes. In the female, this pair is composed of two _____-shaped chromosomes and is designated _____ . In the male, this

pair includes one _____ and one _____ chromosome and is therefore designated _____ .

10. The critical factor in the determination of a zygote's sex is which _____ (sperm/ovum) reaches the other gamete first. In a stressful pregnancy, _____ (XX/XY) embryos are more likely to be expelled in a miscarriage, or _____ .

11. (text and Changing Policy) At birth, the overall sex ratio has always _____ (favored males/favored females/been roughly equal). In countries such as China, prenatal tests that show the sex of the child have been used to _____ .

12. Identical twins, which develop from one _____ (are/are not) genetically identical.

13. Twins who begin life as two separate zygotes created by the fertilization of two ova are called _____ twins. Such twins have approximately _____ percent of their genes in common.

14. Dizygotic births occur naturally about once in every _____ births. Women in their _____ (what age?) are three times as likely to have dizygotic twins than women in their _____ .

15. Within hours after conception, the zygote begins to grow through the process of _____ . At about the eight-cell stage, the cells start to _____ , with various cells beginning to specialize and reproduce at different rates. Genes affect this process through _____–_____ _____ mechanisms that code for specific proteins.

16. The sum total of all the genetic traits that are actually expressed is called the _____ .

17. Most human characteristics are affected by many genes, and so they are _____ ; and by many factors, and so they are _____ .

18. A phenotype that reflects the sum of the contributions of all the genes involved in its determination illustrates the _____ pattern of genetic interaction. Examples include genes that affect _____ and _____ _____ .

19. Less often, genes interact in a _____ fashion. In one example of this pattern, some genes are more influential than others; this is called the _____–_____ pattern. In this pattern, the more influential gene is called _____ , and the weaker gene is called _____ .

20. In one variation of this pattern, the phenotype is influenced primarily, but not exclusively, by the dominant gene; this is the _____ pattern.

21. Some recessive genes are located only on the X chromosome and so are called _____–_____ . Examples of such genes are the ones that determine _____ . Because they have only one X chromosome, _____ (females/males) are more likely to have these characteristics in their phenotype.

22. Complicating inheritance further is the fact that dominant genes sometimes do not completely _____ the phenotype. This may be caused by _____ , _____ , or other factors.

23. Whether a gene is inherited from the mother or the father _____ (does/does not) influence its behavior. This tendency of genes is called _____ , or tagging.

24. When the twenty-three chromosome pairs divide up during the formation of gametes, which of the two pairs will end up in a particular gamete is determined by _____ .

25. Genetic variability is also affected by the _____-_____ of genes, and by the interaction of genetic instructions in ways unique to the individual. Another mechanism of genetic diversity is _____ , which refers to the alteration of genetic information caused by _____ factors.

26. Genetic diversity helps safeguard _____ .

27. (Thinking Like a Scientist) The international effort to map the complete human genetic code is referred to as the _____ _____ _____ . In 2000, they published two drafts, revealing, most importantly, that all living creatures _____ (have different/share) genes.

From Genotype to Phenotype (pp. 70–75)

28. A person who has a gene in his or her genotype that is not expressed in the phenotype but that can be passed on to the person's offspring is said to be a _____ of that gene.

29. The complexity of genetic interaction is particularly apparent in _____ , which is the study of the genetic origins of _____ characteristics. These include traits such as _____ ; psychological disorders such as _____ ; and _____ traits such as _____ .

30. Most behavioral traits are affected by the _____ of large numbers of _____ with _____ factors. Traits that are plastic early in life _____ (always/do not always) remain plastic thereafter.

31. The most-feared form of senility is _____ disease, which occurs when the protein _____ accumulates in the brain and kills cells. When this disease occurs before age _____ , which is referred to as _____-_____ , the cause is entirely _____ . More

common is the _____-_____ form of the disease, which is more prevalent in people over 80 who inherited a particular allele of the _____ gene. Although the gene increases the risk of the disease, other health indicators are also factors, including _____ .

32. Psychopathologies such as _____ are genetically based traits that are also subject to _____ influence.

33. Environmental influences _____ (do/do not) play an important role in the appearance of schizophrenia. One predisposing factor is birth during _____ , probably because a certain _____ is more prevalent at this time of year.

34. Alcoholism _____ (is/is not) partly genetic; furthermore, its expression _____ (is/is not) affected by the environment. Certain temperamental traits correlate with abusive drinking, including _____ .

35. On a practical level, genes and environment affect _____ (most/every/few) human characteristic(s).

Chromosomal and Genetic Abnormalities (pp. 75–88)

Researchers study genetic and chromosomal abnormalities for three major reasons. State them.

36. Chromosomal abnormalities occur during the formation of the _____ , producing a sperm or ovum that does not have the normal complement of chromosomes.

37. The variable that most often correlates with chromosomal abnormalities is _____

_____ . When cells in a zygote end up with more or fewer than 46 chromosomes the result is a person who is _____ .

38. Most fetuses with chromosomal abnormalities are _____ _____ . Nevertheless, about 1 in every _____ newborns has one chromosome too few or one too many, leading to a cluster of characteristics called a _____ .

39. The most common extra-chromosome syndrome is _____ , which is also called _____-_____ . People with this syndrome age _____ (faster/more slowly) than other adults. By middle age, people with Down syndrome almost invariably develop _____ , which severely impairs their already limited _____ skills.

List several of the physical and psychological characteristics associated with Down syndrome.

40. About 1 in every 500 infants is either missing a _____ chromosome or has two or more such chromosomes. One resulting syndrome is _____ , in which a boy inherits the _____ chromosome pattern.

41. Most of the known genetic disorders are _____ (dominant/recessive). Genetic disorders usually _____ (are/are not) seriously disabling. It is much _____ (more/less) likely that a person is a carrier of one or more harmful genes than that he or she has abnormal chromosomes.

42. Two exceptions are the central nervous system disease called _____ and the disorder that causes its victims to exhibit uncontrol-

lable tics and explosive outbursts, called _____ .

43. In some individuals, part of the X chromosome is attached by such a thin string of molecules that it seems about to break off; this abnormality is called _____ _____ syndrome.

44. Genetic disorders that are _____ and _____ claim more victims than dominant ones. Three common recessive disorders are _____ , _____ , and _____-_____ .

45. Through _____ _____ , couples today can learn more about their genes and about their chances of conceiving a child with chromosomal or other genetic abnormalities.

46. List four situations in which genetic counseling is strongly recommended.

    a. _____
    b. _____
    c. _____
    d. _____

47. Among the many reproductive alternatives available to those who are carriers of a serious condition or at high risk because of their age or family history are _____

_____ .

The innovative new prenatal therapy called _____ _____ involves the altering of an organism's genetic instructions.

Testing Yourself

After you have completed the audio and text review questions, see how well you do on the following quiz. Correct answers, with text and audio references, may be found at the end of this chapter.

1. A person who is a "carrier" of a genetic disorder but does not suffer from it manifests the abnormality:
    a. only in his or her genotype.
    b. only in his or her phenotype.
    c. in either the genotype or the phenotype.
    d. in both the genotype and the phenotype.

2. The experimental technique in which normal genes are cultivated and exchanged for abnormal genes is called:
   a. chorionic villi sampling.
   b. gene mapping.
   c. amniocentesis.
   d. gene replacement therapy.

3. In the audio program, Don and Karen decided to have a second child, even though Don was a carrier of a genetic condition in which there was a(n):
   a. dominant gene for Down syndrome.
   b. genetic incompatibility with Karen.
   c. excess of amniotic fluid.
   d. chromosome translocation.

4. Concerning gene mapping and gene replacement therapy, which of the following is true?
   a. At the present time, more advances have been made in gene mapping than in gene replacement therapy.
   b. More advances have been made in gene replacement therapy than in gene sampling.
   c. The technology is not yet sophisticated enough for gene replacement to be used.
   d. All of the above are true.

5. When a sperm and an ovum merge, a one-celled _____ is formed.
   a. zygote
   b. reproductive cell
   c. gamete
   d. monozygote

6. Genes are discrete segments that provide the biochemical instructions that each cell needs to become:
   a. a zygote.
   b. a chromosome.
   c. a specific part of a functioning human body.
   d. deoxyribonucleic acid.

7. In the male, the 23rd pair of chromosomes is designated _____ ; in the female, this pair is designated _____ .
   a. XX; XY
   b. XY; XX
   c. XO; XXY
   d. XXY; XO

8. Since the 23rd pair of chromosomes in females is XX, each ovum carries an:
   a. XX zygote.
   b. X zygote.
   c. XY zygote.
   d. X chromosome.

9. When a zygote splits, the two identical, independent clusters that develop become:
   a. dizygotic twins.
   b. monozygotic twins.
   c. fraternal twins.
   d. trizygotic twins.

10. X-linked recessive genes explain why some traits seem to be passed from:
    a. father to son.
    b. father to daughter.
    c. mother to daughter.
    d. mother to son.

11. Most of the known genetic disorders are:
    a. dominant.
    b. recessive.
    c. seriously disabling.
    d. sex-linked.

12. When we say that a characteristic is multifactorial, we mean that:
    a. many genes are involved.
    b. many environmental factors are involved.
    c. many genetic and environmental factors are involved.
    d. the characteristic is polygenic.

13. Genes are segments of molecules of:
    a. genotype.
    b. deoxyribonucleic acid (DNA).
    c. karyotype.
    d. phenotype.

14. The potential for genetic diversity in humans is so great because:
    a. there are approximately 8 million possible combinations of chromosomes.
    b. when the sperm and ovum unite, genetic combinations not present in either parent can be formed.
    c. just before a chromosome pair divides during the formation of gametes, genes cross over, producing recombinations.
    d. of all the above reasons.

15. A chromosomal abnormality that affects males only involves a(n):
    a. XO chromosomal pattern.
    b. XXX chromosomal pattern.
    c. YY chromosomal pattern.
    d. XXY chromosomal pattern.

16. Polygenic complexity is most apparent in _____ characteristics.
    a. physical
    b. psychological
    c. recessive gene
    d. dominant gene

17. Babies born with trisomy-21 (Down syndrome) are often:
    a. born to older parents.
    b. unusually aggressive.
    c. abnormally tall by adolescence.
    d. blind.

18. To say that a trait is polygenic means that:
    a. many genes make it more likely that the individual will inherit the trait.
    b. several genes must be present in order for the individual to inherit the trait.
    c. the trait is multifactorial.
    d. most people carry genes for the trait.

19. Some genetic diseases are recessive, so the child cannot inherit the condition unless both parents:
    a. have Kleinfelter syndrome.
    b. carry the same recessive gene.
    c. have *XO* chromosomes.
    d. have the disease.

20. Dizygotic twins result when:
    a. a single egg is fertilized by a sperm and then splits.
    b. a single egg is fertilized by two different sperm.
    c. two eggs are fertilized by two different sperm.
    d. either a single egg is fertilized by one sperm or two eggs are fertilized by two different sperm.

21. Genotype is to phenotype as _____ is to _____ .
    a. genetic potential; physical expression
    b. physical expression; genetic potential
    c. sperm; ovum
    d. gamete; zygote

22. A 35-year-old woman who is pregnant is most likely to undergo which type of test for the detection of prenatal chromosomal or genetic abnormalities?
    a. pre-implantation testing
    b. ultrasound
    c. amniocentesis
    d. alpha-fetoprotein assay

NAME _____   INSTRUCTOR _____

LESSON 3: GENETIC LEGACIES

Exercise

As you heard in the audio program, Don was a **carrier** of a genetic condition called a **chromosome translocation**, in which a fragment of one chromosome breaks off and becomes attached to another. In Don's case, chromosomes 3 and 15 were involved. Don inherited one normal chromosome 3 (Normal 3), one abnormally short chromosome 3 (Short 3), one normal chromosome 15 (Normal 15), and one abnormally long chromosome 15 (Long 15) that contained the fragment from chromosome 3. Although he was a carrier of the genetic disorder, it did not appear in his **phenotype**. The disorder is manifest in a person's phenotype only if the abnormally long chromosome is transmitted without the abnormally short one—or vice versa. This condition was manifest in Don's brother and niece, who are severely retarded.

It is important to note that not all genetic disorders are of this kind. Chromo-somal translocations of a different type are involved in disorders such as **Down syndrome**. These disorders are different again from single-gene disorders such as Huntington's disease, cystic fibrosis, sickle-cell anemia, Duchenne's muscular dystrophy, and hemophilia.

If Karen and Don became parents, Karen would transmit normal chromosomes. Their child's condition would therefore depend on Don. There would be four possible legacies. To understand these legacies, fill in the boxes of the figure that follows. The first is filled in for you. Then see if you can answer the questions that follow. Hand the completed exercise in to your instructor.

Genetic Roulette: Don's Four Possible Genetic Legacies

Don's
Chromosome 3
normal 3   or   short 3

	normal 3	short 3
normal 15	Legacy 1: normal 3 normal 15	Legacy 2:
long 15	Legacy 3:	Legacy 4:

Don's
Chromosome 15   or

1. In Legacy 1, the number of genes is normal and they are positioned normally on the chromosomes. Would a baby who receives Legacy 1 be phenotypically normal? _____ Would this baby be a carrier of the genetic defect in his or her genotype? _____

2. In Legacy 2, there are too few genes. Would a baby who receives Legacy 2 be phenotypically normal? _____ Would this baby be a carrier of the genetic defect in his or her genotype? _____

3. In Legacy 3, there are too many genes. Would a baby who receives Legacy 3 be phenotypically normal? _____ Would this baby be a carrier of the genetic defect in his or her genotype? _____

4. In Legacy 4, the number of genes is normal, but some are positioned on the wrong chromosome. Would a baby who receives Legacy 4 be phenotypically normal? _____ Would this baby be a carrier of the genetic defect in his or her genotype? _____

5. Which of the four legacies did Don receive? _____

6. The fetus in Karen and Don's first pregnancy may have received either Legacy _____ or Legacy _____ .

7. The fetus in Karen and Don's second pregnancy received Legacy _____ .

LESSON GUIDELINES

Audio Question Guidelines

1. **Genotype** refers to an individual's entire genetic makeup, including those genes that are not expressed outwardly.

   When a trait is apparent, it means that the genes have expressed themselves in the person's **phenotype**.

2. **Amniocentesis** is a prenatal diagnostic test that can reveal genetic problems in a fetus months before birth. A needle is inserted into the uterus, where the fetus floats in a sac filled with amniotic fluid. Amniotic fluid contains cells shed by the fetus. A sample of fluid is withdrawn and the chromosomes of the cells are magnified, photographed, and examined for chromosomal abnormalities.

   In the case of Karen and Don's unborn fetus, an examination of its chromosomes showed that the child would not only be a carrier of the genetic abnormality called a **chromosome translocation** but would also develop the characteristic physical and mental abnormalities in its phenotype. On the basis of this information they decided to terminate the pregnancy.

3. When any healthy young couple undertakes a pregnancy, there is a two- to three-percent baseline risk that the outcome could be abnormal—for example, a significant birth defect resulting in mental retardation or a shortened life span.

4. As in Karen and Don's case, prenatal diagnosis and counseling are available to prospective parents concerned that a genetic condition may run in their family.

   Pediatric genetic counseling is available to families whose children were born with significant birth defects, and children who, though apparently healthy at birth, later show a decline in development that suggests a genetic condition.

   Counseling for **adult-onset conditions** is available for genetic conditions such as Huntington's disease, presenile dementia, certain neuromuscular disorders, and other problems that do not begin to be expressed until the adult years.

5. **Chorionic villi sampling**: A catheter is inserted into the placenta parallel to the wall of the uterus. A sample of the villi—fingerlike projections that dip into the lining of the uterus—is removed through the catheter.

   The villi are composed of fetal tissue, the cells of which are dividing so rapidly that their chromosomes can be examined directly.

Two advantages of this technique over amniocentesis are that it can be done earlier in the pregnancy, and that the results are available to parents sooner.

Gene mapping: Gene mapping refers to techniques that identify the abnormal genes specifically causing a genetic disorder.

Through gene mapping, abnormal genes have been identified for Huntington's disease, cystic fibrosis, sickle-cell anemia, and other genetic conditions.

Gene replacement therapy: Gene replacement therapy refers to the experimental process in which "good" genes are cultivated and substituted for abnormal genes in a diseased person's tissue.

Still in the experimental stages, and not without possible negative effects, gene replacement therapy may eventually be available to treat some disorders.

Textbook Question Answers

1. proteins; DNA; chromosome; genome
2. 46; 23; genes; protein; amino acids
3. adenine; guanine; cytosine; thymine; three; triplets
4. gametes; sperm; ova
5. zygote
6. 23; 23
7. genotype
8. alleles
9. 23rd; X; XX; X; Y; XY
10. sperm; XY; spontaneous abortion
11. been roughly equal; abort female fetuses
12. zygote; are
13. dizygotic; 50
14. 60; late 30s; early 20s
15. duplication; differentiate; on–off switching
16. phenotype
17. polygenic; multifactorial
18. additive; height; skin color (or hair curliness)
19. nonadditive; dominant–recessive; dominant; recessive;
20. incomplete dominance
21. X-linked; color blindness, many allergies, several diseases, and some learning disabilities; males
22. penetrate; temperature; stress
23. does; parental imprinting

24. chance

25. crossing-over; mutation; environmental

26. health

27. Human Genome Project; share

28. carrier

29. behavior genetics; psychological; personality; sociability, assertiveness, moodiness, and fearfulness; schizophrenia, depression, and attention-deficit/hyperactivity disorder; cognitive; memory for numbers, spatial perception, and fluency of expression

30. interaction; genes; environmental; do not always

31. Alzheimer's; amyloid B; 50; early-onset; genetic; late-onset; ApoE; hypertension, diabetes, and high cholesterol

32. depression, antisocial behavior, phobias, and compulsions, environmental

33. do; late winter; virus

34. is; is; a quick temper, a willingness to take risks, and a high level of anxiety

35. every

They provide insight into the complexities of genetic interactions, knowledge about their origins suggests how to limit their harmful consequences, and misinformation and prejudice compound the problems of people who are affected by such abnormalities.

36. gametes

37. maternal age; mosaic

38. spontaneously aborted; 200; syndrome

39. Down Syndrome; trisomy-21; faster; Alzheimer's disease; communication

Most people with Down syndrome have certain facial characteristics—a thick tongue, round face, slanted eyes—as well as distinctive hands, feet, and fingerprints. Many also have hearing problems, heart abnormalities, muscle weakness, and short stature. Almost all experience some mental slowness.

40. sex; Klinefelter syndrome; XXY

41. dominant; are not; more

42. Huntington's disease; Tourette syndrome

43. fragile X

44. recessive; multifactorial; cystic fibrosis, thalassemia, sickle-cell anemia

45. prenatal genetic counseling

46. Genetic counseling is recommended for (a) those who have a parent, sibling, or child with a serious genetic condition; (b) those who have a history of spontaneous abortions, stillbirths, or infertility; (c) couples who are from the same ethnic group or subgroup; and (d) women over age 35 and men age 40 or older.

47. avoid pregnancy, plan to adopt or use artificial insemination or in vitro fertilization; genetic engineering

Answers to Testing Yourself

1. **a.** is the answer. A carrier manifests the abnormality only in his or her genotype. (audio program; textbook, p. 70)

2. **d.** is the answer. Although still in the experimental stage, gene replacement therapy may someday be a viable form of treatment for many genetic disorders. (audio program)

3. **d.** is the answer. A fragment from Don's chromosome 3 had broken off and become attached to his chromosome 15. (audio program)

4. **a.** is the answer. More advances have been made in genetic mapping. (audio program)

5. **a.** is the answer. (textbook, p. 61)

   b. & c. The reproductive cells (sperm and ova), which are also called gametes, are individual entities.

   d. *Monozygote* refers to one member of a pair of identical twins.

6. **c.** is the answer. (textbook, p. 60)

   a. The zygote is the first cell of the developing person.

   b. Chromosomes are molecules of DNA that *carry* genes.

   d. DNA molecules contain genetic information.

7. **b.** is the answer. (textbook, p. 62)

8. **d.** is the answer. When the gametes are formed, one member of each chromosome pair splits off; because in females both are *X* chromosomes, each ovum must carry an *X* chromosome. (textbook, p. 62)

   a., b., & c. The zygote refers to the merged sperm and ovum that is the first new cell of the developing individual.

9. **b.** is the answer. *Mono* means "one." Thus, monozygotic twins develop from one zygote. (textbook, p. 64)

   a. & c. Dizygotic, or fraternal, twins develop from two (*di*) zygotes.

   d. A trizygotic birth would result in triplets (*tri*), rather than twins.

10. **d.** is the answer. X-linked genes are located only on the *X* chromosome. Because males inherit only one *X* chromosome, they are more likely than

females to have these characteristics in their phenotype. (textbook, p. 66)

11. **a.** is the answer. (textbook, p. 77)

c. & d. Most dominant disorders are neither seriously disabling, nor sex-linked.

12. **c.** is the answer. (textbook, p. 65)

a., b., & d. *Polygenic* means "many genes"; *multifactorial* means "many factors," which are not limited to either genetic or environmental factors.

13. **b.** is the answer. (textbook, p. 60)

a. Genotype is a person's genetic potential.

c. A karyotype is a picture of a person's chromosomes.

d. Phenotype is the actual expression of a genotype.

14. **d.** is the answer. (textbook, p. 68)

15. **d.** is the answer. (textbook, p. 77)

a. & b. These chromosomal abnormalities affect females.

c. There is no such abnormality.

16. **b.** is the answer. (textbook, p. 71)

c. & d. The text does not equate polygenic complexity with either recessive or dominant genes.

17. **a.** is the answer. (textbook, p. 76)

18. **b.** is the answer. (textbook, p. 65)

19. **b.** is the answer. (textbook, p. 77)

a. & c. These abnormalities involve the sex chromosomes, not genes.

d. In order for an offspring to inherit a recessive condition, the parents need only be carriers of the recessive gene in their genotypes; they need not actually have the disease.

20. **c.** is the answer. (textbook, p. 64)

a. This would result in monozygotic twins.

b. Only one sperm can fertilize an ovum.

d. A single egg fertilized by one sperm would produce a single offspring or monozygotic twins.

21. **a.** is the answer. Genotype refers to the sum total of all the genes a person inherits; phenotype refers to the actual expression of the individual's characteristics. (textbook, pp. 61, 65)

22. **c.** is the answer. (textbook, p. 83)

a. Pre-implantation testing is conducted on zygotes grown in vitro.

b. Ultrasound is used to detect visible signs of abnormality.

d. Alpha-fetoprotein assay is used to detect the presences of AFP, an indicator of neural-tube defects.

Prenatal Development and Birth

AUDIO PROGRAM: When to Have a baby

ORIENTATION

Is 21 years of age too young to become a parent? Is 36 years of age too old? There are no simple answers to these questions. As Lesson 4 explains, the answers depend on the settings of three developmental clocks that tick through the seasons of life. The first is the biological clock, which is the body's timetable for growth and decline. The second is the social clock, a culturally set timetable that establishes when various events in life are most appropriate. The third is the psychological clock, our personal timetable of readiness for life's milestones. The clocks, which come into play in every major transition of life, are not always in synchrony. In addition, their settings have been changed over the course of history.

One of the themes of *Seasons of Life* is that the diversity of life-span development is due in part to the fact that the social and psychological clocks are not set the same for everyone. Just as each culture, subculture, and historical period establishes its own social clock, so each individual establishes his or her own psychological clock on the basis of individual life experiences.

In audio program 4, "When to Have a Baby," two couples about to have their first child discuss their impending parenthood. Because one of the expectant mothers is 21 and the other 36, the life-span consequences of their "early" and "late" births will be very different. Their stories, illuminated by the expert commentary of sociologist Alice Rossi and anthropologist Jane Lancaster, illustrate how the three developmental clocks influence the timing of births.

The birth of a child is one of life's most enriching experiences. Nine months of prenatal development culminate in the expectant couple's assuming a new and demanding role as parents, and being transformed from a couple to a family. But, as discussed in Chapter 4 of *The Developing Person Through the Life Span*, 6/e, parental responsibilities begin long before birth, during the prenatal period. This development is outlined, together with a description of some of the problems that can occur, including prenatal exposure to disease, drugs, and environmental hazards, and **preterm** birth and **low birth weight**.

As the program opens we hear the voices of the two couples pondering their imminent transition to parenthood.

LESSON GOALS

By the end of this lesson you should be prepared to:

1. Discuss how the timing of births and the setting of the three developmental clocks have changed over the course of human history, and explain the significance of the three clocks.

2. Outline the rapid and orderly development that occurs between conception and birth.

3. Explain the general risk factors and specific hazards that may affect prenatal development.

4. Describe the normal process of birth and the test used to assess the neonate's condition.

5. Explain the concept of parent–infant bonding and the current view of most developmentalists regarding bonding in humans.

Audio Assignment

Listen to the audio tape that accompanies Lesson 4: "When to Have a Baby."

Write answers to the following questions. You may replay portions of the program if you need to refresh your memory. Answer guidelines may be found in the Lesson Guidelines section at the end of this chapter.

1. Explain how the biological, social, and psychological clocks each affect the timing of births.

2. Discuss whether the settings of the three developmental clocks are different for different generations.

3. Explain how the pattern and timing of childbearing changed as humans shifted from a hunting-and-gathering society to a modern society.

4. Discuss some of the life-span consequences of births that occur early and late in parents' lives.

Textbook Assignment

Read Chapter 4: "Prenatal Development and Birth," pages 91–117 in *The Developing Person Through the Life Span*, 6/e, then work through the material that follows to review it. Complete the sentences and answer the questions. As you proceed, evaluate your performance for each section by consulting the answers on page 50. Do not continue with the next section until you understand each answer. If you need to, review or reread the appropriate section in the textbook before continuing.

From Zygote to Newborn (pp. 91–97)

1. Prenatal development is divided into _____ main periods. The first two weeks of development are called the _____ period; from the _____ week through the _____ week is known as the _____ period; and from this point until birth is the _____ period. Some developmentalists prefer to divide pregnancy into 3-month periods called

_____ .

2. At about the _____-celled stage, clusters of cells begin to take on distinct traits. The first clear sign of this process, called _____ , occurs about _____ week(s) after conception, when the multiplying cells separate into outer cells that will become the _____ and inner cells that will become the

_____ .

3. The next significant event is the burrowing of the outer cells of the organism into the lining of the uterus, a process called _____ . This process _____ (is/is not) automatic.

4. At the beginning of the period of the embryo, a thin line down the middle of the developing individual forms a structure that will become the

_____ _____ , which will develop into the _____

_____ _____ .

Briefly describe the major features of development during the second month.

5. Eight weeks after conception, the embryo weighs about _____ and is about _____ in length. The organism now becomes known as the _____ .

6. The genital organs are fully formed by week _____ . If the fetus has a(n) _____ chromosome, the SRY gene on this chromosome sends a signal that triggers development of the _____ (male/female) sex organs. Without that gene, no signal is sent and the fetus begins to develop _____ (male/female) sex organs.

7. By the end of the _____ month, the fetus is fully formed, weighs approximately _____ , and is about _____ long. These figures _____ (vary/do not vary) from fetus to fetus.

8. During the fourth, fifth, and sixth months the brain increases in size by a factor of _____ . This neurological maturation is essential to the regulation of such basic body functions as _____ and _____ . The brain develops new neurons in a process called _____ and new connections between them in a process called _____ . These developments occur during the _____ trimester.

9. By full term, brain growth is so extensive that the brain's advanced outer areas, called the _____ , must _____ _____ in order to fit into the skull.

10. The age at which a fetus has at least some chance of surviving outside the uterus is called the _____ _____ _____ , which occurs _____ weeks after conception.

11. At about _____ weeks after conception, brain-wave patterns begin to resemble the _____–_____ cycles of a newborn.

12. A 28-week-old fetus typically weighs about _____ and has more than a _____ percent chance of survival.

13. Two crucial aspects of development in the last months of prenatal life are maturation of the _____ and _____ systems.

14. Beginning at _____ (what week?), the fetus hears many sounds, as evidenced by increased fetal _____ and _____ _____ in response to loud noises.

15. (text and Table 4.3) The average newborn weighs _____ .

Risk Reduction (pp. 97–107)

16. The scientific study of birth defects is called _____ . Harmful agents that can cause birth defects, called _____ , include _____ _____ .

17. Substances that impair the child's action and intellect by harming the brain are called _____ _____ .

Approximately _____ percent of all fetuses are born with major structural anomalies, and _____ percent with behavioral difficulties related to prenatal damage.

18. Teratology is a science of _____ _____ , which attempts to evaluate the factors that can make prenatal harm more or less likely to occur.

19. Three crucial factors that determine whether a specific teratogen will cause harm, and of what nature, are the _____ of exposure, the _____ of exposure, and the developing organism's _____

_____ to damage from the substance.

20. The time when a particular part of the body is most susceptible to teratogenic damage is called its _____ _____ . For physical structure and form, this is the entire period of the _____ . However, for _____ teratogens, the entire prenatal period is critical.

21. Some teratogens have a _____ effect—that is, the substances are harmless until exposure reaches a certain frequency or amount. However, the _____ of some teratogens when taken together may make them more harmful at lower dosage levels than when taken separately.

22. Genetic susceptibilities to the prenatal effects of alcohol and to certain birth disorders, such as cleft palate, may involve defective _____ .

23. When the mother-to-be's diet is deficient in _____ _____ , neural-tube defects such as _____ _____ or _____ may result.

24. Genetic vulnerability is also related to the sex of the developing organism. Generally, _____ (male/female) embryos and fetuses are more vulnerable to teratogens. This sex not only has a higher rate of teratogenic birth defects and later behavioral problems, but also a higher rate of _____ _____ , and older members of this sex have more _____ _____ .

25. (Changing Policy) It was once believed that a pregnant woman's _____ prevented all harmful substances from reaching the fetus. This belief was proven wrong when an epidemic

of _____ led to an increase in babies who were born _____ , and an increase in newborns with deformed _____ was traced to maternal use of the drug _____ .

26. (Changing Policy) The most devastating viral teratogen is the _____ _____ _____ , which gradually overwhelms the body's _____ _____ and leads to _____ . Babies who are infected with this virus usually die by age _____ .

27. (Changing Policy) Pregnant women who are HIV-positive can reduce the risk of transmitting the virus to their newborns by giving birth by _____ _____ , by not _____-_____ , and by taking _____ _____ .

State three reasons why almost a million HIV-positive children continue to be born each year.

28. (Changing Policy) The most common teratogen in developed nations is _____ . High doses of this teratogen cause _____ _____ _____ , and less intense doses cause _____ _____ _____ . The damage is increased when alcohol is combined with other _____ _____ .

29. Newborns who weigh less than _____ are classified as _____-_____ babies.

Below 3 pounds, they are called _____-
_____-_____ babies;
at less than 2 pounds they are _____-
_____-_____
babies. Worldwide, rates of this condition
_____ (vary/do not vary) from
nation to nation.

30. Babies who are born 3 or more weeks early are
called _____ .

31. Infants who weigh substantially less than they
should, given how much time has passed since
conception, are called _____
_____ _____
_____ .

32. About 25 percent of all low-birthweight (LBW)
births in the United States are linked to maternal
use of _____ .

33. Two other common reasons for low birthweight
are maternal _____ and
_____ .

The Birth Process (pp. 107–116)

34. At about the 266th day, the fetal brain signals the
release of certain _____ into the
mother's bloodstream, which trigger her
_____ _____
to contract and relax. The normal birth process
begins when these contractions become regular.
The average length of labor is
_____ hours for first births and
_____ hours for subsequent births.

35. The newborn is usually rated on the
_____ _____ , which
assigns a score of 0, 1, or 2 to each of the following five characteristics: _____
_____ . A
score below _____ indicates that the
newborn is in critical condition and requires
immediate attention; if the score is
_____ or better, all is well. This rat-
ing is made twice, at _____

minute(s) after birth and again at
_____ minutes.

36. The birth experience is influenced by several
factors, including _____
_____ .

37. In about 22 percent of U.S. births, a surgical
procedure called a _____
_____ is performed.

38. An increasing number of hospital deliveries occur
in the _____ _____ .
An even more family-oriented environment is the
_____ _____ . In addi-
tion, many North American mothers today use a
professional birth coach, or _____ , to
assist them.

39. The disorder _____
_____ , which affects motor centers
in the brain, often results from
_____ vulnerability, worsened by
exposure to _____ and episodes of
_____ , a temporary lack of
_____ during birth.

40. Another complication is an infection called
_____ _____
_____ , which is often fatal to
newborns if not quickly treated with
_____ .

41. Because they are often confined to intensive-care
nurseries or hooked up to medical machinery,
low-birthweight infants may be deprived of normal kinds of stimulation such as
_____ .

42. Providing extra soothing stimulation to vulnerable infants in the hospital _____
(does/does not) aid weight gain and
_____ (does/does not) increase
overall alertness. One example of this is
_____ _____ , in
which mothers of low-birthweight infants spend
extra time holding their infants.

43. Among the minor developmental problems that
accompany preterm birth are being late to

_____ .

High-risk infants are often more

_____ , less _____ ,

and slower to _____ .

44. The deficits related to low birthweight usually

_____ (can/cannot) be

overcome.

The Beginning of Bonding (pp. 128–130)

45. The rate of LBW births among women born in Mexico and now living in the United states is

_____ (higher/lower) than those of other Americans. This difference has been attributed to _____ , or the strong

_____ _____ that such women experience. Especially important is the role played by a supportive _____ ,

who can help _____

_____ .

46. A crucial factor in the birth experience is the formation of a strong _____

_____ between the prospective parents.

47. Some new mothers experience a profound feeling of sadness called _____

_____ .

48. The term used to describe the close relationship that begins within the first hours after birth is the

_____–_____

_____ .

Testing Yourself

After you have completed the audio and text review questions, see how well you do on the following quiz. Correct answers, with text and audio references, may be found at the end of this chapter.

1. Among other things, the social clock tells us:
   a. the age at which having a child becomes biologically feasible.
   b. the average age for having a first child.
   c. the appropriate or "best" age for having a child in our society.
   d. the age at which having a child best correlates with the parents' well-being later on.

2. In contrast to hunter-gatherer women, sedentary women tend to have:
   a. more children.
   b. fewer children.
   c. fewer menstrual cycles.
   d. a shorter fertile period.

3. The audio program states that for the typical American woman today the biological and social clocks are out of sync. Which of the following statements explains why this is so?
   a. The average teenager today is sexually mature before she is psychologically interested in sexual activity.
   b. Although menarche occurs at a younger age than ever before, it takes longer than ever to achieve the social status of an adult.
   c. Most women today assume the social role of adults before their reproductive systems are optimally suited for childbearing.
   d. Because of the widespread use of oral contraceptives, the biological clock that governs menstruation has effectively been halted.

4. Two patterns of childbearing are common today. The one associated with "early" births favors the _____ clock, while the one associated with "late" births favors the _____ clock.
   a. social; biological
   b. social; psychological
   c. biological; social
   d. psychological; social

5. *Sedentism* refers to:
   a. the tendency for menarche to occur at an earlier age in recent years.
   b. the process by which the biological clock governs the optimal years for childbearing.
   c. the tendency of less active women to have a later menarche.
   d. the shift in human social organization from a nomadic life to a village-dwelling society.

6. The third through the eighth week after conception is called the:
   a. embryonic period.
   b. ovum period.
   c. fetal period.
   d. germinal period.

7. The neural tube develops into the:
   a. respiratory system.
   b. umbilical cord.
   c. brain and spinal column.
   d. circulatory system.

8. To say that a teratogen has a "threshold effect" means that it is:
   a. virtually harmless until exposure reaches a certain level.
   b. harmful only to low-birthweight infants.
   c. harmful to certain developing organs during periods when these organs are developing most rapidly.
   d. harmful only if the pregnant woman's weight does not increase by a certain minimum amount during her pregnancy.

9. By the eighth week after conception, the embryo has almost all the basic organs except the:
   a. skeleton.
   b. elbows and knees.
   c. sex organs.
   d. fingers and toes.

10. The most critical factor in attaining the age of viability is development of the:
   a. placenta.
   b. eyes.
   c. brain.
   d. skeleton.

11. An important nutrient that many women do not get in adequate amounts from the typical diet is:
   a. vitamin A.
   b. zinc.
   c. guanine.
   d. folic acid.

12. An embryo begins to develop male sex organs if _____ , and female sex organs if _____ .
   a. genes on the Y chromosome send a signal; no signal is sent from an X chromosome
   b. genes on the Y chromosome send a signal; genes on the X chromosome send a signal
   c. genes on the X chromosome send a signal; no signal is sent from an X chromosome
   d. genes on the X chromosome send a signal; genes on the Y chromosome send a signal

13. A teratogen:
   a. cannot cross the placenta during the embryonic period.
   b. is usually inherited from the mother.
   c. can be counteracted by good nutrition most of the time.
   d. may be a virus, a drug, a chemical, radiation, or environmental pollutants.

14. (Changing Policy) Among the characteristics of babies born with fetal alcohol syndrome are:
   a. slowed physical growth and behavior problems.
   b. addiction to alcohol and methadone.
   c. deformed arms and legs.
   d. blindness.

15. The birth process begins:
   a. when the fetus moves into the right position.
   b. when the uterus begins to contract at regular intervals to push the fetus out.
   c. about 8 hours (in the case of firstborns) after the uterus begins to contract at regular intervals.
   d. when the baby's head appears at the opening of the vagina.

16. The Apgar scale is administered:
   a. only if the newborn is in obvious distress.
   b. once, just after birth.
   c. twice, one minute and five minutes after birth.
   d. repeatedly during the newborn's first hours.

17. Most newborns weigh about:
   a. 5 pounds.
   b. 6 pounds.
   c. 7 1/2 pounds.
   d. 8 1/2 pounds.

18. Low-birthweight babies born near the due date but weighing substantially less than they should:
   a. are classified as preterm.
   b. are called small for gestational age.
   c. usually have no sex organs.
   d. show many signs of immaturity.

19. Approximately one out of every four low-birthweight births in the United States is caused by maternal use of:
   a. alcohol.
   b. tobacco.
   c. crack cocaine.
   d. household chemicals.

20. The idea of a parent–infant bond in humans arose from:
   a. observations in the delivery room.
   b. data on adopted infants.
   c. animal studies.
   d. studies of disturbed mother–infant pairs.

21. Neurogenesis refers to the process by which:
   a. the fetal brain develops new neurons.
   b. new connections between neurons develop.
   c. the neural tube forms during the middle trimester.
   d. the cortex folds into layers in order to fit into the skull.

22. Synaptogenesis refers to the process by which:
    a. the fetal brain develops new neurons.
    b. new connections between neurons develop.
    c. the neural tube forms during the middle trimester.
    d. the cortex folds into layers in order to fit into the skull.

23. When there is a strong parental alliance:
    a. mother and father cooperate because of their mutual commitment to their children.
    b. the parents agree to support each other in their shared parental roles.
    c. children are likely to thrive.
    d. all of the above are true.

NAME _____   INSTRUCTOR _____

LESSON 4: SAYING WHEN

Exercise

The three developmental clocks come into play in every major transition of life. No transition is greater than the change from being pregnant to being a parent. The setting of the developmental clocks can affect the timing of births and the adjustment of first-time parents to their new roles, and can have long-term life-span consequences on both parents and their children.

The stories of the two couples introduced in audio program 4 illustrate some of these effects and contrast two new patterns of childbearing in our species. Shelley and her husband Charles gave birth when Shelley was 21. Shelley's pregnancy was "on time" biologically, but "off time" socially and psychologically. The pregnancy was unexpected and came at a time when the young couple was still establishing their own relationship, completing their educations, and struggling to make a living.

Brett and Henry's child was born when Brett was 36. This biologically "late" birth is an example of an increasingly common pattern of childbearing that favors the social clock by allowing parents to establish careers and improve their financial security before having children. Brett and Henry's birth may have been "off time" biologically, but it was "on time" psychologically and "on time," or perhaps even a little late, in terms of the social clock.

The experts in the audio program point out that unlike the biological clock, which changes little from generation to generation, the social clock and psychological clocks can be reset. The settings of these clocks reflect each individual's culture, historical context, and life experiences.

To help you integrate the material in Lesson 4 into an actual life story, write answers to the questions that follow, then hand the completed exercise in to your instructor. Before completing the exercise, you may find it helpful to review Audio Guidelines 1–4 to make sure you understand the differences and interrelationships of the three developmental clocks.

1. If you (or your subject) are a parent, please discuss the timing of your child(ren)'s birth(s) by answering the following questions. If you (or your subject) are not a parent, skip to question 2.
   a. According to the settings of your social, biological, and psychological clocks, was the timing of your child(ren)'s, birth(s) "on-time" or "off-time"?
   b. If your child(ren)'s birth(s) was (were) not recent, would its (their) timing be considered different according to the present settings of the developmental clocks and the two new patterns of childbearing mentioned in the audio program?
   c. What factors (career, education, health concerns, and so on) influenced the timing of your child(ren)'s birth(s)?

2. If you (or your subject) are not a parent, but contemplate having children, at what developmental "time" do you foresee these births occurring according to your biological clock? your social clock? your psychological clock? How does this compare with the settings of your parents' developmental clocks when you were born?

3. In your opinion, what is the ideal timing for the birth of a child from the standpoint of the three developmental clocks? You may conclude that the ideal time is never. Whatever the case, please explain your reasoning.

4. What is your current age (or the age of your subject)?

LESSON GUIDELINES

Audio Question Guidelines

1. The biological clock governs physical development through the various mechanisms of heredity and physiology that program growth, fertility, and aging. For women, the biologically optimal period for having a child is between 22 and 32 years; for men the range is between 22 and 40 years.

   The social clock is a culturally set timetable that establishes when various events and behaviors in life are appropriate and called for. Today, the social clock prescribes "later" births, giving couples an opportunity to establish their careers and financial solvency.

   The psychological clock represents each person's inner timetable of development. It is the individual's way of determining when he or she is ready to marry, to become a parent, and to make the other transitions inherent in development.

2. Unlike the two other developmental clocks, which can be reset on the basis of the individual's life experiences, culture, and generation, the biological clock is relatively immutable. For most life events, however, the biological clock specifies a normal *range* of time rather than a precise moment. For example, although the biological clock was unchanged in our transition from a hunter-gatherer society to a sedentary society, because of better nutrition and living conditions in modern times, the average age of menarche has dropped to 12.5 years, which is the lower end of the range set by the biological clock.

   Even as young people are becoming sexually mature at younger ages, the social clock has moved in the opposite direction: it takes longer and longer to achieve the status of an adult in our society. The result is that today's society has created a lengthy period in which an individual may have the reproductive capacity of an adult but the social role of a child.

   The psychological clock, set as it is according to each individual's life experiences, shows the greatest diversity of the three developmental clocks. Because she lives at a time when the biological and social clocks are out of sync, the typical American woman today finds it very difficult to decide when to have a child. The burden generally falls on her individual psychological clock.

3. As recently as 10,000 years ago, our ancestors lived as hunter-gatherers. Unlike modern women, hunter-gatherer women nursed their children for three or four years. This continuous nursing tended to suppress ovulation and limit the number of children born. With the development of agriculture and the shift from a nomadic to a **sedentary** lifestyle, the numbers of children born increased. In addition, the average age of menarche—the beginning of the menstrual cycle—dropped from about age 16 in hunter-gatherer women to age 12.5 in today's sedentary women.

   For hunter-gatherer women, the biological and social clocks were in sync: by the time they had their first child they had already assumed their social role as adults. Because the social and biological clocks are not in sync today, two new patterns of childbearing have emerged. One, favoring the biological clock, is the bearing of children very early in the life cycle (at or before the age of 21). The second, favoring the social clock, is exemplified by women who postpone having children until age 35 or later in order to become established in a career.

4. During most of human history the peak reproductive years were between 20 and 30. The two new patterns of childbearing that have emerged today—"early" births and "late" births—are atypical of our species' history.

   As in the case of Shelley and Charles whom we met in the audio program, an "early" birth is one that may be on-time biologically but off-time socially and psychologically. When the three developmental clocks are out of sync, a difficult period of adjustment may follow.

   Once one moves outside the optimal biological range for having a baby—between 22 and 32 for women and between 22 and 40 for men—there is a greater risk of physiological impairment to the infant. Many early births (to mothers under age 16 or 17) result in low-birth-weight babies. Late births (to mothers over the age of 35) are associated with increased risk of conditions such as Down syndrome.

   Childbearing is delayed most often among better-educated segments of the population, who wish to complete their training or become established in a career before becoming parents. The late-timed baby may benefit from the parents' greater economic security and maturity.

   Because of the advancing ages of today's older parents, late-timed births are often only-births: the one-child family is becoming more and more common.

Textbook Question Answers

1. three; germinal; third; eighth; embryonic; fetal; trimesters

2. eight; differentiation; one; placenta; embryo

3. implantation; is not

4. neural tube; central nervous system

First, the upper arms, then the forearms, palms, and webbed fingers appear. Legs, feet, and webbed toes follow. At eight weeks, the embryo's head is more rounded, and the facial features are fully formed. The fingers and toes are separate.

5. $1/30$ ounce (1 gram); 1 inch (2.5 centimeters); fetus

6. 12; Y; male; female

7. third; 3 ounces (87 grams); 3 inches (7.5 centimeters); vary

8. six; breathing; sucking; neurogenesis; synaptogenesis; middle

9. cortex; fold into layers

10. age of viability; 22

11. 28; sleep–wake

12. 3 pounds (1,300 grams); 95

13. respiratory; cardiovascular

14. 28 weeks; heartbeat; body movements

15. $7^1/2$ pounds (3,400 grams)

16. teratology; teratogens; viruses, drugs, chemicals, pollutants, stressors, and malnutrition

17. behavioral teratogens; 3; 10 to 20

18. risk analysis

19. timing; amount; genetic vulnerability

20. critical period; embryo; behavioral

21. threshold; interaction

22. enzymes

23. folic acid; spina bifida; anencephaly

24. male; spontaneous abortions; learning disabilities

25. placenta; rubella; deaf; limbs; thalidomide

26. human immunodeficiency virus (HIV); immune system; AIDS; 5

27. cesarean section; breast-feeding; antiretroviral drugs

One reason is that the women and their medical providers may not be aware that they have the virus.

Another reason is that the drugs for treating HIV infections are very expensive. A third reason is that the woman's sociocultural context prevents her from admitting she has the disease.

28. alcohol; fetal alcohol syndrome; fetal alcohol effects; psychoactive drugs

29. 2,500 grams ($5^1/2$ pounds); low-birthweight; very-low-birthweight; extremely-low-birthweight; vary

30. preterm

31. small for gestational age

32. tobacco

33. illness; malnutrition

34. hormones; uterine muscles; eight ; three

35. Apgar scale; heart rate, breathing, muscle tone, color, and reflexes; 4; 7; one; five

36. the parents' preparation for birth, the physical and emotional support provided by birth attendants, the position and size of the fetus, the practices of the mother's culture

37. cesarean section

38. labor room; birthing center; doula

39. cerebral palsy; genetic; teratogens; anoxia; oxygen

40. Group B streptococcus (GBS); antibiotics

41. rocking (or regular handling)

42. does; does; kangaroo care

43. smile, hold a bottle, and to communicate; distractible; obedient; talk

44. can

45. lower; familia; family support; father; reduce maternal stress and help ensure the future mother is healthy, well-nourished, and drug free

46. parental alliance

47. postpartum depression

48. parent–infant bond

Answers to Testing Yourself

1. **c.** is the answer. The social clock is a culturally set timetable that establishes when various events and behaviors in life are appropriate and called for. (audio program)

2. **a.** is the answer. The hunter-gatherer society is associated with greater restraint in the production of children. This is due, in part, to the tendency of women in hunter-gatherer societies to nurse continuously, which tends to suppress ovu-

lation and prevent pregnancy. (audio program)

3. **b.** is the answer. Today's society has created a 10-year, or longer, period in which an individual may have the reproductive capacity of an adult but the social role of a child. (audio program)

4. **c.** is the answer. Early births favor the biological clock by occurring during the optimal period of biological fertility. Late births favor the social clock because they allow the couple to establish careers and attain greater financial security before having children. (audio program)

5. **d.** is the answer. The shift from a hunter-gatherer to village-dwelling society is referred to as sedentism. (audio program)

6. **a.** is the answer. (textbook, p. 91)

b. This term, which refers to the germinal period, is not used in the text.

c. The fetal period is from the ninth week until birth.

d. The germinal period covers the first two weeks.

7. **c.** is the answer. (textbook, p. 93)

8. **a.** is the answer. (textbook, p. 98)

b., c., & d. Although low birthweight (b), critical periods of organ development (c), and maternal malnutrition (d) are all hazardous to the developing person during prenatal development, none is an example of a threshold effect.

9. **c.** is the answer. The sex organs do not begin to take shape until the fetal period. (textbook, p. 94)

10. **c.** is the answer. (textbook, p. 95)

11. **d.** is the answer. (textbook, p. 100)

12. **a.** is the answer. (textbook, p. 94)

13. **d.** is the answer. (textbook, p. 97)

a. In general, teratogens can cross the placenta at any time.

b. Teratogens are agents in the environment, not heritable genes (although *susceptibility* to individual teratogens has a genetic component).

c. Although nutrition is an important factor in healthy prenatal development, the text does not suggest that nutrition alone can usually counteract the harmful effects of teratogens.

14. **a.** is the answer. (textbook, p. 103)

15. **b.** is the answer. (textbook, p. 107)

16. **c.** is the answer. (textbook, p. 108)

17. **c.** is the answer. (textbook, p. 96)

18. **b.** is the answer. (textbook, p. 106)

19. **b.** is the answer. (textbook, p. 106)

20. **c.** is the answer. (textbook, p. 115)

21. **a.** is the answer. (textbook, p. 94)

22. **b.** is the answer. (textbook, p. 94)

23. **d.** is the answer. (textbook, p. 114)

The First Two Years: Biosocial Development

AUDIO PROGRAM: The Biography of the Brain

ORIENTATION

This lesson is the first of a three-lesson unit that describes the developing person from birth to age 2 in terms of biosocial, cognitive, and psychosocial development. Lesson 5 examines biosocial development.

Biosocial development during the first two years is so rapid that infants often seem to change before their parents' very eyes. In Chapter 5 of *The Developing Person Through the Life Span*, 6/e, Kathleen Berger describes the typical patterns of growth in the body and nervous system and the timetables for **motor-skill**, **sensory**, and **perceptual development.** Although the developmental sequence is usually the same for all healthy infants, variation in the ages at which certain skills are mastered does occur, in part because development depends on the interaction of biological and environmental forces.

Audio program 5, "The Biography of the Brain," continues the stories of the two couples introduced in program 4. Both couples have now had their babies and in this lesson we follow the early months of the babies' biosocial development. Compared to other mammals, humans are physically quite immature at birth. Evolutionary biologist Stephen Jay Gould and anthropologist Barry Bogin suggest that during the course of human evolution, an increase in the size of the brain and skull required a corresponding reduction in the length of pregnancy. In this way, the infant can be born before its head has grown too large to pass through the birth canal. Brain development influences growth in a variety of ways. Attainment of adult body size and sexual maturity are delayed until the brain, too, is almost fully mature. Brain development continues throughout life, increasingly influenced by environmental factors and learning.

Another issue explored in this lesson is the importance of nutrition to the developing brain. In the program, anthropologist Jane Lancaster notes that mothers and babies store body fat in order to meet the nutritional needs of the developing brain. The mother's fat ensures a rich supply of milk, an ideal food with a special profile of nutrients that exactly matches the developmental needs of the infant.

Neuropsychologist Jill Becker describes brain development at the microscopic level as a process in which individual **neurons** grow and form synapses with other neurons. Laboratory research with animals indicates that being raised in a stimulating environment promotes the development of more of these neural connections.

As the program opens we hear one of the couples describe the birth of their first child and the tight fit of their baby's head through the birth canal.

LESSON GOALS

By the end of this lesson you should be prepared to:

1. Describe the size and proportion of an infant's body, including how they change during the first two years and how they compare with those of an adult.

2. Describe normal patterns of brain, sleep, sensory and perceptual, and motor-skill development during infancy.

3. Discuss how biological and environmental forces interact in the infant's brain maturation, acquisition of motor skills, and sensory and perceptual development.

4. Identify the competing evolutionary pressures that have led some anthropologists to argue that human babies are born "too soon."

5. Outline the nutritional needs of infants during the first year of life. Describe the significance of breast milk and body fat in ensuring adequate nutrition.

Audio Assignment

Listen to the audio tape that accompanies Lesson 5: "The Biography of the Brain."

Write answers to the following questions. You may replay portions of the program if you need to refresh your memory. Answer guidelines may be found in the Lesson Guidelines section at the end of this chapter.

1. Explain why some anthropologists believe that, compared with other mammals, human babies are very immature at birth.

2. Discuss the significance of body fat and breast milk in meeting the nutritional needs of the newborn.

3. Describe the ways in which the nervous system matures during childhood.

4. Compare development of the brain, body, and reproductive system during the first two years.

Textbook Assignment

Read Chapter 5: "The First Two Years: Biosocial Development," pages 121–145 in *The Developing Person Through the Life Span*, 6/e, then work through the material that follows to review it. Complete the sentences and answer the questions. As you proceed, evaluate your performance for each section by consulting the answers on page 61. Do not continue with the next section until you understand each answer. If you need to, review or reread the appropriate section in the textbook before continuing.

Body Changes (pp. 121–125)

1. The average North American newborn measures _____ and weighs a little more than _____ .

2. The phenomenon in which inadequate nutrition causes the body to stop growing but not the brain is called _____-_____ .

3. A standard, or average, of physical development that is derived for a specific group or population is a _____ .

4. By age 2, the typical child weighs about _____ and measures _____ . The typical 2-year-old is almost _____ (what proportion?) of his or her adult weight and _____ (what proportion?) of his or her adult height.

5. A _____ is a point on a ranking scale of _____ (what number?) to _____ (what number?).

6. Throughout childhood, regular and ample _____ correlates with maturation of the _____ , _____ , _____ regulation, and _____ adjustment in school and within the family. Approximately _____ percent of 1-year-olds sleep through the night.

7. Over the first months of life, the relative amount of time spent in the different _____ of sleep changes. The stage of sleep characterized by flickering eyes behind closed lids and

_____ is called _____ _____ . During this stage of sleep brain waves are fairly _____ (slow/rapid). This stage of sleep _____ (increases/decreases) over the first months, as does the dozing stage called _____ _____ . Slow-wave sleep, also called _____ _____ , increases markedly at about _____ months of age.

Early Brain Development (pp. 125–130)

8. At birth, the brain has attained about _____ percent of its adult weight; by age 2 the brain is about _____ percent of its adult weight. In comparison, body weight at age 2 is about _____ percent of what it will be in adulthood.

9. The brain's communication system consists primarily of nerve cells called _____ connected by intricate networks of nerve fibers, called _____ and _____ . About _____ percent of these cells are in the brain's outer layer called the _____ .

10. Each neuron has many _____ but only a single _____ .

11. Neurons communicate with one another at intersections called _____ . After traveling down the length of the _____ , electrical impulses excite chemicals called _____ that carry information across the _____ to the _____ of a "receiving" neuron. Most of the nerve cells _____ (are/are not) present at birth, whereas the fiber networks _____ (are/are not) rudimentary.

12. During the first months of life, brain development is most noticeable in the _____ .

13. From birth until age 2, the density of dendrites in the cortex _____ (increases/ decreases) by a factor of _____ . The phenomenal increase in neural connections over the first two years has been called _____ _____ .

Following this growth process, neurons in some areas of the brain wither in the process called _____ because _____ does not activate those brain areas.

14. Brain functions that require basic common experiences in order to develop are called _____-_____ brain functions; those that depend on particular, and variable, experiences in order to develop are called _____-_____ brain functions.

15. (Thinking Like a Scientist) Neuroscientists once believed that brains were entirely formed by _____ and _____ _____ ; today, most believe in _____ , which is the concept that personality, intellect, habits, and emotions change throughout life for _____ (one/a combination of) reason(s). William Greenough discovered that the brains of rats that were raised in stimulating environments were better developed, with more _____ branching, than the brains of rats raised in barren environments. Orphaned Romanian children who were isolated and deprived of stimulation showed signs of _____ damage. Placed in healthier environments, these children _____ (improved/did not improve); years later, persistent deficits in these children _____ (were/were not) found.

The Senses and Motor Skills (pp. 130–136)

16. The process by which the visual, auditory, and other sensory systems detect stimuli is called _____ ; _____ occurs when the brain tries to make sense out of a stimulus so that the individual becomes aware of it. At birth, both of these processes _____ (are/are not) apparent. In the process called _____ , a person thinks about what he or she has perceived. This process _____ (can/cannot) occur without either sensation or perception.

17. Generally speaking, newborns' hearing _____ (is/is not) very acute. Newborns _____ (can/cannot) perceive differences in voices, rhythms, and language.

18. The least mature of the senses at birth is _____ . Newborns' visual focusing is best for objects between _____ and _____ inches away.

19. Increasing maturation of the visual cortex accounts for improvements in other visual abilities, such as the infant's ability to _____ on an object and _____ to its critical areas. The ability to use both eyes in a coordinated manner to focus on one object, which is called _____ _____ , develops at about _____ of age.

20. Taste, smell, and touch _____ (function/do not function) at birth. The ability to be comforted by the human _____ is a skill tested in the _____ Neonatal Behavioral Assessment Scale.

21. The infant's early sensory abilities seem organized for two goals: _____ _____ and _____ .

22. The most visible and dramatic body changes of infancy involve _____ _____ .

23. An involuntary physical response to a stimulus is called a _____ .

24. The involuntary response that causes the newborn to take the first breath even before the umbilical cord is cut, is called the _____ _____ . Because breathing is irregular during the first few days, other reflexive behaviors, such as _____ , _____ , and _____ , are common.

25. Shivering, crying, and tucking the legs close to the body are examples of reflexes that help to maintain _____ .

26. A third set of reflexes fosters _____ . One of these is the tendency of the newborn to

suck anything that touches the lips; this is the _____ reflex. Another is the tendency of newborns to turn their heads and start to suck when something brushes against their cheek; this is the _____ reflex.

27. Large movements such as running and climbing are called _____ _____ skills.

28. Most infants are able to crawl on all fours (sometimes called creeping) between _____ and _____ months of age.

List the major hallmarks in children's mastery of walking.

29. Abilities that require more precise, small movements, such as picking up a coin, are called _____ _____ skills. By _____ of age, most babies can reach for, grab, and hold onto almost any object of the right size. By _____ months, most infants can transfer objects from one hand to the other.

30. Although the _____ in which motor skills are mastered is the same in all healthy infants, the _____ of acquisition of skills varies greatly.

31. The average ages, or _____ , at which most infants master major motor skills are based on a large sample of infants drawn from _____ (a single/many) ethnic group(s).

32. Motor skill norms vary from one _____ group to another.

33. Motor skill acquisition in identical twins _____ (is/is not) more similar than in fraternal twins, suggesting that genes _____ (do/do not) play an important role. Another influential factor is the _____ .

Public Health Measures (pp. 136–143)

34. In 1900, about 1 in _____ (how many?) children died before age 5. This childhood death rate _____ (varied from one nation to another/was the same throughout the world). Today, in the healthiest nations such as _____ , _____ , and _____ , about 1 in _____ (how many?) children who survive birth die before age 6.

35. A key factor in reducing the childhood death rate was the development of _____—a process that stimulates the body's _____ system to defend against contagious diseases.

36. Another reason for lower infant mortality worldwide is a decrease in _____ _____ _____ , in which seemingly healthy infants die unexpectedly in their _____ .

37. A key factor in SIDS is _____ background. In ethnically diverse nations, babies of _____ descent are more likely, and babies of _____ descent are less likely, to succumb to SIDS than are babies of _____ descent. In ethnic groups with a low incidence of SIDS, babies are put to sleep _____ (in what position?).

Identify several other practices that may explain why certain ethnic groups have a low incidence of SIDS.

38. The ideal infant food is _____ , beginning with the thick, high-calorie fluid called _____ . The only situations in which formula may be healthier for the infant than breast milk are when _____ _____ .

State several advantages of breast milk over cow's milk for the developing infant.

39. The most serious nutritional problem of infancy is _____-_____ _____ .

40. Chronically malnourished infants suffer in three ways: Their _____ may not develop normally; they may have no _____ _____ to protect them against disease, and they may develop the diseases _____ or _____ .

41. Severe protein-calorie deficiency in early infancy causes _____ . In toddlers, protein-calorie deficiency is more likely to cause the disease called _____ , which involves swelling or bloating of the face, legs, and abdomen.

Testing Yourself

After you have completed the audio and text review questions, see how well you do on the following quiz. Correct answers, with text and audio references, may be found at the end of this chapter.

1. According to experts in the audio program, why are human babies born so physically immature?
   a. As a result of better nutrition, the biological clock that times gestation has been reset.
   b. If prenatal development continued longer, infants' large heads would not fit through the birth canal.
   c. Humans are much less active than other mammals.
   d. All of the above are reasons for babies being born so physically immature.

2. In what order do parts of the human body mature?
   a. brain, body, reproductive system
   b. body, brain, reproductive system
   c. body, reproductive system, brain
   d. brain, reproductive system, body

3. Approximately 90 percent of the brain's growth is completed by the age of:
   a. 1 month.
   b. 6 months.
   c. 1 year.
   d. 5 years.

4. Laboratory research with animals has shown that one effect of being raised in a stimulating environment is:
   a. an increase in the number of neurons in the brain.
   b. a shortening of the time required for the brain to reach its full capacity.
   c. a reduction in the number of "extra" nerve cells that die.
   d. a reduction in nerve-cell insulation, which tends to slow neural communication.

5. Compared with that of other species, human milk has a high content of _____, which especially promotes development of _____ .
   a. protein; the brain
   b. protein; muscle
   c. sugar; muscle
   d. sugar; the brain

6. The average North American newborn:
   a. weighs approximately 6 pounds.
   b. weighs approximately 7 pounds.
   c. is "overweight" because of the diet of the mother.
   d. weighs 10 percent less than what is desirable.

7. Compared to the first year, growth during the second year:
   a. proceeds at a slower rate.
   b. continues at about the same rate.
   c. includes more insulating fat.
   d. includes more bone and muscle.

8. The major motor skill most likely to be mastered by an infant before the age of 6 months is:
   a. rolling over.
   b. sitting without support.
   c. turning the head in search of a nipple.
   d. grabbing an object with thumb and forefinger.

9. Norms suggest that the earliest walkers in the world are infants from:
   a. Western Europe.   c. Uganda.
   b. the United States.   d. Denver.

10. Dreaming is characteristic of:
    a. slow-wave sleep.
    b. transitional sleep.
    c. REM sleep.
    d. quiet sleep.

11. Transient exuberance and pruning demonstrate that:
    a. the pace of acquisition of motor skills varies markedly from child to child.
    b. Newborns sleep more than older children because their immature nervous systems cannot handle the higher, waking level of sensory stimulation.
    c. The specifics of brain structure and growth depend partly on the infant's experience.
    d. Good nutrition is essential to healthy biosocial development.

12. Sensation is to perception as _____ is to _____ .
    a. hearing; seeing
    b. detecting a stimulus; making sense of a stimulus
    c. making sense of a stimulus; detecting a stimulus
    d. tasting; smelling

13. Climbing is to using a crayon as _____ is to _____ .
    a. fine motor skill; gross motor skill
    b. gross motor skill; fine motor skill
    c. reflex; fine motor skill
    d. reflex; gross motor skill

14. Compared with formula-fed infants, breast-fed infants tend to have:
    a. greater weight gain.
    b. fewer allergies and digestive upsets.
    c. less frequent feedings during the first few months.
    d. more social approval.

15. Marasmus and kwashiorkor are caused by:
    a. bloating.
    b. protein-calorie deficiency.
    c. living in a developing country.
    d. poor family food habits.

16. The infant's first motor skills are:
    a. fine motor skills.   c. reflexes.
    b. gross motor skills.   d. unpredictable.

17. Regarding the brain's cortex, which of the following is *not* true?
    a. The cortex houses about 70 percent of the brain's neurons.
    b. The cortex is the brain's outer layer.
    c. The cortex is the location of most thinking, feeling, and sensing.
    d. Only primates have a cortex.

18. Which of the following is true of motor-skill development in healthy infants?
    a. It follows the same basic sequence the world over.
    b. It occurs at different rates from individual to individual.
    c. It follows norms that vary from one ethnic group to another.
    d. All of the above are true.

19. All the nerve cells a human brain will ever need are present:
    a. at conception.
    b. about 1 month following conception.
    c. at birth.
    d. at age 5 or 6.

20. Trying to impress his professor, Erik notes that the reason humans have a critical period for learning certain skills might be due to the fact that the brain cannot form new synapses after age 13. Should the professor be impressed with Erik's knowledge of biosocial development?

    a. Yes, although each neuron may have already formed as many as 15,000 connections with other neurons.
    b. Yes, although the branching of dendrites and axons does continue through young adulthood.
    c. No. Although Erik is correct about neural development, the brain attains adult size by about age 7.
    d. No. Synapses form throughout life.

21. Infant sensory and perceptual abilities appear to be especially organized for:
    a. obtaining adequate nutrition and comfort.
    b. comfort and social interaction.
    c. looking.
    d. touching and smelling.

22. Newborns cry, shiver, and tuck their legs close to their bodies. This set of reflexes helps them:
    a. ensure proper muscle tone.
    b. learn how to signal distress.
    c. maintain constant body temperature.
    d. communicate serious hunger pangs.

23. For a pediatrician, the most important factor in assessing a child's healthy growth is:
    a. height in inches.
    b. weight in pounds.
    c. body fat percentage.
    d. the percentile rank of a child's height or weight.

NAME _____   INSTRUCTOR _____

LESSON 5: GROWTH RATES AND MOTOR-SKILL DEVELOPMENT IN THE FIRST TWO YEARS

Exercise

The text notes that weight gain and growth in early infancy are astoundingly rapid. The proportions of the human body change dramatically with maturation, especially in the first year of life. The growth that changes the baby's body shape follows the head-downward (cephalo-caudal) and center-outward (proximo-distal) direction of development. For instance, the percentage of total body length below the belly button is 25 percent at two months after conception, about 45 percent at birth, 50 percent by age 2, and 60 percent by adulthood. Questions 1–5 of this exercise will help you to gain some understanding of how rapid this growth is by projecting the growth patterns of the infant onto an adult, such as yourself or a friend.

Similarly, questions 6–10 of this exercise are designed to help you "feel" the progressively finer coordination achieved by the infant by having you work through the stages of development. A good place to start is with the mastery of motor skills involved in picking up objects. After you have answered the questions, hand the completed exercise in to your instructor.

1. Most newborns seem top-heavy because their heads are equivalent to about one-fourth of their total length, compared with one-fifth at a year and one-eighth in adulthood. Their legs, in turn, represent only about one-fourth of their total body length, whereas an adult's legs account for about one-half. Based on your present height in inches, what would be the lengths of your head and legs if they remained proportionally the same as when you were born?

2. If you were gaining weight at the rate of an infant, your weight would be tripled one year from today. Calculate how much you would weigh.

3. If you, like an infant, grew an inch a month, this would not mark such a significant growth rate—since you are much taller than an infant to begin with. Thus, every inch is a smaller percentage increase for you. Nevertheless, imagine that you are growing at the rate of an infant in the first year, adding an inch a month. What would your height be a year from today?

4. The same kinds of calculations can help you make a less dramatic comparison between growth rates in the first and second years of life. In the first year, weight triples; thus an infant born at a little more than 7 pounds will weigh about 21 pounds at one year. If growth were to continue at this rate, how much would the child weigh at two years? (In fact, the average infant at two years weighs only 30 pounds.)

5. The average infant grows an inch a month in the first year. If a 30-inch one-year-old continued growing at this rate, how tall would he or she be at two years? (In fact, the faster growing child grows only 6 inches, to reach 36 inches at age two.)
   Now try picking up objects as an infant would.

6. Pick up a piece of paper or some other small object with your whole hand, that is, with all fingers curled around it.

7. Now hold the paper between your middle fingers and the palm of your hand.

8. Pick up the paper with your index finger pressed against the side of your palm.

9. Finally, use your thumb and index finger to pick up the paper. When is this type of grasp achieved?

10. Which of these ways of grasping a small object felt most comfortable or natural to you?

LESSON GUIDELINES

Audio Question Guidelines

1. By mammalian standards, the nine-month gestation period in humans is relatively short. As a result, the human infant is exceedingly helpless and relatively less developed compared with most other animals. The relatively short gestation period may be a response to the evolution of a large brain, which, while providing humans with a high level of intelligence and cognitive flexibility, results in a large skull that makes birth difficult.

   Because of **bipedalism** (the upright posture of humans), the duration of prenatal development is somewhat of a compromise. Babies are born at a point when the brain is as big as it can be without requiring a wider birth canal, which would impair a female's ability to walk.

2. Compared with other primates, human infants are remarkably fat when they are born. Fat ensures that the developing brain—which has attained only one-quarter of its mature size at birth—is adequately nourished.

   Even before infants are born, their mothers begin storing fat for them. The mother's fat ensures a rich supply of breast milk for nursing. Each species' milk has a special profile of nutrients that exactly matches the species' specific developmental needs. Human milk is high in sugar, which provides energy for the baby's rapidly developing brain.

3. The brain consists of billions of nerve cells called **neurons**. All the neurons a human will ever possess are already present three months after conception. Some of the neurons will grow while others will die. Neuropsychologists estimate that humans start out with 20 to 40 percent more neurons than they end up with.

   During the first two years of life, neurons in the human brain become coated with insulation (which speeds their chemical communication) and hook up with other neurons by forming connections called synapses. The excess of neurons and synaptic connections creates redundancy that gives humans greater flexibility and insurance: if some neurons die, others can take over their functions.

   While 90 percent of the brain's growth is completed by age 5, synapses will be made and broken throughout life. Laboratory animals respond to stimulating environments by developing more synapses than those raised in normal or deprived environments. Even in old age, nerve cells respond to stimulation by growing extra connections.

4. The biological clock governs every aspect of physical growth. One of the peculiarities of human growth is that we grow slowly. Another is that we do not grow evenly. Development of the body and reproductive system is paced by development of the brain.

   Brain development is rapid, with 90 percent of growth completed by age 5.

   Body growth from birth to two years is very rapid and then levels off to a rate of 3 to 4 inches a year until puberty, when growth in height and weight again accelerates.

   The curve of growth for the reproductive system is very flat until the age of 12 or 14.

Textbook Question Answers

1. 20 inches (51 centimeters); 7 pounds (3.2 kilograms)

2. head-sparing

3. norm

4. 30 pounds (13 kilograms); between 32 and 36 inches inches (81–91 centimeters); one-fifth; half

5. percentile; 1; 99

6. sleep; brain; learning, emotional, psychological; 80

7. stages; dreaming; REM sleep; rapid; decreases; transitional sleep; quiet sleep; 3 or 4

8. 25; 75; 20

9. neurons; axons; dendrites; 70; cortex

10. dendrites; axon

11. synapses; axon; neurotransmitters; synaptic gap; dendrite; are; are

12. cortex

13. increases; five; transient exuberance; pruning; experience

14. experience-expectant; experience-dependent

15. genes; prenatal influences; plasticity; a combination; dendritic; emotional; improved; were

16. sensation; perception; are; cognition; can

17. is; can

18. vision; 4; 30

19. focus; scan; binocular vision; 14 weeks

20. function; touch; Brazelton

21. social interaction; comfort

22. motor skills

23. reflex

24. breathing reflex; hiccups, sneezes, thrashing

25. body temperature

26. feeding; sucking; rooting

27. gross motor

28. 8; 10

On average, a child can walk while holding a hand at 9 months, can stand alone momentarily at 10 months, and can walk well unassisted at 12 months.

29. fine motor; 6 months; 6 months

30. sequence; age

31. norms; many

32. ethnic

33. is; do; pattern of infant care

34. 3; was the same throughout the world; Japan; the Netherlands; France; 200

35. immunization; immune

36. sudden infant death syndrome (SIDS); sleep

37. ethnic; African; Asian; European; on their backs

Chinese parents tend to their babies periodically as they sleep, which makes them less likely to fall into a deep, nonbreathing sleep. Bangladeshi infants are usually surrounded by many family members in a rich sensory environment, making them less likely to sleep deeply for very long.

38. breast milk; colostrum; the mother is HIV-positive, using toxic drugs, or has some other serious condition that makes her milk unhealthy

Breast milk is always sterile and at body temperature; it contains more iron, vitamin C, and vitamin A; it contains antibodies that provide the infant some protection against disease; it is more digestible than any formula; and it decreases the frequency of almost every infant illness and allergy.

39. protein-calorie malnutrition

40. brains; body reserves; marasmus; kwashiorkor

41. marasmus; kwashiorkor

Answers to Testing Yourself

1. **b.** is the answer. Human babies are born at a time when their brains are as big as they can be without requiring a wider birth canal, which would limit females' ability to walk. (audio program)

2. **a.** is the answer. Our slow, uneven growth—first the brain, then the body, then the reproductive system—is directed by the preeminent role of the brain. (audio program)

3. **d.** is the answer. Three-quarters of brain development occurs after birth; this may be the reason why humans store fat—that is, to ensure that the brain has adequate nutrition. (audio program)

4. **c.** is the answer. Environmental stimulation throughout the life span helps individuals, and their brains, grow. (audio program; textbook, Thinking Like a Scientist, p. 129)

5. **d.** is the answer. Human milk has a high sugar content, which provides energy for the baby's rapidly developing brain. (audio program; textbook, p. 141)

6. **b.** is the answer. (textbook, p. 121)

7. **a.** is the answer. (textbook, p. 122)

8. **a.** is the answer. (textbook, p. 134)

   b. The age norm for this skill is 7.8 months.

   c. This is a reflex, rather than an acquired motor skill.

   d. This skill is acquired between 9 and 14 months.

9. **c.** is the answer. (textbook, p. 135)

10. **c.** is the answer. (textbook, p. 123)

11. **c.** is the answer. (textbook, p. 127)

12. **b.** is the answer. (textbook, p. 130)

    a. & d. Sensation and perception operate in all these sensory modalities.

13. **b.** is the answer. (pp. 133, 134)

    c. & d. Reflexes are involuntary responses; climbing and using a crayon are both voluntary responses.

14. **b.** is the answer. This is because breast milk is more digestible than cow's milk or formula. (textbook, p. 141)

    a., c., & d. Breast- and bottle-fed babies do not differ in these attributes.

15. **b.** is the answer. (textbook, pp. 141–142)

16. **c.** is the answer. (textbook, p. 132)

    a. & b. These motor skills do not emerge until somewhat later; reflexes are present at birth.

    d. On the contrary, reflexes are quite predictable.

17. **d.** is the answer. All mammals have a cortex. (p. 125)

18. **d.** is the answer. (textbook, p. 134)

19. **c.** is the answer. (textbook, p. 127)

20. **d.** is the answer. (textbook, p. 127)

21. **b.** is the answer. (p. 132)

22. **c.** is the answer. (p. 132)

23. **d.** is the answer. (p. 122)

The First Two Years: Cognitive Development

AUDIO PROGRAM: First Words

ORIENTATION

During the first two years of life, cognitive development proceeds at a phenomenal pace as the infant is transformed from a baby who can know its world only through a limited set of basic reflexes into a toddler capable of imitating others, anticipating and remembering events, and pretending. Most significant among these advances is the development of language. By age 2, the average toddler has a relatively large vocabulary and is able to converse effectively with others.

Lesson 6 of *Seasons of Life* explores **cognitive development**—the ways in which individuals learn about, think about, and adapt to their surroundings—during the first two years. Chapter 6 of *The Developing Person Through the Life Span*, 6/e, focuses on the various ways in which infant intelligence is revealed: through sensorimotor intelligence, perception, memory, and language development. The chapter begins with a description of Jean Piaget's theory of **sensorimotor intelligence**, which maintains that infants think exclusively with their senses and motor skills. Piaget's six stages of sensorimotor intelligence are examined. It then describes Eleanor and James Gibson's contextual theory of cognitive development.

Audio program 6, "First Words," is concerned with language development from birth until the first word is spoken. As explained by psycholinguist Jill de Villiers, around the world babies and parents move along similar paths as language emerges. In the program, these paths are illustrated by actual examples and the description of linguistic landmarks such as **crying**, **cooing**, **babbling**, and the first true word. Along the way, the listener discovers the importance of the biological clock in the maturation of language and the patterns of speech that adults use to promote linguistic development in children. This issue—the interaction between maturation and learning in cog-

nitive development—is explored further in the textbook, where the theories of language development proposed by B. F. Skinner and Noam Chomsky are described. Skinner argues that language development is the product of conditioning, whereas Chomsky maintains that children have a biological predisposition to acquire language. Most developmental psychologists nevertheless view language development as a social, interactional process that reflects both nature (maturation) and nurture (conditioning).

As the program opens, we hear the voices of English- and Spanish-speaking parents reacting to a milestone in the lives of their children: their first word.

LESSON GOALS

By the end of this lesson you should be prepared to:

1. Outline and evaluate the theory of sensorimotor intelligence proposed by Piaget.

2. Explain the Gibsons' contextual view of perception, and discuss the idea of affordances.

3. Describe perceptual development, particularly in relation to cognitive maturity, during the first two years.

4. Describe language development during the first two years.

5. Contrast the theories of language development proposed by B. F. Skinner and Noam Chomsky, and explain current views on language learning.

Audio Assignment

Listen to the audio tape that accompanies Lesson 6: "First Words."

Write answers to the following questions. You may replay portions of the program if your memory needs to be refreshed. Answer guidelines may be found in the Lesson Guidelines section at the end of this chapter.

1. Outline the basic sequence and landmarks of language development from birth until the first word is spoken.

2. Identify the criteria used by developmental psychologists to determine whether an utterance represents the first actual word. What types of words are likely to be produced first?

3. Identify the characteristics of baby talk (Motherese), the special form of language that adults use to talk to infants.

4. Explain how parents use scaffolding to encourage conversation in their children.

Textbook Assignment

Read Chapter 6: "The First Two Years: Cognitive Development," pages 147–169 in *The Developing Person Through the Life Span*, 6/e, then work through the material that follows to review it. Complete the sentences and answer the questions. As you proceed,

evaluate your performance for each section by consulting the answers on page 73. Do not continue with the next section until you understand each answer. If you need to, review or reread the appropriate section in the textbook before continuing.

Sensorimotor Intelligence (pp. 147–153)

1. Cognition involves _____

   _____ .

   The first major theorist to realize that infants are active learners was _____ .

2. At every stage, people _____ their thinking to their _____ . This is revealed in two ways: by _____ of new information into previously developed mental categories, or _____ ; and by _____ of previous mental categories to incorporate new information.

3. When infants begin to explore the environment through sensory and motor skills, they are displaying what Piaget called _____ intelligence. In number, Piaget described _____ stages of development of this type of intelligence.

4. The first two stages of sensorimotor intelligence are examples of _____ _____ _____ . Stage one begins with newborns' reflexes, such as _____ , _____ , _____ , and _____ . It lasts from birth to _____ of age.

5. Stage two begins when newborns show signs of _____ of their _____ to the specifics of the environment.

Describe the development of the sucking reflex during stages one and two.

6. In stages three and four, development switches to _____ _____ _____ , involving the baby with an object or with another person. During stage three, which occurs between _____ and _____ months of age, infants repeat a specific action that has just elicited a pleasing response.

Describe a typical stage-three behavior.

7. In stage four, which lasts from _____ to _____ months of age, infants can better _____ events. At this stage, babies also engage in purposeful actions, or _____-_____ behavior.

8. (text and Thinking Like a Scientist) A major cognitive accomplishment of infancy is the ability to understand that objects exist even when they are _____ . This awareness is called _____ _____ . To test for this awareness, Piaget devised a procedure to observe whether an infant will _____ for a hidden object. Using this test, Piaget concluded that this awareness does not develop until about _____ of age.

9. During stage five, which lasts from _____ to _____ months, infants begin experimenting in thought and deed. They do so through _____ _____ _____ , which involve taking in experiences and trying to make sense of them.

Explain what Piaget meant when he described the stage-five infant as a little scientist.

10. Stage six, which lasts from _____ to _____ months, is the stage of achieving new means by using _____ _____ .

11. One sign that children have reached stage six is _____ _____ , which is their emerging ability to imitate behaviors they noticed earlier.

12. Two research tools that have become available since Piaget's time are _____ studies and _____ , which reveals brain activity by showing increases in _____ supply to various parts of the brain as cognition occurs.

Information Processing (pp. 154–158)

13. A perspective on human cognition that is modeled on how computers analyze data is the _____-_____ theory. Two aspects of this theory as applied to human development are _____ , which concern perception and so are analogous to computer input, and _____ , which involves storage and retrieval of ideas, or output.

14. Much of the current research in perception and cognition has been inspired by the work of the Gibsons, who stress that perception is a(n) _____ (active/passive/automatic) cognitive phenomenon.

15. According to the Gibsons, any object in the environment offers diverse opportunities for interaction; this property of an object is called an _____ .

16. Which of these an individual perceives in an object depends on the individual's _____ _____ and _____ _____ , on his or her _____ _____ , and on his or her _____ _____ of what the object might be used for.

17. A firm surface that appears to drop off is called a _____ _____ .

Although perception of this drop off was once linked to _____ maturity, later research found that infants as young as _____ are able to perceive the drop off, as evidenced by changes in their _____ _____ and their wide open eyes.

18. Perception that is primed to focus on movement and change is called _____ _____ .

19. Babies have great difficulty storing new memories in their first _____ (how long?).

20. Research has shown, however, that babies can show that they remember when three conditions are met:

   (a) _____

   (b) _____

   (c) _____

21. When these conditions are met, infants as young as _____ months "remembered" events from two weeks earlier if they experienced a _____ _____ prior to retesting.

22. After about _____ months, infants become capable of retaining information for longer periods of time, with less reminding.

23. Most researchers believe there _____ (is one type of memory/are many types of memory).

Language: What Develops in Two Years?
(pp. 158–167)

24. Children the world over _____ (follow/do not follow) the same sequence of early language development. The timing of this sequence _____ (varies/does not vary).

25. Newborns show a preference for hearing _____ over other sounds, including the high-pitched, simplified adult speech called _____ _____ , which is sometimes called _____-_____ speech.

26. By 4 months of age, most babies' verbal repertoire consists of _____ _____ .

27. At _____ months of age, babies begin to repeat certain syllables, a phenomenon referred to as _____ .

28. Deaf babies begin oral babbling _____ (earlier/later) than hearing babies do. Deaf babies may also babble _____ , with this behavior emerging _____ (earlier than/at the same time as/later than) hearing infants begin oral babbling.

29. The average baby speaks a few words at about _____ of age. When vocabulary reaches approximately 50 words, it suddenly begins to build rapidly, at a rate of _____ or more words a month. This language spurt is called the _____ _____ , because toddlers learn a disproportionate number of _____ .

30. Language acquisition may be shaped by our _____ , as revealed by the fact that North American infants learn more _____ than Chinese or Korean infants, who learn more _____ . Alternatively, the entire _____ _____ may determine language acquisition.

31. Another characteristic is the use of the _____ , in which a single word expresses a complete thought.

32. Children begin to produce their first two-word sentences at about _____ months, showing a clearly emerging understanding of _____ , which refers to all the methods that languages use to communicate meaning, apart from the words themselves.

33. Reinforcement and other conditioning processes account for language development, according to the learning theory of _____ .

Support for this theory comes from the fact that there are wide variations in language _____ , especially when children from different cultures are compared. One longitudinal study that followed mother–infant pairs over time found that the frequency of early _____ _____ predicted the child's rate of language acquisition many months later.

34. The theorist who stressed that language is too complex to be mastered so early and easily through conditioning is _____ . This theorist maintained that all children are born with a LAD, or _____ _____ _____ , that enables children to quickly derive the rules of grammar from the speech they hear.

35. Embedded in the LAD, the universal grammar structure of language is _____-_____ , meaning that words are "expected" by the developing brain.

Summarize the research support for theory two.

36. A third, _____-_____ theory of language proposes that _____ _____ foster infant language.

37. A new hybrid theory based on a model called an _____ _____ combines aspects of several theories. A fundamental aspect of this theory is that _____ _____ .

Testing Yourself

After you have completed the audio and text review questions, see how well you do on the following quiz. Correct answers, with text and audio references, may be found at the end of this chapter.

1. Translated literally, the word *infant* means:
   a. little scientist.
   b. not speaking.
   c. innocent one.
   d. explorer.

2. Between 2 and 4 months of age children begin making a pleasant, relaxing speech sound called:
   a. babbling.
   b. cooing.
   c. scaffolding.
   d. baby talk.

3. At about 6 months of age babies begin to repetitively utter certain syllables; they do this more for experimentation than for socializing. This stage of language development is called:
   a. babbling.
   b. cooing.
   c. scaffolding.
   d. baby talk.

4. In order to qualify as a word, a sound must:
   a. serve as a symbol for something.
   b. be used consistently in a number of circumstances.
   c. resemble an adult word.
   d. possess all of the above characteristics.

5. When adults converse with children they usually do all of the following *except*:
   a. exaggerate their intonation.
   b. raise the pitch of their voices.
   c. use shorter sentences.
   d. speak only in the past tense.

6. In general terms, the Gibsons' concept of affordances emphasizes the idea that the individual perceives an object in terms of its:
   a. economic importance.
   b. physical qualities.
   c. function or use to the individual.
   d. role in the larger culture or environment.

7. According to Piaget, when a baby repeats an action that has just triggered a pleasing response from his or her caregiver, a stage _____ behavior has occurred.
   a. one   c. three
   b. two   d. six

8. Sensorimotor intelligence begins with a baby's first:
   a. attempt to crawl.
   b. reflex actions.
   c. auditory perception.
   d. adaptation of a reflex.

9. Piaget and the Gibsons would most likely agree that:
   a. perception is largely automatic.
   b. language development is biologically predisposed in children.
   c. learning and perception are active cognitive processes.
   d. it is unwise to "push" children too hard academically.

10. By the end of the first year, infants usually learn how to:
    a. accomplish simple goals.
    b. manipulate various symbols.
    c. solve complex problems.
    d. pretend.

11. When an infant begins to understand that objects exist even when they are out of sight, she or he has begun to understand the concept of object:
    a. displacement.
    b. importance.
    c. permanence.
    d. location.

12. Today, most cognitive psychologists view language acquisition as:
    a. primarily the result of imitation of adult speech.
    b. a behavior that is determined primarily by biological maturation.
    c. a behavior determined entirely by learning.
    d. determined by both biological maturation and learning.

13. Despite cultural differences, children all over the world attain very similar language skills:
    a. according to ethnically specific timetables.
    b. in the same sequence according to a variable timetable.
    c. according to culturally specific timetables.
    d. according to timetables that vary from child to child.

14. The average baby speaks a few words at about:
    a. 6 months.
    b. 9 months.
    c. 12 months.
    d. 24 months.

15. A single word used by toddlers to express a complete thought is:
    a. a holophrase.
    b. baby talk.
    c. babbling.
    d. an affordance.

16. A fundamental idea of the emergentist coalition model of language acquisition is that:
    a. all humans are born with an innate language acquisition device.
    b. some aspects of language are best learned in one way at one age, others in another way at another age.
    c. language development occurs too rapidly and easily to be entirely the product of conditioning.
    d. imitation and reinforcement are crucial to the development of language.

17. A distinctive form of language, with a particular pitch, structure, etc., that adults use in talking to infants is called:
    a. a holophrase.
    b. the LAD.
    c. baby talk.
    d. conversation.

18. The imaging technique in which the brain's magnetic properties indicate activation in various parts of the brain is called a(n):
    a. PET scan.
    b. EEG.
    c. fMRI.
    d. CAT scan.

19. Which of the following is an example of a secondary circular reaction?
    a. 1-month-old infant staring at a mobile suspended over her crib
    b. a 2-month-old infant sucking a pacifier
    c. realizing that rattles make noise, a 4-month-old infant laughs with delight when his mother puts a rattle in his hand
    d. a 12-month-old toddler licks a bar of soap to learn what it tastes like

20. A toddler who taps on the computer's keyboard after observing her mother sending e-mail is demonstrating:
    a. assimilation.
    b. accommodation.
    c. deferred imitation.
    d. dynamic perception.

21. According to Piaget, assimilation and accommodation are two ways in which:
    a. infants adapt their reflexes to the specifics of the environment.
    b. goal-directed behavior occurs.
    c. infants form mental combinations.
    d. language begins to emerge.

22. A 20-month-old girl who is able to try out various actions mentally without having to actually perform them is learning to solve simple problems by using:
    a. dynamic perception.
    b. object permanence.
    c. affordances.
    d. mental combinations.

23. Like most Korean toddlers, Noriko has acquired a greater number of _____ in her vocabulary than her North American counterparts, who tend to acquire more _____ .
    a. verbs; nouns
    b. nouns; verbs
    c. adjectives; verbs
    d. adjectives; nouns

NAME _____   INSTRUCTOR _____

LESSON 6: BABY TALK

Exercise

To further your understanding of the nature and significance of **baby talk**, make arrangements to listen to an adult conversing with an infant or toddler for ten to fifteen minutes. Your subjects may be family members, other relatives, or friends. The conversation need not be structured in any particular way. The adult might read to the child, play with a favorite toy, or simply carry on a conversation with the child. It is important that you not give the adult clues as to what speech patterns you are looking for. Ask your subject to relax, be candid, and enjoy interacting with the child. If you wish, you might even record the conversation to allow for a more thorough analysis later. After listening to the conversation, answer the questions that follow and hand the completed exercise in to your instructor.

1. Describe the participants and setting that you chose for the baby-talk conversation.

2. Did you encounter any difficulties in completing the exercise (e.g., the adult was nervous; the child did not talk)?

3. Did the adult use baby talk with the child? What aspects of the adult's speech (e.g., intonation, pitch, vocabulary) changed during the conversation with the child?

4. Were there any particular characteristics of the adult's speech (e.g., repetitiveness, exaggerated intonation) that the child seemed particularly responsive to?

5. Based on his or her age and vocalizations, what stage of language development would you say the infant or toddler is in (e.g., cooing, babbling, one-word stage)? If you wish, give examples of the child's utterances that support your assessment.

LESSON GUIDELINES

Audio Question Guidelines

1. Compared with that of other species, human hearing—even for subtle differences in speech sounds—is very sensitive at birth, which contributes to language development.

   Cries are the first speech productions on the way to words.

   Between 2 and 4 months, **cooing** begins. Cooing is a pleasant and relaxing sound with an important social function: it attracts the attention of caregivers.

   At about 6 months infants begin to mix consonants with cooing. As they play with sound, they produce utterances such as "ba, ba, ba, ba," signaling their entrance into the stage of **babbling**. Babbling is not as social as cooing, but represents experimentation with the sounds of language.

   Infants below the age of about 8 months babble in very similar ways, so that the babbling of children from around the world is indistinguishable. At about 10 months babbling begins to take on the characteristics of the language the child will ultimately learn.

   The first true word usually comes at about 12 months of age, although there is wide, and normal, variation in that age.

2. The first criterion is that the sound must be a symbol referring to an object or an event.

   Second, the sound must be used consistently in a number of different circumstances.

   Third, the sound must resemble an adult word.

   The first words are likely to refer to something that moves, something the baby controls, and something that is very interesting. Examples are words for toys, foods, clothing, mothers, fathers, siblings, and pets.

3. **Baby talk** differs from adult speech in several ways: it is distinct in pitch (higher), intonation (more exaggerated and more low-to-high fluctuations), vocabulary (simpler and more concrete), and sentence length (shorter).

   Baby talk is also more repetitive and uses more questions and fewer past tenses, pronouns, and complex sentences.

   An intriguing fact is that people of all ages, including nonparents, use baby talk when conversing with infants.

   In many of the world's cultures, baby words for mother and father—such as "mama" and "dada"—are just the sort of easy-to-produce, repeated syllables that often are a child's first words.

4. **Scaffolding** refers to the tendency of parents and other adults to try to support the young child's conversation. In reading a book, for example, the parent might first read the entire story slowly and with exaggerated intonation to give the child time to process the information. The second time the story is read, the parent might pause at key points and wait for the child to respond in some way. Gradually, the parent removes more and more of the support, or scaffolding, so that the child's role in the conversation becomes more extensive, and precise.

Textbook Question Answers

1. intelligence, learning, memory, and language; Piaget

2. adapt; experiences; assimilation; schemas; accommodation

3. sensorimotor; six

4. primary circular reactions; sucking; grasping; staring; listening; 1 month

5. adaptation; reflexes

Stage-one infants suck everything that touches their lips. At about 1 month, they start to adapt their sucking to specific objects. After several months, they have organized the world into objects to be sucked for nourishment, objects to be sucked for pleasure, and objects not to be sucked at all.

6. secondary circular reactions; 4; 8

A stage-three infant may squeeze a duck, hear a quack, and squeeze the duck again.

7. 8; 12; anticipate; goal-directed

8. no longer in sight; object permanence; search; 8 months

9. 12; 18; tertiary circular reactions

Having discovered some action or set of actions that is possible with a given object, stage-five little scientists seem to ask, "What else can I do with this?"

10. 18; 24; mental combinations

11. deferred imitation

12. habituation; fMRI; oxygen

13. information-processing; affordances; memory

14. active

15. affordance

16. past experiences; current development; immediate motivation; sensory awareness

17. visual cliff; visual; 3 months; heart rate
18. dynamic perception
19. year
20. (a) real-life situations are used; (b) motivation is high; (c) special measures aid memory retrieval
21. 3 months; reminder session
22. six
23. are many types of memory
24. follow; varies
25. speech; baby talk; child-directed
26. squeals, growls, gurgles, grunts, croons, and yells, as well as some speechlike sounds
27. 6 or 7; babbling
28. later; manually; at the same time as
29. 1 year; 50 to 100; naming explosion; nouns
30. culture; nouns; verbs; social context
31. holophrase
32. 21; grammar
33. B. F. Skinner; fluency; maternal responsiveness
34. Noam Chomsky; language acquisition device
35. experience-expectant

Support for this theory comes from the fact that all babies babble a mama and dada sound by 6 months. No reinforcement is needed. All they need is for dendrites to grow, mouth muscles to strengthen, synapses to connect, and speech to be overheard.

36. social-pragmatic; social impulses
37. emergentist coalition; some aspects of language are best learned in one way at one age, others in another way at another age.

Answers to Testing Yourself

1. **b.** is the answer. Translated from its Latin roots, the word "infant" refers to someone who is "not yet speaking." (audio program)
2. **b.** is the answer. Cooing serves the very important social function of attracting the caregiver's attention. (audio program; textbook, p. 159)
3. **a.** is the answer. Babbling is sheer experimentation with the sounds of language. (audio program; textbook, p. 160)
4. **d.** is the answer. To qualify as an actual word, sounds must be symbols, resemble adult words, and be used consistently. (audio program)
5. **d.** is the answer. In speaking to children, adults generally confine their conversation to things in the "here and now." (audio program; textbook, p. 159)
6. **c.** is the answer. (textbook, p. 154)
7. **c.** is the answer. (textbook, p. 149)
8. **b.** is the answer. This was Piaget's most basic contribution to the study of infant cognition—that intelligence is revealed in behavior at every age. (textbook, p. 148)
9. **c.** is the answer. (textbook, pp. 147, 154)
   b. This is Chomsky's position.
   d. This issue was not discussed in the text.
10. **a.** is the answer. (textbook, p. 149)
    b. & c. These abilities are not acquired until children are much older.
    d. Pretending is associated with stage six (18 to 24 months).
11. **c.** is the answer. (textbook, p. 150)
12. **d.** is the answer. (textbook, pp. 165–166)
13. **b.** is the answer. (textbook, p. 159)
    a., c., & d. Children the world over, and in every Piagetian stage, follow the same sequence, but the timing of their accomplishments may vary considerably.
14. **c.** is the answer. (textbook, p. 160)
15. **a.** is the answer. (textbook, p. 161)
    b. Baby talk is the speech adults use with infants.
    c. Babbling refers to the first syllables a baby utters.
    d. An affordance is an opportunity for perception and interaction.
16. **b.** is the answer. (textbook, p. 165)
    a. & c. These ideas are consistent with Noam Chomsky's theory.
    d. This is the central idea of B. F. Skinner's theory.
17. **c.** is the answer. (textbook, p. 180)
    a. A holophrase is a single word uttered by a toddler to express a complete thought.
    b. According to Noam Chomsky, the LAD, or language acquisition device, is an innate ability in humans to acquire language.
    d. These characteristic differences in pitch and structure are precisely what distinguish baby talk from regular conversation.
18. **c.** is the answer. (textbook, p. 152)
19. **c.** is the answer. (textbook, p. 149)

a. & b. These are examples of primary circular reactions.

d. This is an example of a tertiary circular reaction.

20. **c.** is the answer (textbook, p. 152)

    a. & b. In Piaget's theory, these refer to processes by which mental concepts incorporate new experiences (assimilation) or are modified in response to new experiences (accommodation).

    d. Dynamic perception is perception that is primed to focus on movement and change.

21. **a.** is the answer. (textbook, p. 147)

    b. Assimilation and accommodation are cognitive processes, not behaviors.

c. Mental combinations are sequences of actions that are carried out mentally.

d. Assimilation and accommodation do not directly pertain to language use.

22. **d.** is the answer. (textbook, p. 152)

    a. Dynamic perception is perception primed to focus on movement and change.

    b. Object permanence is the awareness that objects do not cease to exist when they are out of sight.

    c. Affordances are the opportunities for perception and interaction that an object or place offers to any individual.

23. **a.** is the answer. (textbook, pp. 160–161)

The First Two Years: Psychosocial Development

AUDIO PROGRAM: Attachment: The Dance Begins

ORIENTATION

Lessons 5 and 6 of *Seasons of Life* examined biosocial and cognitive development during the first two years. Lesson 7, which is concerned with psychosocial development during infancy, explores the individual's emerging self-awareness, personality, emotional expression, and relationship to parents and society.

Chapter 7 of *The Developing Person Through the Life Span*, 6/e describes the emotional and social life of the developing person during the first two years. It begins with a description of the psychoanalytic theories of Freud and Erikson along with behaviorist, cognitive, epigenetic, and sociocultural theories, which help us understand how the infant's emotional and behavioral responses begin to take on the various patterns that form personality. Temperament, which affects later personality and is primarily inborn, is influenced by the individual's interactions with the environment.

The second section explores the infant's emerging emotions and how they reflect mobility and social awareness. The third section explores the social context in which emotions develop. By referencing their caregivers' signals, infants learn when and how to express their emotions.

In the traditional view of personality development, the infant was seen as a passive recipient of the personality created almost entirely by the actions of his or her parents. But it is now apparent that many personality dispositions are present in infants at birth, before parental influence is felt. In addition, active parent-infant interaction within a secure and nurturing environment is now viewed as a central factor in the child's psychosocial development.

Audio program 7, "Attachment: The Dance Begins," explores the who, when, where, and why of **attachment**—the affectional tie between infants and their primary caretakers. In infants the world over, attachment develops at about 7 months, when babies first become aware that other people stay in existence even when they're out of sight. Attachment helps ensure that the relatively helpless human infant receives the adult care it needs in order to survive.

What about infants who do not become securely attached? And what are the effects, for example, of adoption and day care on the development of attachment? Through the expert commentary of psychologists Michael Lamb, Janice Gibson, and Sheldon White, we explore these important issues in attachment—an intricate "interaction" between infant and caregiver that lays the foundation for psychosocial development throughout the subsequent seasons of life.

LESSON GOALS

By the end of this lesson you should be prepared to:

1. Describe Freud's psychosexual stages of infant development and Erikson's psychosocial stages of development.

2. Discuss the epigentic theory explanation of the origins, characteristics, and role of temperament in the child's psychosocial development.

3. Describe the basic emotions expressed by infants during the first days and months.

4. Outline the main developments in the emotional life of the child between 6 months and 2 years.

5. Discuss the significance of parent–infant interaction, particularly as it promotes or hinders attachment, in the infant's psychosocial development.

Audio Assignment

Listen to the audio tape that accompanies Lesson 7: "Attachment: The Dance Begins."

Write answers to the following questions. You may replay portions of the program if you need to refresh your memory. Answer guidelines may be found in the Lesson Guidelines sections at the end of this chapter.

1. Define attachment, outline its development, and explain why experts believe it to be a biologically determined event.

2. Discuss the impact of early mother-infant contact, adoption, and day care on attachment.

3. Discuss the immediate and long-range impact on infants of secure and insecure attachment.

Textbook Assignment

Read Chapter 7: "The First Two Years: Psychosocial Development," pages 171–191 in *The Developing Person Through the Life Span,* 6/e, then work through the material that follows to review it. Complete the sentences and answer the questions. As you proceed, evaluate your performance for each section by consulting the answers on page 85. Do not continue with the next section until you understand each answer. If you need to, review or reread the appropriate section in the textbook before continuing.

Introduction and Theories About Early Psychosocial Development (pp. 172–177)

1. Psychosocial development includes _____ development and _____ development.

2. In Freud's theory, development begins with the _____ stage, so named because the _____ is the infant's prime source of gratification and pleasure.

3. According to Freud, in the second year the prime focus of gratification comes from stimulation and control of the bowels. Freud referred to this period as the _____ stage.

Describe Freud's ideas on the importance of early oral experiences to later personality development.

4. Research has shown that toilet training may take a year or more if it is started before _____ months.

5. The theorist who believed that development occurs through a series of psychosocial crises is _____ . According to his theory, the crisis of infancy is one of

_____ ,

whereas the crisis of toddlerhood is one of

_____ .

6. According to the perspective of _____ , personality is molded through the processes of _____ and _____ of the child's spontaneous behaviors. A strong proponent of this position was _____ .

7. Later theorists incorporated the role of _____ learning, that is, infants' tendency to observe and _____ the personality traits of their parents.

8. According to cognitive theory, a person's _____ , _____ , and _____ determine his or her perspective on the world. More specifically, infants use their early relationships to build a _____ _____ that becomes a frame of reference for organizing perceptions and experiences.

9. According to _____ theory, each infant is born with a _____ predisposition to develop certain emotional traits. Among these are traits of _____ .

10. These traits are similar to _____ . Although these traits are not learned, their expression is influenced by the _____ .

11. The correlations found thus far between neurological measurements and childhood behavior are _____ (large/small). The most famous long-term study of children's temperament is the _____ , begun more than forty years ago. This study found that babies differ in nine characteristics: _____
_____
_____

12. The study found that by two to three months, infants can be clustered into one of three types: _____ , _____ , and _____ . Another study categorized infants on the basis of brain patterns and observable behavior. Most showed consistent patterns of behavior, identified as _____ , _____ , or _____ .

13. An important factor in healthy psychosocial development is _____
_____ _____ between the developing child and the caregiving context.

14. According to _____ theory, the entire _____ context can have a major impact on infant-caregiver relationships and the infant's development.

Emotional Development (pp. 178–180)

15. The first emotions that can be reliably discerned in infants are _____ and _____ . Other early infant emotions include _____ , _____ , and _____ .

16. Fully formed fear emerges at about _____ . One expression of this new emotion is _____ _____ , which becomes full-blown by _____ months; another is _____ _____ , or fear of abandonment, which is most obvious at _____ months. During the second year, anger and fear typically _____ (increase/decrease) and become more _____ toward specific things.

17. Toward the end of the second year, the new emotions of _____ , _____ , _____ , and _____ become apparent. These emotions require an awareness of
_____ .

18. An important foundation for emotional growth is _____ ; very young infants have no sense of _____ . This emerging sense of "me" and "mine" soon becomes linked with _____ . Important in this development is children's ability to form their own positive _____ .

Briefly describe the nature and findings of the classic rouge-and-mirror experiment on self-awareness in infants.

The Development of Social Bonds (pp. 180–189)

19. The coordinated interaction of response between infant and caregiver is called _____ . Partly through this

interaction, infants learn to _____ _____ and to develop some of the basic skills of _____ _____ . Two key factors in this process are the _____ of the interaction and _____ . This process is most evident in _____ interactions.

20. The emotional bond that develops between slightly older infants and their caregivers is called _____ .

21. Approaching, following, and climbing onto the caregiver's lap are signs of _____-_____ behaviors, while clinging and resisting being put down are signs of _____ -_____ behaviors.

22. An infant who derives comfort and confidence from the secure base provided by the caregiver is displaying _____ _____ (Type B). In this type of relationship, the caregiver acts as a secure _____ _____ _____ from which the child is willing to venture forth.

23. By contrast, _____ _____ is characterized by an infant's fear, anger, or seeming indifference to the caregiver. Two extremes of this type of relationship are _____-_____ (Type A) and _____-_____ /_____ (Type C).

(text and Table 7.2) Briefly describe three types of insecure attachment.

24. The procedure developed by Mary Ainsworth to measure attachment is called the _____ _____ .

Approximately _____ (what proportion?) of all normal infants tested with this procedure demonstrate secure attachment. When infant–caregiver interactions are inconsistent, infants are classified as _____ .

25. Attachment status _____(determines/does not determine) future emotional development.

26. It is estimated that _____ percent of mothers of young infants are clinically depressed. This figure is higher for _____-_____ mothers. Attachment appears to be determined by the mother's _____ _____ to her infant's attempts at _____ and _____ .

27. The search for information about another person's feelings is called _____ _____ . For infants, this phenomenon is particularly noticeable at _____ .

28. Although early research on psychosocial development focused on _____–_____ relationships, it is clear that other relatives and unrelated people are crucial to the child's development. Recent studies have shown that infants use their fathers for social referencing _____ (less than/as much as/more than) they do their moms.

29. Although fathers tend to provide less _____ _____ than do mothers, they tend to_____ more, which helps the children master _____ skills and develop _____ control. Fathers, single mothers, and grandparents are capable of providing all necessary _____ and _____ nurturing for a child's healthy psychosocial development. Generally speaking, a father's involvement in infant care also benefits the mother's _____ and the father's _____ strength.

30. Infant day care programs include _____ , when fewer than 6 children are cared for in someone's home, and _____ , in which 15 or more

children are cared for in a separate child care facility. More than _____ (what percentage?) of all 1-year-olds in the United States are in regularly scheduled nonmaternal care.

31. Regarding the impact of nonmaternal care on young children, recent research studies have generally found that _____ _____ .

List several benefits of good preschool education.

32. (Table 7.4) Researchers have identified four factors that seem essential to high-quality day care:

a. _____

b. _____

c. _____

d. _____

33. Early day care may be detrimental when the mother is _____ and the infant spends more than _____ (how many?) hours each week in a poor-quality program.

Conclusions in Theory and Practice (pp. 189–191)

34. Regarding the major theories of development, _____ _____ theory stands out as the best interpretation. Although the first two years are important, early _____ and _____ development is influenced by the _____ behavior, the support provided by the _____ , the quality of _____ _____ , patterns

within the child's _____ , and traits that are _____ .

Testing Yourself

After you have completed the audio and text review questions, see how well you do on the following quiz. Correct answers, with text and audio references, may be found at the end of this chapter.

1. Attachment between infant and primary caregiver typically happens at about what age?
   a. 1 or 2 months
   b. 3 or 4 months
   c. 6 or 7 months
   d. 10 or 11 months

2. Experts believe that the emergence of attachment in infants is:
   a. biologically based and linked to the cognitive ability to represent other individuals.
   b. a learned behavior elicited by responsible caregiving.
   c. largely dependent upon early bonding between mother and infant.
   d. unpredictable and of relative unimportance in later psychosocial development.

3. Infants placed for adoption after 6 months of age:
   a. never form secure attachments.
   b. can still become securely attached to adoptive parents.
   c. are more likely to be abused than infants adopted at an earlier age.
   d. gain weight more slowly than infants adopted at an earlier age.

4. Most infants who are regularly placed in day care:
   a. develop attachments to day-care workers rather than parents.
   b. become insecurely attached, out of confusion over their primary caregivers.
   c. show signs of extreme anxiety when tested in the Strange Situation.
   d. form secure attachments to their parents.

5. Stuffed animals, favorite blankets, and other objects that children keep near them when apart from their primary caregivers are called:
   a. security objects.
   b. transitional objects.
   c. vicarious parents.
   d. symbolic pacifiers.

6. Newborns have two identifiable emotions:
   a. shame and distress.
   b. distress and contentment.
   c. anger and joy.
   d. pride and guilt.

7. Synchrony begins to appear at about what age?
   a. 6 weeks
   b. 2 months
   c. 3 months
   d. 4 months

8. An infant's fear of being left by the mother or other caregiver, called _____ , is most obvious at about _____ .
   a. separation anxiety; 14 months
   b. stranger wariness; 8 months
   c. separation anxiety; 8 months
   d. stranger wariness; 14 months

9. Social referencing refers to:
   a. parenting skills that change over time.
   b. changes in community values regarding, for example, the acceptability of using physical punishment with small children.
   c. the support network for new parents provided by extended family members.
   d. the infant response of looking to trusted adults for emotional cues in uncertain situations.

10. The concept of a working model is most consistent with:
    a. psychoanalytic theory.
    b. behaviorism.
    c. cognitive theory.
    d. sociocultural theory.

11. A key difference between temperament and personality is that:
    a. temperamental traits are learned.
    b. personality includes traits that are primarily learned.
    c. personality is more stable than temperament.
    d. personality does not begin to form until much later, when self-awareness emerges.

12. Freud's oral stage corresponds to Erikson's crisis of:
    a. orality versus anality.
    b. trust versus mistrust.
    c. autonomy versus shame and doubt.
    d. secure versus insecure attachment.

13. Erikson felt that the development of a sense of trust in early infancy depends on the quality of the:
    a. infant's food.
    b. child's genetic inheritance.
    c. maternal relationship.
    d. introduction of toilet training.

14. Keisha is concerned that her 15-month-old daughter, who no longer seems to enjoy face-to-face play, is showing signs of insecure attachment. You tell her:
    a. not to worry; face-to-face play almost disappears toward the end of the first year.
    b. she may be right to worry, because face-to-face play typically increases throughout infancy.
    c. not to worry; attachment behaviors are unreliable until toddlerhood.
    d. that her child is typical of children who spend more than 20 hours in day care each week.

15. (Research Report) "Easy," "slow to warm up," and "difficult" are descriptions of different:
    a. forms of attachment.
    b. types of temperament.
    c. types of parenting.
    d. toddler responses to the Strange Situation.

16. The more physical play of fathers probably helps the children master motor skills and may contribute to the:
    a. infant's self-awareness.
    b. growth of the infant's social skills and emotional expression.
    c. tendency of the infant to become securely attached.
    d. infant's fear of strangers and separation anxiety.

17. *Synchrony* is a term that describes:
    a. the carefully coordinated interaction between parent and infant.
    b. a mismatch of the temperaments of parent and infant.
    c. a research technique involving videotapes.
    d. the concurrent evolution of different species.

18. The emotional tie that develops between an infant and his or her primary caregiver is called:
    a. self-awareness.   c. affiliation.
    b. synchrony.   d. attachment.

19. Secure attachment is directly correlated with the promotion of:
    a. self-awareness.
    b. social skills.
    c. dependency.
    d. all of the above.

20. Interest in people, as evidenced by the social smile, appears for the first time when an infant is _____ weeks old.
    a. 3   c. 9
    b. 6   d. 12

21. When there is goodness of fit, the parents of a slow-to-warm-up boy will:
    a. give him extra time to adjust to new situations.
    b. encourage independence in their son by frequently leaving him for short periods of time.
    c. place their son in regular day care so that other children's temperaments will "rub off" on him.
    d. do all of the above.

22. Emotions such as shame, guilt, embarrassment, and pride emerge at the same time that:
    a. the social smile appears.
    b. aspects of the infant's temperament can first be discerned.
    c. self-awareness begins to emerge.
    d. parents initiate toilet training.

23. Four-month-old Carl and his 13-month-old sister Carla are left in the care of a babysitter. As their parents are leaving, it is to be expected that:
    a. Carl will become extremely upset, while Carla will calmly accept her parents' departure.
    b. Carla will become more upset over her parents' departure than will Carl.
    c. Carl and Carla will both become quite upset as their parents leave.
    d. Neither Carl nor Carla will become very upset as their parents leave.

NAME _____   INSTRUCTOR _____

LESSON 7: ATTACHMENT AND THE STRANGE SITUATION

Exercise

About 7 months after birth—around the time that children develop the ability to represent another person cognitively—infants develop an enduring affectional **attachment** to their primary caregivers.

Attachment can be measured in many ways. Infants express attachment by "proximity-seeking" behaviors, such as approaching, following, and clinging; and "contact-seeking" behaviors, such as crying, smiling, and calling. Parents express their attachment more by eye contact than by physical contact, and by reacting to their child's vocalizations, expressions, and gestures.

On the basis of many naturalistic observations, Mary Ainsworth developed a laboratory procedure in which the infant's reactions to a novel situation and the comings and goings of its caregiver indicate the security of the child's attachment. In this test (called the **Strange Situation**), which is conducted in a well-equipped playroom full of toys, most infants demonstrate **secure attachment**. The presence of their mother gives them the sense of security needed to express their natural curiosity and explore the new room. If their mother attempts to leave the room, securely attached infants will usually stop playing, protest verbally, and demonstrate contact-seeking behaviors.

Approximately one-third of infants show **insecure attachment** in this test situation, clinging nervously to their mother and being unwilling to explore even while she remains in the room. Others seem aloof and engage in little or no interaction with their mothers.

To better understand how attachment is measured, arrange to observe a 1- or 2-year-old and his or her caregiver in a play setting outside the child's home. Ideally, ask a relative or friend and their child to participate. The play setting could be in your home, at a local playground, or at any other mutually agreeable location. If you do not know someone with a young child, you can complete this exercise by visiting a playground or day-care center.

Before your scheduled observation period, read through the questions that follow so that you will know what behaviors to watch for. Observe your participants for 10 to 15 minutes of unstructured play. If possible, during the observation period, ask the adult to make a move as if he or she were going to leave. Observe the child's reaction. After the observation period, answer the questions and hand the completed exercise in to your instructor.

1. Describe the participants and setting that you chose for the attachment observation.

2. Did you encounter any difficulties in completing this exercise?

3. What signs of attachment did you observe in the child's behavior (e.g., contact-seeking, proximity-seeking)?

4. What signs of attachment did you observe in the adult's behavior (e.g., eye contact, responsiveness to child's behavior)?

5. If your observation included a move by the adult to leave the room, describe the child's reactions.

6. On the basis of the material covered in this lesson—and your brief observation—would you say that the child you observed was securely attached or insecurely attached? Give examples of the child's behavior that support your conclusion.

LESSON GUIDELINES

Audio Question Guidelines

1. **Attachment** refers to the process by which infants develop a lasting affectional tie with their primary caregiver. Attachment goes two ways, from parent to child and from child to parent.

   From the parent's point of view, the bonding that leads to attachment begins during pregnancy, includes the special memories of birth, and continues to develop indefinitely.

   Babies give their first **social smiles** at about 4 to 6 weeks of age, which clearly contributes to attachment with the caregiver.

   Attachment emerges in children the world over at about 7 months of age. This regularity implies that it is a biologically based event.

   Attachment ensures that the relatively immature and helpless human newborn will receive the adult help it needs in order to survive.

   The signs of attachment to a particular person are clear. The baby turns to that person when distressed and protests when that person leaves. Babies may also cry when strangers appear.

2. There is no good evidence that early mother-infant contact has a major impact on attachment. In most cases, researchers report no reduction in the quality of the relationship formed between mothers and babies when contact in the first few weeks of life does not take place.

   Because babies form their first attachment at about 7 months of age, it is somewhat easier to place a child for adoption before that time. A child placed with adoptive parents after that age may have to go through a process of grieving the loss of an earlier attachment figure before investing emotionally in a new one.

   In most circumstances, babies form more than one attachment in the course of growing up.

   Approximately two-thirds of babies in this country form secure attachments to their mothers whether or not they are in regular day care. An important variable in day care is the quality of care that the child receives and the extent to which it matches the style of the parents.

   Because their children may develop attachments to day-care workers, day care may be a more difficult adjustment for parents than it is for children.

3. Three-year-old children who were **securely attached** at one year are more mature and significantly more independent, self-confident, cooperative, and sociable than those who were **insecurely attached**.

   Securely attached children are more likely to be persistent and resilient in challenging situations.

   The developmental advantages of securely attached children seem to continue to age 5 or 6, when children start school. Most likely, the reason is that their home has been consistently nurturant.

Textbook Question Answers

1. emotional; social

2. oral; mouth

3. anal

Freud believed that the oral and anal stages are fraught with potential conflict that can have long-term consequences for the infant. If nursing is a hurried or tense event, for example, the child may become fixated at the oral stage, excessively eating, drinking, chewing, biting, or talking in quest of oral satisfaction.

4. 27

5. Erikson; trust versus mistrust; autonomy versus shame and doubt

6. behaviorism; reinforcement; punishment; John Watson

7. social; imitate

8. thoughts; perceptions; memories; working model

9. epigenetic; genetic; temperament

10. personality; environment

11. small; New York Longitudinal Study (NYLS); activity level, rhythmicity, approach–withdrawal, adaptability, intensity of reaction, threshold of responsiveness, quality of mood, distractibility, attention span

12. easy; difficult; slow to warm up; positive; inhibited; negative

13. goodness of fit

14. sociocultural; social

15. distress; contentment; curiosity; pleasure; anger

16. 9 months; stranger wariness; 10 to 14; separation anxiety; 9 to 14; decrease; targeted

17. pride, shame, embarrassment, guilt; what other people might be thinking

18. self-awareness; self; self-concept; self-evaluations

In the classic self-awareness experiment, babies look in a mirror after a dot of rouge is put on their nose. If the babies react to the mirror image by touching their nose, it is clear they know they are seeing their own face. Most babies demonstrate this self-awareness between 15 and 24 months of age.

19. synchrony; read other people's emotions; social interaction; timing; imitation; play

20. attachment

21. proximity-seeking; contact-maintaining

22. secure attachment; base for exploration

23. insecure attachment; insecure-avoidant; insecure-resistant/ambivalent

Some infants are avoidant: They engage in little interaction with their mother before and after her departure. Others are anxious and resistant: They cling nervously to their mother, are unwilling to explore, cry loudly when she leaves, and refuse to be comforted when she returns. Others are disorganized: They show an inconsistent mixture of behavior toward the mother.

24. Strange Situation; two-thirds; disorganized

25. does not determine

26. 10; low-income; overt responses; synchrony; attachment

27. social referencing; mealtime

28. mother–infant; as much as

29. basic care; play; motor; muscle; emotional; cognitive; self-confidence; emotional

30. family day care; center care; 50

31. children are not harmed by, and sometimes benefit from, professional day care

Good preschool education helps children learn more language, think with more perspective, develop better social skills, and achieve more in the long term.

32. (a) adequate attention to each child; (b) encouragement of sensorimotor exploration and language development; (c) attention to health and safety; (d) well-trained and professional caregivers.

33. insensitive; 20

34. no single; emotional; social; mothers'; father; day care; culture; inborn

Answers to Testing Yourself

1. **c.** is the answer. In children throughout the world, attachment emerges at 6 or 7 months. (audio program)

2. **a.** is the answer. Attachment emerges at about the same age that infants develop the cognitive ability to maintain the image of another person in their minds. (audio program)

3. **b.** is the answer. Infants who are placed for adoption after the age of 6 or 7 months may first grieve the loss of an earlier attachment, but they can still develop new secure attachments. (audio program)

4. **d.** is the answer. Infants placed regularly in day care may develop attachments to day-care workers, but they still become attached to their parents. (audio program)

5. **b.** is the answer. Transitional objects help fill an emotional need in the time between when a child is physically near the parent and when he or she can be away from the parent completely. (audio program)

6. **b.** is the answer. (textbook, p. 178)

   a., c., & d. These emotions emerge later in infancy, at about the same time as self-awareness emerges.

7. **c.** is the answer. (textbook, p. 180)

8. **a.** is the answer. (textbook, p. 178)

   b. & d. This fear, which is also called fear of strangers, peaks by 10 to 14 months.

9. **d.** is the answer. (textbook, p. 185)

10. **c.** is the answer. (textbook, p. 174)

11. **b.** is the answer. (textbook, p. 175)

12. **b.** is the answer. (textbook, p. 173)

    a. Orality and anality refer to personality traits that result from fixation in the oral and anal stages, respectively.

    c. According to Erikson, this is the crisis of toddlerhood, which corresponds to Freud's anal stage.

    d. This is not a developmental crisis in Erikson's theory.

13. **c.** is the answer. (textbook, p. 173)

14. **a.** is the answer. (textbook, p. 181)

c. Attachment behaviors are reliably found during infancy.

d. There is no indication that the child attends day care.

15. **b.** is the answer. (textbook, pp. 175–176)

a. "Secure" and "insecure" are different forms of attachment.

c. The chapter does not describe different types of parenting.

d. The Strange Situation is a test of attachment, rather than of temperament.

16. **b.** is the answer. (textbook, p. 187)

17. **a.** is the answer. (textbook, p. 180)

18. **d.** is the answer. (textbook, p. 181)

a. Self-awareness refers to the infant's developing sense of "me and mine."

b. Synchrony describes the coordinated interaction between infant and caregiver.

c. Affiliation describes the tendency of people at any age to seek the companionship of others.

19. **b.** is the answer. (textbook, pp. 181–184)

a. The text does not link self-awareness to secure attachment.

c. On the contrary, secure attachment promotes *independence* in infants and children.

20. **b.** is the answer. (textbook, p. 178)

21. **a.** is the answer. (textbook, p. 177)

22. **c.** is the answer. (textbook, p. 179)

a. & b. The social smile, as well as temperamental characteristics, emerge well before the first signs of self-awareness.

d. Contemporary developmentalists link these emotions to self-consciousness, rather than any specific environmental event such as toilet training.

23. **b.** is the answer. The fear of being left by a caregiver (separation anxiety) is most obvious at 9 to 14 months. For this reason, 4-month-old Carl can be expected to become less upset than his older sister. (textbook, p. 178)

The Play Years: Biosocial Development

AUDIO PROGRAM: "How to" Time

ORIENTATION

Lesson 8 is the first of a three-lesson unit that describes the developing person from 2 to 6 years in terms of biosocial, cognitive, and psychosocial development. Lesson 8 examines biosocial development during the play years.

Children grow steadily taller and slimmer during the preschool years, with their genetic background and nutrition being responsible for most of the variation seen in children from various parts of the world. The most significant aspect of growth is the continued maturation of the nervous system and the refinement of the visual, muscular, and cognitive skills that will be necessary for the child to function in school. The brain becomes more specialized as it matures, with the left side usually becoming the center for speech, and the right the center for visual, spatial, and artistic skills.

Chapter 8 of *The Developing Person Through the Life Span*, 6/e, also discusses these refinements in physical development. In addition, it includes a thorough discussion of a tragedy in child development: child abuse and neglect, including the prevalence of maltreatment, its causes, consequences, treatment, and prevention.

Play is especially appropriate for the extended period of childhood that has been programmed into the biological clock. Audio program 8, "'How To' Time," explores the evolutionary origins of this period and the use to which humans have put it.

The human biological clock delays the onset of reproductive maturity and gives children time to acquire what Erik Erikson referred to as a sense of industry. Childhood is the time to pretend, to play, and to learn how to do things. And herein lies the key to our extended childhood. More than any other species, we humans are dependent upon complex, learned behavior for our survival. Through the expert commentary of pediatrician Howard Weinblatt, endocrinologist Inese Beitins, anthropologist Barry Bogin, and evolutionary biologist Stephen Jay Gould, the significance of "how to" time is explored.

The program opens with the voice of a girl explaining how to ride a tricycle, a skill rarely used by adults but never forgotten.

LESSON GOALS

By the end of this lesson you should be prepared to:

1. Describe normal physical growth during the play years, and account for variations in height and weight.

2. Discuss brain growth and development, its effect on development during the play years, and the development of school readiness.

3. Outline the development of gross and fine motor skills during early childhood, and describe activities that foster these skills.

4. Discuss the significance of the extended period of human childhood and the importance of play in development.

5. Discuss various issues concerning child maltreatment, including its prevalence, causes, consequences, treatment, and prevention.

Audio Assignment

Listen to the audio tape that accompanies Lesson 8: "'How To' Time."

Write answers to the following questions. You may replay portions of the program if you need to refresh your memory. Answer guidelines may be found in the Lesson Guidelines section at the end of this chapter.

1. Outline the biological clock's hormonal program for the timing of sexual maturity.

2. Cite two possible evolutionary explanations for the extended period of childhood in humans.

3. Explain the "down-and-out" principle of physical development.

Textbook Assignment

Read Chapter 8: "The Play Years: Biosocial Development," pages 197–215 in *The Developing Person Through the Life Span*, 6/e, then work through the material that follows to review it. Complete the sentences and answer the questions. As you proceed, evaluate your performance for each section by consulting the answers on page 97. Do not continue with the next section until you understand each answer. If you need to, review or reread the appropriate section in the textbook before continuing.

Body and Brain (pp. 197–203)

1. During the preschool years, from age _____ to _____ , children add almost _____ in height and gain about _____ in weight per year. By age 6, the average child in a developed nation weighs about _____ and measures _____ in height. In num-bers, _____ are more useful than _____ in monitoring growth.

2. The range of normal physical development is quite _____ (narrow/broad).

3. In multiethnic countries, children of _____ descent tend to be tallest, followed by _____ , then _____ , and then _____ . The impact of _____ patterns on physical development can be seen in families in South Asia and India, where _____ (which gender?) are better fed and cared for than the other sex.

4. Of the many factors that influence height and weight, the most influential are the child's _____ , _____ , and _____ .

5. The dramatic differences between physical development in developed and underdeveloped nations are largely due to differences in the average child's _____ .

6. During the preschool years, annual height and weight gain is much _____ (greater/less) than during infancy. This means that children need _____ (fewer/more) calories per pound during this period.

7. The most prevalent nutritional problem in early childhood is an insufficient intake of _____ , _____ , and _____ .

8. An additional problem for American children is that they consume too many _____ .

9. By age 2, most pruning of the brain's _____ has occurred and the brain weighs _____ percent of its adult weight. By age 5, the brain has attained about _____ percent of its adult weight; by age 7 it is almost _____ percent.

10. Part of the brain's increase in size during child-hood is due to the continued proliferation of _____ pathways and the ongoing process of _____ . This process, which is influenced by _____ , is essential for communication that is _____ and _____ . During the play years, this process proceeds most rapidly in brain areas dedicated to _____ and _____ .

11. The band of nerve fibers that connects the right and left sides of the brain, called the _____ _____ , grows and _____ rapidly during the play years. This helps children better coordinate func-tions that involve _____ _____ .

12. The two sides of the body and brain _____ (are/are not) identical. The specialization of the two sides of the body and brain, which begins before _____ , is called _____ . Throughout the world, societies are organized to favor _____-handedness. Training of one side of the body is easier _____ (before/after) the process of _____ is complete.

13. Damage to the left side of the brain, where most _____ functions are located, is more serious in _____ than in _____ .

14. The left hemisphere of the brain controls the _____ side of the body and contains areas dedicated to _____ , _____ , and _____ . The right hemisphere controls the _____ side of the body and contains brains areas dedicated to _____ and _____ impulses.

15. The corpus callosum _____ (is/is not) fully developed in young children, which partly explains why their behaviors sometimes are _____ .

16. The final part of the brain to reach maturity is the _____ _____ . Development of this brain area is not completed until _____ .

17. Two signs of an undeveloped prefrontal cortex are _____ and _____ , which is the tendency to stick to a thought or action even after it has become inappropriate.

18. Brain development _____ (is/is not) smooth and linear, and brain functions _____ (improve/do not improve) at the same age for every child.

19. During the school years, many deficiencies in _____ , _____ _____ , _____ _____ , and _____ . _____ are directly tied to inadequate lateralization and to _____ and _____ of the frontal cortex.

Motor Skills and Avoidable Injuries (pp. 203–208)

20. Large body movements such as running, climb-ing, jumping, and throwing are called _____ _____ skills. These skills, which improve dramatically during the preschool years, require guided _____ , as well as a certain level of _____ _____ .

21. Most children learn these skills from _____ (other children/parents).

22. Skills that involve small body movements, such as pouring liquids and cutting food, are called _____ _____ skills. Preschoolers have greater difficulty with these skills primarily because they have not developed the _____ control, patience, or _____ needed—in part because the _____ of the central nervous system is not complete.

23. Many developmentalists believe that _____ _____ is a form of play that enhances the child's sense of accom-plishment. The pictures children draw often

reveal their _____ and

_____ .

24. Except in times of famine, the leading cause of childhood death is _____ . Injuries and accidental deaths are _____ (more/less) frequent among boys than girls.

25. Not until age _____ does any disease become a greater cause of mortality.

26. Instead of "accident prevention," many experts speak of _____

_____

(or _____ _____), an approach based on the belief that most accidents _____ (are/are not) preventable.

27. Preventive community actions that reduce everyone's chance of injury are called

_____ _____ .

Preventive actions that avert harm in the immediate situation constitute _____

_____ . Actions aimed at minimizing the impact of an adverse event that has already occurred constitute _____

_____ .

28. One risk factor in accident rates is

_____ , with children in the

_____ countries being more likely than other children to die from _____

or an _____ .

29. (Changing Policy) The accidental death rate for American children between the ages of 1 and 5 has _____ (increased/ decreased) over the past 20 years.

Child Maltreatment (pp. 208–214)

30. Until a few decades ago, the concept of child maltreatment was mostly limited to obvious

_____ assault, which was thought to be the outburst of a mentally disturbed person. Today, it is known that most perpetrators of maltreatment _____ (are/are not) mentally ill.

31. Intentional harm to, or avoidable endangerment of, someone under age 18 defines child _____ . Actions that are deliberately harmful to a child's well-being are classified as _____ . A failure to act appropriately to meet a child's basic needs is classified as

_____ .

32. One sign of maltreatment is called _____

_____ _____ , in which an infant or young child gains little or no _____ , despite apparently normal health. Another sign is _____ , in which an older child seems too nervous to concentrate on anything. These phenomena are symptoms of _____ _____

_____ _____ , which was first described in combat victims. Children can also suffer from _____ neglect or from _____ neglect.

33. Since 1993, the ratio of the number of cases of

_____ _____ , in which authorities have been officially notified, to cases of _____ _____ , which have been reported and verified, has been about _____ (what ratio?).

34. Laws requiring teachers, social workers, and other professionals to report possible maltreatment _____ (have/have not) resulted in increased reporting.

35. Maltreated children have difficulty learning in part because they may develop abnormal _____ patterns that make learning difficult. The most serious of these is

_____ _____

_____ , which can cause the child's neck to break and damage

_____ _____ and _____ _____ in the brain.

36. Abnormal brain development in an abused child may result in impaired _____ and delayed _____

_____ . In children who are

neglected because their mothers are clinically depressed, the _____ (right/left) side of the prefrontal cortex develops more than the other side.

Describe other deficits of children who have been maltreated.

37. Public policy measures and other efforts designed to prevent maltreatment from ever occurring are called _____ _____ .
An approach that focuses on spotting and treating the first symptoms of maltreatment is called _____ _____ . Last-ditch measures such as removing a child from an abusive home, jailing the perpetrator, and so forth constitute _____

_____ .

38. Some children are officially removed from their parents and placed in a _____ _____ arrangement with another adult or family who is paid to nurture them.

39. The number of children needing foster placement has _____ (increased/decreased) over the past decade in the United States.

40. In another type of foster care, called _____ _____ , a relative of the maltreated child becomes the approved caregiver. A final option is _____ .

After you have completed the audio and text review questions, see how well you do on the following quiz. Correct answers, with text and audio references, may be found at the end of this chapter.

1. The primary sex hormones are _____ in females and _____ in males.
   a. testosterone; estrogen
   b. estrogen; testosterone
   c. adrenaline; noradrenaline
   d. progesterone; testosterone

2. Which of the following most accurately describes how the levels of sex hormones change from birth to puberty?
   a. In both males and females, levels of sex hormones increase from birth until puberty.
   b. In males only, levels of sex hormones increase from birth until puberty.
   c. In females only, levels of sex hormones increase from birth until puberty.
   d. In both males and females, levels of sex hormones are very high at birth, drop at about 18 months, and become high again at puberty.

3. Anthropologists have proposed that an extended period of childhood evolved in humans because:
   a. humans need this time to learn the many complex behaviors critical for survival.
   b. babysitting by older children conferred such an advantage on humans that our biological clock evolved to keep childhood as lengthy as possible.
   c. both a. and b. are true.
   d. none of the above is true.

4. The "down-and-out" principle of development would explain why:
   a. reproductive maturity does not occur until puberty.
   b. babies can sit up before their color vision is mature.
   c. babies can sit up before they can stand.
   d. physical development is more rapid in girls than in boys.

5. According to developmental psychologists, the play of "how to" time is an important way in which children:
   a. perfect motor skills.
   b. develop a sense of being useful and competent.
   c. develop what Erikson referred to as a sense of industry.
   d. do all of the above.

6. During the preschool years, the most common nutritional problem in developed countries is:
   a. serious malnutrition.
   b. excessive intake of sweets.
   c. insufficient intake of iron, zinc, and calcium.
   d. excessive caloric intake.

7. The brain center for speech is usually located in the:
   a. right brain.
   b. left brain.
   c. corpus callosum.
   d. space just below the right ear.

8. Which of the following is an example of tertiary prevention of child maltreatment?
   a. removing a child from an abusive home
   b. home visitation of families with infants by health professionals
   c. new laws establishing stiff penalties for child maltreatment
   d. public-policy measures aimed at creating stable neighborhoods

9. (Changing Policy) Which of the following is *not* true regarding injury control?
   a. Broad-based television announcements do not have a direct impact on children's risk taking.
   b. Unless parents become involved, classroom safety education has little effect on children's actual behavior.
   c. Safety laws that include penalties are more effective than educational measures.
   d. Accidental deaths of 1- to 5-year-olds have held steady in the United States over the past two decades.

10. Children tend to have too much _____ in their diet, which contributes to _____ .
    a. iron; anemia
    b. sugar; tooth decay
    c. fat; delayed development of fine motor skills
    d. carbohydrate; delayed development of gross motor skills

11. Skills that involve large body movements, such as running and jumping, are called:
    a. activity-level skills.
    b. fine motor skills.
    c. gross motor skills.
    d. left-brain skills.

12. The brain's ongoing myelination and overall maturation during childhood helps children:
    a. control their actions more precisely.
    b. react more quickly to stimuli.
    c. control their emotions.
    d. do all of the above.

13. The leading cause of death in childhood is:
    a. accidents.
    b. untreated diabetes.
    c. malnutrition.
    d. iron deficiency.

14. Regarding lateralization, which of the following is *not* true?
    a. Some cognitive skills require only one side of the brain.
    b. Brain centers for generalized emotional impulses can be found in the right hemisphere.
    c. The left hemisphere contains brain areas dedicated to spatial reasoning.
    d. The right side of the brain controls the left side of the body.

15. Which of the following factors is *most* responsible for differences in height and weight between children in developed and developing countries?
    a. the child's genetic background
    b. health care
    c. nutrition
    d. age of weaning

16. The area of the brain that directs and controls the other areas is the:
    a. corpus callosum.
    b. myelin sheath.
    c. prefrontal cortex.
    d. temporal lobe.

17. The relationship between accident rate and income can be described as:
    a. a positive correlation.
    b. a negative correlation.
    c. curvilinear.
    d. no correlation.

18. Which of the following is true of the corpus callosum?
    a. It enables short-term memory.
    b. It connects the two halves of the brain.
    c. It must be fully myelinated before gross motor skills can be acquired.
    d. All of the above are correct.

19. The improvements in eye–hand coordination that allow preschoolers to catch and then throw a ball occur, in part, because:
    a. the brain areas associated with this ability become more fully myelinated.
    b. the corpus callosum begins to function.
    c. fine motor skills have matured by age 2.
    d. gross motor skills have matured by age 2.

20. Adoption is most likely to be successful as an intervention for maltreatment when:
    a. children are young and biological families are inadequate.
    b. efforts at tertiary prevention have already failed.
    c. children have endured years of maltreatment in their biological family.
    d. foster care and kinship care have failed.

21. Which of the following is an example of perseveration?
    a. 2-year-old Jason sings the same song over and over
    b. 3-year-old Kwame falls down when attempting to kick a soccer ball
    c. 4-year-old Kara pours water very slowly from a pitcher into a glass
    d. None of the above is an example.

22. During the play years, children's appetites seem _____ they were in the first two years of life.
    a. larger than
    b. smaller than
    c. about the same as
    d. erratic, sometimes smaller and sometimes larger than

23. Jason is a three-year-old child, whose hyperactivity and hypervigilance may be symptoms of:
    a. post-traumatic stress disorder.
    b. an immature corpus callosum.
    c. an immature prefrontal cortex.
    d. normal development.

NAME _____ INSTRUCTOR _____

LESSON 8: PLAY SPACES AND PLAYGROUNDS

Exercise

A major theme of this lesson is that "play is the work of childhood." According to most developmental psychologists, both work and play are important activities at every stage of life. But the line between play and work is not clear-cut, especially in the play years. Rather than thinking about the two as opposites, many developmentalists argue that it is more profitable to think of them as endpoints along a continuum, from the most whimsical, spontaneous, nonproductive play on the one side, to the most deliberate, planned, productive work on the other.

Developmental psychologists view play as the major means through which physical, cognitive, and social skills are mastered. Unfortunately, many adults are so imbued with the work ethic that they tend to denigrate children's play. Some even punish their children for "horsing around," criticize nursery school teachers for letting children play "too much," or schedule their children's lives so heavily with lessons, homework, and chores that there is little time left for play.

Every age has its own special forms of play. Play that captures the pleasures of using the senses and motor abilities is called **sensorimotor play**. Associated most closely with infants, this type of play actually continues throughout childhood. Much of the physical play of childhood is **mastery play**, which refers to play that helps children to master new skills. This type of play is most obvious when physical skills are involved, but increasingly comes to include intellectual skills as children grow older. A third type of play is the **rough-and-tumble** wrestling, chasing, and hitting that occur purely in fun, with no intent to harm.

Young children need safe, adequate play space and the opportunity to play with children their own age. To increase your awareness of the play and play needs of children in your neighborhood, the exercise for Lesson 8 asks you to locate and observe play spaces within walking distance of your home. If there are none, what alternatives exist for preschoolers in your neighborhood? For example, do they play in backyards? Or are most preschoolers enrolled in nursery schools that have their own play spaces? Once you have answered the following questions, hand the completed exercise in to your instructor.

1. Describe a public or school playground within walking distance of your home. List the play equipment provided that is designed to be used by younger children (especially preschoolers).

2. Describe the population of children who visit the playground. (For example, are the children of different ages, or ethnic or racial backgrounds?)

3. Spend some time, if you can, observing the way in which preschoolers play. What types of play can you identify? Give several examples of each type.

4. If you can, observe the way in which preschoolers attempt to master the larger, more exciting structures on the playground. For example, observe their uses of the jungle gym, slide, or "big" swings. How do parents or caregivers respond to the exploration and risk-taking of their preschoolers? Identify differences in parenting styles you have seen.

LESSON GUIDELINES

Audio Question Guidelines

1. The biological clock is a metaphor for the body's mechanisms for the timing of physical development.

   Hormones are chemical messengers secreted into the bloodstream by glands and have a variety of effects on the body. **Sex hormones**, such as **estrogen** in females and **testosterone** in males, are responsible for triggering development of the reproductive system.

   By the end of the third month of prenatal development, the human fetus has sex organs and is producing sex hormones. At birth, sex hormones are present in a baby's bloodstream at levels equivalent to those at puberty.

   At about 18 months of age, the high levels of sex hormones drop and remain at a very low level until puberty, when there is another surge and reproductive maturity is attained.

2. Anthropologists have suggested that one reason humans have a much longer childhood than other animals (and that the development of their reproductive system is delayed) is to provide an opportunity for children to learn the many complex behaviors that gave our species its great cognitive capacity. This explanation is supported by the fact that our species' survival depends to a much greater extent on learned behavior than does that of any other species.

   Another possible explanation is that an extended childhood allows older children to take care of younger children. In hunting-and-gathering societies throughout the world, the prime job of children is to take care of younger children. In animal societies, by contrast, the mother must care for the young herself and is therefore limited in her capacity to produce more offspring.

3. The **"down-and-out" principle** of development is that maturation begins with the head and brain and works its way down the spine and out to the extremities. In the textbook (page 99), this pattern is referred to as cephalo-caudal (head to tail) and proximo-distal (near to far, or inside out) development.

   The down-and-out principle explains why babies are able to lift their heads before they can sit up, and can sit before they are able to stand. It also explains the normal progression of gross-motor-skill development. For example, younger children throw balls with their entire arms. Older children are able to control a throw more precisely by

adding, successively, motion of the wrist, hand, and fingers.

Textbook Question Answers

1. 2; 6; 3 inches (7 centimeters); 4.5 pounds (2 kilograms); 46 pounds (21 kilograms); 46 inches (117 centimeters); percentiles; norms
2. broad
3. African; Europeans; Asians; Latinos; cultural; boys
4. genes; health; nutrition
5. nutrition
6. less; fewer
7. iron; zinc; calcium
8. sweetened cereals and drinks
9. dendrites; 75; 90; 100
10. communication; myelination; experience; fast; complex; memory; reflection
11. corpus callosum; myelinates; both sides of the brain and body
12. are not; birth; lateralization; right; before; lateralization
13. language; adults; children
14. right; logic; analysis; language; left; emotional; creative
15. is not; clumsy, wobbly, and slow
16. prefrontal cortex; mid-adolescence
17. impulsiveness; perseveration
18. is not; do not improve
19. cognition, peer relationships; emotional control; classroom learning; immaturity; asymmetry
20. gross motor; practice; brain maturation
21. other children
22. fine motor; muscular; judgment; myelination
23. artistic expression; perception; cognition
24. accidents; more
25. 40
26. injury control; harm reduction; are
27. primary prevention; secondary prevention; tertiary prevention
28. income; poorest; disease; accident
29. decreased
30. physical; are not
31. maltreatment; abuse; neglect
32. failure to thrive; weight; hypervigilance; post-traumatic stress disorder; medical; educational

33. reported maltreatment; substantiated maltreatment; 3-to-1

34. have

35. brain; shaken baby syndrome; blood vessels; neural connections

36. memory; logical thinking; right

37. primary prevention; secondary prevention; tertiary prevention

Maltreated children tend to regard other people as hostile and exploitative, and hence are less friendly, more aggressive, and more isolated than other children. As adolescents and adults they often use drugs or alcohol, choose unsupportive relationships, become victims or aggressors, sabotage their own careers, eat too much or too little, and generally engage in self-destructive behavior.

38. foster care

39. increased

40. kinship care; adoption

Answers to Testing Yourself

1. **b.** is the answer. Estrogen is the primary female sex hormone; testosterone, the primary male hormone. (audio program; see also text Chapter 14, p. 342)

2. **d.** is the answer. At birth, the level of sex hormones in both sexes is as high as it will be at puberty. In the years in between, however, levels drop precipitously. (audio program)

3. **c.** is the answer. Anthropologists believe that the benefits of both learning and babysitting resulted in the evolution of an extended childhood in humans. (audio program)

4. **c.** is the answer. The muscles that permit sitting develop before those that permit standing, following the head-down principle of development. (audio program)

5. **d.** is the answer. Play is the "work" of childhood. (audio program)

6. **c.** is the answer. (textbook, p. 198)

   a. Serious malnutrition is much more likely to occur in infancy or in adolescence than in early childhood.

   b. Although an important health problem, eating too much candy or other sweets is not as serious a problem as this.

   d. Since growth is slower during the preschool years, children need fewer calories per pound during this period.

7. **b.** is the answer. (textbook, p. 200)

   a. & d. The right brain is the location of areas associated with generalized emotional and creative impulses

   c. The corpus callosum helps integrate the functioning of the two halves of the brain; it does not contain areas specialized for particular skills.

8. **a.** is the answer. (textbook, p. 213)

   b. This is an example of secondary prevention.

   c. & d. These are examples of primary prevention.

9. **d.** is the answer. Accident rates have *decreased* during this time period. (textbook, p. 207)

10. **d.** is the answer. (textbook, pp. 198–199)

11. **c.** is the answer. (textbook, p. 203)

12. **d.** is the answer. (textbook, pp. 199, 201)

13. **a.** is the answer. (textbook, p. 205)

14. **c.** is the answer. (textbook, p. 201)

    b. The proportions are more adultlike in both girls and boys.

    d. Nutrition is a bigger factor in growth at this age than either heredity or health care.

15. **c.** is the answer. (textbook, p. 198)

16. **c.** is the answer. (p. 201)

    a. The corpus callosum is the band of fibers that link the two halves of the brain.

    b. The myelin sheath is the fatty insulation that surrounds some neurons in the brain.

    d. The temporal lobes of the brain contain the primary centers for hearing.

17. **b.** is the answer. Children with *lower* SES have *higher* accident rates. (textbook, p. 206)

18. **b.** is the answer. (textbook, p. 200)

    a. The corpus callosum is not directly involved in memory.

    c. Myelination of the central nervous system is important to the mastery of *fine* motor skills.

19. **a.** is the answer. (textbook, p. 199)

    b. The corpus callosum begins to function long before the play years.

    c. & d. Neither fine nor gross motor skills have fully matured by age 2.

20. **a.** is the answer. (textbook, p. 214)

    b. Removing a child from an abusive home is itself a form of tertiary prevention.

    c. Such children tend to fare better in group homes.

d. Although adoption is the final option, children who have been unable to thrive in foster care or kinship care will probably not thrive in an adoptive home either.

21. a. is the answer. (p. 201)

b. Kicking a ball is a gross motor skill.

c. Pouring is a fine motor skill.

22. b. is the answer. (p. 198)

23. a. is the answer. (p. 209)

The Play Years: Cognitive Development

AUDIO PROGRAM: **Then Sentences**

ORIENTATION

Each season of life has its particular perspective on the world. At no age is this more apparent than during the play years. Young children think and speak very differently from older children and adults. In countless everyday instances, as well as in the findings of numerous research studies, preschoolers reveal themselves to be remarkably thoughtful, insightful, and perceptive thinkers whose grasp of the causes of everyday events, memory of the past, and mastery of language is sometimes astounding.

Chapter 9 of *The Developing Person Through the Life Span*, 6/e, begins by comparing Piaget's and Vygotsky's views of cognitive development at this age. According to Piaget, young children's thought is prelogical: Between the ages of 2 and 6, they are unable to perform many logical operations and are limited by irreversible, centered, and static thinking. Lev Vygotsky, a contemporary of Piaget's, saw learning as a social activity more than as a matter of individual discovery. Vygotsky focused on the child's "zone of proximal development" and the relationship between language and thought.

Audio program 9, "Then Sentences," picks up where program 6, "First Words," left off in describing the path children follow in acquiring language. With the expert commentary of psycholinguist Jill de Villiers, the audio program examines how children come to produce their first primitive sentences and then move on to produce more complex, grammatically correct speech.

The journey from cries to words to articulate speech is an intricate one unique to human beings. The similar developmental course of children the world over points to the importance of the biological clock in language development. The grammatical errors, abbreviations, and overextensions of rules in children's speech suggest that humans have a natural propensity to acquire language and that children master its complicated rules by actively experimenting with them, rather than merely by imitating the speech that they hear.

As the program opens, we hear audio snapshots of one child at three different ages. The snapshots reveal the remarkable transition from words to sentences.

LESSON GOALS

By the end of this lesson you should be prepared to:

1. Describe and discuss the major characteristics of preoperational thought, according to Piaget.

2. Discuss Vygotsky's views on cognitive development, focusing on the concept of guided participation.

3. Discuss young children's memory abilities and limitations.

4. Outline the main accomplishments and limitations of language development during the play years.

5. Discuss why the play years are a prime period for learning, and identify the kinds of experiences that best foster cognitive development during early childhood.

Audio Assignment

Listen to the audio tape that accompanies Lesson 9: "Then Sentences."

Write answers to the following questions. You may replay portions of the program if you need to refresh your memory. Answer guidelines may be found in the Lesson Guidelines section at the end of this chapter.

1. Outline the course of language development during the year after the child's production of his or her first word.

2. What evidence is there that the biological clock sets a common timetable for language development?

3. Describe the ways in which young children and adults speak to each other and how this interaction promotes the child's acquisition of the rules of language.

4. Compare and contrast the state of readiness of the auditory system, nervous system, and vocal tract for language acquisition during early childhood.

5. What evidence does the program present that humans have a natural propensity for learning sign language?

Textbook Assignment

Read Chapter 9: "The Play Years: Cognitive Development," pages 217–235 in *The Developing Person Through the Life Span*, 6/e, then work through the material that follows to review it. Complete the sentences and answer the questions. As you proceed, evaluate your performance for each section by consulting the answers on page 109. Do not continue with the next section until you understand each answer. If you need to, review or reread the appropriate section in the textbook before continuing.

How Young Children Think: Piaget and Vygotsky
(pp. 217–225)

1. For many years, researchers maintained that young children's thinking abilities were sorely limited by their _____ .

2. Piaget referred to cognitive development between the ages of 2 and 6 as _____ thought.

3. Young children's tendency to think about one aspect of a situation at a time is called _____ . One particular form of this characteristic is children's tendency to contemplate the world exclusively from their personal perspective, which is referred to as _____ . They also tend to focus on _____ to the exclusion of other attributes of objects and people.

4. Preschoolers' understanding of the world tends to be _____ (static/dynamic), which means that they tend to think of their world as _____ . A closely related characteristic is _____—the inability to recognize that reversing a process will restore the original conditions from which the process began.

5. The idea that amount is unaffected by changes in appearance is called _____ . In the case of _____ _____ _____ , preschoolers who are shown pairs of checkers in two even rows and who then observe one row being spaced out will say that the spaced-out row has more checkers.

6. The term _____-_____ highlights the idea that children attempt to construct theories to explain everything they see and

hear. The idea that children are "apprentices in thinking" emphasizes that children's intellectual growth is stimulated by their _____ _____ in _____ experiences of their environment. The critical element in this process is that the mentor and the child _____ to accomplish a task.

7. Much of the research from the sociocultural perspective on the young child's emerging cognition is inspired by the Russian psychologist _____ . According to this perspective, an adult can most effectively help a child solve a problem by offering _____ , _____ successes, maintaining _____ , providing _____ , and helping the child to recognize that together they are progressing toward accomplishing their goal.

8. Unlike Piaget, this psychologist believed that cognitive growth is a _____ _____ more than a matter of individual discovery.

9. Vygotsky suggested that for each developing individual there is a _____ _____ _____ , a range of skills that the person can exercise with assistance but is not yet able to perform independently.

10. How and when new skills are developed depends, in part, on the willingness of tutors to _____ the child's participation in learning encounters.

11. Vygotsky believed that language is essential to the advancement of thinking in two crucial ways. The first is through the internal dialogue in which a person talks to himself or herself, called _____ _____ . In preschoolers, this dialogue is likely to be _____ (expressed silently/uttered aloud).

12. According to Vygotsky, another way language advances thinking is as the _____ of the social interaction.

13. As a result of their experiences with others, young children acquire a _____ _____ _____ that reflects their developing concepts about human mental processes.

Describe the theory of mind of children between the ages of 3 and 6.

14. Most 3-year-olds _____ (have/do not have) difficulty realizing that a belief can be false.

15. Research studies reveal that theory-of-mind development depends as much on general _____ ability as it does on _____ _____ . A third helpful factor is having at least one _____ . Finally, _____ may be a factor.

Language (pp. 225–230)

16. The skills a child needs in order to learn to read are called _____ _____ . Two aspects of development that make ages 2 to 6 the prime time for learning language are _____ and _____ in the language areas of the brain.

17. Although early childhood does not appear to be a _____ period for language development, it does seem to be a _____ period for the learning of vocabulary, grammar, and pronunciation.

18. During the preschool years, a dramatic increase in language occurs, with _____ increasing exponentially.

19. Through the process called _____

_____ preschoolers often learn words after only one or two hearings. A closely related process is _____

_____ , by which children are able to apply newly learned words to other objects in the same category.

20. Abstract nouns and metaphors are _____ (more/no more) difficult for preschoolers to understand.

21. Because preschool children tend to think in absolute terms, they have difficulty with words that express _____ , as well as words expressing relativities of _____ and _____ .

22. The structures, techniques, and rules that a language uses to communicate meaning define its _____ . By age _____ , children typically demonstrate extensive understanding of this aspect of language.

23. Preschoolers' tendency to apply rules of grammar when they should not is called _____ .

Give several examples of this tendency.

24. Most developmentalists agree that bilingualism _____ (is/is not necessarily) an asset to children in today's world.

25. Children who speak two languages by age 5 often are less _____ in their understanding of language and more advanced in their

_____ _____

_____ . Advocates of monolingualism point out that bilingual proficiency comes at the expense of _____

_____ in the dominant language, slowing down the development of

_____ _____ .

26. Some immigrant parents are saddened when their children make a _____

_____ and become more fluent in their new language than that of their home culture. The best solution is for children to become

_____ _____ , who are fluent in both languages. This is easiest for children when their parents _____

_____ .

Early-Childhood Education (pp. 230–234)

27. A century ago, _____

_____ opened the first structured nursery schools for poor children in Rome. Many new programs use an educational model inspired by _____ that allows children to

_____ .

Other, often _____ (more/less) structured programs, stress _____ .

28. The new early-childhood curriculum called

_____ _____ encourages children to master skills not usually seen until about age _____ .

29. Early-childhood education _____ (has/has not) always been deemed important in most cultures. Today, developmentalists _____ (agree/disagree) about the value of national programs for quality early education.

30. In 1965, _____ _____

_____ was inaugurated to give low-income children some form of compensatory education during the preschool years. Longitudinal research found that graduates of similar but more intensive, well-evaluated programs scored _____ (higher/no higher) on achievement tests and were more likely to attend college and less likely to go to jail.

List several characteristics of high-quality early childhood education.

Testing Yourself

After you have completed the audio and text review questions, see how well you do on the following quiz. Correct answers, with text and audio references, may be found at the end of this chapter.

1. Concerning the acquisition of language during early childhood, which of the following is true?
   a. The first true sentences do not occur until about age 3.
   b. Children's two-word sentences show a lack of knowledge of grammatical rules.
   c. Grammatical rules are evident even in the first two-word sentences of children.
   d. In acquiring language, children merely imitate the speech they hear.

2. Young children's abbreviated "telegrams" show that:
   a. they do not yet possess a knowledge of grammar.
   b. they are actively experimenting with the rules of grammar.
   c. they are imitating the sloppy grammar of the adults they listen to.
   d. adults tend to rush the acquisition of language before children are truly ready.

3. In terms of a child's readiness for hearing and producing sentences, which is the correct order in which the three structures indicated mature?
   a. auditory system; nervous system; vocal tract
   b. nervous system; auditory system; vocal tract
   c. vocal tract; auditory system; nervous system
   d. auditory system; vocal tract; nervous system

4. Children usually produce their first two-word sentences at about age:
   a. 1 year.
   b. 1 1/2 or 2.
   c. 2 1/2 or 3.
   d. 3 1/2 or 4.

5. Concerning the acquisition of the rules of language, which of the following is true?
   a. Rule-learning is quicker with sign language than with spoken language.
   b. Children learn the rules of language without being explicitly taught.
   c. Two-word sentences appear at the same time in all the world's cultures.
   d. All of the above are true.

6. Piaget believed that children are in the preoperational stage from ages:
   a. 6 months to 1 year.   c. 2 to 6 years.
   b. 1 to 3 years.   d. 5 to 11 years.

7. Which of the following is *not* a characteristic of preoperational thinking?
   a. focus on appearance
   b. static reasoning
   c. abstract thinking
   d. centration

8. Which of the following provides evidence that early childhood is a sensitive period, rather than a critical period, for language learning?
   a. People can and do master their native language after early childhood.
   b. Vocabulary, grammar, and pronunciation are acquired especially easily during early childhood.
   c. Neurological characteristics of the young child's developing brain facilitate language acquisition.
   d. a. and b.
   e. a., b., and c.

9. Emergent literacy refers to the:
   a. skills needed to learn to read.
   b. "teachability" of pre-K children.
   c. best time for learning a second or third language.
   d. learning experiences provided to children by skilled tutors.

10. Reggio Emilia is:
    a. the educator who first opened nursery schools for poor children in Rome.
    b. the early-childhood curriculum that allows children to discover ideas at their own pace.
    c. a new form of early-childhood education that encourages children to master skills not usually seen until age 7 or so.
    d. the Canadian system for promoting bilingualism in young children.

11. The vocabulary of preschool children consists primarily of:
    a. metaphors.
    b. self-created words.
    c. abstract nouns.
    d. verbs and concrete nouns.

12. Preschoolers sometimes apply the rules of grammar even when they shouldn't. This tendency is called:
    a. overregularization.   c. practical usage.
    b. literal language.   d. single-mindedness.

13. The Russian psychologist Vygotsky emphasized that:
    a. language helps children form ideas.
    b. children form concepts first, then find words to express them.
    c. language and other cognitive developments are unrelated at this stage.
    d. preschoolers learn language only for egocentric purposes.

14. Private speech can be described as:
    a. a way of formulating ideas to oneself.
    b. fantasy.
    c. an early learning difficulty.
    d. the beginnings of deception.

15. The child who has not yet grasped the principle of conservation is likely to:
    a. insist that a tall, narrow glass contains more liquid than a short, wide glass, even though both glasses actually contain the same amount.
    b. be incapable of egocentric thought.
    c. be unable to reverse an event.
    d. do all of the above.

16. In later life, High/Scope graduates showed:
    a. better report cards, but more behavioral problems.
    b. significantly higher IQ scores.
    c. higher scores on math and reading achievement tests.
    d. alienation from their original neighborhoods and families.

17. The best preschool programs are generally those that provide the greatest amount of:
    a. behavioral control.
    b. positive social interactions among children and adults.
    c. instruction in conservation and other logical principles.
    d. demonstration of toys by professionals.

18. According to Vygotsky, language advances thinking through private speech, and by:
    a. helping children to privately review what they know.
    b. helping children explain events to themselves.
    c. serving as a mediator of the social interaction that is a vital part of learning.
    d. facilitating the process of fast mapping.

19. Preschoolers *can* succeed at tests of conservation when:
    a. they are allowed to work cooperatively with other children.
    b. the test is presented as a competition.
    c. the children are informed that they are being observed by their parents.
    d. the test is presented in a simple, gamelike way.

20. Through the process called fast mapping, children:
    a. immediately assimilate new words by connecting them through their assumed meaning to categories of words they have already mastered.
    b. acquire the concept of conservation at an earlier age than Piaget believed.
    c. are able to move beyond egocentric thinking.
    d. become skilled in the practical use of language.

21. Balanced bilingualism is easiest for children to attain when:
    a. the parents themselves speak two languages.
    b. the second language is not taught until the child is fluent in the first.
    c. fast mapping is avoided.
    d. overregularization is discouraged.

22. Overregularization indicates that a child:
    a. is clearly applying rules of grammar.
    b. persists in egocentric thinking.
    c. has not yet mastered the principle of conservation.
    d. does not yet have a theory of mind.

23. Regarding the value of preschool education, most developmentalists believe that:
    a. most disadvantaged children will not benefit from an early preschool education.
    b. most disadvantaged children will benefit from an early preschool education.
    c. the early benefits of preschool education are likely to disappear by grade 3.
    d. the relatively small benefits of antipoverty measures such as Head Start do not justify their huge costs.

NAME _____   INSTRUCTOR _____

LESSON 9: PRESCHOOL LITERATURE

Exercise

You can learn much about the language and thought processes of young children by examining the literature written for them. Obtain a "classic" or well-loved storybook written for children from 2 to 6 years old. Some possibilities include the *I Can Read* books by Arnold Lobel, the *Amelia Bedelia* books by Peggy Parish, the Mr. books by Roger Hargreaves, and books for younger children by such well-known authors as Maurice Sendak, Charlotte Zolotow, and Dr. Seuss.

   Examine the book carefully. If possible, read it aloud to a child or someone else. Then complete the questions that follow and hand the completed exercise in to your instructor.

1. Give the title, name of the author and illustrator, and date of publication of the book.

2. Write down examples of the following elements that appear in the book.

   a. rhyme and repetition in the story

   b. egocentrism (e.g., animals that dress and talk like a child; misunderstandings that arise from the main character's egocentric viewpoint)

c. centration (e.g., stories about characters who have only one prominent feature; stories about a child focusing on one special goal, trait, or object)

d. effects that depend on literal or figurative language (e.g, jokes that come from a character taking a figure of speech literally)

e. story elements that reassure the child about the strong ties of family and friendship

f. story elements that reflect the young child's fear of separation

3. If you read this book aloud to another person, give the age of the person and describe her or his reaction. If you recall reading the book yourself as a child, describe your own reaction.

LESSON GUIDELINES

Audio Question Guidelines

1. The first word is usually said around the time of the first birthday, the first two-word sentence between 1 1/2 and 2 years.

   Two-word utterances are not always sentences, however. The words must appear in isolation, and then in combination with one another to produce different meanings in order to qualify as true sentences.

   Early sentences are in effect "telegrams," in that they omit articles, conjunctions, prepositions, and other parts of speech that are not essential to meaning.

   During the next year the child actively experiments with the grammatical rules of language. Vocabulary increases rapidly and the two-word sentences soon become three- and four-word sentences.

   The slow-to-develop vocal tract of humans results in the same accommodations to language in children throughout the world. These include reducing consonant clusters to a single consonant and a preference for certain kinds of pronunciations.

2. The fact that deaf and hearing children babble at about the same age suggests a maturational basis for language development.

   The evidence for a common biological timetable in the maturation of language also includes the fact that the stage of two-word sentences comes at about the same age in every culture.

   The slow maturation of the human vocal tract results in the same accommodations in language pronunciation in children of similar age throughout the world.

3. The two- and three-word "telegrams" of children during these years are abbreviations of adult speech in which articles, conjunctions, prepositions, and other unessential words are dropped.

   At the same time that children abbreviate their speech, adults often restate their ideas and expand them into complete, grammatically correct utterances. This process implicitly calls the child's attention to the rules of language and indicates that children are experimenting with language, rather than merely imitating it.

   Another illustration of the creative and experimental process of language learning comes from the **overextensions** of grammatical rules that are typical of children during this stage.

4. The auditory system is mature and ready for hearing at birth.

   Between 1 1/2 and 2 years of age the brain and nervous system reach a point of maturation that permits the combination of words into primitive sentences.

   The vocal tract lags behind the auditory system and nervous system in maturing. Until it matures, children are unable to articulate complex sounds.

5. The evidence that humans have a natural propensity for acquiring sign language includes the fact that although deaf and hearing children babble at about the same age, deaf children produce their first signs sooner than hearing children produce their first words. This developmental advantage is maintained when it comes to forming two-word or two-sign combinations.

Textbook Question Answers

1. perspective (or egocentrism)

2. preoperational

3. centration; ego-centration or egocentrism; appearances

4. static; unchanging; irreversibility

5. conservation; conservation of number

6. theory-theory; guided participation; social; interact

7. Lev Vygotsky; assistance; praising; enthusiasm; instruction

8. social activity

9. zone of proximal development

10. scaffold

11. private speech; uttered aloud

12. mediator

13. theory of mind

Between the ages of 3 and 6, young children come to realize that mental phenomena may not reflect reality and that individuals can believe various things and, therefore, can be deliberately deceived or fooled.

14. have

15. language; brain maturation; brother or sister; culture

16. emergent literacy; maturation; myelination

17. critical; sensitive

18. vocabulary

19. fast mapping; logical extension

20. more

21. comparisons; time; place

22. grammar; 3

23. overregularization

Many preschoolers overapply the rule of adding "s" to form the plural, as well as the rule of adding "ed" to form the past tense. Thus, preschoolers are likely to say "foots" and "snows" and that someone "broked" a toy.

24. is

25. egocentric; theories of mind; vocabulary development; emergent literacy

26. language shift; balanced bilinguals; speak two languages themselves

27. Maria Montessori; Piaget; discover ideas at their own pace; more; readiness (or academics)

28. Reggio Emilia; 7

29. has not; agree

30. Project Head Start; higher

High-quality preschools are characterized by (a) a low adult–child ratio, (b) a trained staff (or educated parents) who are unlikely to leave the program, (c) positive social interactions among children and adults, (d) adequate space and equipment, and (e) safety.

Answers to Testing Yourself

1. **c.** is the answer. Even the two- and three-word "telegrams" of preschoolers show evidence of a rudimentary understanding of grammar. (audio program; textbook, p. 228)

2. **b.** is the answer. Children master the rules of grammar by experimenting and testing hypotheses, often overextending rules and making errors that cannot be attributed to imitation. (audio program; textbook, p. 226)

3. **a.** is the answer. The slow-to-mature vocal tract forces accommodations in pronunciation that are similar the world over. (audio program)

4. **b.** is the answer. Although there is wide variation in normal development, the first primitive sentences usually occur between 1 1/2 and 2 years of age. (audio program)

5. **d.** is the answer. All of these statements are true, indicating a common timetable in the maturation of language and the natural propensity of chil-

dren for acquiring language, including sign language. (audio program)

6. **c.** is the answer. (textbook, p. 218)

7. **c.** is the answer. Preoperational children have great difficulty understanding abstract concepts. (textbook, p. 218)

8. **e.** is the answer. (textbook, p. 225)

9. **a.** is the answer. (textbook, p. 225)

10. **c.** is the answer. (textbook, p. 231)

    a. This describes Maria Montessori.

    b. This refers to Piaget's approach.

    d. The program originated in Italy.

11. **d.** is the answer. (textbook, pp. 227–228)

    a. & c. Preschoolers generally have great difficulty understanding, and therefore using, metaphors and abstract nouns.

    b. Other than the grammatical errors of overregularization, the text does not indicate that preschoolers use a significant number of self-created words.

12. **a.** is the answer. (textbook, p. 228)

    b. & d. These terms are not identified in the text and do not apply to the use of grammar.

    c. Practical usage, which also is not discussed in the text, refers to communication between one person and another in terms of the overall context in which language is used.

13. **a.** is the answer. (textbook, p. 222)

    b. This expresses the views of Piaget.

    c. Because he believed that language facilitates thinking, Vygotsky obviously felt that language and other cognitive developments are intimately related.

    d. Vygotsky did not hold this view.

14. **a.** is the answer. (textbook, p. 222)

15. **a.** is the answer. (textbook, p. 219)

    b., c., & d. Failure to conserve is the result of thinking that is centered on appearances. Egocentrism and irreversibility are also examples of centered thinking.

16. **c.** is the answer. (textbook, p. 232–233)

    b. This is not discussed in the text.

    a. & d. There was no indication of greater behavioral problems or alienation in graduates of this program.

17. **b.** is the answer. (textbook, p. 224)

18. **c.** is the answer. (textbook, p. 222)

    a. & b. These are both advantages of private speech.

d. Fast mapping is the process by which new words are acquired, often after only one hearing.

19. **d.** is the answer. (textbook, pp. 219–220)

20. **a.** is the answer. (textbook, p. 226)

21. **a.** is the answer. (textbook, p. 230)

b. Although there are many different approaches to promoting bilingualism, the text does not suggest that children should master one language before being exposed to another.

c. & d. Fast mapping and overregularization are normal aspects of language development that stimulate the development of vocabulary and grammar.

22. **a.** is the answer. (textbook, p. 228)

b., c., & d. Overregularization is a *linguistic* phenomenon rather than a characteristic type of thinking (b. and d.), or a logical principle (c.).

23. **b.** is the answer. (textbook, p. 232)

The Play Years: Psychosocial Development

AUDIO PROGRAM: Because I Wear Dresses

ORIENTATION

As we learned in Lessons 8 and 9, the biosocial and cognitive development that occurs between the ages of 2 and 6 is extensive. Body proportions begin to resemble those of adults; language develops rapidly; and the capacity to use mental representation and symbols increases dramatically. Lesson 10 concludes the unit on the play years by exploring ways in which preschool children relate to others in their ever-widening social environment.

During the preschool years a child's self-confidence, social skills, and social roles become more fully developed. This growth coincides with the child's increased capacity for communication, imagination, and understanding of his or her social context. Chapter 10 of *The Developing Person Through the Life Span*, 6/e, explores the ways in which young children begin to relate to others in an ever-widening social environment. The chapter begins where social understanding begins, with the emergence of the sense of self. With their increasing social awareness, children become more concerned with how others evaluate them and better able to regulate their emotions. The chapter concludes with a description of children's emerging gender identity.

Audio program 10, "Because I Wear Dresses," focuses on how children develop gender identity as boys or girls. Through the expert commentary of psychologists Michael Stevenson and Jacquelynne Eccles, we discover that by the time children begin elementary school they have developed a strong sense of their gender. During these years children segregate themselves according to sex and become quite stereotyped in their thinking and behavior regarding gender.

Are the psychological differences between males and females a result of our biology or are they something we learn? One way of looking at this question is to examine how gender differences change across the life span. According to psychologist David Gutmann, masculinity and femininity mean different things at different ages. Although gender differences in such characteristics as aggressiveness may have a biological basis, the difference may not be the same for the entire life cycle. Researchers are finding that men and women become more alike in their actions and attitudes as they get older.

Social guidelines for males and females may be blurred in old age, but if you ask children about gender differences, you are likely to hear the kind of answers that open this program.

LESSON GOALS

By the end of this lesson you should be prepared to:

1. Discuss the relationship between the child's developing sense of self and social awareness.

2. Discuss emotional development during early childhood, focusing on emotional regulation, and how it relates to attachment.

3. Differentiate four types of aggression during the play years and explain why certain types are more troubling to developentalists.

4. Compare and contrast three classic patterns of parenting and their effect on children.

5. Summarize five theories of gender-role development during the play years, noting important contributions of each.

Audio Assignment

Listen to the audio tape that accompanies Lesson 10: "Because I Wear Dresses."

Write answers to the following questions. You may replay portions of the program if you need to

refresh your memory. Answer guidelines may be found in the Lesson Guidelines section at the end of this chapter.

1. Describe the development of gender identity in preschoolers.

2. Explain some of the gender differences that are usually apparent in the first ten years of life.

3. Explain how gender differences in aggression change over the life span.

Textbook Assignment

Read Chapter 10: "The Play Years: Psychosocial Development," pages 237–260 in *The Developing Person Through the Life Span, 6/e*, then work through the material that follows to review it. Complete the sentences and answer the questions. As you proceed, evaluate your performance for each section by consulting the answers on page 125. Do not continue with the next section until you understand each answer. If you need to, review or reread the appropriate section in the textbook before continuing.

Emotional Development (pp. 237–245)

1. Between 3 and 6 years of age, according to Erikson, children are in the stage of

_____ _____

_____ . Unlike the earlier stage of

_____ _____

_____ , children in this stage want to begin *and* _____ something. Erikson also believed that during this stage children begin to feel _____ when their efforts result in failure or criticism.

2. Psychologists emphasize the importance of children's developing a positive _____

and feelings of pride that enable concentration and _____ and

_____ .

3. The ability to direct or modify one's feelings is called _____ _____ . This ability begins with the control of _____ . Children who have _____ problems and lash out at other people or things are said to be _____ (overcontrolled/undercontrolled). Children who have _____ problems tend to be inhibited, fearful, and withdrawn.

4. Genetic influences _____ (are/are not) a source of variation in emotional regulation in young children. One research study found that fearful children had greater activity in the

_____ _____

_____ of their brains, while those who were less withdrawn had greater activity in their _____ _____

_____ .

5. Repeated exposure to extreme stress can kill _____ and make some young children physiologically unable to regulate their emotions. Extreme stress can also affect the release of stress hormones such as _____ . One study found _____ (higher-than-normal/lower-than-normal) levels of this hormone in abused children.

Give several examples of early stress that can inhibit young children's emotional regulation.

6. Another set of influences on emotional regulation is the child's early and current

   _____ _____ .

7. According to _____ , the ability to direct emotions is crucial to the development of

   _____ _____ .

8. The ability to truly understand the emotions of another, called _____ , often leads to sharing, cooperating, and other examples of

   _____ _____ . In contrast, dislike for others, or _____ , may lead to actions that are destructive or deliberately hurtful. Such actions are called _____

   _____ .

9. The most antisocial behavior of all is active

   _____ .

10. Developmentalists distinguish four types of physical aggression: _____ , used to obtain or retain an object or privilege;

   _____ , used in angry retaliation against an intentional or accidental act committed by a peer; _____ , which takes the form of insults or social rejection; and

   _____ , used in an unprovoked attack on a peer.

11. (Table 10.1) The form of aggression that is most likely to increase from age 2 to 6 is _____

   _____ . Of greater concern are

   _____ _____ , because it can indicate a lack of _____

   _____ , and _____

   _____ , which is most worrisome overall.

12. Emotions are ultimately expressed in behavior related to _____ , who are other people of about the same _____ and

   _____ as the child.

13. Play is both _____ and

   _____ by culture, gender, and age.

14. The type of physical play that mimics aggression is called _____-_____-

   _____ play. A distinctive feature of this form of play, which _____ (occurs only

in some cultures/is universal), is the positive facial expression that characterizes the

"_____ _____ ." Age differences are evident, because this type of play relies on the child's _____

   _____ . Gender differences

   _____ (are/are not) evident in rough-and-tumble play.

15. In _____ play, children act out various roles and themes in stories of their own creation.

   _____ (Girls/Boys) tend to engage in this type of play more often than do

   _____ (girls/boys).

Parenting Patterns (pp. 246–252)

16. A significant influence on early psychosocial growth is the style of _____

   that characterizes a child's family life.

17. The early research on parenting styles, which was conducted by _____ , found that parents varied in their _____

   toward offspring, in their strategies for

   _____ , in how well they

   _____ , and in their expectations for

   _____ .

18. Parents who adopt the _____

   style demand unquestioning obedience from their children. In this style of parenting, nurturance tends to be _____ (low/high), maturity demands are _____

   (low/high), and parent–child communication tends to be _____ (low/high).

19. Parents who adopt the _____

   style make few demands on their children and are lax in discipline. Such parents

   _____ (are/are not very) nurturant, communicate _____ (well/poorly), and make _____ (few/extensive) maturity demands.

20. Parents who adopt the _____

   style set limits and enforce rules but also listen to their children. Such parents make _____

   (high/low) maturity demands, communicate

   _____ (well/poorly), and

_____ (are/are not) nurturant. Two other styles of parenting that have been identified are _____ parenting, in which parents don't seem to care at all about their children, and _____ parenting, in which parents give in to a child's every whim.

21. Follow-up studies indicate that children raised by _____ parents are likely to be obedient but unhappy and those raised by _____ parents are likely to lack self-control. Those raised by _____ parents are more likely to be successful, happy with themselves, and generous with others; these advantages _____ (grow stronger/weaken) over time.

22. An important factor in the effectiveness of parenting style is the child's _____ . In addition, _____ and _____ _____ influence the child's perception of the quality of parenting. The crucial factors in how children perceive their parents are _____ _____ , _____ , and _____ for the child.

23. Culture _____ (exerts/does not exert) a strong influence on disciplinary techniques. Japanese mothers tend to use _____ as disciplinary techniques more often than do North American mothers, who are more likely to encourage _____ expressions of all sorts in their children. A disciplinary technique in which a child is required to stop all activity and sit quietly for a few minutes is the _____-_____ . This technique is widely used in _____ _____ .

(Table 10.3) State four specific recommendations for the use of punishment that are derived from developmental research findings.

a. _____

b. _____

c. _____

d. _____

24. Physical punishment of children is against the law for parents and teachers in _____ . In contrast, in some _____ nations, all parents are expected to physically punish their children.

25. Throughout the world, most parents _____ (believe/do not believe) that spanking is acceptable at times. Although spanking _____ (is/is not) effective, it may teach children to be more _____ .

26. Six major organizations concerned with the well-being of children urge parents to

_____

in order to avoid exposing their children to _____ _____ . Those who advocate the opposite viewpoint contend that the media are merely reflecting _____ .

27. In comparison to broadcast television programs, video games are more _____ , _____ , and _____ .

28. Longitudinal research demonstrates that children who watched educational programs as young children became teenagers who had _____ . This finding was especially true for _____ (boys/girls). Teenagers who, as children who watched violent television programs, had _____ , especially if they were _____ (boys/girls).

29. Developmentalists agree that video games and violent television programs perpetuate _____ , _____ , and _____ stereotypes; depict _____ solutions to problems with no expression of _____ ; and encourage _____ emotions rather than thoughtful _____ .

Boy or Girl: So What? (pp. 253–259)

30. Social scientists distinguish between biological, or _____ , differences between males and females, and cultural, or _____ , differences in the _____ and behaviors of males and females.

31. True sex differences are _____ (more/less) apparent in childhood than in adulthood; _____ differentiation seems more significant to children than to adults.

32. By age _____ , children can consistently apply gender labels and have a rudimentary understanding of the permanence of their own gender. By age _____ , children are convinced that certain toys and roles are appropriate for one gender but not the other. Awareness that sex is a fixed biological characteristic does not become solid until about age

    _____ .

33. Freud called the period from age 3 to 6 the _____ _____ . According to his view, boys in this stage develop sexual feelings about their _____ and become jealous of their _____ . Freud called this phenomenon the _____

    _____ .

34. In Freud's theory, preschool boys resolve their guilty feelings defensively through _____ with their father. Boys also develop, again in self-defense, a powerful conscience called the _____ .

35. According to Freud, during the phallic stage little girls may experience the _____ _____ , in which they want to get rid of their mother and become intimate with their father. Alternatively, they may become jealous of boys because they have a penis; this emotion Freud called _____ _____ .

36. According to behaviorism, preschool children develop gender-role ideas by being _____ for behaviors deemed appropriate for their sex and _____ for behaviors deemed inappropriate.

37. Behaviorists also maintain that children learn gender-appropriate behavior not only through direct reinforcement but also by _____ .

38. Cognitive theorists focus on children's _____ of male–female differences.

39. Gender education varies by region, socioeconomic status, and historical period, according to the _____ theory. Gender distinctions are emphasized in many _____ cultures. This theory points out that children can maintain a balance of male and female characteristics, or _____ , only if their culture promotes that idea.

40. According to _____ theory, gender attitudes and roles are the result of interaction between _____ and _____

    _____ .

41. The idea that is supported by recent research is that some gender differences are _____ based because of differences between male and female _____ .

42. These differences probably result from the differing _____ _____ that influence brain development. However, the theory maintains that the manifestations of biological origins are shaped, enhanced, or halted by _____ _____ . One example of such a factor is that prehistorically, female brains apparently favored _____ , which may have created a genetically inclined tendency for girls to _____ earlier than boys.

Testing Yourself

After you have completed the audio and text review questions, see how well you do on the following quiz. Correct answers, with text and audio references, may be found at the end of this chapter.

1. Children apply gender labels and have definite ideas about how boys and girls behave as early as age:
   a. 2.   c. 5.
   b. 4.   d. 7.

2. Concerning gender roles during later life, David Gutmann believes that:
   a. gender roles are the same as those in earlier life.
   b. during middle and late adulthood, each sex moves toward a middle ground between the traditional gender roles.

c. once the demands of parenting are removed, traditional gender roles are reestablished.

d. gender roles are unrelated to cultural experiences.

3. The greater aggressiveness of boys compared to girls is:

a. due to boys having a higher natural level of testosterone.

b. found in virtually all known cultures.

c. maintained throughout the life cycle.

d. such that a. and b. are true.

4. Concerning children's concept of gender, which of the following statements is true?

a. Until the age of 5 or so, children think that boys and girls can change gender as they get older.

b. Children as young as 18 months have a clear understanding of the anatomical differences between girls and boys.

c. Children are inaccurate in labeling others' gender until about age 5.

d. All of the above are true.

5. Which of the following most accurately summarizes the audio program's explanation of the psychological differences between males and females?

a. Most differences are biologically determined.

b. Most differences are learned.

c. Most differences are jointly determined by learning and biology.

d. None of the above is true.

6. Preschool children have a clear (but not necessarily accurate) self-concept. Typically, the preschooler believes that she or he:

a. owns all objects in sight.

b. is great at almost everything.

c. is much less competent than peers and older children.

d. is more powerful than her or his parents.

7. According to Freud, the third stage of psychosexual development, during which the penis is the focus of psychological concern and pleasure, is the:

a. oral stage.   **c.** phallic stage.

b. anal stage.   **d.** latency period.

8. Because it helps children rehearse social roles, work out fears and fantasies, and learn cooperation, an important form of social play is:

a. sociodramatic play.

b. mastery play.

c. rough-and-tumble play.

d. sensorimotor play.

9. The three *basic* patterns of parenting described by Diana Baumrind are:

a. hostile, loving, and harsh.

b. authoritarian, permissive, and authoritative.

c. positive, negative, and punishing.

d. indulgent, neglecting, and traditional.

10. Authoritative parents are receptive and loving, but they also normally:

a. set limits and enforce rules.

b. have difficulty communicating.

c. withhold praise and affection.

d. encourage aggressive behavior.

11. Children who watch a lot of violent television or play violent video games:

a. are more likely to be violent.

b. do less reading.

c. tend to have lower grades in school.

d. have all of the above characteristics.

12. (Table 10.1) Between 2 and 6 years of age, the form of aggression that is most likely to increase is:

a. reactive.

b. instrumental.

c. relational.

d. bullying.

13. During the play years, a child's self-concept is defined largely by his or her:

a. expanding range of skills and competencies.

b. physical appearance.

c. gender.

d. relationship with family members.

14. Behaviorists emphasize the importance of _____ in the development of the preschool child.

a. identification   **c.** initiative

b. praise and blame   **d.** a theory of mind

15. Children of permissive parents are *most* likely to lack:

a. social skills.   **c.** initiative and guilt.

b. self-control.   **d.** care and concern.

16. Psychologist Daniel Goleman believes that emotional regulation is especially crucial to the preschooler's developing:
    a. sense of self.
    b. social awareness.
    c. emotional intelligence.
    d. sense of gender.

17. Six-year-old Leonardo has superior verbal ability rivaling that of most girls his age. Dr. Laurent believes this is due to the fact that although his sex is predisposed to slower language development, Leonardo's upbringing in a linguistically rich home enhanced his biological capabilities. Dr. Laurent is evidently a proponent of:
    a. cognitive theory.
    b. psychoanalytic theory.
    c. sociocultural theory.
    d. epigenetic theory.

18. Three-year-old Jake, who lashes out at the family pet in anger, is displaying signs of _____ problems, which suggests that he is emotionally _____ .
    a. internalizing; overcontrolled
    b. internalizing; undercontrolled
    c. externalizing; overcontrolled
    d. externalizing; undercontrolled

19. Compared to Japanese mothers, North American mothers are more likely to:
    a. use reasoning to control their preschoolers' social behavior.
    b. use expressions of disappointment to control their preschoolers' social behavior.
    c. encourage emotional expressions of all sorts in their preschoolers.
    d. do all of the above.

20. When her friend hurts her feelings, Maya shouts that she is a "mean old stinker!" Maya's behavior is an example of:
    a. instrumental aggression.
    b. reactive aggression.
    c. bullying aggression.
    d. relational aggression.

21. Which of the following best summarizes the current view of developmentalists regarding gender differences?
    a. Developmentalists disagree on the proportion of gender differences that are biological in origin.
    b. Most gender differences are biological in origin.
    c. Nearly all gender differences are cultural in origin.
    d. There is no consensus among developmentalists regarding the origin of gender differences.

22. Antipathy refers to a person's:
    a. understanding of the emotions of another person.
    b. self-understanding.
    c. feelings of anger or dislike toward another person.
    d. tendency to internalize emotions or inhibit their expression.

23. A parent who wishes to use a time-out to discipline her son for behaving aggressively on the playground would be advised to:
    a. have the child sit quietly indoors for a few minutes.
    b. tell her son that he will be punished later at home.
    c. tell the child that he will not be allowed to play outdoors for the rest of the week.
    d. choose a different disciplinary technique since time-outs are ineffective.

LESSON 10 EXERCISE: GENDER-ROLE DEVELOPMENT

During the play years, children acquire not only their gender identities but also many masculine or feminine behaviors and attitudes. These behaviors and attitudes largely reflect gender roles. A role is a set of social expectations that prescribes how those who occupy the role should act.

To what extent is your own gender identity a reflection of the behaviors modeled by your parents? Have gender roles become less distinct in recent generations? Should parents encourage gender-stereotyped behaviors in their children? These are among the many controversial questions regarding gender roles that researchers today are grappling with.

The exercise for this lesson asks you to reflect on the kinds of gender models your parents provided and to ask a friend or relative who is presently in a different season of life to do the same. After you and your respondent have completed the Gender Role Quizzes on the next two pages, answer the questions that follow and hand the completed exercise (only) in to your instructor.

Gender Role Quiz: Respondent #1

For each question, check whether the behavior described was more typical of your mother or father as you were growing up.

	Mother	Father
1. When your family went out, who drove?		
2. Who filled out the income tax forms?		
3. Who wrote the "thank you" notes for gifts?		
4. Who was more likely to ask, "Where are my socks/stockings?"		
5. When the car needed to be repaired, who took it to the garage?		
6. Who did the laundry?		
7. Who dusted and vacuumed your house?		
8. When you had a fever, who knew where to find the thermometer?		
9. When the sink needed fixing, who knew where to find the pipe wrench?		
10. Who knew where the summer clothes were packed away?		
11. When you had guests for dinner, who made the drinks?		
12. Who watered the house plants?		
13. Who mowed the lawn?		
14. When you went on a trip, who packed the car?		

Source: Adapted from Doyle, J. A., & Paludi, M. A. (1995). *Sex and gender: The human experience* (3rd ed.). © 1995 WCB/McGraw-Hill. Used with permission of the McGraw-Hill Companies.

Gender Role Quiz: Respondent #2

For each question, check whether the behavior described was more typical of your mother or father as you were growing up.

	Mother	Father
1. When your family went out, who drove?		
2. Who filled out the income tax forms?		
3. Who wrote the "thank you" notes for gifts?		
4. Who was more likely to ask, "Where are my socks/stockings?"		
5. When the car needed to be repaired, who took it to the garage?		
6. Who did the laundry?		
7. Who dusted and vacuumed your house?		
8. When you had a fever, who knew where to find the thermometer?		
9. When the sink needed fixing, who knew where to find the pipe wrench?		
10. Who knew where the summer clothes were packed away?		
11. When you had guests for dinner, who made the drinks?		
12. Who watered the house plants?		
13. Who mowed the lawn?		
14. When you went on a trip, who packed the car?		

Sources: Adapted from Doyle, J. A., & Paludi, M. A. (1995). *Sex and gender: The human experience* (3rd ed.). © 1995 WCB/McGraw-Hill. Used with permission of the McGraw-Hill Companies.

NAME _____   INSTRUCTOR _____

LESSON 10: GENDER-ROLE DEVELOPMENT

Exercise

1. In what seasons of life were your quiz respondents?

2. **a.** Is there evidence of gender-stereotyped behaviors in the respondents' answers? Explain.

   b. Were items 1, 2, 4, 5, 9, 11, 13 and 15 checked as more typical of fathers?

   c. Were items 3, 6, 7, 8, 10, 12, and 14 checked as more typical of mothers?

   d. For each respondent, indicate the total number of responses (out of 15) that are *in agreement* with the traditional gender-role breakdown in this list.

	Younger Respondent	Older Respondent
Number of items in agreement with traditional gender roles (maximum = 15)		

   e. If there is a difference in responses given by your younger and older respondents, please explain the difference.

3. To what extent do you believe your own gender identity and gender-role development were influenced by the behaviors modeled by your parents? In what ways is your own behavior modeled after that of your same-sex parent? In what ways is it different?

4. To what extent is your concept of the ideal person of the opposite sex a reflection of the behaviors modeled by your opposite-sex parent? In what ways is it different?

5. In your estimation, should parents encourage or discourage traditional gender-role development in their children? Please explain your reasoning.

LESSON GUIDELINES

Audio Question Guidelines

1. It is likely that children begin to recognize the categories of male and female as early as 18 months of age.

   Most 2-year-olds know whether they are boys or girls, but they have not yet mastered **gender constancy**. They may think that their sex can change when they grow older or wear different clothes.

   Before the age of 5, most children do not understand the anatomical differences between boys and girls. Instead, they are likely to identify the sexes on the basis of hair length, clothing, or whether a person cooks or goes to work.

   By the time children start school they have developed a very strong sense of their own **gender identity**, and they know that it will remain constant.

2. Although both biology and environment contribute to differences between the sexes, these differences are slight. There is more variation between individuals *of the same sex* than there is between the sexes.

   As infants, boys are more likely than girls to have been born prematurely, to suffer from birth trauma, to show delayed development, and to be subject to colic and nonrhythmic behaviors that make them somewhat harder to deal with.

   Male infants tend to be less easily cuddled, more resistant to being wrapped up, and more active.

   Perhaps as a consequence of their exposure to higher prenatal levels of testosterone, boys are more likely than girls to get into aggressive encounters.

   From very early on, girls may be more sensitive than boys to faces and to language cues.

   Boys and girls may also develop different play styles as they go through childhood, with a greater emphasis on competition in boys' games and a greater emphasis on cooperation in girls' games.

3. In nearly every known culture, boys play more aggressively than girls. Boys also have higher levels of testosterone, a hormone linked to aggressiveness.

   David Gutmann believes that males evolved into the more aggressive sex because from the standpoint of species survival, men are more expendable than women. Gutmann also believes that women are responsible for instilling in their children a sense of basic trust—a task facilitated by reduced levels of aggression.

As men and women get beyond what Gutmann calls the "chronic emergency of parenting," changes in their dispositions become evident. In men, there is an ebbing away of aggressiveness and a flowing in of affiliative and nurturant qualities.

In women the reverse occurs. Freed of the responsibility for their children's emotional security, women's natural aggressiveness begins to surface. The net result of these changes is that the two sexes become more alike in later life.

Textbook Question Answers

1. initiative versus guilt; autonomy versus shame; complete; guilt

2. self-concept; persistence; a willingness to try new experiences

3. emotional regulation; impulses; externalizing; undercontrolled; internalizing

4. are; right prefrontal cortex; left prefrontal cortex

5. neurons; cortisol; lower-than-normal

Prenatal examples of early stress that can inhibit emotional regulation include pregnant women who experience stress, suffer illness, or are heavy drug users. Postnatal examples include chronic infant malnourishment, injury, or fear.

6. care experiences

7. Daniel Goleman; emotional intelligence

8. empathy; prosocial behaviors; antipathy; antisocial behavior

9. aggression

10. instrumental; reactive; relational; bullying

11. instrumental aggression; reactive aggression; emotional regulation; bullying aggression

12. peers; age; status

13. universal; variable

14. rough-and-tumble; is universal; play face; social experience; are

15. sociodramatic; Girls; boys

16. parenting

17. Diana Baumrind; nurturance; discipline; communicate; maturity

18. authoritarian; low; high; low

19. permissive; are; well; few

20. authoritative; high; well; are; neglectful; indulgent

21. authoritarian; permissive; authoritative; grow stronger

22. temperament; community; cultural differences; parental warmth; support; concern

23. exerts; reasoning; emotional; time-out; North America

    a. Remember theory of mind.
    b. Remember emerging self-concept.
    c. Remember the language explosion and fast mapping.
    d. Remember that young children are not yet logical.

24. Sweden; Caribbean

25. believe; is; aggressive

26. turn off the TV; video violence; reality

27. violent, sexist, racist

28. higher grades; boys; lower grades; girls

29. sexist, ageist, and racist stereotypes; violent; empathy; quick, reactive; regulation

30. sex; gender; roles

31. less; gender

32. 2; 4; 8

33. phallic stage; mothers; fathers; Oedipus complex

34. identification; superego

35. Electra complex; penis envy

36. reinforced; punished

37. modeling

38. understanding

39. sociocultural; traditional; androgyny

40. epigenetic; genes; early experience

41. biologically; brains

42. sex hormones; environmental factors; language; speak

Answers to Testing Yourself

1. **a.** is the answer. (audio program; textbook, p. 253)

2. **b.** is the answer. David Gutmann believes that gender roles become less distinct as we grow older. (audio program)

3. **d.** is the answer. Boys have a greater natural endowment of testosterone and are more aggressive in virtually all cultures. (audio program)

4. **a.** is the answer. Before age 5, many children think their gender may change as they get older. (audio program)

5. **c.** is the answer. (audio program)

6. **b.** is the answer. (textbook, pp. 237–238)

7. **c.** is the answer. (textbook, p. 254)

a. & b. In Freud's theory, the oral and anal stages are associated with infant and early childhood development, respectively.

d. In Freud's theory, the latency period is associated with development during the school years.

8. **a.** is the answer. (textbook, pp. 244–245)

    b. & d. These two types of play are not discussed in this chapter. Mastery play is play that helps children develop new physical and intellectual skills. Sensorimotor play captures the pleasures of using the senses and motor skills.

    c. Rough-and-tumble play is physical play that mimics aggression.

9. **b.** is the answer. (textbook, pp. 246–247)

    d. Traditional is a variation of the basic styles uncovered by later research. Indulgent and neglecting are abusive styles and clearly harmful, unlike the styles initially identified by Baumrind.

10. **a.** is the answer. (textbook, p. 247)

    b. & c. Authoritative parents communicate very well and are quite affectionate.

    d. This is not typical of authoritative parents.

11. **d.** is the answer. (textbook, pp. 251–252)

12. **b.** is the answer. (textbook, p. 243)

13. **a.** is the answer. (textbook, pp. 237–238)

14. **b.** is the answer. (textbook, p. 256)

    a. This is the focus of Freud's phallic stage.

    c. This is the focus of Erikson's psychosocial theory.

    d. This is the focus of cognitive theorists.

15. **b.** is the answer. (textbook, p. 247)

16. **c.** is the answer. (textbook, p. 241)

17. **d.** is the answer. In accounting for Leonardo's verbal ability, Dr. Laurent alludes to both genetic and environmental factors, a dead-giveaway for epigenetic theory. (textbook, p. 258)

    a., b., & c. These theories do not address biological or genetic influences on development.

18. **d.** is the answer. (textbook, p. 239)

    a. & b. Children who display internalizing problems are withdrawn and bottle up their emotions.

    c. Jake is displaying an inability to control his negative emotions.

19. **c.** is the answer. (textbook, pp. 248–249)

    a., & b. These strategies are more typical of Japanese mothers.

20. **d.** is the answer. (textbook, p. 243)

21. **a.** is the answer. (p. 254)

22. **c.** is the answer. (p. 241)

    a. This describes empathy.

    b. This describes self-concept.

    d. This describes an internalizing problem.

23. **a.** is the answer. (p. 249)

    b. & c. Time-outs involve removing a child from a situation in which misbehavior has occurred.

Moreover, these threats of future punishment would likely be less effective because of the delay between the behavior and the consequence.

d. Although developmentalists stress the need to prevent misdeeds instead of punishing them and warn that time-outs may have unintended consequences, they nevertheless can be an effective form of discipline.

The School Years: Biosocial Development

AUDIO PROGRAM: Everything Is Harder

ORIENTATION

For most boys and girls, the years of middle childhood are a time when physical growth is smooth and uneventful. Body maturation coupled with sufficient practice enables school-age children to master many motor skills. Chapter 11 of *The Developing Person Through the Life Span*, 6/e, introduces middle childhood, the years from 7 to 11. Changes in physical size and shape are described, and the problems of **obesity** and **asthma** are addressed. The discussion then turns to the continuing development of motor and intellectual skills during the school years, culminating in an evaluation of intelligence testing. A final section examines the experiences of children with special needs, such as autistic children, those diagnosed as having an attention-deficit disorder, and those with learning disabilities. The causes of and treatments for these problems are discussed, with emphasis placed on insights arising from the new **developmental psychopathology** perspective. This perspective makes it clear that the manifestations of any special childhood problem will change as the child grows older and that treatment must often focus on all three domains of development.

Audio program 11, "Everything Is Harder," introduces Sean Miller and Jenny Hamburg, each of whom is disabled by **cerebral palsy**. Through their stories, illuminated by the expert commentary of physical rehabilitation specialist Dr. Virginia Nelson, we discover that when physical development does not go as expected, everything is "off-time" and harder for all concerned. For **disabled** children, **handicapped** by the world around them, nothing—from getting around to meeting the ordinary developmental tasks of life—comes smoothly or easily.

LESSON GOALS

By the end of this lesson you should be prepared to:

1. Describe patterns of normal physical growth and development during middle childhood, and account for the usual variations among children.

2. Identify the causes and problems of obesity, and discuss the physical and psychological impact of asthma.

3. Describe brain maturation and motor-skill development during the school years, focusing on variations due to culture, practice, and genetics.

4. Explain how achievement and aptitude tests are used in evaluating individual differences in cognitive growth, and discuss why use of such tests is controversial.

5. Discuss the diagnosis and possible causes and treatment of specific learning disabilities, as well as autism and attention-deficit hyperactivity disorders.

Audio Assignment

Listen to the audio tape that accompanies Lesson 11: "Everything Is Harder: Children with Disabilities."

Write answers to the following questions. You may replay portions of the program if you need to refresh your memory. Answer guidelines may be found in the Lesson Guidelines section at the end of this chapter.

1. Identify the causes and characteristics of cerebral palsy.

2. Differentiate physical disabilities from social handicaps and cite several reasons that development is harder for disabled children.

Textbook Assignment

Read Chapter 11: "The School Years: Biosocial Development," pages 265–287 in *The Developing Person Through the Life Span*, 6/e, then work through the material that follows to review it. Complete the sentences and answer the questions. As you proceed, evaluate your performance for each section by consulting the answers on page 137. Do not continue with the next section until you understand each answer. If you need to, review or reread the appropriate section in the textbook before continuing.

1. The biggest influence on development from age 7 to 11 is the changing _____ context.

A Healthy Time (pp. 267–271)

2. Compared with biosocial development during other periods of the life span, biosocial development during this time, known as _____ _____ , is _____ (relatively smooth/often fraught with problems). For example, disease and death during these years are _____ (more common/rarer) than during any other period.

3. Children grow _____ (faster/more slowly) during middle childhood than they did earlier or than they will in adolescence. The typical child gains about _____ pounds and at least _____ inches per year.

Describe several other features of physical development during the school years.

4. Variations in growth during middle childhood are caused by differences in _____ , _____ and _____ .

5. Children are said to be overweight when their body weights are _____ (what percent?) above ideal weight for their age and height and obese when when their body weights are _____ (what percent?) above their ideal weights. Experts estimate that nearly _____ (what proportion?) of North American children are obese.

6. Childhood obesity, which is _____ (increasing/decreasing) in the United States, is hazardous to children's health because it reduces _____ and increases _____ _____ , both of which are associated with serious health problems in middle adulthood. Obese children who do not lose weight in adolescence are more likely to experience _____ and _____ health problems, especially _____ . Too much pressure, however, may contribute to the development of an _____ disorder, such as _____ or _____ .

7. Adopted children are more often overweight when their _____ (adoptive/biological) parents are obese. However, _____ factors are the main reasons for the recent increase in childhood obesity. The most significant of these is lack of _____ .

8. Compared to the past, middle childhood is now a healthier time _____ (in every nation of the world/only in developed nations).

9. During middle childhood, children are _____ (more/less) aware of one another's, or their own, physical imperfections.

10. A chronic inflammatory disorder of the airways is called _____ . This disorder is _____ (more common/less common) today than in the past.

11. The causes or triggers of asthma include

    _____ , _____ , and

    exposure to _____ such as pet hair.

12. The use of injections, inhalers, and pills to treat
    asthma is an example of _____ pre-
    vention. Less than _____ (how
    many?) asthmatic children in the United States
    benefit from this type of treatment. The best
    approach to treating childhood diseases is

    _____ _____ , which

    in the case of asthma includes proper

    _____ of homes and schools,

    decreased _____ , eradication of

    cockroaches, and safe outdoor

    _____ _____ .

Brain Development (pp. 271–276)

13. The brain reaches adult size at about age
    _____ . Advances in brain develop-
    ment during middle childhood enable the control

    over _____ _____ ,

    _____ , _____ , and

    _____ .

    Ongoing maturation of the _____

    _____ allows children to analyze

    the _____ of their behaviors before

    engaging in them.

14. Two other advances in brain function at this time

    include the ability to _____

    _____ , called

    _____ _____ , and the

    _____ of thoughts and actions that

    are repeated in sequence.

15. The length of time it takes a person to respond to
    a particular stimulus is called _____

    _____ .

16. Other important abilities that continue to develop

    during the school years are _____–

    _____ _____ , balance,

    and judgment of _____ .

17. Motor habits that rely on coordinating both sides

    of the body improve because the _____

    _____ between the brain's hemi-

    spheres continues to mature. Animal research

also demonstrates that brain development is stim-

ulated through _____ .

In addition, _____ play may help

boys overcome their genetic tendencies toward

_____ and _____

_____ because it helps with regula-

tion and coordination in the _____

_____ of the brain.

18. Along with brain maturation, _____ ,

    _____ , and _____ are

    important factors in the development of motor

    skills. Approximately _____ percent

    of all children have a motor coordination disabili-

    ty serious enough to interfere with school

    achievement.

19. The potential to learn a particular skill or body of

    knowledge is a person's _____ . The

    most commonly used tests of this type are

    _____ _____ . In the

    original version of the most commonly used test

    of this type, a person's score was calculated as a

    _____ (the child's _____

    _____ divided by the child's

    _____ _____ and mul-

    tiplied by 100 to determine his or her

    _____).

20. Tests that are designed to measure what a child
    has learned are called _____ tests.
    Tests that are designed to measure learning
    potential are called _____ tests.

21. Two highly regarded IQ tests are the

    _____ _____

    _____ _____

    _____ and the

    _____-_____ .

22. IQ tests are quite reliable in predicting
    _____ achievement.

23. IQ testing is controversial in part because no test
    can measure _____ without also
    measuring _____ or without reflect-
    ing the _____ . Another reason is
    that a child's intellectual potential
    _____ (changes/does not change)
    over time.

24. Robert Sternberg believes that there are three distinct types of intelligence:_____ , _____ , and _____ . Similarly, Howard Gardner describes _____ (how many?) distinct intelligences.

Children with Special Needs (pp. 276–286)

25. Among the conditions that give rise to "special needs" are _____ _____ .

26. Down syndrome and other conditions that give rise to "special needs" begin with a _____ anomaly.

27. The process of formally identifying a child with special needs usual begins with a teacher _____ , which may ultimately lead to agreement on an _____ _____ _____ for the child.

28. The field of study that is concerned with childhood psychological disorders is _____ _____ . This perspective has provided several lessons that apply to all children. Three of these are that _____ is normal; disability _____ (changes/does not change) over time; and adolescence and adulthood may be _____ .

29. This perspective also has made diagnosticians much more aware of the _____ _____ of childhood problems. This awareness is reflected in the official diagnostic guide of the American Psychiatric Association, which is the _____ _____ .

30. The most severe disturbance of early childhood is _____ , which is used to describe children who are _____ . Autism is an example of a _____ _____ _____ .

31. Autism is more common in _____ (boys/girls).

32. Children who have autistic symptoms that are less severe than those in the classic syndrome are sometimes diagnosed with _____ _____ , also called _____-_____ _____ .

33. In early childhood autism, severe deficiencies appear in three areas: _____ ability, _____ _____ , and _____ _____ .

34. Some autistic children engage in a type of speech called _____ , in which they repeat, word for word, things they have heard.

35. The unusual play patterns of autistic children are characterized by repetitive _____ or _____ play.

36. As children with pervasive developmental disorders grow older their strongest cognitive skills tend to be in the area of _____ reasoning, and their weakest, in the area of _____ cognition.

37. A disability that manifests itself in a difficulty in concentrating for more than a few moments is called _____-_____ _____ . The most common type of this disorder, which includes a need to be active, often accompanied by excitability and impulsivity, is called _____-_____/ _____ _____ . Children suffering from this disorder can be _____ , _____ , and _____ . The crucial problem in these conditions seems to be a neurological difficulty in paying _____ .

38. Researchers have identified several factors that may contribute to AD/HD. These include _____ _____ , prenatal damage from _____ , and postnatal damage, such as from _____ .

39. Children who have difficulty in school that
_____ (is/is not) attributable to an
overall intellectual slowness, a physical handicap,
or a severely stressful situation are said to have a
_____ _____ . The
crucial factor is a _____
_____ between expected learning
and actual accomplishment.

40. A disability in reading is called
_____ . Other specific academic
subjects that may show a learning disability are
_____ , _____ , and
_____ .

41. In childhood, the most effective forms of treatment for AD/HD are _____ ,
_____ therapy, and changes in the
_____ .

42. Certain drugs that stimulate adults, such as
_____ and _____ ,
have a reverse effect on many hyperactive children.

43. In response to a 1975 act requiring that children
with special needs be taught in the
_____ _____
_____ , the strategy of not separat-
ing special-needs children into special classes,
called _____ , emerged. More
recently, some schools have developed a
_____ _____ , in
which such children spend part of each day with
a teaching specialist. In the most recent approach,
called _____ , learning-disabled
children receive targeted help within the setting
of a regular classroom.

Testing Yourself

After you have completed the audio and text review
questions, see how well you do on the following quiz.
Correct answers, with text and audio references, may
be found at the end of this chapter.

1. A movement disorder that results from brain
injury occurring at birth is called:
   a. epilepsy.
   b. Huntington's disease.
   c. Parkinson's disease.
   d. cerebral palsy.

2. According to experts in the audio program, disabilities are _____ imposed and handicaps
are _____ imposed.
   a. physically; socially
   b. socially; physically
   c. physically; physically
   d. socially; socially

3. Which of the following was *not* cited in the program as a developmental obstacle faced by disabled children and their parents?
   a. There are few good role models with physical
disabilities.
   b. Because many things take more time, difficult
choices between activities must sometimes be
made.
   c. Parents of disabled children experience many
stresses that other parents do not.
   d. Counselors of disabled children are unwilling
to let them make their own choices.

4. According to the experts heard in the audio program, the most difficult season of life for a disabled person is likely to be:
   a. early childhood.
   b. early adolescence.
   c. early adulthood.
   d. all seasons of life.

5. As children move into middle childhood:
   a. the rate of accidental death increases.
   b. sexual urges intensify.
   c. the rate of weight gain increases.
   d. biological growth slows and steadies.

6. Ongoing maturation of which brain area contributes most to left–right coordination?
   a. corpus callosum
   b. prefrontal cortex
   c. brainstem
   d. temporal lobe

7. In the earliest aptitude tests, a child's score was calculated by dividing the child's _____ age by his or her _____ age to find the _____ quotient.

   a. mental; chronological; intelligence
   b. chronological; mental; intelligence
   c. intelligence; chronological; mental
   d. intelligence; mental; chronological

8. A factor that is *not* primary in the development of motor skills during middle childhood is:

   a. practice.   c. brain maturation.
   b. gender.   d. heredity.

9. Dyslexia is a learning disability that affects the ability to:

   a. do math.   c. write.
   b. read.   d. speak.

10. Today, approximately _____ of North American children are obese.

    a. one-eighth
    b. one-fourth
    c. one-third
    d. one-half

11. The developmental psychopathology perspective is characterized by its:

    a. contextual approach.
    b. emphasis on the unchanging nature of developmental disorders.
    c. emphasis on the cognitive domain of development.
    d. concern with all of the above.

12. The time—usually measured in fractions of a second—it takes for a person to respond to a particular stimulus is called:

    a. the interstimulus interval.
    b. reaction time.
    c. the stimulus-response interval.
    d. response latency.

13. Ongoing maturation of which brain area enables schoolchildren to more effectively analyze the potential consequences of their actions?

    a. corpus callosum
    b. prefrontal cortex
    c. brainstem
    d. temporal lobe

14. The underlying problem in attention-deficit/hyperactivity disorder appears to be:

    a. low overall intelligence.
    b. a neurological difficulty in paying attention.
    c. a learning disability in a specific academic skill.
    d. the existence of a conduct disorder.

15. During the years from 7 to 11, the average child:

    a. becomes slimmer.
    b. gains about 12 pounds a year.
    c. has decreased lung capacity.
    d. is more likely to become obese than at any other period in the life span.

16. Among the factors that are known to contribute to obesity are body type, quantity and types of food eaten, and:

    a. metabolism.
    b. activity level.
    c. taste preferences.
    d. all of the above.

17. Autistic children generally have severe deficiencies in all but which of the following?

    a. social skills
    b. imaginative play
    c. echolalia
    d. communication ability

18. Although asthma has genetic origins, several environmental factors contribute to its onset, including:

    a. urbanization.
    b. airtight windows.
    c. dogs and cats living inside the house.
    d. all of the above.

19. Psychoactive drugs are most effective in treating attention-deficit/hyperactivity disorder when they are administered:

    a. before the diagnosis becomes certain.
    b. for several years after the basic problem has abated.
    c. as part of the labeling process.
    d. with psychological therapy and changes at home and at school.

20. Tests that measure a child's potential to learn a new subject are called _____ tests.

    a. aptitude   c. vocational
    b. achievement   d. intelligence

21. Which of the following is true of children with a diagnosed learning disability?

    a. They are, in most cases, average in intelligence.

    b. They often have a specific physical handicap, such as hearing loss.

    c. They often lack basic educational experiences.

    d. All of the above are true.

22. Which approach to education may best meet the needs of learning-disabled children in terms of both skill remediation and social interaction with other children?

    a. mainstreaming

    b. special education

    c. inclusion

    d. resource rooms

23. Asperger syndrome is a disorder in which:

    a. body weight fluctuates dramatically over short periods of time.

    b. verbal skills seem normal, but social perceptions and skills are abnormal.

    c. an autistic child is extremely aggressive.

    d. a child of normal intelligence has difficulty mastering a specific cognitive skill.

LESSON 11: EVERYTHING IS HARDER

Exercise

A major theme of Lesson 11 is that when biosocial, cognitive, or psychosocial development does not proceed normally, life becomes more difficult for everyone involved. Parents find that it takes more time and effort to raise a **disabled** child and that other people often are hurtful in their comments and behavior toward the child. Disabled children may need extra self-confidence, self-esteem, and persistence to master tasks that are routine for other children. Later, during adolescence, when young people want to be like everyone else, disabled adolescents find that they cannot do the same things, look the same, or keep up with their friends.

Throughout the series, the developmental theory of Erik Erikson has been discussed as an important model for studying life-span changes. As you will recall from Lesson 2, Erikson's theory identifies eight important psychosocial crises, or challenges, in life and, hence, eight stages of development. Each crisis can be resolved either positively, in a growth-promoting way, or negatively, in a way that disrupts healthy development.

The exercise for Lesson 11 asks you to reflect on Erikson's stages of development as they relate to the special problems of people with physical disabilities. How might a disability make it more difficult for the individual to experience a positive outcome for each crisis? Note that although Lesson 11 focuses on development during middle childhood, this exercise requires you to integrate material from earlier seasons of life and to anticipate later developmental issues. Please answer the following questions and hand the completed exercise in to your instructor.

For each of Erik Erikson's eight psychosocial crises, note how a disability might make it more difficult to achieve a positive outcome. Base your answers on material from the audio program and the text, your own experiences, or the experiences of someone you know.

Trust versus mistrust:

Autonomy versus shame and doubt:

Initiative versus guilt:

Industry versus inferiority:

Identity versus role confusion:

Intimacy versus isolation:

Generativity versus self-absorption:

Identity versus despair:

LESSON GUIDELINES

Audio Question Guidelines

1. **Cerebral palsy** is a movement disorder that results from a brain injury, usually one that occurs at birth.

   Although the most obvious symptom of cerebral palsy is the person's inability to move body parts the way he or she normally would, other associated symptoms may occur. These include seizures, mental retardation, and hearing and vision problems.

   Unlike many disorders, cerebral palsy is nonprogressive—it does not become worse as the person gets older.

2. **Disabilities** are the result of injury or heredity. **Handicaps** are imposed by society. Social handicaps, such as an environmental obstacle that prevents wheelchair access to a building or attitudes that are prejudicial, are, in many cases, more disabling than physical disabilities.

   Development is harder for children with disabilities for many reasons. One is the additional stresses the disability places on parents and other family members.

   Another obstacle to development is the lack of good role models for disabled children.

   Children with disabilities may need greater self-confidence, self-esteem, and "stick-to-itiveness" than normal children simply because most things are more difficult and take longer.

   Social attitudes often become obstacles for disabled individuals, particularly during adolescence when they want to be like everyone else and discover they are not.

Textbook Question Answers

1. social
2. middle childhood; relatively smooth; rarer
3. more slowly; 5 to 7; 2

During the school years, children generally become slimmer, muscles become stronger, and lung capacity increases.

4. genes; gender; nutrition
5. 20; 30; one-third
6. increasing; exercise; blood pressure; physical; psychological; depression; eating; bulimia; anorexia nervosa
7. biological; environmental; exercise
8. in every nation of the world
9. more
10. asthma; more common
11. genes; infections; allergens
12. tertiary; half; primary prevention; ventilation; pollution; play spaces
13. 7; emotional outbursts; perseveration, inattention, the insistence on routines; prefrontal cortex; consequences
14. pay special heed to one source of information among many; selective attention; automatization
15. reaction time
16. hand–eye coordination; movement
17. corpus callosum; play; rough-and-tumble; hyperactivity; learning disabilities; frontal lobes
18. culture, practice, heredity; 6
19. aptitude; IQ tests; quotient; mental age; chronological age; IQ
20. achievement; aptitude
21. Wechsler Intelligence Scale for Children (WISC); Stanford-Binet
22. school
23. aptitude; achievement; culture; changes
24. academic; creative; practical; eight
25. aggression, anxiety, autism, conduct disorder, depression, developmental delay, learning disability, Down syndrome, attachment disorder, attention-deficit disorder, bipolar disorder, and Asperger syndrome
26. biological
27. referral; individual education plan (IEP)
28. developmental psychopathology; abnormality; changes; better or worse
29. social context; *Diagnostic and Statistical Manual of Mental Disorders* (DSM-IV-R)
30. autism; self-absorbed; pervasive developmental disorder
31. boys
32. Asperger syndrome; high-functioning autism
33. communication; social skills; imaginative play
34. echolalia
35. movements; compulsive
36. abstract; social
37. attention-deficit disorder; attention deficit/hyperactivity disorder; inattentive; impulsive; overactive; attention
38. genetic vulnerability; teratogens; lead poisoning
39. is not; learning disability; measured discrepancy
40. dyslexia; math; spelling; handwriting
41. medication; psychological; family and school environment

42. amphetamines; methylphenidate (Ritalin)

43. least restrictive environment (LRE); mainstreaming; resource room; inclusion

Answers to Testing Yourself

1. **d.** is the answer. (audio program)

2. **a.** is the answer. Social handicaps are often more disabling than physical difficulties. (audio program)

3. **d.** is the answer. Rehabilitation specialist Virginia Nelson encourages her clients to make their own decisions with regard to walking and driving, for example. (audio program)

4. **b.** is the answer. Because of the particular pressures of adolescence—such as wanting to be like everyone else—this may be the most difficult season for the disabled person. (audio program)

5. **d.** is the answer. (textbook, p. 267)

6. **a.** is the answer. (textbook, p. 271)

7. **a.** is the answer. (textbook, p. 274)

8. **b.** Gender is not mentioned as a factor in the development of motor skills. (textbook, p. 273)

9. **b.** is the answer. (textbook, p. 282)

   a. Though not mentioned in the text, this is dyscalcula.

   c. & d. The text does not give labels for learning disabilities in writing or speaking.

10. **c.** is the answer. (textbook, p. 268)

11. **a.** is the answer. (textbook, p. 277)

    b. & c. Because of its contextual approach, developmental psychopathology emphasizes *all* domains of development. Also, it points out that behaviors change over time.

12. **b.** is the answer. (textbook, p. 273)

13. **b.** is the answer. (textbook, p. 272)

    a. Maturation of the corpus callosum contributes to left–right coordination.

c. & d. These brain areas, which were not discussed in this chapter, play important roles in regulating sleep–waking cycles (brainstem) and hearing and language abilities (temporal lobe).

14. **b.** is the answer. (textbook, p. 282)

15. **a.** is the answer. (textbook, p. 268)

    b. & c. During this period children gain about 5 pounds per year and experience increased lung capacity.

    d. Although childhood obesity is a common problem, the text does not indicate that a person is more likely to become obese at this age than at any other.

16. **d.** is the answer. (textbook, p. 268)

17. **c.** is the answer. Echolalia *is* a type of communication difficulty, a characteristic form of speech of many autistic children. (textbook, pp. 280–281)

18. **d.** is the answer. (textbook, p. 270)

19. **d.** is the answer. (textbook, p. 284)

20. **a.** is the answer. (textbook, p. 274)

    b. Achievement tests measure what has already been learned.

    c. Vocational tests, which, as their name implies, measure what a person has learned about a particular trade, are achievement tests.

    d. Intelligence tests measure general aptitude, rather than aptitude for a specific subject.

21. **a.** is the answer. (textbook, p. 282)

22. **c.** is the answer. (textbook, p. 284)

    a. Many general education teachers are unable to cope with the special needs of some children.

    b. & d. These approaches undermined the social integration of children with special needs.

23. **b.** is the answer. (textbook, p. 280)

The School Years: Cognitive Development

AUDIO PROGRAM: **Piaget and the Age of Reason**

ORIENTATION

Cognitive development between the ages of 7 and 11 is impressive, as attested to by children's reasoning strategies, mastery of school-related skills, and use of language. Lesson 12 explores these changes and their significance to the developing person.

Chapter 12 of *The Developing Person Through the Life Span*, 6/e, examines the development of cognitive abilities in children from ages 7 to 11. The first section discusses the views of Piaget and Vygotsky regarding the child's cognitive development, which involves a growing ability to use logic and reasoning (as emphasized by Piaget) and to benefit from social interactions with skilled mentors (as emphasized by Vygotsky). Because the school years are also a time of expanding moral reasoning, this section also examines Kohlberg's stage theory of moral development as well as current evaluations of his theory.

The second section focuses on changes in the child's processing speed and capacity, control processes, knowledge base, and metacognition. It also looks at language development during middle childhood. During this time, children develop a more analytic understanding of words and show a marked improvement in their language skills.

The last section covers educational and environmental conditions that are conducive to learning by schoolchildren, including how reading, math, and science are best taught, and fluency in a second language.

Audio program 12, "Piaget and the Age of Reason," focuses on a description and critique of Piaget's stages of preoperational and concrete operational thought. Piaget's famous **conservation** experiments are illustrated with children of several ages, and expert commentary is provided by psychologist David Elkind. Several landmarks of the transition from preoperational to concrete operational thought are illustrated, including the disappearance of **egocentric** thinking, and the emergence of abilities to classify, deal with rules, consider two dimensions at once, and take another's perspective. Professor Elkind also discusses the contemporary concept of the **competent child** and why the efforts of many modern parents to accelerate cognitive development in their children may be futile.

As the program opens we hear the voices of two children—one who has not yet attained what philosophers once called "The Age of Reason," and one who has.

LESSON GOALS

By the end of this lesson you should be prepared to:

1. Discuss the logical structures of concrete operational thought, according to Piaget, and describe Vygotsky's views regarding the influence of the sociocultural context on learning during middle childhood.

2. Outline Kohlberg's stage theory of moral reasoning, and evaluate criticisms of his theory.

3. Describe the components of the information-processing system, noting how they interact.

4. Discuss advances in selective attention, metacognition, and processing speed during middle childhood.

5. Describe how children's language abilities change between the ages of 7 and 11.

6. Discuss variations in the schooling of children, focusing on the impact of cultural needs and standards for how schoolchildren spend their time.

Audio Assignment

Listen to the audio tape that accompanies Lesson 12: "Piaget and the Age of Reason."

Write answers to the following questions. You may replay portions of the program if you need to refresh your memory. Answer guidelines may be found in the Lesson Guidelines section at the end of this chapter.

1. Identify and describe the major characteristics of preoperational thinking.

2. Explain the conservation-of-liquid task and identify the cognitive abilities that enable children to succeed in this task.

3. Identify the cognitive gains that come with concrete operational thought. In what ways is thinking still limited among children in this stage?

4. Discuss some of the psychological and social effects of preoperational and concrete operational thought on children.

5. Discuss how some of Piaget's ideas have been modified recently and how the social revolutions of the past 25 years have changed parents' expectations of children.

Textbook Assignment

Read Chapter 12: "The School Years: Cognitive Development," pages 289–311 in *The Developing Person Through the Life Span,* 6/e, then work through the material that follows to review it. Complete the sentences and answer the questions. As you proceed, evaluate your performance for each section by consulting the answers on page 149. Do not continue with the next section until you understand each answer. If you need to, review or reread the appropriate section in the textbook before continuing.

Building on Piaget and Vygotsky (pp. 289–295)

1. According to Piaget, between ages 7 and 11, children are in the stage of _____ _____ _____ . Unlike Piaget, Vygotsky regarded instruction by _____ as crucial to cognitive development.

2. The concept that objects can be organized into categories according to some common property is _____ .

3. The logical principle that certain characteristics of an object remain the same even when other characteristics change is _____ . The idea that a transformation process can be reversed to restore the original condition is _____ . The logical principle that two things can change in opposite ways to balance each other out is _____ .

4. Cross-cultural studies of classification and other logical processes demonstrate that these principles _____ (apply/do not apply) throughout the world.

5. Contemporary developmentalists believe that Piaget underestimated the influence of

_____ , _____ , and _____ on cognitive development. In doing so, he also underestimated the _____ in development from one child to another.

6. The theorist who has extensively studied moral development by presenting subjects with stories that pose ethical dilemmas is

_____ . According to his theory, the three levels of moral reasoning are

_____ , _____ , and _____ .

7. (Table 12.1) In preconventional reasoning, emphasis is on getting _____ and avoiding _____ . "Might makes right" describes stage _____ (1/2), whereas "look out for number one" describes stage _____ (1/2).

8. (Table 12.1) In conventional reasoning, emphasis is on _____ _____ , such as being a dutiful citizen, in stage _____ (3/4), or winning approval from others, in stage _____ (3/4).

9. (Table 12.1) In postconventional reasoning, emphasis is on_____ _____ , such as _____ _____ (stage 5) and _____ _____ _____ (stage 6).

10. During middle childhood, children's moral reasoning generally falls at the _____ and _____ levels.

11. One criticism of Kohlberg's theory is that the later stages reflect values associated with _____ intellectual values. Another is that Kohlberg ignored the moral development of _____ .

12. It is now well established that different cultures _____ (have/do not have) distinctive morals and values.

13. Carol Gilligan believes that females develop a

_____ _____ _____ , based on concern for the well-being of others, more than a _____ _____ _____ , based on depersonalized standards of right and wrong.

Information Processing (pp. 296–301)

14. The idea that the advances in thinking that accompany middle childhood occur because of basic changes in how children take in, store, and process data is central to the _____- _____ theory.

15. Incoming stimulus information is held for a split second in the _____ _____ , after which most of it is lost.

16. Meaningful material is transferred into

_____ _____ , which is sometimes called _____- _____ _____ . This part of memory handles mental activity that is

_____ .

17. The part of memory that stores information for days, months, or years is _____- _____ _____ . Crucial in this component of the system is not only storage of the material but also its _____ .

18. Children in the school years are better learners and problem solvers than younger children are, because they have faster _____ _____ , and they have a larger _____ _____ .

19. One reason for the cognitive advances of middle childhood is _____ maturation, especially the _____ of nerve pathways and the development of the

_____ _____ .

20. Processing capacity also becomes more efficient through _____ , as familiar mental activities become routine.

21. Memory ability improves during middle childhood in part because of the child's expanded

_____ _____ .

22. The knowledge base also depends on

_____ and _____ .

23. The mechanisms of the information-processing system that regulate the analysis and flow of information are the _____

_____ .

24. The ability to use _____

_____—to screen out distractors and concentrate on relevant information—improves steadily during the school years and beyond.

25. The ability to evaluate a cognitive task to determine what to do—and to monitor one's performance—is called _____ . This ability becomes evident by age _____ .

26. The practical application of linguistic knowledge is called the _____ of language.

27. During middle childhood, some children learn as many as _____ new words a day. Unlike the vocabulary explosion of the play years, this language growth is distinguished by _____ , _____ , and the ability to make connections between one bit of knowledge and another and later vocabulary performance in school.

28. Schoolchildren's love of words is evident in their _____ , secret _____ , and _____ that they tell.

Teaching and Learning (pp. 301–311)

29. There _____ (is/is not) universal agreement on how best to educate schoolchildren. Internationally and historically, there has been agreement that schools should teach _____ , _____ , and _____ .

30. Some researchers distinguish among the _____ curriculum, which refers to the content endorsed by _____ _____ ; the _____ curriculum, which refers

to what is actually offered; and the _____ curriculum, that the students actually learn.

31. (text and Thinking Like a Scientist) Every culture creates its own _____ _____ , the unofficial priorities that influence every aspect of school learning. Two aspects of this curriculum are the _____ , and the number of _____ . The evidence supporting the popular assumption that smaller class size results in better learning is _____ (strong/weak).

32. Two distinct approaches to teaching reading are the _____ approach, in which children learn the sounds of letters first, and the _____-_____ approach, in which children are encouraged to develop all their language skills at the same time. Most developmentalists believe that _____ (both approaches/neither approach/only the phonics approach/only the whole-language approach) make(s) sense.

33. The lower the family income, the less developed a child's _____ and _____ . This indicates that language development and reading attainment _____ (correlate/do not correlate) with _____ status. The crucial factor in this relationship is the child's actual _____ to language.

34. The best predictor of school achievement and overall intelligence is _____ _____ .

35. Worldwide, literacy has _____ (increased/decreased/not changed) over the past 50 years.

36. Many nations have decided that _____ and _____ are the key areas of the curriculum, perhaps because advances in these areas seem to be connected to a nation's _____ development.

37. In the United States, math was traditionally taught through _____ _____ . A more recent approach replaces this type of learning by emphasizing _____ _____ , estimating and _____ .

38. Cross-cultural research reveals that North American teachers present math at a lower level with more _____ but less _____ to other learning. In contrast, teachers in Japan work more _____ to build children's knowledge.

39. The gap between rich and poor families in their access to computers has been called the _____ . Students who never use computers score _____ (much lower/much higher/almost the same) in math and science as students who often use computers.

40. Most of the world's children _____ (learn/do not learn) a second language. The best time to learn a second language by listening and talking is during _____ , and the best time to teach a second language is during _____ _____ .

41. The approach to bilingual education in which the child's instruction occurs entirely in the second language is called _____ _____ . In _____ _____ programs, the child is taught first in his or her native language, until the second language is taught as a "foreign" language.

42. (Table 12.4) In ESL, or _____ _____ programs, children must master the basics of English before joining regular classes with other children. In contrast, _____ _____ requires that teachers instruct children in both their native language and in English.

43. Immersion programs were successful in _____ , when English-speaking children were initially placed in French-only classrooms. Immersion tends to fail if the child feels _____ , _____ , or _____ _____ .

44. The crucial difference between success and failure in second-language learning rests with _____ _____ , who indicate to the children whether learning a second language is really valued. When both languages are valued, _____ _____ is likely to occur. When second-language learning fails and neither language is learned well, a child is said to be _____ .

Testing Yourself

After you have completed the audio and text review questions, see how well you do on the following quiz. Correct answers, with text and audio references, may be found at the end of this chapter.

1. The kind of thinking that does not allow one to see the world from another's point of view is called:
   a. centration.
   b. egocentrism.
   c. concrete operations.
   d. preoperational thought.

2. Although Piaget believed that children could not take another's point of view before the age of _____ , some contemporary researchers believe that children as young as age _____ can grasp this concept.
   a. 4; 2
   b. 9; 5
   c. 6; 4
   d. 7; 3

3. Preoperational children lack the concept of conservation because they fail to realize that:
   a. a change in one dimension of an object brings about a change in another dimension, too.
   b. matter can neither be created nor destroyed.
   c. rules are not immutable and can be modified.
   d. a transformation can be reversed to restore the original form.

4. The principle that properties such as volume, number, and area remain the same despite changes in the appearance of objects is called:
   a. constancy.
   b. reversibility.
   c. conservation.
   d. reciprocity.

5. Current research on cognitive development indicates that:
   a. Piaget's theory is applicable only to upper-class children.
   b. Piaget overlooked the importance of social development on cognition.
   c. certain cognitive abilities may be acquired at an earlier age than Piaget believed.
   d. Piaget may have overestimated the competence of young children.

6. According to Piaget, the stage of cognitive development in which a person understands specific logical ideas and can apply them to concrete problems is called:
   a. preoperational thought.
   b. operational thought.
   c. concrete operational thought.
   d. formal operational thought.

7. Which of the following is the *most* direct reason that thinking speed continues to increase throughout adolescence?
   a. the increasing myelination of neural axons
   b. the continuing development of the frontal cortex
   c. learning from experience
   d. neurological maturation

8. The idea that an object that has been transformed in some way can be restored to its original form by undoing the process is:
   a. identity.
   b. reversibility.
   c. reciprocity.
   d. automatization.

9. Information-processing theorists contend that major advances in cognitive development occur during the school years because:
   a. the child's mind becomes more like a computer as he or she matures.
   b. children become better able to process and analyze information.
   c. most mental activities become automatic by the time a child is about 13 years old.
   d. the major improvements in reasoning that occur during the school years involve increased long-term memory capacity.

10. The ability to filter out distractions and concentrate on relevant details is called:
    a. metacognition.
    b. information processing.
    c. selective attention.
    d. decentering.

11. Concrete operational thought is Piaget's term for the school-age child's ability to:
    a. reason logically about things and events he or she perceives.
    b. think about thinking.
    c. understand that certain characteristics of an object remain the same when other characteristics are changed.
    d. understand that moral principles may supersede the standards of society.

12. The term for the ability to monitor one's cognitive performance—to think about thinking—is:
    a. pragmatics.
    b. information processing.
    c. selective attention.
    d. metacognition.

13. Long-term memory is _____ permanent and _____ limited than working memory.
    a. more; less
    b. less; more
    c. more; more
    d. less; less

14. In making moral choices, according to Gilligan, females are more likely than males to:
    a. score at a higher level in Kohlberg's system.
    b. emphasize the needs of others.
    c. judge right and wrong in absolute terms.
    d. formulate abstract principles.

15. Compared to more advantaged children, children from low-income families show deficits in their development of:
    a. vocabulary.
    b. grammar.
    c. sentence length.
    d. all the above.

16. The best predictor of a child's achievement in school is:
    a. the school achievement of the child's parents.
    b. vocabulary size.
    c. the child's socioeconomic status.
    d. class size.

17. Which of the following is *not* an approach used in the United States to avoid the shock of complete immersion in the teaching of English?
    a. reverse immersion
    b. English as a second language
    c. bilingual education
    d. total immersion

18. The idea that two things can change in opposite directions, yet balance each other out is:
    a. identity.
    b. reversibility.
    c. reciprocity.
    d. automatization.

19. Between 9 and 11 years of age, children are most likely to demonstrate moral reasoning at which of Kohlberg's stages?
    a. preconventional
    b. conventional
    c. postconventional
    d. It is impossible to predict based only on a child's age.

20. Of the following, which was *not* identified as an important factor in the difference between success and failure in second-language learning?
    a. the age of the child
    b. the attitudes of the parents
    c. community values regarding second language learning
    d. the difficulty of the language

21. The increase in processing speed that occurs during middle childhood is partly the result of:
    a. ongoing myelination of axons.
    b. neurological development in the limbic system.
    c. the streamlining of the knowledge base.
    d. all of the above.

22. According to Kohlberg, a person who is a dutiful citizen and obeys the laws set down by society would be at which level of moral reasoning?
    a. preconventional stage one
    b. preconventional stage two
    c. conventional
    d. postconventional

23. An example of schoolchildren's growth in metacognition is their understanding that:
    a. transformed objects can be returned to their original state.
    b. rehearsal is a good strategy for memorizing, but outlining is better for understanding.
    c. objects may belong to more than one class.
    d. they can use different language styles in different situations.

NAME _____   INSTRUCTOR _____

LESSON 12: PREOPERATIONAL AND CONCRETE OPERATIONAL THOUGHT

Exercise

According to Piaget, preoperational and concrete operational children think about the world in very different ways. The **preoperational** child (4- to 5-year-old) sees the world from his or her own perspective (**egocentrism**), and has not yet mastered the principle of **conservation**: the idea that properties such as mass, volume, and number remain the same despite changes in appearance. The **concrete operational** child (6- to 11-year-old) is less egocentric and demonstrates mastery of logical thought, including conservation, with tangible objects.

These Piagetian concepts can be demonstrated if you know a 4- or 5-year-old and a 7- or 8-year-old—perhaps the children of relatives, friends, or neighbors—who are willing to participate. First try several of the conservation tasks described in the audio program and in the text (p. 219). Choose from the tests for the conservation of liquid, number, matter, length, volume, and area.

Then probe your subjects' ability to take another person's point of view. Asked why the sun shines, the preoperational child might answer, "So that I can see." Try asking your subjects the following questions and any others that you can think of. Why does the sun shine? Why is there snow? Why does it rain? Also have your subjects shut their eyes, then ask if they think that you can still see them. The preoperational child is likely to say no. As Professor Kotre did in the program, inquire how many brothers and sisters each child has. Follow up by asking how many children her or his parents have. The preoperational child is likely to know the number of siblings but not the number of children his or her parents have.

After you have conducted your tests, answer the questions that follow and hand the completed exercise in to your instructor.

1. Describe the participants (ages, sex, relationship to you) and setting that you chose for the interview.

2. Briefly describe each child's response to the conservation test you attempted.

   a. Conservation of _____

   Younger child's response

   Older child's response

    b. Conservation of _____

    Younger child's response

    Older child's response

    c. Conservation of _____

    Younger child's response

    Older child's response

3. Briefly describe each child's response to the test of egocentric thought. Was egocentric thinking evident in any of the answers given? If so, give examples.

    Younger child's response

    Older child's response

4. Do your subjects' ages and test responses support Piaget's stage theory of cognitive development? Why or why not?

LESSON GUIDELINES

Audio Question Guidelines

1. Preoperational children possess the notion of **phenomenalistic causality**, mistakenly believing that two things that happen together are related causally.

   Preoperational thought is also **egocentric**, making it difficult for young children to take the perspective of someone else. Egocentrism is lost gradually as the preschooler learns to keep track of two dimensions at once.

2. **Conservation** refers to the principle that an entity remains the same despite changes in its appearance. Preoperational children fail tests for conservation of volume, number, and area.

   In the test for conservation of volume, for example, the same amount of water is poured into a short fat glass and a tall skinny glass. Failing to conserve, the preoperational child judges that the tall skinny glass contains more water.

   The failure to conserve is due to the child's failure to realize that a change in one dimension of an object brings about a change in another dimension too. Preoperational children **center** their attention on the height of the water and forget about the width of the glass.

   Children who are able to conserve take both dimensions into consideration. They have entered the stage of **concrete operations**.

3. Around the age of 6 or 7 children enter the stage of concrete operations. Now, logical operations—the workings of reason—are evident in their handling of concrete objects.

   The newly found abilities include mastery of conservation and the emergence of **classification**, which is the ability to sort objects into categories and subcategories.

   The logic of **concrete operational thinking** means that children are also able to deal with rules. Rule-regulated thinking is evident in children's symbolic play and in the typical school curriculum (math rules, reading rules, science rules, etc.).

   Another characteristic of concrete operational thinking is the loss of egocentrism.

   Although children are able to think logically, this is true only for tangible objects. They are not yet capable of reasoning in the abstract.

4. Preoperational children's notion of cause and effect and their egocentrism have profound psychological effects. Their concepts of birth and death, for example, reflect the absence of any biological awareness of where babies come from or of the finality of death. Their sense that co-occurring events cause one another may lead them to believe that some particular act of theirs may have been the cause of their parents' divorce.

   There are many social ramifications to the attainment of concrete operations, including the newly found concern with rules in symbolic play and games, and the emerging ability to take the perspective of another person.

5. Although Piaget believed that children acquire the ability to perform concrete operations around 6 or 7, contemporary researchers have found otherwise. When experiments on conservation, classification, and egocentrism are simplified, younger children are often able to respond correctly.

   Other research has shown that the transition from preoperational thought to concrete operational thought is not as sudden or abrupt as Piaget believed.

   Professor Elkind notes that society's concept of the child is constructed to meet the needs of adults. During the past few decades, as adults have become more "liberated," the concept of the **competent child** has emerged. Many parents have responded by trying too hard to hurry their children's development.

   Professor Elkind notes that there is no evidence that the stages of cognitive development can be accelerated, and that indeed it may be a mistake to hurry children along the path of development.

Textbook Question Answers

1. concrete operational thought; others (or peers, schools, and teachers)
2. classification
3. identity; reversibility; reciprocity
4. apply
5. context; instruction; culture; variability
6. Kohlberg; preconventional; conventional; postconventional
7. rewards; punishments; 1; 2
8. social rules; 4; 3
9. moral principles; social contracts; universal ethical principles
10. preconventional; conventional
11. Western; women

12. have
13. morality of care; morality of justice
14. information-processing
15. sensory memory (register)
16. working memory; short-term memory; conscious
17. long-term memory; retrieval
18. processing speed; processing capacity
19. neurological; myelination; frontal cortex
20. automatization
21. knowledge base
22. opportunity; motivation
23. control processes
24. selective attention
25. metacognition; 8 or 9
26. pragmatics
27. 20; logic; memory
28. poems; languages; jokes
29. is not; reading; writing; arithmetic
30. intended; political and educational leaders; implemented; attained
31. hidden curriculum; length of the school day and year; students per teacher; weak
32. phonics; whole-language; both approaches
33. vocabulary; grammar; correlate; socioeconomic; exposure
34. vocabulary size
35. increased
36. math; science; economic
37. rote learning; concepts; problem solving; probability
38. definitions; connection; collaboratively
39. digital divide; almost the same
40. learn; early childhood; middle childhood
41. total immersion; reverse immersion
42. English as a second language; bilingual education
43. Canada; shy; stupid; socially isolated
44. the attitudes of parents, teachers, and the community; additive bilingualism; semilingual

Answers to Testing Yourself

1. **b.** is the answer. "Egocentrism" is self-defining. Thought is centered (centrism) on the self, or ego. (audio program)
2. **d.** is the answer. When Piaget's original experiments are simplified, younger children are remarkably successful at them. (audio program)
3. **a.** is the answer. In the conservation of liquid experiment, younger children center their attention on the height of the water and do not consider the width of the glass. (audio program)
4. **c.** is the answer. Attainment of conservation marks the transition from preoperational to concrete operational thinking. (audio program)
5. **c.** is the answer. Using simpler tasks for measuring conservation, classification, and egocentrism, researchers have found that younger children are able to respond correctly. (audio program)
6. **c.** is the answer. (textbook, p. 289)
   a. Preoperational thought is "pre-logical" thinking.
   b. There is no such stage in Piaget's theory.
   d. Formal operational thought extends logical reasoning to abstract problems.
7. **c.** is the answer. (textbook, p. 297)
   a., b., & d. Although myelination and the development of the frontal cortex, which are both examples of neurological maturation, partly account for increasing speed of processing, learning is a more direct cause.
8. **b.** is the answer. (textbook, p. 291)
   a. This is the concept that certain characteristics of an object remain the same even when other characteristics change.
   c. This is the concept that two things can change in opposite directions to balance each other out.
   d. This is the process by which familiar mental activities become routine and automatic.
9. **b.** is the answer. (textbook, p. 296)
   a. Information-processing theorists use the mind-computer metaphor at every age.
   c. Although increasing automatization is an important aspect of development, the information-processing perspective does not suggest that most mental activities become automatic by age 13.
   d. Most of the important changes in reasoning that occur during the school years are due to the improved processing capacity of the person's *working memory.*
10. **c.** is the answer. (textbook, p. 298)
    a. This is the ability to evaluate a cognitive task and to monitor one's performance on it.
    b. Information processing is a perspective on cognitive development that focuses on how the mind analyzes, stores, retrieves, and reasons about information.

d. Decentering, which refers to the school-age child's ability to consider more than one aspect of a problem simultaneously, is not discussed in this chapter.

11. **a.** is the answer. (textbook, p. 289)

b. This refers to metacognition.

c. This refers to Piaget's concept of identity.

d. This is characteristic of Kohlberg's postconventional moral reasoning.

12. **d.** is the answer. (textbook, p. 299)

a. Pragmatics refers to the practical use of language to communicate with others.

b. The information-processing perspective views the mind as being like a computer.

c. This is the ability to screen out distractions in order to focus on important information.

13. **a.** is the answer. (textbook, p. 296)

14. **b.** is the answer. (textbook, pp. 294–295)

15. **d.** is the answer. (textbook, p. 304)

16. **b.** is the answer. (textbook, p. 305)

17. **a.** is the answer. (textbook, p. 309)

18. **c.** is the answer. (textbook, p. 291)

19. **b.** is the answer. (textbook, p. 293)

20. **d.** is the answer. (textbook, p. 309)

21. **a.** is the answer. (textbook, p. 297)

b. Neurological development in the frontal cortex facilitates processing speed during middle childhood. The limbic system, which was not discussed in this chapter, is concerned with emotions.

c. Processing speed is facilitated by *growth*, rather than streamlining, of the knowledge base.

22. **c.** is the answer. (textbook, p. 293)

23. **b.** is the answer. (textbook, p. 299)

The School Years: Psychosocial Development

AUDIO PROGRAM: **The First Day**

ORIENTATION

This lesson on psychosocial development brings to a close the unit on the school years. Lessons 11 and 12 noted that from ages 6 to 11 children become stronger and more competent as they master the biosocial and cognitive skills important in their cultures. Their psychosocial development during these years is no less impressive.

Chapter 13 of *The Developing Person Through the Life Span*, 6/e, begins by exploring the growing social competence of children, as described by Freud and Erikson and behaviorist, cognitive, sociocultural, and epigenetic theorists. The section continues with a discussion of the growth of social cognition and self-understanding.

Children's interaction with peers and others in their ever-widening social world is the subject of the next section. Although the peer group often is a supportive, positive influence on children, some children are rejected by their peers or become the victims of bullying.

The next section explores the problems and challenges often experienced by school-age children in our society, including the experience living in single-parent, stepparent, and blended families. The chapter closes with a discussion of the ways in which children cope with stressful situations.

Audio program 13, "The First Day," focuses on the universal experience of children taking their first step onto a new stage of life: a stage where the world outside the family becomes very important. As children begin school, they confront a much more complex social world than they have previously experienced. It is a world with a new authority figure: the teacher. It is also a world with a large number of peers who provide opportunities for conversation, play, exploration, and the shared joy of friendship. Through the expert commentary of psychologists Steven Asher and Sheldon White, we discover both the problems and the promise of this world of school and friends and its landmark status in the life story of the developing person.

As the program opens, the host speaks with 5-year-old Hannah who, like the main character in her favorite book, is about to embark on a journey beyond the security of home and family. In Hannah's case, the journey into the world of school and friends begins with her first day of kindergarten.

LESSON GOALS

By the end of this lesson you should be prepared to:

1. Identify the common themes or emphases of different theoretical views of the psychosocial development of school-age children.

2. Describe the development of self-understanding during middle childhood and its implications for children's self-esteem.

3. Discuss the impact that peers have on psychosocial development during middle childhood, focusing on how friendship circles change and on the plight of rejected children.

4. Identify the various ways in which functional families nurture school-age children, and discuss the impact of different family sructures on the psychosocial development of the school-age child.

5. Describe the problems that may cause stress in middle childhood and factors that help to alleviate the effects of stress.

Audio Assignment

Listen to the audio tape that accompanies Lesson 13: "The First Day."

Write answers to the following questions. You may replay portions of the program if you need to

refresh your memory. Answer guidelines may be found in the Lesson Guidelines section at the end of this chapter.

1. Summarize the cognitive and social skills of the 5- to 7-year-old child that make possible the important transition that takes place at this age.

2. Discuss the important role that friends play in the psychosocial development of school-age children.

3. (Audio and text) Discuss the plight of the rejected child during the school years.

Textbook Assignment

Read Chapter 13: "The School years: Psychosocial Development," pages 313–336 in *The Developing Person Through the Life Span*, 6/e, then work through the material that follows to review it. Complete the sentences and answer the questions. As you proceed, evaluate your performance for each section by consulting the answers on page 161. Do not continue with the next section until you understand each answer. If you need to, review or reread the appropriate section in the textbook before continuing.

The Child's Emotions and Concerns (pp. 313–316)

1. Freud describes middle childhood as the period of _____ , when emotional drives are _____ , psychosexual needs are _____ , and unconscious conflicts are _____ .

2. According to Erikson, the crisis of middle childhood is _____ _____ _____ .

3. Developmentalists influenced by behaviorism are more concerned with children's _____ of new cognitive abilities; those influenced by the cognitive perspective focus on _____ . One offshoot of the grand theories, _____ _____ theory, stresses the combination of _____ and _____ that allows children to understand themselves and to be effective and competent. In addition to comparing children from different parts of the world, _____ theory examines various _____ within one nation. Epigenetic theory notes that not only are schoolchildren _____ driven to master the skills they will need in adulthood, but girls and boys have different visions and _____ _____ for adulthood.

4. As their self-understanding sharpens, children gradually become _____ (more/less) self-critical, and their self-esteem _____ (rises/dips). One reason is that they more often evaluate themselves through _____ _____ .

5. One example of how culture influences social comparison is the tendency of many social groups to teach children not to be too _____ . Research demonstrates that academic and social competence are fostered more by _____ evaluation of achievement than by artificially high _____ .

The Peer Group (pp. 317–323)

6. A peer group is defined as _____ _____ .

Difficulties with peers _____ (place/do not place) children at risk for developing psychological problems.

7. During middle childhood, children care _____ (more/less) about the opinions of their peers than they did when they were younger. They also become _____ (more/less) dependent on each other and must learn to _____ , _____ , _____ , and defend themselves.

8. Having a personal friend is _____ (more/less) important to children than acceptance by the peer group.

9. Friendships during middle childhood become more _____ and _____ . As a result, older children _____ (change/do not change) friends as often and find it _____ (easier/harder) to make new friends.

10. Middle schoolers tend to choose best friends whose _____ , _____ , and _____ are similar to their own.

11. Children who are not really rejected but not picked as friends are _____ . Children who are actively rejected tend to be either _____-_____ or _____-_____ .

Give an example of the immaturity of rejected children.

12. Bullying is defined as _____ efforts to inflict harm through _____ , _____ , or _____ attacks. A key aspect in the definition of bullying is that harmful attacks are _____ .

13. Contrary to the public perception, in middle childhood bullies usually _____ (have/do not have) friends who admire them.

14. Victims of bullying are often _____-rejected children. Less often, _____-rejected children become _____-_____ . Bullies

and their victims _____ (are/are not) usually of the same gender.

15. Boys who are bullies are often above average in _____ , whereas girls who are bullies are often above average in _____ _____ . Boys who are bullies typically use _____ aggression, whereas girls use _____ aggression. Bullying may also be _____ , and obvious, or _____ .

16. Culture _____ (is/is not) a major factor in the incidence of bullying. For instance, a child's _____ status and behavior change from year to year and from place to place. For another, changes in the extent and type of bullying are common in the _____ grades.

Describe the effects of bullying on children.

17. Bullying is _____ (fairly easy/difficult) to change. The origins of bullying and other kinds of _____ behavior may lie in _____ _____ that are present at birth and then strengthened by _____ _____ , poor _____ _____ , and other deficits.

18. (Thinking Like a Scientist) An effective intervention in controlling bullying is to change the _____ _____ within the school so that bully–victim cycles are not allowed to persist.

Families and Children (pp. 323–330)

19. There is an ongoing debate between those who believe that _____ and _____ are more important influences on children's psychosocial development and those who believe that a child's _____ are much more powerful. Even so, all researchers agree that both

_____ and _____ are important.

20. Research demonstrates that _____ (shared/nonshared) influences on most traits are far greater than _____ (shared/non-shared) influences.

21. Family function refers to how well the family

_____

_____ .

22. A functional family nurtures school-age children by meeting their basic _____ , encouraging _____ , fostering the development of _____ , nurturing peer _____ , and providing _____ and _____ .

23. (text and Table 13.2) Family structure is defined as the _____

_____ .

Identify each of the following family structures:

a. _____ A family that includes three or more biologically related generations, including parents and children.

b. _____ A family that consists of the father, the mother, and their biological children.

c. _____ A family that consists of one parent with his or her biological children.

d. _____ A family consisting of two parents, at least one with biological children from another union.

e. _____ A family that consists of children living in their grandparents' home, either with our without their parents.

f. _____ A family that consists of one or more nonbiological children whom adults have legally taken to raise as their own.

g. _____ A family that consists of one or more orphaned, neglected, abused, or delinquent children who are tem-

porarily cared for by an adult to whom they are not biologically related.

h. _____ A family that consists of a parent, his or her biological children, and his or her spouse, who is not biologically related to the children.

i. _____ A family that consists of one or two grandparents and their grandchildren.

j. _____ A family that consists of a homosexual couple and the biological or adopted children of one or both partners.

24. Longitudinal research studies demonstrate that children can thrive _____ (only in certain family structures/in almost any family structure).

Give several reasons for the benefits of the nuclear family structure.

25. When researchers control for differences in wealth, education, health, and hostility, the developmental differences between children raised in different family structures _____ (persist/disappear).

26. Children in every type of family structure grow up very well and sometimes run into trouble. Thus, family _____ seems more critical than family _____ .

27. Family income _____ (correlates/does not correlate) with optimal child development. A second factor that has a crucial impact on children is the _____ that characterizes family interaction. This latter factor explains why _____ families are problematic for many children.

28. Single parents tend to be _____ (older/younger) than married parents.

29. Parents who use harsh discipline are usually categorized as _____ . In the United States, however, many _____-, _____-, and _____-American families use harsh discipline yet are also warm and accepting of their children. An important factor in the impact of this pattern on children is how _____ or _____ the family is.

Coping with Problems (pp. 330–335)

30. Some children are better able to adapt within the context of adversity, that is, they seem to be more _____ . This trait is a _____ process that represents a _____ adaptation to stress.

31. The impact of a given stress on a child (such as divorce) depends on three factors:

    a. _____

    b. _____

    c. _____

32. The importance of daily _____ explains why _____ is so difficult for children. An important factor in the impact of a given stressor is the child's _____ . One study found that children's coping depended more on their _____ of events than on the nature of the events themselves.

33. Another element that helps children deal with problems is the _____ _____ they receive.

34. During middle childhood, there are typically _____ (fewer/more) sources of social support. This can be obtained from grandparents or siblings, for example, or from _____ and _____ . In addition, _____ can also be psychologically protective for children in difficult circumstances.

Testing Yourself

After you have completed the audio and text review questions, see how well you do on the following quiz. Correct answers, with text and audio references, may be found at the end of this chapter.

1. By age 5, the preschooler's brain has attained approximately _____ percent of its eventual adult size.
    a. 65
    b. 75
    c. 85
    d. 90

2. The transition from the family environment of a young child into the broader world beyond the immediate family:
    a. occurs in children between 5 and 7 years of age throughout the world.
    b. is characteristic only of well-educated, pluralistic societies.
    c. occurs at different ages in different societies.
    d. reflects a relatively recent setting of the social clock.

3. The "vision quest" refers to:
    a. a Native American rite of passage in which young children make a journey to seek their totemic animal.
    b. a friendship game played by children the world over.
    c. the efforts of rejected children to make friends.
    d. the developmental process by which school-age children attain a sense of industry.

4. Because it highlights how school-age children advance in learning, cognition, and culture, _____ theory is particularly relevant to middle childhood.
    a. Freud's psychoanalytic
    b. Erikson's psychosocial
    c. sociocultural
    d. social cognitive

5. A common thread running through the five major developmental theories is that cultures throughout history have selected ages 7 to 11 as the time for:
    a. a period of latency.
    b. the emergence of a theory of mind.
    c. more independence and responsibility.
    d. intellectual curiosity.

6. The best strategy for helping children who are at risk of developing serious psychological problems because of multiple stresses would be to:
   a. obtain assistance from a psychiatrist.
   b. increase the child's competencies or social supports.
   c. change the household situation.
   d. reduce the peer group's influence.

7. In explaining psychosocial development during the school years, Professor Wilson stresses the combination of maturation and experience that allows children to understand themselves and to be effective and competent. Professor Wilson is evidently working from the perspective of:
   a. behaviorism.
   b. Erik Erikson's theory of development.
   c. social cognitive theory.
   d. psychoanalytic theory.

8. Girls who are bullies are often above average in _____ , whereas boys who are bullies are often above average in _____ .
   a. size; verbal assertiveness
   b. verbal assertiveness; size
   c. intelligence; aggressiveness
   d. aggressiveness; intelligence

9. As rejected children get older:
   a. their problems often get worse.
   b. their problems usually decrease.
   c. their friendship circles typically become larger.
   d. their peer group becomes less important to their self-esteem.

10. Compared with average or popular children, rejected children tend to be:
    a. brighter and more competitive.
    b. affluent and "stuck-up."
    c. economically disadvantaged.
    d. socially immature.

11. Compared to middle school boys, middle school girls are more likely to emphasize _____ in their friendship networks.
    a. fewer but closer friends
    b. friendships with members of the opposite sex
    c. similar interests and values
    d. friendships with others who are not the same age or sex

12. Artificially high self-esteem in schoolchildren:
    a. fosters academic competence.
    b. fosters social competence.
    c. fosters both academic and social competence.
    d. is less beneficial in fostering academic and social competence than a more objective evaluation of achievement.

13. Older schoolchildren tend to be _____ vulnerable to the stresses of life than children who are just beginning middle childhood because they _____ .
    a. more; tend to overpersonalize their problems
    b. less; have better developed coping skills
    c. more; are more likely to compare their well-being with that of their peers
    d. less; are less egocentric

14. Bully-victims are typically children who would be categorized as:
    a. aggressive-rejected.
    b. withdrawn-rejected.
    c. isolated-rejected.
    d. immature-rejected.

15. Bullying during middle childhood:
    a. occurs only in certain cultures.
    b. is more common in rural schools than in urban schools.
    c. seems to be universal.
    d. is rarely a major problem, because other children usually intervene to prevent it from getting out of hand.

16. During the school years, children become _____ selective about their friends, and their friendship groups become _____ .
    a. less; larger
    b. less; smaller
    c. more; larger
    d. more; smaller

17. Which of the following was *not* identified as a pivotal issue in determining whether divorce or some other problem will adversely affect a child during the school years?
    a. how many other stresses the child is already experiencing
    b. how many protective buffers are in place
    c. how much the stress affects the child's daily life
    d. the specific structure of the child's family

18. Erikson's crisis of the school years is that of:
    a. industry versus inferiority.
    b. acceptance versus rejection.
    c. initiative versus guilt.
    d. male versus female.

19. Children who are categorized as _____ are particularly vulnerable to bullying.
   a. aggressive-rejected
   b. passive-aggressive
   c. withdrawn-rejected
   d. passive-rejected

20. Environmental influences on children's traits that result from contact with different teachers and peer groups are classified as:
   a. shared influences.
   b. nonshared influences.
   c. epigenetic influences.
   d. nuclear influences.

21. Compared to parents in other family structures, parents in a nuclear family tend to be:
   a. wealthier.
   b. better educated.
   c. healthier.
   d. all of the above.

22. Which of the following most accurately describes the relationship between family income and child development?
   a. Adequate family income allows children to own whatever possessions help them to feel accepted.
   b. Because parents need not argue about money, household wealth provides harmony and stability.
   c. the basic family functions are enhanced by adequate family income.
   d. Family income is not correlated with child development.

23. Two factors that most often help the child cope well with multiple stresses are social support and:
   a. social comparison.
   b. religious faith.
   c. remedial education.
   d. referral to mental health professionals.

NAME _____   INSTRUCTOR _____

LESSON 13: SCHOOL-AGE FRIENDSHIPS

Exercise

A central theme of Lesson 13 is that middle childhood is a developmental period characterized by the child's growing inclusion in the social world beyond the family. This world is a complex social environment that includes a large number of peers at school and the shared joy of a smaller network of friends.

To help you apply the material from this lesson to your own life experiences, the exercise asks you to recall the social organization of your own elementary school days and to reflect on the importance of your own friendships. You may, of course, ask the questions of someone other than yourself.

After you have noted your responses, hand the completed exercise in to your instructor.

Think back to the social organization of your own elementary school days in answering the following questions.

1. Under what circumstances outside of school (e.g., birthday parties, outings, slumber parties, "sleep overs") did you and your friends get together?

2. Describe any social groups that formed on your street, in your apartment building, or around activities such as scouting, sports, lessons, or school activities.

3. Describe any special feelings that you have regarding the socializing you did as a child. For example, in what lasting ways did you benefit from the friendships you had in your school years?

4. Everyone experiences social rejection at one time or another. If you remember being teased, rejected, or called a derogatory name during grade school, describe your feelings about this experience. If you do not recall such an experience, describe someone you knew who suffered rejection, explain why he or she was rejected, and suggest how the person might have improved his or her popularity.

LESSON GUIDELINES

Audio Question Guidelines

1. In children between 5 and 7 years of age, the biological and social clocks are in sync, preparing the child to take his or her first step into the world of school and friends.

   By age 5 the brain has reached 90 percent of its eventual adult size, children have acquired the basic vocabulary and grammar of their language, and they are on the threshold of reaching the "age of reason."

   Socially, children are able to be away from their families for relatively long periods of time, and they are able to get along with other children, forming friendships, alliances, and other social groupings.

   Among some Native American tribes, children mark this transition with the "vision quest," a journey in which they go alone into the woods to search for a totem animal that will remain associated with them for the rest of their lives. As children become connected to nature, they also become connected to the world outside their families.

2. An important task that children face during the school years is making friends.

   As children grow older, their friendships become more important, more intense, and more intimate.

   School-age children become choosier about their friends and demand more of a smaller network of friends.

   The way that children think and talk about friendship changes as they get older. Younger children describe a friend in terms of the things they do together. Older children stress the importance of the help and emotional support their friends provide.

   Forming friendships can be very important to the child's psychological development. Children confide in their friends, and their friends help to reassure them about fears or feelings of inadequacy they might have.

   Friends offer comfort and security as children try a new task or approach a new situation.

   Children also learn new skills from their friends.

3. All children are rejected at some time.

   An estimated 5 to 15 percent of all schoolchildren experience serious difficulty in their peer relationships.

   Such children can be grouped into several cate-
gories: aggressive children; those who are shy, withdrawn, and have feelings that are easily hurt; and those who simply lack positive social skills.

Rejected children typically are lonely and immature in social cognition, and have low self-esteem.

Children who have poor peer relationships in elementary school run a higher risk of having problems coping later in life.

Teaching rejected children social skills may help them to form stable friendships.

Children should also be encouraged to develop their own interests and confidence apart from the social scene.

Research has shown that children who improve their academic skills are likely to improve in self-esteem as well.

Textbook Question Answers

1. latency; quieter; repressed; submerged
2. industry versus inferiority
3. acquisition; self-understanding; social cognitive; maturation; experience; sociocultural; subcultures; genetically; role models
4. more; dips; social comparison
5. outstanding; objective; self-esteem
6. a group of individuals of similar age and social status who play, work, or learn together; place
7. more; more; negotiate, compromise, share
8. more
9. intense; intimate; do not change; harder
10. interests; values; backgrounds
11. neglected; aggressive-rejected; withdrawn-rejected

Rejected children often misinterpret social situations—considering a compliment to be sarcastic, for example.

12. systematic; physical, verbal, social; repeated
13. have
14. withdrawn; aggressive; bully-victims; are
15. size; verbal assertiveness; physical; relational; direct; indirect
16. is; social; transitional

Bullied children are anxious, depressed, and underachieving and have lower self-esteem and painful memories.

17. difficult; antisocial; brain abnormalities; insecure attachment; emotional regulation
18. social climate
19. genes; peers; parents; nature; nurture
20. nonshared; shared

21. works to meet the needs of its members
22. needs; learning; self-esteem; friendships; harmony; stability
23. genetic and legal relationships among the members of a family
    a. extended family
    b. nuclear family
    c. one-parent family
    d. blended family
    e. grandparent family
    f. adoptive family
    g. foster family
    h. stepparent family
    i. grandparents alone
    j. homosexual family
24. in almost any family structure

Parents in a nuclear family tend to be wealthier, better educated, psychologically and physically healthier, more willing to compromise, and less hostile than other parents.

25. disappear
26. function; structure
27. correlates; warmth or conflict; blended
28. younger
29. authoritarian; Asian; African; Mexican; isolated; supported
30. resilient; dynamic; positive
31. a. how many other stresses the child is experiencing
    b. how the stress affects the child's daily life
    c. how the child interprets the stress
32. routines; homelessness; attitude; appraisal
33. social support
34. more; peers; pets; religion

Answers to Testing Yourself

1. **d.** is the answer. (audio program)
2. **a.** is the answer. The transition from immediate family to the larger social world is a universal phenomenon. (audio program)
3. **a.** is the answer. In the vision quest, young Native American children search for their totemic animal, marking their connection with nature and the larger world outside the family. (audio program)

4. **d.** is the answer. (textbook, p. 314)
   a. Freud described middle childhood as a period of emotional latency.
   b. Erikson emphasized children's efforts to develop feelings of competency.
   c. Sociocultural theory emphasizes the impact of the children's cultures and subcultures on their development.
5. **b.** is the answer. (textbook, pp. 314–315)
6. **b.** is the answer. (textbook, pp. 332–333)
7. **c.** is the answer. (textbook, p. 314)
8. **b.** is the answer. (textbook, p. 320)
9. **a.** is the answer. (textbook, p. 319)
10. **d.** is the answer. (textbook, p. 319)
11. **a.** is the answer. (textbook, p. 318)
    b. & c. Both boys and girls form same-sex groups, and both choose friends with similar interests and values.
12. **d.** is the answer. (textbook, p. 316)
13. **b.** is the answer. (textbook, p. 334)
14. **a.** is the answer. (textbook, p. 320)
    b. Withdrawn-rejected children are frequently the victims of bullies but rarely become bullies themselves.
    c. & d. There are no such categories.
15. **c.** is the answer. (textbook, p. 321)
    d. In fact, children rarely intervene, unless a best friend is involved.
16. **d.** is the answer. (textbook, p. 318)
17. **d.** is the answer. (textbook, p. 331)
18. **a.** is the answer. (textbook, p. 313)
19. **c.** is the answer. (textbook, p. 320)
    a. These are usually bullies.
    b. & d. These are not subcategories of rejected children.
20. **b.** is the answer. (textbook, p. 324)
    a. Shared influences are those that occur because children are raised by the same parents in the same home.
    c. & d. There are no such influences.
21. **d.** is the answer. (textbook, p. 327)
22. **c.** is the answer. (textbook, p. 328)
23. **b.** is the answer. (textbook, p. 334)

Adolescence: Biosocial Development

ORIENTATION

For most people, adolescence is an eventful season that brings dramatic changes in the ticking of each of the three developmental clocks—biological, psychological, and social. Along with physical growth that occurs at a more rapid rate than at any time since early childhood, the changes associated with sexual maturation contribute a new dimension to the ways in which adolescents think about themselves and relate to others. Lesson 14, which focuses on the nature and consequences of biosocial development during adolescence, begins a three-lesson unit on development between the ages of 10 and 20—the season when young people cross the boundary between childhood and adulthood.

Chapter 14 of *The Developing Person Through the Life Span*, 6/e, focuses on the dramatic changes that occur in the biosocial domain, beginning with puberty and the growth spurt. The biosocial metamorphosis of the adolescent is discussed in detail, with emphasis on factors that affect the age of puberty and sexual maturation.

Although adolescence is, in many ways, a healthy time of life, the text addresses three health hazards that too often affect adolescence: poor nutrition, sexual misbehavior and sexual abuse, and the use of alcohol, tobacco, and other drugs.

In audio program 14, "Changing Bodies, Changing Selves," the mechanisms by which the biological clock programs puberty are discussed. In this century, children are entering puberty earlier and earlier. Around the age of 9 in girls and 10 in boys, puberty begins when the **pituitary gland** in the brain releases hormones that affect the ovaries in girls and the testes in boys. Dr. Inese Beitins, a pediatric endocrinologist, explains the intricate sequence of bodily changes triggered by this hormonal surge. In

boys and girls, the sequences are nearly opposite, with fertility arriving late in the pubertal cycle of girls and early in that of boys. The possible explanations for this sex difference are explored by anthropologists Jane Lancaster and Barry Bogin, and psychologist Laurence Steinberg. According to one view, the male-female difference was shaped by our evolutionary past, at a time when the biological and social clocks were in sync. Today, however, fertility often arrives a decade before society confers on the young person the status of adult, bringing with it a time when the biological clock says "ready," but the social clock says "wait."

For all of us, the changes of adolescence have a memorable and lifelong impact on our bodies and self-images. Perhaps we can recall the excitement and embarrassment of an event like the one that opens the program.

LESSON GOALS

By the end of this lesson you should be prepared to:

1. Outline the biological changes of puberty, and discuss the emotional and psychological impact of pubertal hormones.

2. Compare and contrast the development of the primary and secondary sex characteristics in adolescent males and females.

3. Discuss the evolutionary perspective on male–female differences in development during puberty.

4. Describe the possible problems faced by boys and girls during adolescence, including dissatisfaction with body image, sexual abuse, and drug use.

Audio Assignment

Listen to the audio tape that accompanies Lesson 14: "Changing Bodies, Changing Selves."

Write answers to the following questions. You may replay portions of the program if you need to refresh your memory. Answer guidelines may be found in the Lesson Guidelines section at the end of this chapter.

1. Outline what is known of the neural and hormonal mechanisms that govern the onset of puberty.

2. Explain why, according to some anthropologists, the biological clock programs fertility to arrive late in the pubertal sequence for girls, and early in the sequence for boys.

3. Contrast the effects of early and late maturation on boys and girls in today's society.

Textbook Assignment

Read Chapter 14: "Adolescence: Biosocial Development," pages 341–361 in *The Developing Person Through the Life Span*, 6/e, then work through the material that follows to review it. Complete the sentences and answer the questions. As you proceed, evaluate your performance for each section by consulting the answers on page 173. Do not continue with the next section until you understand each answer. If you need to, review or reread the appropriate section in the textbook before continuing.

Puberty Begins (pp. 341–350)

1. The period of rapid physical growth and sexual maturation that ends childhood and brings the young person to adult size, shape, and sexual potential is called _____ . The physical changes of puberty typically are complete _____ (how long?) after puberty begins. Although puberty begins at various ages, the _____ is almost always the same.

   List, in order, the major physical changes of puberty in

   Girls: _____

   _____

   Boys: _____

   _____

2. Puberty begins when a hormonal signal from the _____ triggers hormone production in the _____ _____ , which in turn triggers increased hormone production by the _____ _____ and by the _____ , which include the _____ in males and the _____ in females. This route, called the _____ _____ , also triggers the development of the _____ and _____ sexual characteristics.

3. The hormone _____ causes the gonads to dramatically increase their production of sex hormones, especially _____ in girls and _____ in boys.

4. The increase in the hormone _____ is dramatic in boys and slight in girls, whereas the increase in the hormone _____ is marked in girls and slight in boys. Conflict, moodiness, and sexual urges _____ (usually do/do not usually) increase during adolescence. This is due in part to the increasingly high levels of hormones such as _____ . During puberty, hormonal levels have their greatest emotional impact

_____ (directly/indirectly), via the

_____

_____

of _____

_____ .

5. The age of puberty is _____ (highly variable/quite consistent from child to child).

6. Normal children begin to notice pubertal changes between the ages of _____ and

_____ .

7. The average American girl experiences her first menstrual period, called _____ , between ages _____ and

_____ , with age _____ the average.

8. Genes are an important factor in the timing of menarche, as demonstrated by the fact that

_____ and _____

reach menarche at very similar ages.

9. Stocky individuals tend to experience puberty

_____ (earlier/later) than those with taller, thinner builds.

10. Menarche seems to be related to the accumulation of a certain amount of body _____ .

11. For both sexes, fat is limited by chronic

_____ , which therefore delays puberty by several years.

12. Another influence on the age of puberty is

_____ .

13. Research from many nations suggests that family stress may _____ (accelerate/ delay) the onset of puberty.

14. Stress may cause production of the hormones that cause _____ . Support for this hypothesis comes from a study showing that early puberty was associated with

_____ and

_____ .

15. An evolutionary explanation of the stress-puberty hypothesis is that ancestral females growing up in stressful environments may have increased

their _____ _____ by accelerating physical maturation.

16. For girls, _____ (early/late) maturation may be especially troublesome.

Describe several common problems and developmental hazards experienced by early-maturing girls.

17. For boys, _____ (early/late) maturation is usually more difficult.

Describe several characteristics and/or problems of late-maturing boys.

18. A major _____ spurt occurs in late childhood and early adolescence, during which growth proceeds from the _____ (core/extremities) to the _____ (core/extremities). At the same time, children begin to _____ (gain/lose) weight at a relatively rapid rate.

19. The change in weight that typically occurs between 10 and 12 years of age is due primarily to the accumulation of body _____ .

20. The amount of weight gain an individual experiences depends on several factors, including

_____ , _____ ,

_____ , and _____ .

21. During the growth spurt, a greater percentage of fat is retained by _____ (males/ females), who naturally have a higher proportion of body fat in adulthood.

22. About a year after the height and weight changes occur, a period of _____ increase occurs, causing the pudginess and clumsiness of an earlier age to disappear. In boys, this increase is particularly notable in the _____ body.

23. Internal organs also grow during puberty. The _____ increase in size and capacity, the _____ doubles in size, heart rate _____ (increases/decreases), and blood volume _____ (increases/ decreases). These changes increase the adolescent's physical _____ .

24. During puberty, one organ system, the _____ system, decreases in size, making teenagers _____ (more/less) susceptible to respiratory ailments.

Explain why the physical demands placed on a teenager, as in athletic training, should not be the same as those for a young adult of similar height and weight.

25. The hormones of puberty also affect the _____ rhythm, causing changes in when the teenager needs the most sleep. In addition, hormones cause many relatively minor physical changes that can have significant emotional impact. These include increased activity in _____ , _____ , and _____ glands.

26. Changes in _____

_____ _____ involve the sex organs that are directly involved in reproduction. By the end of puberty, reproduction _____ (is/is still not) possible.

Describe the major changes in primary sex characteristics that occur in both sexes during puberty.

27. In girls, the event that is usually taken to indicate sexual maturity is _____ . In boys, the indicator of reproductive potential is the first ejaculation of seminal fluid containing sperm, which is called _____ . In both sexes, full reproductive maturity occurs _____ (at this time/several years later).

28. Sexual features other than those associated with reproduction are referred to as _____

_____ _____ .

Describe the major pubertal changes in the secondary sex characteristics of both sexes.

29. Two secondary sex characteristics that are mistakenly considered signs of womanhood and manliness, respectively, are _____ _____ and

_____ .

Hazards to Health (pp. 350–360)

30. The minor illnesses of childhood, including _____ , _____ , _____ , and _____ _____ , are _____ (less common/more common) during adolescence. The diseases of adulthood are _____ (common/rare). Death rates caused by _____ and _____ increase markedly from ages 10 to 25.

31. Due to rapid physical growth, the adolescent needs a higher daily intake of

_____ , _____ , and _____ . Specifically, the typical adolescent needs about 50 percent more of the minerals _____ , _____ , and _____ during the growth spurt. Inadequate consumption of _____ is particularly troubling because it is a good source of the _____ needed for bone growth.

32. Most teenagers eat _____ (few / most) meals at home. As a result, they are likely to consume too much _____ , _____ , and _____ .

33. Because of menstruation, adolescent females need additional _____ in their diets and are more likely to suffer _____ - _____ _____ than any other subgroup of the population.

34. Adolescents' mental conception of, and attitude toward, their physical appearance is referred to as their _____ _____ . Most girls think they look too _____ , and many boys think they look too _____ . These distorted perceptions may lead to the life-threatening diseases _____ and _____ in girls; for boys, they can lead to _____ _____ .

35. Because puberty occurs _____ (earlier/later) than it used to and marriage occurs _____ (earlier/later), one-fourth of all adolescents are sexually active by age _____ , and about one-half are active _____ .

36. Sexually active teenagers have higher rates of _____ _____ _____ such as _____ , _____ _____ , _____ , and _____ .

37. Risk of exposure to HIV increases if a person:

a. _____

b. _____

c. _____

38. A second developmental risk for sexually active adolescent girls is _____ . If this happens within a year or two of menarche, girls are at increased risk of many complications, including _____ _____ . Teenage motherhood slows _____ achievement and restricts _____ growth. Babies of young teenagers have a higher risk of _____ and _____ complications, including _____ _____ and _____ .

39. Any activity in which an adult uses an unconsenting person for his or her own sexual stimulation or pleasure is considered _____ _____ . When such activity involves a young person, whether or not genital contact is involved, it is called _____ _____ _____ .

40. The damage done by sexual abuse depends on many factors, including how often it is _____ , how much it distorts _____ - _____ , if it is _____ , or if it impairs the child's relationships with _____ .

41. Sexual victimization often begins in _____ and typically is committed by _____ . Overt sexual abuse typically begins at _____ .

42. An estimated _____ percent of child molesters are _____ _____ .

43. Adolescent problems, such as pregnancy, drug abuse, and suicide often are tied to past _____ _____ .

44. Drug _____ always harms physical and psychological development, whether or not the drug becomes _____ . Drug _____ may or may not be harmful, depending on the reasons for, and the effects of, that use.

45. Tobacco, alcohol, and marijuana may act as _____ _____ , opening the door not only to regular use of multiple drugs but also to other destructive behaviors, such as risky _____ , school _____ , and _____ .

46. By decreasing food consumption and the absorption of nutrients, tobacco can limit the adolescent _____ _____ .

47. Because alcohol loosens _____ and impairs _____ , even moderate use can be destructive in adolescence. Alcohol also impairs _____ and _____ by damaging the brain's _____ and _____ _____ .

48. Marijuana _____ (slows/accelerates) thinking processes, particularly those related to _____ and _____ reasoning.

49. About _____ (how many?) high school seniors admit to using at least one drug in the last month, with _____ being the most common.

50. Whether a particular teenager uses drugs, and what drugs he or she uses, depends largely on his or her _____ , the _____ , and the national _____ .

51. (Changing Policy) Students who participate in Project D.A.R.E. are _____ (more/no more) likely to abstain from drugs over the high school years than those who do not.

52. (Changing Policy) Three factors that protect against drug use are

    a. _____

    b. _____

    c. _____

Testing Yourself

After you have completed the audio and text review questions, see how well you do on the following quiz. Correct answers, with text and audio references, may be found at the end of this chapter.

1. Which of the following is true regarding the pubertal sequence of physical changes in boys and girls?
   a. For both boys and girls, fertility comes very early in the pubertal sequence.
   b. Fertility comes earlier in the pubertal sequence for girls than for boys.
   c. Fertility comes earlier in the pubertal sequence for boys than for girls.
   d. For both boys and girls, fertility comes very late in the pubertal sequence.

2. Compared to the turn of the century, today the average age at which children enter puberty is:
   a. younger.
   b. older.
   c. no different.
   d. less predictable and more dependent on factors such as diet and exercise.

3. One evolutionary perspective on sex differences in pubertal development holds that for our ancestors:
   a. males who retained boyish features for a while after they became fertile were more successful reproductively than those who did not.
   b. females who did not become fertile until after they were physically mature were more successful reproductively than those who became fertile earlier.
   c. the biological clock programmed fertility to occur at about the same time in males and females, with the bodily changes of puberty beginning about one year earlier in females.
   d. all of the above statements are true.

4. Regarding the effects of early and late maturation on boys and girls, which of the following is *not* true?
   a. Early maturation is usually easier for boys to manage than it is for girls.
   b. Late maturation is usually easier for girls to manage than it is for boys.
   c. Early-maturing girls may be drawn into older peer groups and may become involved in problem behaviors such as drug use and early sexual activity.
   d. Late-maturing boys do not "catch up" physically, or in terms of their self-images, for many years.

5. Which of the following most accurately describes the sequence of pubertal development in girls?
   a. breast buds and pubic hair; growth spurt in which fat is deposited on hips and buttocks; first menstrual period; ovulation
   b. growth spurt; breast buds and pubic hair; first menstrual period; ovulation
   c. first menstrual period; breast buds and pubic hair; growth spurt; ovulation
   d. breast buds and pubic hair; growth spurt; ovulation; first menstrual period

6. Although both sexes grow rapidly during adolescence, boys typically gain more than girls in their:
   a. muscle strength.
   b. body fat.
   c. internal organ growth.
   d. lymphoid system.

7. For girls, the first readily observable sign of the onset of puberty is:
   a. the onset of breast growth.
   b. the appearance of facial, body, and pubic hair.
   c. a change in the shape of the eyes.
   d. a lengthening of the torso.

8. More than any other group in the population, adolescent girls are likely to have:
   a. asthma.
   b. acne.
   c. iron-deficiency anemia.
   d. testosterone deficiency.

9. The HPA axis is the:
   a. route followed by many hormones to regulate stress, growth, sleep, and appetite.
   b. pair of sex glands in humans.
   c. cascade of sex hormones in females and males.
   d. area of the brain that regulates the pituitary gland.

10. For males, the secondary sex characteristic that usually occurs last is:
    a. breast enlargement.
    b. the appearance of facial hair.
    c. growth of the testes.
    d. the appearance of pubic hair.

11. For girls, the specific event that is taken to indicate fertility is _____ ; for boys, it is _____ .
    a. the growth of breast buds; voice deepening
    b. menarche; spermarche
    c. anovulation; the testosterone surge
    d. the growth spurt; pubic hair

12. The most significant hormonal changes of puberty include an increase of _____ in _____ and an increase of _____ in _____ .
    a. progesterone; boys; estrogen; girls
    b. estrogen; boys; testosterone; girls
    c. progesterone; girls; estrogen; boys
    d. estrogen; girls; testosterone; boys

13. In general, most adolescents are:
    a. overweight.
    b. satisfied with their appearance.
    c. dissatisfied with their appearance.
    d. unaffected by cultural attitudes about beauty.

14. Estrogen is to ovaries as:
    a. testosterone is to adrenals
    b. testosterone is to testes.
    c. GnRH is to ovaries.
    d. GnRH is to testicles.

15. The damage caused by sexual abuse depends on all of the following factors *except*:
    a. repeated incidence.
    b. the gender of the perpetrator.
    c. distorted adult–child relationships.
    d. impairment of the child's ability to relate to peers.

16. Early physical growth and sexual maturation:
    a. tend to be equally difficult for girls and boys.
    b. tend to be more difficult for boys than for girls.
    c. tend to be more difficult for girls than for boys.
    d. are easier for both girls and boys than late maturation.

17. Pubertal changes in growth and maturation typically are complete how long after puberty begins?
    a. one year
    b. two years
    c. three or four years
    d. The variation is too great to generalize.

18. Use of gateway drugs is:
    a. more typical of affluent teenagers who are experiencing an identity crisis.
    b. both a cause and a symptom of adolescent problems.
    c. less likely to result in alcohol-abuse problems later on.
    d. less helpful to teens trying to resist later peer pressure leading to long-term addiction.

19. Compounding the problem of sexual abuse of boys, abused boys:
    a. feel shame at the idea of being weak.
    b. have fewer sources of emotional support.
    c. are more likely to be abused by fathers.
    d. have all of the above problems.

20. Nutritional deficiencies in adolescence are frequently the result of:
    a. eating red meat.
    b. poor eating habits.
    c. anovulatory menstruation.
    d. excessive exercise.

21. Nonreproductive sexual characteristics, such as the deepening of the voice and the development of breasts, are called:
    a. gender-typed traits.
    b. primary sex characteristics.
    c. secondary sex characteristics.
    d. pubertal prototypes.

22. Which of the following does *not* typically occur during puberty?
    a. The lungs increase in size and capacity.
    b. The heart's size and rate of beating increase.
    c. Blood volume increases.
    d. The lymphoid system decreases in size.

23. Teenagers' susceptibility to respiratory ailments typically _____ during adolescence, due to a(n) _____ in the size of the lymphoid system.
    a. increases; increase
    b. increases; decrease
    c. decreases; increase
    d. decreases; decrease

NAME _____   INSTRUCTOR _____

LESSON 14: BODY IMAGES IN ADOLESCENCE

Exercise

A major theme of Lesson 14 is that the biosocial changes of puberty have a profound impact on our self-images. Most people are able to remember at least one event, attitude, misconception, or worry they experienced in connection with the biosocial changes of puberty: having had big feet; having been the first or the last to experience **menarche**; having been concerned about having a small penis or being oversexed; having worried about acne, or voice change.

The young people who have the most difficulty are those who must adjust to these changes earlier or later than the majority of their peers. Early or late maturation may be difficult because one of the things an adolescent does not want to do is stand out from the crowd in a way that is not admirable. Early-maturing girls who are taller and more developed are often teased about their bodies by boys and accused of being "boy crazy" by girls. Late-maturing boys may compensate for being physically outdistanced by peers by becoming the class "brain," clown, or trouble-maker.

Several studies have found that early-maturing girls and late-maturing boys may experience problems that reflect their difficulty in adjusting to their bodies. Early-maturing girls may be drawn to an older peer group and be more likely to engage in problem behaviors, such as drug use and early sexual activity. Follow-up studies of late-maturing boys during adulthood found that although most of them had reached average or above average height, some of the personality patterns of their adolescence persisted. Compared to early- or average-maturing boys, men who had been late-maturers tended to be less controlled and less responsible, and to harbor feelings of inferiority or rejection.

To help you recall your own adolescent preoccupation with appearance, the exercise for Lesson 14 asks you to respond to questions about your body image during your own adolescence. Once you have worked through the items, hand the completed exercise in to your instructor. If you prefer, you may base your answers to the questions on the experiences of a friend or relative.

Think back to your opinion about your physical appearance when you were in the eighth or ninth grade—when you were 14 or 15 years old.

1. What did you consider your "best feature"?

2. What did others (such as your parents) tell you was your "best feature"?

3. What did you consider your "worst feature"—the aspect of your appearance that you felt required the most care or upgrading?

4. Compared to your classmates and friends, were you an average-maturing, early-maturing, or late-maturing individual? What impact do you feel the timing of your puberty had on you at the time? What impact has it had on who you are today?

5. Do the ideas you had about your physical appearance at age 14 or 15 reflect your current body image? Why or why not (or to what extent)?

LESSON GUIDELINES

Audio Question Guidelines

1. The term **puberty** refers to the set of biological changes that occur at the start of adolescence and result in sexual maturity.

   Although infants have high levels of sex hormones, an unknown biological switch lowers the hormone level by the age of 2 and slows children's sexual development.

   At about the age of 9 in girls and 10 in boys, the **pituitary gland** in the brain releases hormones that affect the ovaries in girls and the testes in boys. In response, the ovaries and testes release sex hormones, and a year or so later the first outward signs of sexual maturation appear.

   In girls, the development of breast buds and pubic hair is followed by a **growth spurt**, in which fat is deposited on the hips and buttocks; by the first menstrual period; and finally, by **ovulation**—the release of the first egg.

   In boys, the normal sequence of events at puberty is nearly the reverse: First, the sex organs grow larger and pubic hair appears; followed by the first **ejaculation** of semen; then the growth spurt; and, finally, a lowering of the voice and appearance of facial hair.

2. Although girls start the sequence of puberty a year or so earlier than boys, both sexes become fertile at about the same time.

   Some anthropologists believe that puberty occurs earlier today than in previous eras because of the high fat and sugar levels in our diets.

   Other experts see the biological clock as being shaped by social needs. According to this view, early in human history, females who developed a mature appearance early in life, prior to their becoming fertile, may have had more opportunities to practice the various skills needed to take on the soon-to-be-attained social role of adult. Females who followed this growth pattern may have been more successful in having babies and rearing more of those babies to adulthood. In this way, the timing of the female pubertal sequence may have become coded into their biological clocks.

   In boys, according to this viewpoint, early development of the physical characteristics of stature, muscles, facial hair, and a deep voice, prior to their becoming fertile, might have been dangerous. If boys looked like men before they were fertile, they might have been perceived as competitors by older men. Such individuals would probably have been less successful reproductively, leading to the coding of mature appearance late in the pubertal sequence of boys' biological clocks.

3. The adolescents who have the most difficult time with puberty are early-maturing girls and late-maturing boys.

   Early-maturing girls are often teased and may suffer a loss of self-esteem.

   Early-maturing girls may be drawn into an older peer group and be more likely to engage in problem behavior, such as drinking, drug use, and early sexual activity.

   Late-maturing boys are at a disadvantage because, being smaller and less muscular, they tend to be less competitive at sports—the ticket to popularity for boys in most junior and senior high schools. This may have a continuing negative impact on the late-maturing boy's self-image.

Textbook Question Answers

1. puberty; three or four years; sequence

   Girls: onset of breast growth, initial pubic hair, peak growth spurt, widening of the hips, first menstrual period, completion of pubic-hair growth, and final breast development

   Boys: growth of the testes, initial pubic hair, growth of the penis, first ejaculation, peak growth spurt, voice deepening, beard development, and completion of pubic-hair growth

2. hypothalamus; pituitary gland; adrenal glands; gonads (sex glands); testes; ovaries; HPA axis; primary; secondary
3. GnRH (gonadotropin-releasing hormone); estrogen; testosterone
4. testosterone; estrogen; usually do; testosterone; indirectly; visible signs; sexual maturation
5. highly variable
6. 8; 14
7. menarche; 9; 15; 12
8. mothers; daughters
9. earlier
10. fat
11. malnutrition
12. stress
13. accelerate
14. puberty; conflicted relationships within the family; an unrelated man living in the home
15. reproductive success
16. early

Early-maturing girls may be teased about their big feet or developing breasts. Those who date early may begin "adult" activities at an earlier age, may be pressured by their dates to be sexually active, and may suffer a decrease in self-esteem.

17. late

Late-maturing boys who are short and skinny and who are not athletic are likely to be shunned by girls. They tend to be academically successful. However, the timing of puberty is not so crucial for boys as for girls.

18. growth; extremities; core; gain

19. fat

20. sex; heredity; diet; exercise

21. females

22. muscle; upper

23. lungs; heart; decreases; increases; endurance

24. lymphoid; less

The fact that the more visible spurts of weight and height precede the less visible ones of the muscles and organs means that athletic training and weight lifting should match the young person's size of a year or so earlier.

25. circadian; oil; sweat; odor

26. primary sex characteristics; is

Girls: growth of ovaries and uterus and thickening of the vaginal lining

Boys: growth of testes and lengthening of penis; also scrotum enlarges and becomes pendulous

27. menarche; spermarche; several years later

28. secondary sex characteristics

Males grow taller than females and become wider at the shoulders than at the hips. Females take on more fat all over and become wider at the hips, and their breasts begin to develop. About 65 percent of boys experience some temporary breast enlargement. As the lungs and larynx grow, the adolescent's voice (especially in boys) becomes lower. Head and body hair become coarser and darker in both sexes. Facial hair (especially in boys) begins to grow.

29. breast development; facial and body hair

30. flu; colds; earaches; childhood diseases; less common; rare; violence; injury

31. calories; vitamins; minerals; calcium; iron; zinc; milk; calcium

32. few; salt; sugar; fat

33. iron; iron-deficiency anemia

34. body image; fat; weak; anorexia; bulimia nervosa; drug use

35. earlier; later; 14; before they graduate from high school

36. sexually transmitted infections; gonorrhea; genital herpes; syphilis; chlamydia

37. a. is already infected with other STIs

     b. has more than one sexual partner within a year

     c. does not use condoms during intercourse

38. pregnancy; spontaneous abortion, high blood pressure, stillbirth, cesarean section, and a low-birthweight baby; educational; personal; prenatal; birth; low birthweight; brain damage

39. sexual abuse; child sexual abuse

40. repeated; adult–child relationships; coercive; peers

41. childhood; fathers or stepfathers; puberty

42. 30 to 50 percent; adolescent boys who had been abused themselves

43. sexual abuse

44. abuse; addictive; use

45. gateway drugs; sex; failure; violence

46. growth rate

47. inhibitions; judgment; memory; self-control; hippocampus; prefrontal cortex

48. slows; memory; abstract

49. half; alcohol

50. peers; community; culture

51. no more

52. a. active, problem-solving style of coping

     b. competence and well-being

     c. cognitive maturity

Answers to Testing Yourself

1. **c.** is the answer. Although pubertal changes begin a year earlier for girls than for boys, fertility occurs near the end of the sequence in girls and near the beginning of the sequence in boys. (audio program)

2. **a.** is the answer. For the past 100 years or so, each generation has experienced puberty at an earlier age than the preceding generation. (audio program)

3. **d.** is the answer. All of these are true according to the evolutionary perspective discussed in the program. (audio program)

4. **d.** is the answer. Late-maturing boys generally do catch up physically within a relatively short period of time. (audio program)

5. **a.** is the answer. (textbook, p. 341)

6. **a.** is the answer. (textbook, p. 347)

     b. Girls gain more body fat than boys do.

c. & d. The text does not indicate that these are different for boys and girls.

7. **a.** is the answer. (textbook, p. 341)

8. **c.** is the answer. This is because each menstrual period depletes some iron from the body. (textbook, p. 351)

9. **a.** is the answer. (textbook, p. 342)

   b. This describes the gonads.

   c. These include estrogen and testosterone.

   d. This is the hypothalamus.

10. **b.** is the answer. (textbook, p. 341)

11. **b.** is the answer. (textbook, p. 345)

12. **d.** is the answer. (textbook, p. 342)

13. **c.** is the answer. (textbook, p. 351)

   a. Although some adolescents become over-weight, many diet and lose weight in an effort to attain a desired body image.

   d. On the contrary, cultural attitudes about beauty are an extremely influential factor in the formation of a teenager's body image.

14. **b.** is the answer. (textbook, p. 342)

15. **b.** is the answer. (textbook, p. 354)

16. **c.** is the answer. (textbook, p. 346)

17. **c.** is the answer. (textbook, p. 341)

18. **b.** is the answer. (textbook, p. 355)

19. **a.** is the answer. (textbook, p. 354)

   b. This was not discussed in the text.

   c. This is true of girls.

20. **b.** is the answer. (textbook, pp. 350–351)

21. **c.** is the answer. (textbook, p. 349)

   a. Although not a term used in the textbook, a gender-typed trait is one that is typical of one sex but not of the other.

   b. Primary sex characteristics are those involving the reproductive organs.

   d. This is not a term used by developmental psychologists.

22. **b.** is the answer. Although the size of the heart increases during puberty, heart rate *decreases*. (textbook, p. 347)

23. **d.** is the answer. (textbook, p. 347)

Adolescence: Cognitive Development

AUDIO PROGRAM: **All Things Possible**

ORIENTATION

Lesson 14 explored the biosocial changes that transform children into adolescents, giving them adult size, shape, and reproductive capacity. But equally important psychological and social changes occur during this sometimes tumultuous season. Lesson 15, which focuses on cognitive development, is the second of a three-lesson unit on adolescent development.

As explained in the first section of Chapter 15 of *The Developing Person Through the Life Span*, 6/e, during adolescence, young people become increasingly able to speculate, hypothesize, and use logic. Unlike younger children, whose thinking is tied to **concrete operations**, adolescents with the ability to think in terms of formal operations are able to consider possibilities as well as reality. Even those who reach the stage of formal operational thought spend much of their time thinking at less advanced levels. The discussion of adolescent egocentrism supports this generalization in showing that adolescents have difficulty thinking rationally about themselves and their immediate experiences. Adolescent egocentrism makes them see themselves as psychologically unique and more socially significant than they really are.

The second section explores the adolescent decision-making process in relation to school, jobs, sex, and risk taking in general. The discussion relates choices made by adolescents to their cognitive abilities and typical shortcomings. As adolescents enter secondary school, their grades often suffer and their level of participation decreases. The rigid behavioral demands and intensified competition of most secondary schools do not, unfortunately, provide a supportive learning environment for adolescents.

Adolescent thinking has its limitations, however. As psychologist David Elkind notes in audio program 15, "All Things Possible," adolescents often create for themselves an **imaginary audience** and a **personal fable**, as they fantasize about how they appear to others, imagine their own lives as heroic, and feel that they are immune to danger.

The audio program also explores a new theory of intelligence proposed by psychologist Robert Sternberg. Professor Sternberg believes that **practical intelligence** reflects an ability to function effectively in everyday life. The emergence of practical intelligence may help adolescents to develop a more realistic picture of who they are.

Perhaps most significantly, the logical, idealistic, and egocentric thinking of adolescence represents a significant step in the process of creating a life story. Such is the view of psychologist Dan McAdams, who sees this season as a time when individuals begin to define that which makes them unique. As discussed in the audio program and in Chapter 16 of the textbook, Erik Erikson views adolescence as a time when young people struggle to form an **identity**. As they do, they create a background of ideology and write the first draft of their own life stories.

LESSON GOALS

By the end of this lesson you should be prepared to:

1. Describe the cognitive abilities of the typical adolescent.

2. Discuss adolescent egocentrism and the significance of adolescent thinking in the formation of identity and the process of creating a life story.

3. Evaluate the typical secondary school's ability to meet the cognitive needs of the typical adolescent.

4. Discuss the typical adolescent's inability to make major life decisions.

5. Explain how adolescent thinking contributes to adolescent pregnancy and sexually transmitted disease.

Audio Assignment

Listen to the audio tape that accompanies Lesson 15: "All Things Possible."

Write answers to the following questions. You may replay portions of the program if you need to refresh your memory. Answer guidelines may be found in the Lesson Guidelines section at the end of this chapter.

1. Explain how the development of formal operational thinking influences adolescents' attitudes toward family and society.

2. Compare and contrast formal operational thought with practical intelligence.

3. Discuss the significance of the imaginary audience and personal fable in the adolescent's formation of identity and creation of a life story.

Textbook Assignment

Read Chapter 15: "Adolescence: Cognitive Development," pages 363–383 in *The Developing Person Through the Life Span*, 6/e, then work through the material that follows to review it. Complete the sentences and answer the questions. As you proceed, evaluate your performance for each section by consulting the answers on page 185. Do not continue with the next section until you understand each answer. If you need to, review or reread the appropriate section in the textbook before continuing.

Intellectual Advances (pp. 363–372)

1. Adolescent thinking advances in three ways: basic _____ _____

continue to develop, _____

emerges, and _____ thinking becomes quicker and more compelling. The basic skills of thinking, learning, and remembering that advance during the school-age years _____ (continue to progress/stabilize) during adolescence.

2. Advances in _____ _____ improve concentration, while a growing _____ _____ and memory skills allow teens to connect new ideas to old ones, and strengthened _____ help them become better students. Brain maturation _____ (is complete/continues).

3. Reaction time _____ (improves/slows) as a result of ongoing _____ , and the brain's _____ _____ becomes more densely packed. This latter development results in significant advances in the _____ _____ of the brain.

4. Improvements in language include a better understanding of the nuances of _____ and _____ choice, which makes _____- _____ more sophisticated.

5. Piaget's term for the fourth stage of cognitive development is _____ _____ thought. Other theorists may explain adolescent advances differently, but virtually all theorists agree that adolescent thought _____ (is/is not) qualitatively different from children's thought.

6. (Thinking Like a Scientist) Piaget devised a number of famous tasks involving _____ principles to study how children of various ages reasoned hypothetically and deductively.

(Thinking Like a Scientist) Briefly describe how children reason differently about the "balance beam" problem at ages 7, 10, and 13.

7. The kind of thinking in which adolescents consider unproven possibilities that are logical but not necessarily real is called _____-_____ thinking.

8. During adolescence, they become more capable of _____ reasoning—that is, they can begin with a general _____ or _____ and draw logical _____ from it. This type of reasoning is a hallmark of formal operational thought.

9. They also make great strides in _____ (inductive/deductive) reasoning.

10. In addition to advances in the formal, logical, _____-_____ thinking described by Piaget, adolescents advance in their _____ cognition.

11. Theorists refer to hypothetical-deductive reasoning as _____ thought. The second mode of thinking, which begins with a prior _____, is called _____. The brain pathways that enable these two types of thinking are variously called _____ _____.

12. The adolescent's belief that he or she is uniquely significant and that the social world revolves around him or her is a psychological phenomenon called _____ _____.

13. An adolescent's tendency to feel that he or she is somehow immune to the consequences of dangerous or illegal behavior is expressed in the _____ _____.

14. An adolescent's tendency to imagine that her or his own life is unique, heroic, or even legendary, and that she or he is destined for great accomplishments, is expressed in the _____ _____.

15. Adolescents, who believe that they are under constant scrutiny from nearly everyone, create for themselves an _____ _____.

16. Although intuitive thinking generally is _____ and _____, it is also often _____.

17. Together, the _____ thinking that is used in school and the _____ thinking used in one's personal life create a type of _____ _____.

Adolescent Decision Making (pp. 372–382)

18. Adults try to protect teenagers from poor judgment for three reasons:

    a. _____
       _____

    b. _____
       _____

    c. _____
       _____

Cite several benefits of graduating from high school.

19. Instead of there being a good fit between adolescents' needs and the schools, there is often a _____ _____.

20. Compared to elementary schools, most secondary schools feature _____ _____, rigid _____ _____, and _____ _____ that do not meet adolescents' needs.

21. Internationally, education systems vary in _____, _____, and average _____ _____.

22. In general, teenagers in the United States work _____ (more/less) and learn _____ (more/less) than teenagers elsewhere. Attitudes regarding after-school jobs _____ (vary/do not vary) from country to country.

23. In some nations, such as _____ , almost no adolescent is employed or even does significant chores at home. In many _____ countries, many older adolescents have jobs as part of their school curriculum. Most parents in the United States _____ (approve/do not approve) of youth employment.

24. Perhaps because many of today's jobs for adolescents are not _____ , research finds that when adolescents are employed more than _____ hours a week, their grades suffer.

25. The teen birth rate is _____ (increasing/decreasing) since the 1980s. In the United States, this trend has occurred in _____ (every/most) ethnic and age group, but most dramatically among _____-_____ . At the same time, condom use has _____ (increased/decreased).

26. Sexual activity among adolescents _____ (is/is not) more diverse than it was 10 years ago.

27. Most secondary schools _____ (provide/do not provide) sex education.

Testing Yourself

After you have completed the audio and text review questions, see how well you do on the following quiz. Correct answers, with text and audio references, may be found at the end of this chapter.

1. Many psychologists consider the distinguishing feature of adolescent thought to be the ability to think in terms of:
   a. moral issues.
   b. concrete operations.
   c. possibility, not just reality.
   d. logical principles.

2. The imaginary audience refers to:
   a. the concrete operational child's preoccupation with performing for everyone, including toys and imaginary people.
   b. the adolescent's fear of being spied on.
   c. the ability of adolescents to empathize with others by putting themselves in their shoes.
   d. the egocentric fantasy of adolescents that their behavior and appearance are constantly being monitored by others.

3. According to Piaget, the final stage of cognitive development is that of:
   a. concrete operations.
   b. practical intelligence.
   c. formal operations.
   d. postformal operations.

4. A chief executive officer of a major company who does poorly on standardized intelligence tests, yet is very successful professionally, would probably be described by Robert Sternberg as possessing considerable:
   a. practical intelligence.
   b. fluid intelligence.
   c. crystallized intelligence.
   d. egocentrism.

5. The personal fable refers to adolescents imagining that:
   a. they are immune to the dangers of risky behaviors.
   b. they are always being scrutinized by others.
   c. their own lives are unique, heroic, or even legendary.
   d. the world revolves around their actions.

6. Analytic thinking is to _____ thinking as emotional force is to _____ thinking.
   a. intuitive; egocentric
   b. egocentric; intuitive
   c. formal; intuitive
   d. intuitive; formal

7. Teenagers need protection from poor judgment because:
   a. they are particularly likely to overrate the joys of the moment.
   b. adolescent choices can be long-lasting.
   c. the younger a person is, the more serious are the consequences of risk taking.
   d. of all of the above reasons.

8. Advances in metacognition deepen adolescents' abilities in:
   a. studying.
   b. the invincibility fable.
   c. the personal fable.
   d. adolescent egocentrism.

9. The adolescent who takes risks and feels immune to the laws of mortality is showing evidence of the:
   a. invincibility fable.
   c. imaginary audience.
   b. personal fable.
   d. death instinct.

10. Imaginary audiences, invincibility fables, and personal fables are expressions of adolescent:
    a. morality.
    c. decision making.
    b. thinking games.
    d. egocentrism.

11. The typical adolescent is:
    a. tough-minded.
    b. indifferent to public opinion.
    c. self-absorbed and hypersensitive to criticism.
    d. all of the above.

12. When adolescents enter secondary school, many:
    a. experience a drop in their academic performance.
    b. are less motivated than they were in elementary school.
    c. are less conscientious than they were in elementary school.
    d. experience all of the above.

13. During adolescence, which area of the brain becomes more densely packed and efficient, enabling adolescents to analyze possibilities and to pursue goals more effectively?
    a. hypothalamus
    b. brain stem
    c. adrenal glands
    d. prefrontal cortex

14. Thinking that begins with a general premise and then draws logical conclusions from it is called:
    a. inductive reasoning.
    b. deductive reasoning.
    c. intuitive thinking.
    d. hypothetical reasoning.

15. Serious reflection on important issues is a wrenching process for many adolescents because of their newfound ability to reason:
    a. inductively.
    c. hypothetically.
    b. deductively.
    d. symbolically.

16. Hypothetical-deductive thinking is to heuristic thinking as:
    a. rational analysis is to intuitive thought.
    b. intuitive thought is to rational analysis.
    c. experiential thinking is to intuitive reasoning.
    d. intuitive thinking is to analytical reasoning.

17. Many adolescents seem to believe that *their* love-making will not lead to pregnancy. This belief is an expression of the:
    a. personal fable.
    c. imaginary audience.
    b. invincibility fable.
    d. "game of thinking."

18. A parent in which of the following countries is *least* likely to approve of her daughter's request to take a part-time job after school?
    a. the United States
    c. Great Britain
    b. Germany
    d. Japan

19. Sex education classes today tend to:
    a. focus on practice with emotional expression and social interaction.
    b. be based on scare tactics designed to discourage sexual activity.
    c. be more dependent upon bringing the parents and other authoritative caregivers into the education process.
    d. have changed in all of the above ways.

20. To estimate the risk of a behavior, such as unprotected sexual intercourse, it is most important that the adolescent be able to think clearly about:
    a. universal ethical principles.
    b. personal beliefs and self-interest.
    c. future consequences.
    d. peer pressure.

21. Adolescents who fall prey to the invincibility fable may be more likely to:
    a. engage in risky behaviors.
    b. suffer from depression.
    c. have low self-esteem.
    d. drop out of school.

22. Research has shown that adolescents who work at after-school jobs more than 20 hours per week:
    a. are more likely to use drugs as adults.
    b. have lower grades.
    c. are more likely to engage in unprotected sex.
    d. have all of the above characteristics.

23. To avoid a volatile mismatch, a school should:
    a. focus on cooperative rather than competitive learning.
    b. base grading on individual test performance.
    c. establish the same goals for every student.
    d. vary its settings and approach according to children's developmental stages and cognition.

LESSON 15: LOGICAL VERSUS PRACTICAL INTELLIGENCE

Exercise

During adolescence, **formal operational thought**—including **scientific reasoning**, logical construction of arguments, and critical thought—becomes possible. Piaget's finding that adolescents are more logical and systematic than preadolescents has been replicated in experiments many times. But not all problems encountered by adolescents and adults require thinking at this level. Also, while many adolescents and adults are capable of thinking logically, they do not always do so. Indeed, older adults often find that a formal approach to solving problems is unsatisfactory and oversimplified.

One theme of this lesson is that a new kind of **practical intelligence** begins to emerge during late adolescence and early adulthood. This type of thinking is more applicable to everyday situations than formal thought. It recognizes that for many problems there may be no single correct answer, and that "logical" answers are often impractical. Some researchers believe that this new way of thinking reflects the greater cognitive maturity of adults in reconciling formal thought with the reality of their lives. If this is true, measuring adult intelligence by the same standards used to assess the "pure" logic of the adolescent is clearly inappropriate.

To stimulate your own thinking about the difference between formal thought and practical intelligence, consider the following problems. After you have answered the questions, hand the completed exercise in to your instructor.

1. In audio program 12, several children were presented with a Piagetian conservation-of-area task. Five "houses" were arranged in different ways on two "meadows." In one arrangement, representing a town, the houses were placed in a single group in one corner of the meadow. In another, representing the country, the houses were scattered about the meadow. Children were asked whether the spatial arrangement of the houses would affect the amount of grass each house's residents needed to mow. Would there be more grass to cut in the "town" or in the "country"?

   a. What is the *logically* correct answer to this question?

   b. What *practical* reasons might lead one to think differently about this question?

2. A woman threatens to leave her drunkard husband if he comes home drunk one more time. One week later, he comes home drunk. What should the woman do?

    a. What is the *logical* answer to this question?

    b. What is a more *practical* answer to this problem, and why?

3. Consider the following domestic scene:

Downstairs, there are three rooms: the kitchen, the dining room, and the sitting room. The sitting room is in the front of the house, and the kitchen and dining room face onto the vegetable garden at the back of the house. The noise of the traffic is very disturbing in the front of the house. Mother is in the kitchen cooking and Grandfather is reading the paper in the sitting room. The children are at school and won't be home until tea time. Who is being disturbed by the traffic noise?*

    a. What is the *logical* answer to this question?

    b. What *practical* considerations might lead one to a different answer to this question?

---

*The example is from Cohen, G. (1979). Language and comprehension in old age. *Cognitive Psychology, 11*, pp. 412–429. One practical consideration suggested by psychologist Gisela Labouvie-Vief is Grandfather's hearing ability.
Labouvie-Vief, G. (1985). Intelligence and cognition. In J. E. Birren & K. W. Schaie (Eds.), *Handbook of the psychology of aging* (2nd ed., pp. 500–530). New York: Van Nostrand.

4. Describe or create a "real-life" problem in which the logical answer may differ from a practical answer.

    a. State the problem.

    b. State the *logical* answer.

    c. State a *practical* answer that differs from the logical answer.

LESSON GUIDELINES

Audio Question Guidelines

1. The development of **formal operational thought** enables adolescents to move beyond the concrete operational world of "here and now" to a world of possibility, where abstract, logical, and scientific thinking becomes typical.

   Because they are able to speculate about possibilities, adolescents often think about ideal parents and an ideal society. This idealism may cause some teenagers to become dissatisfied with their present situation and want to change it. Adolescents are also able to imagine ideal mates, and so they are susceptible to "crushes."

2. Formal operational thought is hypothetical, logical, and abstract. This kind of thinking is emphasized by schools and teachers.

   According to Robert Sternberg, most of the everyday problems people face do not have clear correct or incorrect solutions that can be arrived at by using formal operational thinking.

   In addition to academic intelligence, a valuable kind of thinking that educators generally overlook is **practical intelligence**. This is the ability to adapt, shape, and select real-world environments. It represents an ability to function effectively in the everyday world.

   Many people who have relatively low scores on standardized tests of academic intelligence may nevertheless be very successful in careers in which practical intelligence is especially useful.

3. According to David Elkind, **adolescent egocentrism**, which is different from childhood egocentrism, leads young people to see themselves as being much more central to their social world than they really are. Adolescents often create an **imaginary audience** for themselves and fantasize about how others will react to their appearance and behavior.

   Egocentrism may also lead adolescents to develop their own **personal fable**, in which they imagine their lives as heroic or destined for fame and fortune, and an **invincibility fable**, in which they see themselves as immune to dangers.

   These cognitive tendencies prepare the way for the process of forming a life story. Through them the teenager begins to define how he or she is different from others, which leads to the formation of an **identity**. Over time, the early fantasies and fables become more realistic. The older adoles-

cent develops a belief and value system that serves as an **ideological** background for his or her life story.

Textbook Question Answers

1. cognitive skills; logic; intuitive; continue to progress

2. selective attention; knowledge base; metacognition; continues

3. improves; myelination; prefrontal cortex; executive functions

4. grammar; vocabulary; code-switching

5. formal operational; is

6. scientific

Preschoolers have no understanding of how to solve the problem. By age 7, children understand balancing the weights but don't know that distance from the center is also a factor. By age 10, they understand the concepts but are unable to coordinate them. By ages 13 or 14, they are able to solve the problem.

7. hypothetical-deductive

8. deductive; premise; theory; conclusions

9. inductive

10. hypothetical-deductive; intuitive

11. analytic; belief or assumption; intuitive (or heuristic or experiential); conscious/unconscious, explicit/implicit; factual/creative

12. adolescent egocentrism

13. invincibility fable

14. personal fable

15. imaginary audience

16. quick; emotional; wrong

17. analytic; experiential; cognitive economy

18. **a.** The consequences of risk taking are more serious the younger a person is

    b. Adolescent choices are long-lasting

    c. Adolescents overrate the joys of the moment and ignore future costs

High school graduates stay healthier, live longer, are richer, and are more likely to marry, vote, stay out of jail, and buy homes than their less educated contemporaries.

19. volatile mismatch

20. intensified competition; behavioral demands; academic standards

21. expectations; curriculum; class size

22. more; less; vary
23. Japan; European; approve
24. meaningful; 20
25. decreasing; every; African-Americans; increased
26. is
27. provide

Answers to Testing Yourself

1. **c.** is the answer. (audio program; textbook, p. 366)

    a. Although moral reasoning becomes much deeper during adolescence, it is not limited to this stage of development.

    b. & d. Concrete operational thought, which *is* logical, is the distinguishing feature of childhood thinking.

2. **d.** is the answer. The imaginary audience is an especially vivid expression of adolescent egocentrism. (audio program; textbook, p. 368)

3. **c.** is the answer. (audio program; textbook, p. 364)

4. **a.** is the answer. Practical intelligence is the ability to function effectively in the everyday world. (audio program)

5. **c.** is the answer. (audio program; textbook, p. 368)

    a. This describes the invincibility fable.

    b. This describes the imaginary audience.

    d. This describes adolescent egocentrism in general.

6. **c.** is the answer. (textbook, p. 367)

7. **d.** is the answer. (textbook, p. 372)

8. **a.** is the answer. (textbook, p. 363)

    b., c., & d. These are examples of limited reasoning ability during adolescence.

9. **a.** is the answer. (textbook, p. 368)

    b. This refers to adolescents' tendency to imagine their own lives as unique, heroic, or even mythical.

    c. This refers to adolescents' tendency to fantasize about how others will react to their appearance and behavior.

    d. This is a concept in Freud's theory.

10. **d.** is the answer. These thought processes are manifestations of adolescents' tendency to see themselves as being much more central and important to the social scene than they really are. (textbook, p. 368)

11. **c.** is the answer. (textbook, p. 363)

12. **d.** is the answer. (textbook, p. 375)

13. **d.** is the answer. (textbook, p. 364)

    a., b., & c. These "lower" brain centers and endocrine glands, which are not involved in conscious reasoning, control hunger and thirst (hypothalamus); sleep and arousal (brainstem); and the production of stress hormones (adrenal glands).

14. **b.** is the answer. (textbook, p. 366)

    a. Inductive reasoning moves from specific facts to a general conclusion.

    c. By its very nature, intuitive thinking does not move logically either from a general conclusion to specific facts or from specific facts to a general conclusion.

    d. Hypothetical reasoning involves thinking about possibilities rather than facts.

15. **c.** is the answer. (textbook, p. 366)

16. **a.** is the answer. (textbook, p. 367)

    c. Heuristic thinking is both experiential *and* intuitive.

17. **b.** is the answer. (textbook, p. 368)

    a. This refers to adolescents' tendency to imagine their own lives as unique, heroic, or even mythical.

    c. This refers to adolescents' tendency to fantasize about how others will react to their appearance and behavior.

    d. This is the adolescent ability to suspend knowledge of reality in order to think playfully about possibilities.

18. **d.** is the answer. Japanese adolescents almost never work after school. (textbook, p. 376)

    a. American parents generally approve of adolescent employment.

    b. & c. Jobs are an important part of the school curriculum in many European countries.

19. 14. **a.** is the answer. (textbook, pp. 378–379)

    b. Scare tactics were often a central feature of earlier sex education classes.

    c. Generally speaking, parents are not effective sex educators.

20. **c.** is the answer. (textbook, pp. 372–373)

21. **a.** is the answer. (textbook, p. 368)

b., c., & d. The invincibility fable leads some teens to believe that they are immune to the dangers of risky behaviors; it is not necessarily linked to depression, low self-esteem, or the likelihood that an individual will drop out of school.

22. d. is the answer. (textbook, p. 377)

23. d. is the answer. (textbook, pp. 373, 376)

Adolescence: Psychosocial Development

AUDIO PROGRAM: Second Chances

ORIENTATION

As discussed in Lessons 14 and 15, the biosocial changes of adolescence transform the child's body into that of an adult, while the cognitive changes enable the young person to think logically and more practically. These changes set the stage for psychosocial development, which is the subject of Lesson 16.

According to Erik Erikson, adolescence brings the dawning of commitment to a personal **identity** and future, to other people, and to ideologies (see also Lesson 15). Friends, family, community, and culture are powerful social forces that act to help or hinder the adolescent's transition from childhood to adulthood.

Chapter 16 of *The Developing Person Through the Life Span,* 6/e, focuses on the adolescent's psychosocial development, particularly the formation of **identity,** which is required for the attainment of adult status and maturity. Depression, self-destruction, and suicide—the most perplexing problems of adolescence—are then explored. The special problems posed by adolescent lawbreaking are discussed, and suggestions for alleviating or treating these problems are given. The final section examines the influences of family and friends on adolescent psychosocial development, including the development of romantic relationships. The chapter concludes with the message that although no other period of life is characterized by so many changes in the three domains of development, for most young people the teenage years are happy ones. Furthermore, serious problems in adolescence do not necessarily lead to lifelong problems.

Audio program 16, "Second Chances," examines the psychosocial challenges of adolescence, emphasizing the particular vulnerability of today's teenagers. This vulnerability is dramatically illustrated by the stories of two teenage "casualties." Although Valerie and Tony have troubled beginnings, both teenagers were afforded "second chances" and seem to be taking advantage of them.

While many of today's teenagers are visibly damaged by the problems of this tumultuous season, the image of the troubled adolescent as irretrievable is not accurate. Through the expert commentary of psychologists Ruby Takanishi and Richard Jessor, we discover that although peer group pressure is often the initial trigger for problem behaviors in adolescence, the socializing role of peers has many potentially positive effects—in particular, peers facilitate identity formation, independence, and the development of social skills that help the young person eventually attain adult status and maturity.

As adolescents forge an identity and attempt to make wise choices about the future, their social context encourages some paths to identity and forecloses others. The result of this interaction will be, in the ideal case, young people who are sure of themselves and are able to pass through these vulnerable years of adolescence successfully.

LESSON GOALS

By the end of this lesson you should be prepared to:

1. Describe the development of identity during adolescence, focusing on four identity statuses.

2. Discuss adolescent suicide, noting its incidence and prevalence, contributing factors, warning signs, and gender, ethnic, and national variations.

3. Discuss delinquency among adolescents today, noting its prevalence, significance for later development, and best approaches for prevention or treatment.

4. Discuss parental influence on identity formation, including the effect of parent–adolescent conflict and other aspects of family functioning.

5. Discuss the constructive functions of peer relationships and close friendships during adolescence.

Audio Assignment

Listen to the audio tape that accompanies Lesson 16: "Second Chances."

Write answers to the following questions. You may replay portions of the program if you need to refresh your memory. Answer guidelines can be found in the Lesson Guidelines section at the end of this chapter.

1. Explain why early adolescence is considered a period of particular vulnerability for young people today.

2. Discuss the issue of retrievability in adolescence and who is most likely to receive a "second chance."

3. Identify and explain the kinds of interventions that have helped adolescents take advantage of such second chances.

Textbook Assignment

Read Chapter 16: "Adolescence: Psychosocial Development," pages 385–408 in *The Developing Person Through the Life Span*, 6/e, then work through the material that follows to review it. Complete the sentences and answer the questions. As you proceed, evaluate your performance for each section by con-

sulting the answers on page 197. Do not continue with the next section until you understand each answer. If you need to, review or reread the appropriate section in the textbook before continuing.

The Self and Identity (pp. 385–391)

1. The momentous changes that occur during the teen years challenge adolescents to find their own _____ . In this process, many adolescents experience _____ _____ , or various fantasies about what their futures might be if one or another course of action is followed.

2. Adolescents may take on a _____ _____ ; that is, they act in ways they know to be contrary to their true nature. Three variations on this identity status are the

_____ _____ _____ , the _____ _____ _____ , and the _____ _____ _____ .

3. According to Erikson, the challenge of adolescence is _____ _____ _____ _____ .

4. The ultimate goal of adolescence is to establish a new identity that involves both repudiation and assimilation of childhood values; this is called

_____ _____ .

5. The young person who prematurely accepts earlier roles and parental values without exploring alternatives or truly forging a unique identity is experiencing identity _____ .

6. An adolescent who adopts an identity that is the opposite of the one he or she is expected to adopt has taken on a _____

_____ .

7. The young person who has few commitments to goals or values and is apathetic about defining his or her identity is experiencing

_____ _____ .

8. A time-out period during which a young person experiments with different identities, postponing important choices, is called an identity _____ . An obvious institutional example of this in the United States is attending _____ .

9. The psychologist who developed a set of questions to measure identity statuses is _____ _____ .

   Generally speaking, developmentalists are more interested in ongoing identity _____ than in _____ .

10. People _____ (can/generally cannot) achieve identity in one domain and still be searching for their identity in another. Identity is formed both from _____ , as when a person recognizes his or her true nature, and from _____ , in response to _____ forces.

11. A person's identification as either male or female is called _____ _____ . This includes accepting all the _____ and _____ that society assigns to that biological category.

12. Gender identity and _____ identity are often connected because male and female roles are defined differently by different _____ .

13. In general, ethnic identity becomes more important when adolescents see their background as _____ .

    Today, about _____ percent of all teenagers are not of European descent.

Sadness and Anger (pp. 391–397)

14. Psychologists categorize emotional problems in two ways: _____ problems, which are directed inward and include _____ ; and _____ problems, which include _____ . Both types of problems _____ (increase gradually/increase suddenly/decrease gradually/decrease suddenly) at adolescence.

15. Cross-sequential research studies show that, from ages 6 to 18, people generally feel _____ (more/less) competent each year in most areas of their lives.

16. Clinical depression _____ (increases/decreases) at puberty, especially among _____ (males/females).

17. Thinking about committing suicide, called _____ _____ , is _____ (common/relatively rare) among high school students.

18. Adolescents under age 20 are _____ (more/less) likely to kill themselves than adults are.

19. Most suicide attempts in adolescence _____ (do/do not) result in death. A deliberate act of self-destruction that does not result in death is called a _____ .

20. List five factors that affect whether thinking about suicide leads to a self-destructive act or to death.

    a. _____

    b. _____

    c. _____

    d. _____

    e. _____

21. The rate of suicide is higher for adolescent _____ (males/females). The rate of parasuicide is higher for _____ (males/females).

22. Around the world, cultural differences in the rates of suicidal ideation and completion _____ (are/are not) apparent.

23. When a town or school sentimentalizes the "tragic end" of a teen suicide, the publicity can trigger _____ _____ .

(Table 16.3) Briefly describe ethnic differences in suicide rates in the United States.

Breaking the Law (pp. 512–516)

24. Psychologists influenced by the _____ perspective believe that adolescent rebellion and defiance are normal, particularly for adolescent _____ (boys/girls).

25. Arrests are far more likely to occur during the _____ _____ of life than during any other time period. Although statistics indicate that the _____ (incidence/prevalence) of arrests is highest among this age group, they do not reveal how widespread, or _____, lawbreaking is among this age group.

26. If all acts of "juvenile delinquency" are included, the prevalence of adolescent crime is _____ (less/greater) than official records report.

Briefly describe data on gender and ethnic differences in adolescent arrests.

27. The victims of crime tend to be _____ (teenagers/adults).

28. Experts find it useful to distinguish _____-_____ offenders, whose criminal activity stops by age 21, from _____-_____-_____ offenders, who become career criminals.

29. Developmentalists have found that it _____ (is/is not) currently possible to distinguish children who actually will become career criminals.

30. Adolescents who later become career criminals are among the first of their cohort to _____.

They also are among the least involved in _____ activities and tend to be _____ in preschool and elementary school. At an even earlier age, they show signs of _____ _____, such as being slow in _____ development, being _____, or having poor _____ control.

31. For most delinquents, residential incarceration in a prison or reform school usually _____ (is/is not) the best solution.

Family and Friends (pp. 397–406)

32. People who focus on differences between the younger and older generations speak of a _____ _____. An exception occurs when the parents grow up in a very different _____.

33. The idea that family members in different developmental stages have a natural tendency to see the family in different ways is called the _____ _____.

34. Parent–adolescent conflict is most common in _____ (early/late) adolescence and is particularly notable with _____ (mothers/fathers) and their _____ (early/late)-maturing _____ (sons/daughters). This conflict often involves _____, which refers to repeated, petty arguments about daily habits.

35. Among Chinese-, Korean-, and Mexican-American teens, conflict tends to arise in _____ (early/late) adolescence, possibly because these cultures encourage _____ in their children and emphasize family _____.

36. Four other elements of family functioning that have been heavily researched include _____, _____, _____, and _____.

37. In terms of family control, a powerful deterrent to delinquency, risky sex, and drug abuse is _____ _____.

Too much interference, however, may contribute to adolescent _____. Particularly harmful to teens are threats to withdraw love and support, or _____.

38. The largely constructive role of peers runs counter to the notion of _____
_____ . Social pressure to conform _____ (falls/rises) dramatically in early adolescence, until about age _____ , when it begins to _____ (fall/rise).

39. Adolescents whose parents are immigrants comprise a(n) _____ (increasing/decreasing) proportion of all teenagers in almost every nation of the world.

Briefly outline the four-stage progression of heterosexual involvement.

40. Cultural patterns _____ (affect/do not affect) the _____ and _____ of these stages, but the basic _____ seems to be based on _____ factors.

41. For gay and lesbian adolescents, added complications usually _____ (slow down/speed up) romantic attachments. In cultures that are _____ , many young men and women with homosexual or lesbian feelings may _____ their feelings or try to _____ or _____ them.

42. Most parents _____ (overestimate/underestimate) the significance of romantic relationships during adolescence.

Conclusion (pp. 406–407)

43. For most young people, the teenage years overall are _____ (happy/unhappy) ones.

44. Adolescents who have one serious problem _____ (often have/do not usually have) others.

45. In most cases, adolescent problems stem from earlier developmental events such as

_____ .

Testing Yourself

After you have completed the audio and text review questions, see how well you do on the following quiz. Correct answers, with text and audio references, may be found at the end of this chapter.

1. As discussed in the audio program, "retrievability" refers specifically to the:
   a. cognitive capacity of adolescents to remember their own internalized ideologies.
   b. ability of troubled adolescents to bounce back from problem behaviors and benefit from "second chances."
   c. influence of authoritarian parenting on adolescent identity formation.
   d. permanent mark left on identity by problem behaviors during adolescence.

2. According to Erikson, the primary task of adolescence is that of establishing:
   a. basic trust.   c. intimacy.
   b. an identity.   d. integrity.

3. According to developmentalists who study identity formation, foreclosure involves:
   a. accepting an identity prematurely, without exploration.
   b. taking time off from school, work, and other commitments.
   c. opposing parental values.
   d. failing to commit oneself to a vocational goal.

4. When adolescents adopt an identity that is the opposite of the one they are expected to adopt, they are considered to be taking on a:
   a. foreclosed identity.
   b. diffused identity.
   c. negative identity.
   d. reverse identity.

5. The main sources of emotional support for most young people who are establishing independence from their parents are:
   a. older adolescents of the opposite sex.
   b. older siblings.
   c. teachers.
   d. peer groups.

6. For members of minority ethnic groups, identity achievement may be particularly complicated because:
   a. their cultural ideal clashes with the Western emphasis on adolescent self-determination.
   b. peers, themselves torn by similar conflicts, can be very critical.
   c. parents and other relatives tend to emphasize ethnicity and expect teens to honor their roots.
   d. of all of the above reasons.

7. In a crime-ridden neighborhood, parents can protect their adolescents by keeping close watch over activities, friends, and so on. This practice is called:
   a. generational stake.
   b. foreclosure.
   c. peer screening.
   d. parental monitoring.

8. Conflict between adolescent girls and their mothers is most likely to involve:
   a. bickering over hair, neatness, and other daily habits.
   b. political, religious, and moral issues.
   c. peer relationships and friendships.
   d. relationships with boys.

9. If there is a "generation gap," it is likely to occur in _____ adolescence and to center on issues of _____ .
   a. early; morality
   b. late; self-discipline
   c. early; self-control
   d. late; politics

10. Which of the following best describes how identity is formed?
    a. It is almost always formed "from without" as social forces push a teenager to adopt a particular identity.
    b. Identity is a process of discovery.
    c. For most teens, identity is blindly accepted, as parents, culture, and other sociocultural factors create their impact.
    d. Identity is constructed from within, when a person recognizes his or her true nature, or from without, in response to social forces.

11. Fifteen-year-old Cindy, who has strong self-esteem and is trying out a new, artistic identity "just to see how it feels," is apparently exploring:
    a. an acceptable false self.
    b. a pleasing false self.
    c. an experimental false self.
    d. none of the above.

12. If the vast majority of cases of a certain crime are committed by a small number of repeat offenders, this would indicate that the crime's:
    a. incidence is less than its prevalence.
    b. incidence is greater than its prevalence.
    c. incidence and prevalence are about equal.
    d. incidence and prevalence are impossible to calculate.

13. Adolescents who adopt an acceptable false self:
    a. report greater self-understanding than those whose false self arises from a wish to impress others.
    b. report higher self-esteem than those whose false self arises from a wish to "see how it feels."
    c. tend to feel depressed and hopeless.
    d. have all of the above characteristics.

14. The early signs of life-course-persistent offenders include all of the following except:
    a. signs of brain damage early in life.
    b. antisocial school behavior.
    c. delayed sexual intimacy.
    d. use of alcohol and tobacco at an early age.

15. Regarding gender differences in self-destructive acts, the rate of parasuicide is _____ and the rate of suicide is _____ .
    a. higher in males; higher in females
    b. higher in females; higher in males
    c. the same in males and females; higher in males
    d. the same in males and females; higher in females

16. Conflict between parents and adolescent offspring is:
    a. most likely to involve fathers and their early-maturing offspring.
    b. more frequent in single-parent homes.
    c. more likely between early-maturing daughters and their mothers.
    d. likely in all of the above situations.

17. Thirteen-year-old Adam, who never has doubted his faith, identifies himself as an orthodox member of a particular religious group. A developmentalist would probably say that Adam's religious identity is:
    a. achieved.
    b. foreclosed.
    c. in moratorium.
    d. oppositional in nature.

18. Parent–teen conflict among Chinese-, Korean-, and Mexican-American families often surfaces late in adolescence because these cultures:
    a. emphasize family closeness.
    b. value authoritarian parenting.
    c. encourage autonomy in children.
    d. do all of the above.

19. Thinking about committing suicide is called:
    a. cluster suicide.
    b. parasuicide.
    c. suicidal ideation.
    d. fratracide.

20. Cross-sequential studies of individuals from ages 6 to 18 show that:
    a. children feel less competent each year in most areas of their lives.
    b. the general emotional trend in adolescence is more downward than upward.
    c. self-esteem generally begins to decrease at about age 12.
    d. all of the above are true.

21. Crime statistics show that during adolescence:
    a. males and females are equally likely to be arrested.
    b. males are more likely to be arrested than females.
    c. females are more likely to be arrested than males.
    d. males commit more crimes than females but are less likely to be arrested.

22. Which of the following is *not* true regarding the rate of clinical depression among adolescents?
    a. At puberty the rate more than doubles.
    b. It affects a higher proportion of teenage boys than girls.
    c. Genetic vulnerability is a predictor of teenage depression.
    d. The adolescent's school setting is a factor.

23. According to a review of studies from various nations, suicidal ideation is:
    a. not as common among high school students as is popularly believed.
    b. more common among males than females.
    c. more common among females than among males.
    d. so common among high school students that it might be considered normal.

NAME _____   INSTRUCTOR _____

LESSON 16: IDENTITY THROUGH THE SEASONS

Exercise

A central theme of the three-lesson unit on adolescence is that **identity** formation is a primary task of this season. Ideally, adolescents develop a clear picture of their unique standing in the larger social world to which they belong.

But the development of identity is not confined to one season of life. Like the life story itself, it continues to evolve over the life span. To help you apply this truth to your own life story, this exercise asks you to respond to the deceptively simple question, "Who am I?" You may respond in terms of your social roles, responsibilities, or commitments; the groups to which you belong; your beliefs and values; your personality traits and abilities; and your needs, feelings, and behavior patterns. List only things that are really important to you—things that, if lost, would make a real difference in your sense of who you are. Limit your answer to 10 definitions of your identity.

After you have completed your list, you are asked to consider each item separately and assign a number from 1 (most important) to 10 (least important) to each item, indicating its importance to your identity today. Then rank the items again, based on their importance to you 10 years ago. What differences do you see?

As always, you may ask someone else to answer the questions on this exercise. After you have finished, hand the completed exercise in to your instructor.

Part 1.
Following the instructions above, write ten answers to the question, "Who am I?" (See the next page for instructions regarding ranking, which is to be done *after* the list is complete.)

		Rank Today	**Rank Ten Years Ago**
1.	I am:	_____	_____
2.	I am:	_____	_____
3.	I am:	_____	_____
4.	I am:	_____	_____
5.	I am:	_____	_____

	Rank Today	Rank Ten Years Ago
6. I am:	_____	_____
7. I am:	_____	_____
8. I am:	_____	_____
9. I am:	_____	_____
10. I am:	_____	_____

My current age is: _____

Part 2.

After you have listed your answers, rank the importance of each to your identity today by assigning a number from 1 (most important) to 10 (least important) in the blank next to each item. Then do the same for your identity ten years ago. In the space below, briefly explain any changes you observed in your rankings. What makes the item ranked 1 each time the most important?

LESSON GUIDELINES

Audio Question Guidelines

1. The biological changes associated with puberty are occurring among young people today earlier than in the past. Society, however, has not adapted to this change. The result is a relatively long period of time during which young people are physically mature, yet socially denied the privileges and responsibilities of adults.

There is great diversity in biosocial development during early adolescence; some individuals continue to look like children, while others already resemble adults. This diversity is itself challenging for adolescents.

Today there may be greater opportunity in the adolescent environment for experimentation and risk taking. This includes pressure from peers to experiment with risky behaviors such as delinquent acts, early sexual activity, and use of alcohol and other drugs.

Compared to previous generations, adolescents today are exposed to much more lethal substances. This may account for the fact that the leading cause of death among young adolescents is accidents, often related to the diminished judgment that accompanies the use of drugs.

2. Approximately 75 percent of adolescents move through this season relatively easily; about 25 percent are at risk and do not make the transition as successfully.

For those in early or middle adolescence who come from disadvantaged backgrounds and have already begun to experiment with risky behaviors, opportunities for "second-chance" interventions are especially important.

Individuals who have been at risk need to perceive that they have a promising future economically and psychologically.

Many young people have reserves of resiliency that make them eminently "retrievable" from their disadvantaged beginnings. For young people who do not possess this inner tenacity, early provision of social programs may make a major difference.

3. Peer counseling may help adolescents to learn about the dangers of high-risk behaviors, develop independence and social skills, forge a clearer sense of **identity**, and promote self-esteem. It can be helpful both to those who give it and those who receive it.

Programs that link young people to consistent, caring adults have proven to be beneficial. So has the continuing involvement of parents.

Textbook Question Answers

1. identity; possible selves
2. false self; acceptable false self; pleasing false self; experimental false self
3. identity versus role confusion
4. identity achievement
5. foreclosure
6. negative identity
7. identity diffusion
8. moratorium; college
9. James Marcia; processes; statuses
10. can; within; without; social
11. gender identity; roles; behaviors
12. ethnic; cultures
13. more; negative; foreclose; different from that of others; 40
14. internalizing; depression, eating disorders, self-mutilation, overuse of sedative drugs, clinical depression, and suicide; externalizing; injuring others, destroying property, and defying authority; increase suddenly
15. less
16. increases; females
17. suicidal ideation; common
18. less
19. do not; parasuicide
20. a. the availability of lethal methods
    b. the extent of parental supervision
    c. the use of alcohol and other drugs
    d. gender
    e. the attitudes about suicide held by the adolescent's culture
21. males; females
22. are
23. cluster suicides

American Indian and Alaskan Native males have the highest rates, followed by European-American males, Hispanic-American and African-American males, American Indian females, Asian-American males, and so on.

24. psychoanalytic; boys
25. second decade; incidence; prevalent

26. greater

Adolescent males are three times as likely to be arrested as females, and African-American youth are three times as likely to be arrested as European-Americans, who are three times as likely to be arrested as Asian-Americans. However, confidential self-reports find much smaller gender and ethnic differences.

27. teenagers

28. adolescent-limited; life-course-persistent

29. is

30. have sex and use gateway drugs; school; antisocial; brain damage; language; hyperactive; emotional

31. is not

32. generation gap; place

33. generational stake

34. early; mothers; early; daughters; bickering

35. late; dependency; closeness

36. communication; support; connectedness; control

37. parental monitoring; depression; psychological control

38. peer pressure; rises; 14; fall

39. increasing

The progression begins with groups of same-sex friends. Next, a loose, public association of a girl's group and a boy's group forms. Then, a smaller, heterosexual group forms from the more advanced members of the larger association. Finally, more intimate heterosexual couples peel off.

40. affect; timing; manifestation; sequence; biological

41. slow down; homophobic; deny; change; conceal

42. underestimate

43. happy

44. often have

45. genetic vulnerability, prenatal injury, family disruptions and discord, learning difficulties, lack of emotional regulation in elementary school, inadequate community intervention

Answers to Testing Yourself

1. **b.** is the answer. A major theme of the audio program is that the image of the troubled adolescent as irretrievable is incorrect. (audio program)

2. **b.** is the answer. (textbook, p. 385)

    a. According to Erikson, this is the crisis of infancy.

c. & d. In Erikson's theory, these crises occur later in life.

3. **a.** is the answer. (textbook, p. 387)

    b. This describes an identity moratorium.

    c. This describes a negative identity.

    d. This describes identity diffusion.

4. **c.** is the answer. (textbook, p. 388)

5. **d.** is the answer. (textbook, p. 390)

6. **d.** is the answer. (textbook, p. 390)

7. **d.** is the answer. (textbook, p. 399)

    a. The generational stake refers to differences in how family members from different generations view the family.

    b. Foreclosure refers to the premature establishment of identity.

    c. Peer screening is an aspect of parental monitoring, but it was not specifically discussed in the text.

8. **a.** is the answer. (textbook, p. 398)

9. **c.** is the answer. (textbook, pp. 397–398)

10. **d.** is the answer. (textbook, p. 389)

11. **c.** is the answer. (tetxbook, p. 386)

    a. & b. Teenagers who try out these false selves tend to feel either worthless and depressed (acceptable false self) or experience the psychological consequences of living an identity just to impress or please others (pleasing false self).

12. **b.** is the answer. Incidence is how often a particular circumstance (such as lawbreaking) occurs; prevalence is how widespread the circumstance is. A crime that is committed by only a few repeat offenders is not very prevalent in the population. (textbook, p. 395)

13. **c.** is the answer. (textbook, p. 386)

14. **c.** is the answer. Most life-course persistent offenders are among the earliest of their cohort to have sex. (textbook, p. 396)

15. **b.** is the answer. (textbook, p. 394)

16. **c.** is the answer. (textbook, p. 398)

    a. In fact, parent-child conflict is more likely to involve mothers and their early-maturing offspring.

    b. The text did not compare the rate of conflict in two-parent and single-parent homes.

17. **b.** is the answer. Foreclosed members of a religious group have, like Adam, never really doubted. (textbook, pp. 388–389)

a. Because there is no evidence that Adam has asked the "hard questions" regarding his religious beliefs, a developmentalist would probably say that his religious identity is not achieved.

c. Adam clearly does have a religious identity.

d. There is no evidence that Adam's religious identity was formed in opposition to expectations.

18. **a.** is the answer. For this reason, autonomy in their offspring tends to be delayed. (textbook, p. 398)

19. **c.** is the answer. (textbook, p. 393)

20. **d.** is the answer. (textbook, pp. 391–392)

21. **b.** is the answer. (textbook, p. 396)

22. **b.** is the answer. (textbook, p. 392)

23. **d.** is the answer. (textbook, p. 393)

Early Adulthood: Biosocial Development

AUDIO PROGRAM: Seasons of Eros

ORIENTATION

This is the first of a three-lesson unit on development between the ages of 20 and 40, the period of early adulthood. Lesson 17 focuses on biosocial development during this season.

In terms of our overall health, these years are the prime of life. However, with the attainment of maturity, a new aspect of physical development comes into play—that is, decline. Chapter 17 of *The Developing Person Through the Life Span*, 6/e, takes a look at how people perceive changes that occur as the body ages as well as how decisions they make regarding lifestyle affect the course of their overall development. The chapter begins with a description of the growth, strength, and health of the individual during adulthood, as well as both visible age-related changes, such as wrinkling, and less obvious changes, such as declines in the efficiency of the body's systems. Sexual-reproductive health, a matter of great concern to young adults, is also discussed, with particular attention paid to trends in sexual responsiveness during adulthood and fertility problems that may develop. The second section looks at several emotional problems that are more prevalent during young adulthood than at any other period of the life span: destructive dieting, eating disorders, drug abuse and addiction, psychopathology, and violence.

Audio program 17, "Seasons of Eros," explores how the expressions and meanings of sexuality, or **eros**, change over the life span. In a round table discussion featuring psychologists Janice Gibson, David Gutmann, and June Reinisch, psychiatrists Robert Butler and Thomas Carli, and psychotherapist Laura Nitzberg, it becomes clear that eros is more than intercourse; it is a capacity for pleasure that pervades the entire body and reflects the particular developmental needs of each individual and each age. The emerging life-span perspective makes it clear that,

although its expressions and meanings may change, the life-giving force of eros manifests itself throughout the seasons of life.

LESSON GOALS

By the end of this lesson you should be prepared to:

1. Describe the changes in growth, strength, overall health, and physical appearance that occur during early adulthood.

2. Identify age-related trends in sexual responsiveness of women and men during early adulthod, the main causes of infertility in men and women, and techniques used to treat this problem.

3. Discuss the causes and consequences of repeated dieting during adulthood, and describe the typical victims of anorexia nervosa and bulimia nervosa, noting possible explanations for these disorders.

4. Discuss the causes and consequences of drug abuse during early adulthood.

5. Discuss the nature and causes of major depression and schizophrenia.

Audio Assignment

Listen to the audio tape that accompanies Lesson 17: "Seasons of Eros."

Write answers to the following questions. You may replay portions of the program if you need to refresh your memory. Answer guidelines may be found in the Lesson Guidelines section at the end of this chapter.

1. Define "eros," and tell how its meaning changes from the beginning of life through adolescence.

2. Discuss the concept of sexual orientation and how experts believe it emerges in the individual.

3. Describe the ways in which the meaning and expression of eros change during adulthood.

Textbook Assignment

Read Chapter 17: "Early Adulthood: Biosocial Development," pages 413–433 in *The Developing Person Through the Life Span*, 6/e, then work through the material that follows to review it. Complete the sentences and answer the questions. As you proceed, evaluate your performance for each section by consulting the answers on page 213. Do not continue with the next section until you understand each answer. If you need to, review or reread the appropriate section in the textbook before continuing.

1. The beginning of young adulthood is the best time for _____

   _____

   _____

   (three categories) .

Growth, Strength, and Health (pp. 413–422)

2. Girls usually reach their maximum height by age _____ , and boys by age

   _____ .

3. Growth in _____ and increases in _____ continue into the 20s.

4. Physical strength reaches a peak at about age _____ and then decreases.

5. Medical attention in early adulthood is more often necessitated by _____ than by illness.

6. Of the fatal diseases, _____ is the leading killer of adults under age 75, with fewer than 1 in 10,000 being adults between _____ and _____ years of age. However, young adulthood is the most dangerous time for _____ death.

7. When overall growth stops, _____ , or age-related gradual physical decline, begins. The rate of this decline is influenced by _____ , the _____ , and _____ _____ .

8. The earliest signs of aging include wrinkles, caused by loss of _____ in facial skin, and the first _____

   _____ , caused by a loss of pigment-producing cells in the head.

9. Lung efficiency, as measured by

   _____ _____ , decreases about _____ percent per decade beginning in the 20s.

10. The kidneys begin to lose their efficiency at about age _____ , declining about _____ percent per decade.

11. Notable decline occurs in the ability of the eye's _____ to focus on _____ (near/far) objects. At about age _____ this decline reaches the point where it is labeled _____ , and reading glasses are needed. Age-related hearing loss, or _____ , generally becomes apparent at about age _____ .

12. Aging occurs more quickly among people who are _____ , low _____ _____ , and from _____ _____ .

13. Females generally _____ (are healthier/are not healthier) than men. Compared to men, females have better _____ in early adulthood, fewer _____ _____ in middle age, and live on average _____ years (how many?) longer than men.

14. Two ways in which females are at a health disadvantage compared to males are _____ and _____- _____ problems.

15. The imbalance in elderly women and men is due to the fact that more _____ (younger/older) _____ (males/females) die.

16. Three types of explanations have been proposed for why there is an imbalance of elderly women and elderly men. One _____ explanation is based on the evolutionary need for females to _____ . Another, _____ explanation suggests that the difference is due to the fact that men take more _____ than women. A third, _____ explanation, suggests that women are more likely to engage in _____ , _____ , _____ , and _____ activities—all of which are protective of health

17. Many of the body's functions serve to maintain _____ ; that is, they keep physiological functioning in a state of balance. Many of these mechanisms are regulated by the _____ , which is often referred to as the brain's _____ gland.

18. For body weight, there is a homeostatic _____ _____ that is

affected by _____ , _____ , _____ , _____ , and _____ . The older a person is, the _____ (less time/longer) it takes for these adjustments to occur. This makes it more difficult for older bodies to adapt to, and recover from _____ .

19. For most of us, our bodies, if adequately maintained, are capable of functioning quite well until we are at least age _____ . The declines of aging primarily affect our _____ , which is defined as _____ .

20. The muscles of the body _____ (do/do not) have the equivalent of an organ reserve.

21. The average maximum heart rate _____ (declines/remains stable/increases) with age. Resting heart rate _____ (declines/remains stable/increases) with age.

Briefly explain why most of the age-related biological changes that occur during the first decades of adulthood are of little consequence to the individual.

22. Age-related biological changes are particularly noticeable in professional _____ and serious weekend players.

23. Performance in sports that demand vigorous _____ motor skills peaks _____ (earlier/later) than those that demand _____ motor skills. An important factor in the impact of aging on athletic performance, however, is the individual's _____ .

24. Male and female bodies _____ (do/do not) follow a similar sequence of sexual activation at every age.

25. The sequence of sexual activation begins with _____ , followed by _____ _____ , release through _____ , followed by _____ and _____ .

26. During the early years of manhood, sexual excitement, which includes

_____

_____

and _____

_____ , can occur very quickly and frequently. As men grow older, they often need stimulation that is more _____ or _____ to initiate sexual excitement.

27. Age-related trends in sexual responsiveness _____ (are/are not) as clear-cut for women. As they mature from adolescence toward middle adulthood, women become more likely to experience _____ .

State four possible reasons for this age-related trend in women.

28. In the United States in 2000, 85 percent of newborns had a mother younger than _____ and a father younger than _____ .

29. Between _____ and _____ percent of all married couples experience infertility, which is defined as _____

_____

30. The most common fertility problems in men lie in abnormalities in the _____ , _____ , or _____ of sperm.

List several factors that can alter normal sperm development.

31. The most common fertility problem in women is difficulty with _____ . This may result from anything that impairs a woman's normal bodily functioning, including being _____ or _____ .

32. Most women find that ovulation becomes _____ (more/less) regular as middle age approaches. Older women take _____ (longer/less time) to conceive, and they are more likely to give birth to _____ when they do.

33. The other common fertility problem for women is blocked _____ _____ , often caused by _____ _____ _____ that was not treated promptly.

34. Most physicians recommend that women begin their childbearing before age _____ and would-be fathers before age

_____ .

35. Many infertility problems can also be overcome by modern medical techniques, such as _____ to open blocked genital ducts or fallopian tubes, or the use of _____ to stimulate ovulation. Another possibility is _____ _____ _____ , in which ova are fertilized outside the ovaries. This technique is successful about _____ percent of the time.

Techniques such as this are called

_____ _____

_____ , and are generally most
effective with couples under age

_____ .

Emotional Problems in Early Adulthood
(pp. 423–432)

36. Although young adults are generally healthy,
they are more likely than older adults to use
_____ and to suffer from
_____ . Two problems that are more
common in females are _____
and _____ . A problem that is more
common among young adult males is
_____ .

37. To measure whether a person is too fat or too
thin, clinicians calculate his or her

_____ _____

_____ , defined as the ratio of
_____ (in kilograms) divided by
_____ (in meters squared).

38. The subset of the population that is most likely to
connect self-concept to body image is women
of _____ ancestry.

39. One survey of North American dieters reported
that the average woman during early adulthood
would like to weigh _____ pounds
less, and the average man about
_____ pounds more.

40. Dieting may also trigger physiological changes
that lead to an eating disorder such as

_____ _____ , an

affliction characterized by _____ .

41. Anorexia nervosa is diagnosed on the basis of
four symptoms:

   a. _____

   b. _____

   c. _____

   d. _____

42. Anorexia is a disease of the _____
context that was rare before _____ .

43. The other major eating disorder is

_____ _____ , which is

_____ (more/less) common disor-
der and involves successive bouts of binge eating
followed by purging through vomiting or mas-
sive doses of laxatives.

44. Binge-purge eating can cause a wide range of
health problems, including damage to the
_____ _____ and
_____ _____ from the
strain of electrolyte imbalance. A group that is at
particular risk for eating disorders is

_____ _____ .

Briefly summarize how each of the major theories
of development views eating disorders.

Psychoanalytic theory

Behaviorism

Cognitive theory

Sociocultural theory

Epigenetic theory

45. Drug abuse is defined as using a drug in a manner that is _____

46. When the absence of a drug in a person's system
causes physiological or psychological craving,
_____ is apparent.

47. Women use drugs _____ (less often
than/as often as/more often than) men do.

Internationally, _____-_____ countries have the highest rates of drug use.

48. State four reasons for the high rate of drug use and abuse in the first years of adulthood.

    a. _____

    b. _____

    c. _____

    d. _____

49. Drug use generally _____ (increases/ decreases) during young adulthood, in part due to _____ norms. Other factors that discourage drug use are

    _____ .

50. Compared to others their age, young adult drug users are more likely to _____

    _____ .

51. Major depression is more common among _____ (women/men). People who have more activity in the _____

    _____ cortex of the brain, or in the emotional hotspot of the _____ , are more vulnerable to depression.

52. Three neurotransmitters that are involved in depression are _____ ,

    _____ , and _____ .

53. The disorder characterized by bizarre thoughts, delusions, and hallucinations is

    _____ , which is usually caused by

    _____ .

54. Worldwide, young men are far more likely than women to die a _____

    _____ . One reason for this difference may be the fact that higher levels of the hormone _____ correlate with angry reactions to events. Another reason has to do with the way in in which males are

    _____ .

55. Some experts believe that aggression is the result of an "explosive combination" of high

    _____ and dashed

    _____ . A blow to the individual's

    _____ is more likely to result in vio-

lence when the individual is under the influence of _____ ; when there is a

_____ present; and when the individual lacks _____ .

Testing Yourself

After you have completed the audio and text review questions, see how well you do on the following quiz. Correct answers, with text and audio references, may be found at the end of this chapter.

1. *Eros* is most broadly defined as:
   a. the biological drive to reproduce.
   b. the drive to obtain pleasure and avoid pain.
   c. our species' natural attraction to members of the opposite sex.
   d. the desire for sexual and sensual pleasure.

2. Approximately _____ percent of the population is estimated to have a homosexual orientation.
   a. 1
   b. 5
   c. 10
   d. 20

3. Which of the following is true regarding the development of a homosexual orientation?
   a. Homosexuality is the product of a combination of biological and environmental influences.
   b. Homosexuality arises out of fear of the opposite sex.
   c. Most homosexuals were sexually molested as children.
   d. Homosexuality develops most readily in families with domineering mothers and weak, ineffectual fathers.

4. During which season(s) of life does eros tend to be diffused throughout the body and sense organs?
   a. adolescence
   b. early adulthood
   c. later adulthood
   d. both a. and b.

5. During which season(s) of life does eros tend to be most narrowly focused?
   a. childhood
   b. early adulthood
   c. later adulthood
   d. both b. and c.

6. Senescence refers to:
   a. a loss of efficiency in the body's regulatory systems.
   b. age-related gradual physical decline.
   c. decreased physical strength.
   d. vulnerability to disease.

7. When do noticeable increases in height stop?
   a. at about the same age in men and women
   b. at an earlier age in women than in men
   c. at an earlier age in men than in women
   d. There is such diversity in physiological development that it is impossible to generalize regarding this issue.

8. A difference between men and women during early adulthood is that men have:
   a. a higher percentage of body fat.
   b. lower metabolism.
   c. proportionately more muscle.
   d. greater organ reserve.

9. The majority of young adults rate their own health as:
   a. very good or excellent.
   b. average or fair.
   c. poor.
   d. worse than it was during adolescence.

10. The automatic adjustment of the body's systems to keep physiological functions in a state of equilibrium, even during heavy exertion, is called:
    a. organ reserve.   c. stress.
    b. homeostasis.   d. muscle capacity.

11. Which of the following temperamental characteristics was *not* identified as being typical of drug abusers?
    a. attraction to excitement
    b. intolerance of frustration
    c. extroversion
    d. vulnerability to depression

12. (A Life-Span View) As men grow older:
    a. they often need more direct stimulation to initiate sexual excitement.
    b. a longer time elapses between the beginning of sexual excitement and full erection.
    c. a longer time elapses between orgasm and the end of the refractory period.
    d. all of the above occur.

13. It is estimated that infertility affects:
    a. at least half of all married couples in which the woman is in her early 30s.

    b. men more than women.
    c. about one-third of all married couples.
    d. about 15 percent of all married couples.

14. The decrease in physical strength that occurs during the decade of the 30s:
    a. occurs more rapidly in the arm and upper torso than in the legs.
    b. occurs more rapidly in the back and leg muscles than in the arm.
    c. occurs at the same rate throughout the body.
    d. varies from individual to individual.

15. Endometriosis is:
    a. a sexually transmitted disease.
    b. lack of ovulation or irregular ovulation in an older woman.
    c. a disease characterized by the presence of uterine tissue on the surface of the ovaries or the Fallopian tubes.
    d. a condition that invariably results from pelvic inflammatory disease.

16. In vitro fertilization is a solution for infertility that is caused by:
    a. sperm motility problems.
    b. low sperm count.
    c. low sperm count or ovulatory problems.
    d. PID.

17. A 50-year-old woman can expect to retain what percentage of her strength at age 20?
    a. 25
    b. 50
    c. 75
    d. 90

18. According to epigenetic systems theory, eating disorders such as anorexia nervosa are more common in young women who are genetically susceptible to:
    a. depression.
    b. alcohol abuse.
    c. obesity.
    d. suicide.

19. Major depression is likely to be diagnosed when an individual displays:
    a. a loss of interest or pleasure in activities lasting two weeks or more.
    b. social withdrawal accompanied by self-destructive behaviors.
    c. disorganized emotions and thoughts.
    d. delusions.

20. Which of the following was *not* suggested as a reason for the high rate of drug use and abuse in the first years of adulthood?

a. Young adults often have friends who use drugs.

b. Young adults are trying to imitate their parents' behavior.

c. Young adults may use drugs as a way of relieving job or educational stress.

d. Young adults often fear social rejection.

21. A technique that involves fertilization of the ovum outside the uterus is referred to as:

a. varicoceles.

b. artificial insemination.

c. in vitro fertilization.

d. surrogate fertilization.

22. The typical bulimic patient is a:

a. college-age woman.

b. woman who starves herself to the point of emaciation.

c. woman in her late 40s.

d. woman who suffers from life-threatening obesity.

23. Which of the following was *not* identified as a cause of schizophrenia?

a. genes

b. severe early trauma

c. anoxia at birth

d. low birthweight

NAME _____   INSTRUCTOR _____

LESSON 17: EROS IN THE MEDIA

Exercise

When sexuality is broadly defined as eros, it becomes clear that every season of life is sexual. Audio program 17 outlines the changing meanings of eros over the seasons of life.

Sexuality at various ages is often depicted in the popular media of television, magazines, motion pictures, novels, and radio. Television programs and advertising, for example, often employ sexual themes and stereotypes targeted to certain age groups.

The exercise for Lesson 17 asks you to look in the popular media for examples of advertising or programming that include portrayals of eros in various seasons. You may choose examples from current media sources or from your recollections of media portrayals in earlier seasons of your own life. After you have answered the following questions, hand the completed exercise in to your instructor.

Pick three stages of life (from infancy, childhood, adolescence, early adulthood, middle adulthood, or late adulthood) and, for each stage, find two contrasting portrayals of sexuality in the popular media. One portrayal, for example, might show someone in late adulthood as a "dirty old man"; a contrasting portrayal would show an older adult as being asexual. Then answer the following questions for each example.

1. Stage: _____

   a. Describe one portrayal of sexuality.

   b. Describe a contrasting portrayal of sexuality.

   c. Is sexual stereotyping present in either example? If so, in what ways?

    d. What aspects of sexuality during this stage of life are missing or misrepresented in the samples you have chosen?

2. Stage: _____

    a. Describe one portrayal of sexuality.

    b. Describe a contrasting portrayal of sexuality.

    c. Is sexual stereotyping present in either example? If so, in what ways?

    d. What aspects of sexuality during this stage of life are missing or misrepresented in the samples you have chosen?

3. Stage: _____

    a. Describe one portrayal of sexuality.

    b. Describe a contrasting portrayal of sexuality.

    c. Is sexual stereotyping present in either example? If so, in what ways?

    d. What aspects of sexuality during this stage of life are missing or misrepresented in the samples you have chosen?

LESSON GUIDELINES

Audio Question Guidelines

1. When sexuality is broadly defined as **eros**, it becomes clear that every season of life is sexual. Children derive pleasure from touching their bodies, and from the sensory experiences of their eyes, ears, and mouths. In this first season, pleasure is diffused throughout the body.

   As children grow older, they become interested in each other's bodies and curious about where babies come from.

   Around the age of 6, children come to understand that our society is uncomfortable about sexuality and so they become more private, entering what Freud called the period of **latency**.

   In adolescence and early adulthood, eros is directed at others and concentrated in the sexual organs. Sexuality centers on mating and reproduction, although it may not be focused on a particular partner or necessarily coupled with intimacy.

2. In addition to forging a personal identity, each individual develops a sexual orientation toward intimacy with members of the same or opposite sex. Approximately 10 percent of the population is homosexual.

   Experts still do not agree on what causes a person to develop a homosexual or heterosexual orientation. Some suggest that a biological predisposition is involved. One point of agreement is that sexual orientation does *not* appear to be learned. Children who grow up with gay or lesbian parents are no more likely themselves to be gay or lesbian than children who grow up with heterosexual parents. In all probability, it is a combination of certain biological factors and environmental influences that lead to the development of sexual orientation.

3. During early adulthood, eros is coupled with intimacy. A relationship with one special person becomes the basis for marriage and the bearing of children.

   Many couples report that the years of middle adulthood are the most sensual and sexual of their lives, as partners rediscover each other after the children have left home.

   Sex may become less frequent as one gets older, but it tends to be savored more fully, with pleasure diffused over all the senses, just as it was at the beginning of life.

Textbook Question Answers

1. hard physical work, problem-free reproduction, peak athletic performance
2. 16; 18
3. muscle; fat
4. 30
5. injuries
6. cancer; 20; 34; violent
7. senescence; genes; environment; personal choices
8. elasticity; gray hairs
9. vital capacity; 5
10. 30; 4
11. lens; near; 60; presbyopia; presbycusis; 60
12. male; socioeconomic status; ethnic minorities
13. are healthier; health habits; fatal diseases; five
14. undernourishment; reproductive-system
15. younger; males
16. biological; reproduce and care for young children; cognitive; risks; psychosocial; marriage; family life; friendship; help-seeking
17. homeostasis; pituitary; master
18. set point; genes; diet; age; hormones; exercise; longer; physical stress
19. 70; organ reserve; the extra capacity that each organ has for responding to unusually stressful events or conditions that demand intense or prolonged effort
20. do
21. declines; remains stable

The declines of aging primarily affect our organ reserve. In the course of normal daily life, adults seldom have to call upon this capacity, so the deficits in organ reserve generally go unnoticed.

22. athletes
23. gross; earlier; fine; lifestyle
24. do
25. arousal; peak excitement; orgasm; refraction; recovery
26. faster heartbeat; penile erection; direct (or explicit); prolonged
27. are not; orgasm

Four reasons are:

   a. The slowing of the man's responses lengthens the sex act, providing the more prolonged stimulation that many women need to reach orgasm.

b. With experience, both partners may be more likely to recognize and focus on those aspects of love-making that intensify the woman's sexual responses.

c. The culture may teach women that sex is violent and that they should say no to it. It may take years for women to acknowledge and appreciate their sexuality.

d. According to the ethological perspective, age-related increases in sexual passions among women are the result of the reduced likelihood of reproduction.

28. 35; 45

29. 2; 30; being unable to conceive a child after a year or more of intercourse without contraception

30. number; shape; motility

Anything that impairs normal body functioning, such as illness with a high fever; medical therapy involving radiation or prescription drugs; exposure to environmental toxins; unusual stress; or drug abuse, alcoholism, or cigarette smoking can affect the number, shape, and motility of the sperm.

31. ovulation; underweight; obese

32. less; longer; twins

33. fallopian tubes; pelvic inflammatory disease (PID)

34. 30; 40

35. surgery; drugs; in vitro fertilization (IVF); 30; assisted reproductive technology (ART); 35

36. drugs; psychopathologies; dieting; eating disorders; violence

37. body mass index (BMI); weight; height

38. European

39. eight; five

40. anorexia nervosa; self-starvation

41. a. refusal to maintain body weight at least 85 percent of normal for age

b. an intense fear of gaining weight

c. disturbed body perception

d. lack of menstruation

42. social; 1950

43. bulimia nervosa; more

44. gastrointestinal system; cardiac arrest; college women

According to psychoanalytic theory, women with eating disorders have a conflict with their mothers, who provided their first nourishment. According to behaviorism, disordered eating may set up a stimulus–response chain in which self-starvation relieves

emotional stress and tension. Cognitive theory suggests that as women enter the workplace they try to project a strong, self-controlled, "masculine" image. Sociocultural explanations focus on the contemporary cultural pressures to be model-like in appearance. Epigenetic theory suggests that because self-starvation may cause menstruation to cease and sexual hormones to decrease, girls who are genetically susceptible to depression or addiction may resort to this self-destructive behavior to relieve the pressures to marry and reproduce.

45. harmful to physical, cognitive, or psychosocial well-being

46. drug addiction

47. less often than; English-speaking

48. a. For some young adults, drug abuse is a way of striving for independence from parents and helps them escape the life stresses that cluster during the 20s.

b. Genes that predispose to drug use include attraction to excitement and vulnerability to depression—traits that increase in adolescence and young adulthood.

c. The group activities of young adults, including large parties, concerts, and sports events, often promote drug use.

d. Young adults are the group least likely to be regularly exposed to religious faith and practice.

49. decreases; social; medical advice, marriage, and religious involvement

50. avoid, fail, or drop out of college; lose or quit jobs; be employed below their potential; be involved in transitory, uncommitted sexual relationships; die violently; and experience serious psychological difficulties

51. women; right prefrontal; amygdala

52. dopamine; norepinephrine; serotonin

53. schizophrenia; genes

54. violent death; testosterone; socialized

55. self-esteem; expectations; self-concept; alcohol; weapon; self-restraint

Answers to Testing Yourself

1. **d.** is the answer. (audio program)

2. **c.** is the answer. About 10 percent of the population will eventually identify itself as homosexual. (audio program)

3. **a.** is the answer. (audio program)

4. **c.** is the answer. During later adulthood, as in childhood, eros is spread throughout the body and senses. (audio program)

5. **b.** is the answer. During early adulthood, eros tends to be focused on mating and reproduction. (audio program)

6. **b.** is the answer. (textbook, p. 414)

   a., c., & d. Each of these is a specific example of the more general process of senescence.

7. **b.** is the answer. (textbook, p. 413)

8. **c.** is the answer. (textbook, p. 413)

   a. & b. These are true of women.

   d. Men and women do not differ in this characteristic.

9. **a.** is the answer. (textbook, p. 414)

10. **b.** is the answer. (textbook, p. 417)

    a. This is the extra capacity that each organ of the body has for responding to unusually stressful events or conditions that demand intense or prolonged effort.

    c. Stress, which is not defined in this chapter, refers to events or situations that tax the body's resources.

    d. This simply refers to a muscle's potential for work.

11. **c.** is the answer. (textbook, p. 428)

12. **d.** is the answer. (textbook, p. 420)

13. **d.** is the answer. (textbook, p. 421)

    b. Until middle age, infertility is equally likely in women and men.

14. **b.** is the answer. (textbook, p. 413)

15. **b.** is the answer. (textbook, p. 423)

16. **c.** is the answer. (textbook, p. 422)

17. **d.** is the answer. (textbook, p. 418)

18. **a.** is the answer. Depression and low self-esteem often serve as stimulus triggers for fasting, bingeing, and purging, which may temporarily relieve these states of emotional distress. (textbook, p. 427)

19. **a.** is the answer. (textbook, p. 430)

    c. & d. These are possible symptoms of schizophrenia.

    b. This combination of behaviors is not indicative of any particular form of psychopathology.

20. **b.** is the answer. In fact, just the opposite is true. Young adults may use drugs to express independence from their parents. (textbook, p. 428)

21. **c.** is the answer. (textbook, p. 421)

    a. These are varicose veins in the testes and partially blocked genital ducts.

    b. In this technique, sperm collected from a male donor are artificially inserted into the uterus.

    d. In this technique, fertilization occurs outside the uterus but it involves another woman who carries the fetus.

22. **a.** is the answer. (textbook, p. 426)

    b. This describes a woman suffering from anorexia nervosa.

    c. Eating disorders are much more common in younger women.

    d. Most women with bulimia nervosa are usually close to normal in weight.

23. **d.** is the answer. (textbook, p. 431)

Early Adulthood: Cognitive Development

AUDIO PROGRAM: The Development of Faith

ORIENTATION

Lesson 18 of the audio program is the fifth in a sequence of lessons that track cognitive development from infancy to late adulthood. The first two of these, Lessons 6 and 9, explored the acquisition of language. The next two, Lessons 12 and 15, presented the theory of Jean Piaget, who identified four stages of cognitive development culminating in the abstract logic of formal operations. In this lesson we step beyond Piaget and explore other ways of thinking.

As people grow from adolescence into adulthood, the commitments, demands, and responsibilities of adult life produce a new type of **postformal thinking** that is better suited than formal operations to solving the practical problems of daily life. Postformal thought is more adaptive, flexible, and **dialectical**. Dialectical thought, which some researchers consider the most advanced form of cognition, recognizes that most of life's important questions do not have single, unvarying, correct answers. It is grounded in the ability to consider both sides of an issue simultaneously.

Chapter 18 of *The Developing Person Through the Life Span*, 6/e, begins by describing how adult thinking differs from adolescent thinking. The experiences and challenges of adulthood result in a new, postformal thought, evidenced by practical, flexible, and dialectical thinking—the dynamic, in-the-world cognitive style that adults typically use to solve the problems of daily life.

The second section explores how the events of early adulthood can affect moral development. Of particular interest are Fowler's six stages in the development of faith.

The third section examines the effect of the college experience on cognitive growth; findings here indicate that years of education correlate with virtually every measure of cognition as thinking becomes progressively more flexible and tolerant.

Thinking about questions of **faith** and ethics may also progress during adulthood, especially in response to significant life experiences such as participating in higher education and becoming a parent. Both the text and audio program 18, "The Development of Faith," present James Fowler's theory of how faith changes throughout the seasons of life. Fowler, a Christian minister and professor of theology, has bridged the fields of psychology and religion by creating a model in which faith is broadly conceived. Building on the cognitive and personality theories of Jean Piaget and Erik Erikson, Fowler's model extends the concept of faith beyond religious faith to include whatever each person really cares about—his or her "ultimate concern." Fowler's theory describes six stages, each of which has distinct features and is classified as typical of a certain age.

Although Fowler's theory is not without its critics, its emphasis on faith as a developmental process rings true. If Fowler is correct, faith, like other aspects of cognition, may mature from the simple self-centered and one-sided perspective of the child to the much more complex, altruistic, and multifaceted perspective of many adults.

LESSON GOALS

By the end of this lesson you should be prepared to:

1. Describe three approaches to the study of adult cognition.

2. Identify the main characteristics of postformal and dialectical thought, and describe how it differs from formal operational thought.

3. Explain Carol Gilligan's view of how moral reasoning changes during adulthood.

4. Outline James Fowler's stage theory of the development of faith.

5. Describe the relationship of adult cognitive growth to higher education.

Audio Assignment

Listen to the audio tape that accompanies Lesson 18: "The Development of Faith."

Write answers to the following questions. You may replay portions of the program if you need to refresh your memory. Answer guidelines may be found in the Lesson Guidelines section at the end of this chapter.

1. (Audio Program and text) List and describe the six stages in the development of faith proposed by James Fowler.

2. Discuss the relationship between cognitive development and faith.

3. Cite several criticisms of Fowler's theory.

Textbook Assignment

Read Chapter 18: "Early Adulthood: Cognitive Development," pages 435–457 in *The Developing Person Through the Life Span*, 6/e, then work through the material that follows to review it. Complete the sentences and answer the questions. As you proceed, evaluate your performance for each section by consulting the answers on page 225. Do not continue with the next section until you understand each answer. If you need to, review or reread the appropriate section in the textbook before continuing.

1. Unlike the relatively "straightforward" cognitive growth of earlier ages, cognitive development during adulthood is _____ and _____ . Developmentalists have used three approaches to explain this development: the _____ approach, the _____ approach, and the _____-_____ approach.

Postformal Thought (pp. 436–445)

2. Compared to adolescent thinking, adult thinking is more _____ , _____ , and _____ .

3. Reasoning that is adapted to the subjective real-life contexts to which it is applied is called _____ _____ . It is characterized by problem _____ rather than problem _____ .

4. Developmentalists distinguish between _____ thinking, which arises from the _____ experiences and _____ of an individual, and _____ thinking, which follows abstract _____ . The latter kind of thinking is _____ (more/less) adaptive for schoolchildren, adolescents, and young adults than for mature adults.

5. The difference between adolescent and young adult reasoning is particularly apparent for reasoning involving _____ questions.

6. In contrast to adolescent _____-_____ regarding personal experiences, adults are more likely to demonstrate _____ _____ when suggesting solutions to real-life problems.

7. When the mere possibility of being negatively stereotyped arouses emotions that disrupt cognition, _____ _____ has occurred. This is especially common during _____ , when _____ and/or _____ is being developed. Strong identification with a group to which one belongs, even when that group is discriminated against, is

healthier than _____ or

_____ .

8. (Thinking Like a Scientist) Stereotype threat can make _____ and _____ doubt their academic ability. As a result they may become _____ in academic contexts and _____ with intellectual achievement.

9. (Thinking Like a Scientist) Adults today _____ (have/do not have) fewer sexist and racial stereotypes than they did in the past. Research studies have shown that intellectual performance among students increases if they _____ the concept that intelligence is plastic and can be changed.

10. Some theorists consider _____ _____ the most advanced form of cognition. This thinking recognizes that every idea, or _____ , implies an opposing idea, or _____ ; these are then forged into a(n) _____ of the two. This type of thinking fosters a worldview that recognizes that most of life's important questions _____ (have/do not have) single, unchangeable, correct answers.

11. Some researchers believe that some _____ encourage flexible, dialectical reasoning more than others. According to this view, ancient _____ philosophy has led Europeans to use _____ _____ , whereas and _____ have led Asians to think more _____ .

12. Although all adults _____ (think/ do not think) in a postformal manner, life experiences _____ (can/cannot) move a person's thinking past the formal operational stage.

Adult Moral Reasoning (pp. 445–449)

13. According to James Rest, one catalyst for propelling young adults from a lower moral stage to a higher one is _____ .

14. Other researchers maintain that in order to be capable of "truly ethical" reasoning, a person must have experienced sustained responsibility for _____ .

15. Carol Gilligan believes that in matters of moral reasoning _____ (males/ females) tend to be more concerned with the question of rights and justice, whereas _____ (males/females) are more concerned with personal relationships. Other moral issues that contemporary adults are likely to confront arise from increasing _____ and _____ . They also arise from television, popular music, and the _____ .

16. The current approach to research on moral reasoning is based on a series of questions about moral reasoning called the _____ _____ _____ . In general, scores on this test increase with _____ and with each year of _____ .

17. The theorist who has outlined six stages in the development of faith is _____ .

18. In the space below, identify and briefly describe each stage in the development of faith.

Stage One: _____

_____

Stage Two: _____

_____

Stage Three: _____

_____

Stage Four: _____

_____

Stage Five: _____

_____

Stage Six: _____

_____

19. Although Fowler's stage theory of faith _____ (is/is not) totally accepted, the idea that religion plays an important role in human development _____ (is/is not).

Cognitive Growth and Higher Education
(pp. 449–456)

20. Years of education _____ (are/are not) strongly correlated with most measures of adult cognition.

Briefly outline the year-by-year progression in how the thinking of college students becomes more flexible and tolerant.

21. William Perry found that the thinking of students, over the course of their college careers, progressed through _____ levels of complexity.

22. Research has shown that the more years of higher education a person has, the deeper and more _____ that person's reasoning is likely to become.

23. Worldwide, the number of students who receive higher education _____ (has increased/ has not increased) since the first half of the twentieth century.

24. Collegiate populations have become _____ (more/less) diverse in recent years. The values and _____ of students are also _____ (the same/ different). The structure of higher education also _____ (has changed/remains the same).

25. Some developmentalists believe that a college education today is a _____ (more powerful/less powerful) force in producing cognitive growth than it might have been. Among the factors that may explain why are _____ effects, _____ effects, and _____ rates.

26. One cohort difference is that most of today's college students _____ (work/do not work) during their college years. Selection effects refer to the possibility that advanced cognition doesn't result directly from a college education but from factors that _____ with college attendance. Only about _____ (how many?) of the students who enroll in college actually graduate.

27. (In Person) Young full-time students living on campus are _____ (more/less) likely to accept cheating than are students who commute. Many students have a _____ (broader/more limited) definition of cheating than professors. For example, many students seem unaware of the rules defining _____ .

28. (In Person) Dr. Berger's analysis of cheating behavior led her to suspect that students may have a different _____ _____ that encourages cheating in order to cope with institutions that penalize those who are _____ _____ and those who are educationally _____ .

Testing Yourself

After you have completed the audio and text review questions, see how well you do on the following quiz. Correct answers, with text and audio references, may be found at the end of this chapter.

1. According to James Fowler, the simplest stage of faith is the stage of:
   a. universalizing faith.
   b. intuitive-projective faith.
   c. mythic-literal faith.
   d. synthetic-conventional faith.

2. At one stage in the development of faith, people learn to question the practices and philosophies of significant persons in their lives. This is the stage of:
   a. conjunctive faith.
   b. individual-reflective faith.
   c. synthetic-conventional faith.
   d. intuitive-projective faith.

3. At the highest stages in the development of faith, people have incorporated a powerful vision of compassion and human brotherhood into their lives. This stage is called:
   a. conjunctive faith.
   b. individual-reflective faith.
   c. synthetic-conventional faith.
   d. universalizing faith.

4. The stage of faith that corresponds with the age at which most individuals achieve concrete operational thought is called:
   a. mythic-literal faith.
   b. individual-reflective faith.
   c. synthetic-conventional faith.
   d. universalizing faith.

5. Fowler's theory of faith has been criticized for:
   a. focusing primarily on religious faith.
   b. proposing that faith develops in stages, rather than continuously.
   c. proposing stages of faith that many people will never reach.
   d. all of the above reasons.

6. Differences in the reasoning maturity of adolescents and young adults are most likely to be apparent when:
   a. low-SES and high-SES groups are compared.
   b. ethnic-minority adolescents and adults are compared.
   c. ethnic-majority adolescents and adults are compared.
   d. emotionally charged issues are involved.

7. Which of the following is *not* one of the major approaches to the study of adult cognition described in the text?
   a. the information-processing approach
   b. the postformal approach
   c. the systems approach
   d. the psychometric approach

8. Compared to adolescent thinking, adult thinking tends to be:
   a. more personal.   c. more dialectical.
   b. more practical.   d. all of the above.

9. A hallmark of mature adult thought is the:
   a. ability to engage in dialectical thinking.
   b. reconciliation of both objective and subjective approaches to real-life problems.
   c. adoption of conjunctive faith.
   d. all of the above.

10. According to James Fowler, the experience of college often is a springboard to:
    a. intuitive-projective faith.
    b. mythic-literal faith.
    c. individual-reflective faith.
    d. synthetic-conventional faith

11. Which approach to adult cognitive development focuses on life-span changes in the efficiency of encoding, storage, and retrieval?
    a. postformal
    b. information-processing
    c. psychometric
    d. dialectical

12. Postformal thinking is most useful for solving _____ problems.
    a. science   c. everyday
    b. mathematics   d. abstract, logical

13. The term for the kind of thinking that involves the consideration of both poles of an idea and their reconciliation, or synthesis, in a new idea is:
    a. subjective thinking.
    b. postformal thought.
    c. adaptive reasoning.
    d. dialectical thinking.

14. Thesis is to antithesis as _____ is to _____ .
    a. a new idea; an opposing idea
    b. abstract; concrete
    c. concrete; abstract
    d. provisional; absolute

15. Which of the following adjectives best describe(s) cognitive development during adulthood?
    a. multidirectional and multicontextual
    b. linear
    c. steady
    d. tumultuous

16. Which of the following most accurately describes postformal thought?
    a. subjective thinking that arises from the personal experiences and perceptions of the individual
    b. objective reasoning that follows abstract, impersonal logic
    c. a form of logic that combines subjectivity and objectivity
    d. thinking that is rigid, inflexible, and fails to recognize the existence of other potentially valid views

17. The Defining Issues Test is a:
    a. standardized test that measures postformal thinking.
    b. projective test that assesses dialectical reasoning.
    c. series of questions about moral dilemmas.
    d. test that assesses the impact of life events on cognitive growth.

18. According to Carol Gilligan:
    a. in matters of moral reasoning, females tend to be more concerned with the question of rights and justice.
    b. in matters of moral reasoning, males tend to put human needs above principles of justice.
    c. moral reasoning advances during adulthood in response to the more complex moral dilemmas that life poses.
    d. all of the above are true.

19. Which of the following was *not* identified as a factor in why college education is a less powerful force in producing cognitive growth?
    a. selection effects   c. grade inflation
    b. dropout rates   d. cohort effects

20. Research has revealed that a typical outcome of college education is that students become:
    a. very liberal politically.
    b. less committed to any particular ideology.
    c. more committed to a particular ideology.
    d. less open-minded.

21. As adult thinking becomes more focused on occupational and interpersonal demands, it also becomes less inclined toward:
    a. single-mindedness.
    b. dialectical thought.
    c. adaptive thought.
    d. all of the above.

22. Formal operational thinking is most useful for solving problems that:
    a. involve logical relationships or theoretical possibilities.
    b. require integrative skills.
    c. involve the synthesis of diverse issues.
    d. require seeing perspectives other than one's own.

23. Many of the problems of adult life are characterized by ambiguity, partial truths, and extenuating circumstances, and therefore are often best solved using _____ thinking.
    a. formal   c. postformal
    b. reintegrative   d. executive

NAME _____   INSTRUCTOR _____

LESSON 18: THINKING DURING ADULTHOOD

Exercise

One theme of the *Seasons of Life* series is that every age brings a different way of knowing. The cognitive patterns that emerge during adulthood are propelled by the commitments each individual makes during this time. These include commitments to personal achievement, family concerns, and the community at large. Such commitments give the individual a new understanding of the complexity of most of life's daily problems.

In this lesson we have explored several types of thinking, including formal and **post-formal thought, dialectical reasoning**, and **faith.** Test your understanding of these ways of thinking by writing answers to the following questions. Hand the completed exercise in to your instructor.

1. Many different kinds of problems arise in daily life. Based on your own experiences, or those of a typical college student or person in your season of life, give an example of a problem likely to benefit from formal operational thinking. Why is a logical answer to this problem appropriate?

2. Imagine that you are a religious leader attempting to convince the members of your congregation to become more involved in their community's religious life. What kind of appeal might be most effective with members at Fowler's stage of "mythic-literal faith"? with members at the stage of "individual-reflective faith"?

3. Dialectical thinking involves the constant integration of one's beliefs and experiences with the contradictions and inconsistencies of daily life. Give an example of the use of dialectical thinking in your own life, or that of a typical person in your season.

4. The idea that personal commitment and assuming responsibility for others are hallmarks of adult thinking is central to several theories of adult cognition. Why would becoming a parent foster cognitive growth? In what ways might being a stepparent or grandparent influence cognitive growth? What other life experiences have influenced your own cognitive development?

LESSON GUIDELINES

Audio Question Guidelines

1. Stage One: **Intuitive-projective faith** refers to the imaginative faith that emerges as children acquire the use of symbols and language.

   Stage Two: **Mythic-literal faith** corresponds to Piaget's stage of concrete operations. In this stage children become interested in learning the stories of their culture, and often take these stories literally.

   Stage Three: **Synthetic-conventional faith** often emerges during adolescence as a result of young people's new awareness of who they are and what they believe in. Faith is characterized by a conformist, nonintellectual acceptance of the values and ideals of people who are important to the young person.

   Stage Four: **Individual-reflective faith** often begins in early adulthood, as individuals become critically reflective of their beliefs. Characterized by intellectual detachment from the values of the culture and the approval of others, faith in this stage may represent God in the abstract or as a philosophical concept. In the audio program, Fowler refers to this stage as "individuative."

   Stage Five: **Conjunctive faith** rarely develops before middle age. Considered the highest stage that most people experience, conjunctive faith recognizes the many paradoxes and inconsistencies of life.

   Stage Six: **Universalizing faith** refers to the behavior of rare individuals who develop a vision of universal compassion, justice, and love that often leads to the denial of their personal welfare in an effort to serve those beliefs.

2. James Fowler has delineated six stages of faith that progress from a simple, self-centered perspective to a more complex, altruistic, and multifaceted view.

   In developing this theory, Fowler was strongly influenced by Piaget's stages of cognitive development. Although Fowler's stages are not considered exclusive to a given age range, each is classified as typical of a certain age group and a certain stage of cognitive development. In the first stage of faith (intuitive-projective faith), for example, egocentric preschoolers, who are unable to take the perspective of another person, often form a highly imaginative and nonhuman image of God. In the second stage (mythic-literal faith)—equivalent to Piaget's stage of concrete operations—children begin to understand cause-and-effect rela-

tionships, but are limited to the concrete reality of the here and now. Their faith puts a correspondingly literal interpretation on the stories and myths of their religion and culture.

Later in adulthood, the development of faith is also paced by cognitive development. When **postformal thought** is achieved, for example, faith can become dialectical in nature and recognize the often paradoxical nature of life. This is what happens in the conjunctive stage. At each season of life, therefore, the development of faith and thinking go hand in hand.

3. Like any pioneer, James Fowler is not without his critics. One criticism is that although Fowler defines faith broadly, he overemphasizes religious faith.

   Another criticism is that faith may develop continuously rather than in stages as Fowler proposed.

   A third objection is based on the reluctance of some critics to accept the notion that some stages of faith are higher than others.

Textbook Question Answers

1. multidirectional; multicontextual; postformal; psychometric; information-processing
2. practical; flexible; dialectical
3. postformal thought; finding; solving
4. subjective; personal; perceptions; objective; logic; more
5. emotional
6. single-mindedness; cognitive flexibility (or flexible problem solving)
7. stereotype threat; adolescence; ethnic identity; gender identity; disidentification; counteridentification
8. women; minorities; anxious; disidentify
9. have; internalize
10. dialectical thought; thesis; antithesis; synthesis; do not have
11. cultures; Greek; analytic logic; Confucianism and Taoism; dialectically
12. do not think; can
13. college
14. the welfare of others
15. males; females; globalization; immigration; Internet
16. Defining Issues Test; age; education
17. James Fowler

18. Intuitive-projective faith is magical, illogical, filled with fantasy, and typical of children ages 3 to 7.

    Mythic-literal faith, which is typical of middle childhood, is characterized by taking the myths and stories of religion literally.

    Synthetic-conventional faith is a nonintellectual acceptance of cultural or religious values in the context of interpersonal relationships.

    Individual-reflective faith is characterized by intellectual detachment from the values of culture and the approval of significant others.

    Conjunctive faith incorporates both powerful unconscious ideas and rational, conscious values.

    Universalizing faith is characterized by a powerful vision of universal compassion, justice, and love that leads people to put their own personal welfare aside in an effort to serve these values.

19. is not; is
20. are

First-year students often believe that there are clear and perfect truths to be found. This phase is followed by a wholesale questioning of values. Finally, after considering opposite ideas, students become committed to certain values, at the same time realizing the need to remain open-minded.

21. nine
22. dialectical
23. has increased
24. more; attitudes; different; has changed
25. less powerful; cohort; selection; dropout
26. work; correlate; half
27. more; more limited; plagiarism
28. value system; culturally different; underprepared

Answers to Testing Yourself

1. **b.** is the answer. In this stage faith is magical, illogical, imaginative, and filled with fantasy. (audio program; textbook, p. 448)

2. **b.** is the answer. A person's ability to articulate his or her own values, separately from family and friends, is characteristic of individual-reflective faith. In the audio program, Fowler calls this stage "individuative." (audio program; textbook, p. 448)

3. **d.** is the answer. Persons reaching stage six in the development of faith (examples include Mahatma Gandhi, Martin Luther King, Jr., and Mother Teresa) are exceedingly rare. (audio program; textbook, p. 448)

4. **a.** is the answer. At this stage, the individual takes the myths and stories of his or her religion literally. (audio program; textbook, p. 448)

5. **d.** is the answer. (audio program)

6. **d.** is the answer. (textbook, p. 437)

   a., b., & c. Socioeconomic status and ethnicity do not predict reasoning maturity.

7. **c.** is the answer. (textbook, p. 435)

8. **d.** is the answer (textbook, p. 436)

9. **b.** is the answer. (textbook, p. 437)

10. **c.** is the answer. (textbook, p. 448)

11. **b.** is the answer. (textbook, p. 435)

    a. This approach emphasizes the emergence of a new stage of thinking that builds on the skills of formal operational thinking.

    c. This approach analyzes the measurable components of intelligence.

    d. This is a type of thinking rather than an approach to the study of cognitive development.

12. **c.** is the answer. (textbook, p. 436)

    a., b., & d. Because of its more analytical nature, formal thinking is most useful for solving these types of problems.

13. **d.** is the answer. (textbook, p. 443)

    a. Thinking that is subjective relies on personal reflection rather than objective observation.

    b. Although dialectical thinking *is* characteristic of postformal thought, this question refers specifically to dialectical thinking.

    c. Adaptive reasoning, which also is characteristic of postformal thought, goes beyond mere logic in solving problems to also explore real-life complexities and contextual circumstances.

14. **a.** is the answer (textbook, p. 443)

15. **a.** is the answer. (textbook, p. 435)

    b. & c. Comparatively speaking, linear and steady are *more* descriptive of childhood and adolescent cognitive development.

16. **b.** is the answer. (textbook, p. 436)

17. **d.** is the answer. (textbook, p. 447)

18. **c.** is the answer. (textbook, p. 447)

    a. In Gilligan's theory, this is more true of males than females.

    b. In Gilligan's theory, this is more true of females than males.

19. **c.** is the answer. (textbook, p. 455)

20. **c.** is the answer. Although they become more committed, they realize they need to remain open-minded. (textbook, p. 451)

21. **a.** is the answer. (textbook, p. 439)

    b. & c. During adulthood, thinking typically becomes more dialectical and adaptive.

22. **a.** is the answer. (textbook, p. 437)

b., c., & d. Postformal thought is most useful for solving problems such as these.

23. **c.** is the answer. (textbook, p. 436)

    a. Formal thinking is best suited to solving problems that require logic and analytical thinking.

Early Adulthood: Psychosocial Development

AUDIO PROGRAM: Not Being First

ORIENTATION

Lesson 19 of *Seasons of Life* is concerned with psychosocial development in early adulthood and the changing composition of the American family. Chapter 19 of *The Developing Person Through the Life Span*, 6/e, begins with a discussion of the two basic psychosocial needs of adulthood, love and work. The next section addresses the need for intimacy in adulthood, focusing on the development of friendship, love, and marriage. The impact of divorce on families is also discussed. The final section is concerned with generativity, or the motivation to achieve during adulthood. It highlights the importance of work and parenthood and addresses the special challenges facing stepparents, adoptive parents, and foster parents.

For some, the question "Who's in your family?" is difficult to answer. Although many people tend to form very close-knit nuclear families consisting of a mother, a father, and one or more children, the number of **stepfamilies** is increasing. This increase is not due, as it was in the past, to death and remarriage, but to divorce and remarriage. For the first time in 1974 more marriages in the United States were ended by divorce than by death. Since people are living longer now than at any other time in history, divorced persons have more opportunities to remarry.

These trends in the composition of American families have created new notions about the words *family*, *mother*, and *father*. Unlike nuclear families, stepfamilies usually include children who are members of two households. Extra sets of in-laws and grandparents and the stress of the competition that often exists between a stepparent and the ex-spouse all serve to complicate family relationships.

Audio program 19, "Not Being First," poignantly illustrates the particular dilemma of the stepparent by introducing the listener to Penny and Lyn Beesley. Married for six years, both Penny and Lyn have had previous marriages that ended in divorce. As the program unfolds, we hear of Lyn's struggles to form a bond with Heather, Penny's daughter from her first marriage. We also hear commentary from counselor Elaine Horigian, a clinical psychologist, and Helen Weingarten, a professor of social work.

LESSON GOALS

By the end of this lesson you should be prepared to:

1. Discuss the ways in which adults meet their needs for love/affiliation and work/achievement during early adulthood.

2. Explain how the social clock influences the timing of important events during adulthood.

3. Review the developmental course of friendship during adulthood, and discuss the issues facing adults in meeting the need for intimacy.

4. Discuss the impact of the social context on divorce, the reasons for today's rising divorce rate, and the usual impact of divorce on families.

5. Describe the typical stages of the family life cycle, and discuss the special challenges facing stepparents, adoptive parents, and foster parents.

Audio Assignment

Listen to the audio tape that accompanies Lesson 19: "Not Being First."

Write answers to the following questions. You may replay portions of the program if you need to refresh your memory. Answer guidelines may be found in the Lesson Guidelines section at the end of this chapter.

1. In what ways do nuclear families and stepfamilies differ?

2. How and why has the prevalence of stepfamilies changed from the seventeenth century to the present day? Do experts predict that the current trend will continue?

3. Name and describe the three stages in stepfamily development described by clinical psychologist Elaine Horigian.

4. What are some of the typical problems faced by the members of stepfamilies?

5. Why is it that "every person in a stepfamily has experienced a significant loss"?

Textbook Assignment

Read Chapter 19: "Early Adulthood: Psychosocial Development," pages 459–486 in *The Developing Person Through the Life Span*, 6/e, then work through the material that follows to review it. Complete the sentences and answer the questions. As you proceed, evaluate your performance for each section by consulting the answers on page 239. Do not continue with the next section until you understand each answer. If you need to, review or reread the appropriate section in the textbook before continuing.

Theories of Adulthood (pp. 459–464)

1. Developmentalists generally agree that two psychosocial needs must be met during adulthood. These are _____ _____ _____ .

2. According to Freud, the healthy adult was one who could _____ and _____ .

3. According to Maslow, the need for _____ and _____ was followed by a need for _____ and _____ .

4. In Erikson's theory, the identity crisis of adolescence is followed in early adulthood by the crisis of _____ _____ _____ , and then later by the crisis of _____ _____ _____ .

5. Today, most social scientists regard adult lives as less _____ and _____ than stage models suggest.

Briefly describe what was in the 1950s the most common pattern of development during the early and middle 20s.

6. Although most developmentalists

_____ (take/do not take) a strict

stage view of adulthood, they do recognize that

development is influenced by the

_____ _____ ,

which is defined as _____

_____ .

7. A prime influence on the social clock is

_____ _____ . The

lower a person's SES, the _____

(younger/older) the age at which he or she is

expected to leave school, begin work, marry, have

children, and so forth.

8. The influence of SES is particularly apparent with

regard to the age at which _____

(men/women) are expected to

_____ and finish _____ .

9. Women from low-SES backgrounds may feel

pressure to marry by age _____ ,

and most stop childbearing by age _____ ,

whereas wealthy women may not feel pressure to

marry until age _____ or to stop

childbearing until age _____ .

Intimacy (pp. 464–476)

10. Two main sources of intimacy in early adulthood

are _____ _____

and _____ _____ .

11. As a buffer against stress, as guides to self-aware-

ness, and as a source of positive feelings,

_____ are particularly important.

Briefly state why this is so.

12. Young adulthood is the prime time to solidify

friendships and make new ones for two reasons:

a. _____

_____

b. _____

_____

13. Four factors that promote friendship by serving

as _____ _____

_____ are

a. _____

b. _____

c. _____

d. _____

14. When it comes to our close confidants, most of us

have two or three basic _____ , and

everyone who has those traits is _____

from consideration.

15. (In Person) Gender differences in friendship

_____ (are/are not) especially

apparent during adulthood. In general, men's

friendships are based on _____

_____ and _____ ,

whereas friendships between women tend to be

more _____ and _____ .

Briefly contrast the types of conversations men and

women are likely to have with their friends.

16. Research has shown that

_____ (women/men) are more like-

ly to reveal their weaknesses to friends, whereas

when _____ (women/men) do so,

they expect practical advice rather than

sympathy.

17. The typical _____

(female/male) friendship pattern seems to be bet-

ter in terms of meeting intimacy needs.

18. Robert Sternberg has argued that love has three

distinct components—_____ ,

_____ , and _____ —

that often occur in a _____

_____ .

19. Sternberg believes that the relative absence or presence of these components gives rise to _____ (how many?) different forms of love.

20. Relationships grow because _____ _____ intensifies, leading to the gradual establishment and strengthening of _____ .

21. When commitment is added to passion and intimacy, the result is _____ love.

22. With time, _____ tends to fade and _____ tends to stabilize, even as _____ develops.

23. Arranged marriages are _____ (rare today/still common in many nations).

24. Increasingly common among young adults in many countries is the living pattern called _____ , in which two unrelated adults of the opposite sex live together in a committed sexual relationship.

25. Cohabitation _____ (does/does not) seem to benefit the participants. Cohabitants tend to be less _____ , less _____ , and less satisfied with their _____ _____ than married people. Research also demonstrates that cohabitation increases _____ .

26. In the United States today, the proportion of adults who are unmarried is _____ (higher/lower) than in the previous 100 years; only _____ percent of brides are virgins; nearly _____ percent of all first births are to unmarried mothers; and the divorce rate is _____ percent of the marriage rate.

27. Adults in many developed nations spend about _____ of the years between 20 and 40 single.

28. Compared to those who are single, married people are _____ , _____ , and _____ .

29. The younger marriage partners are when they first wed, the _____ (more/ less)

likely their marriage is to succeed. According to Erikson, this may be because intimacy is hard to establish until _____ is secure.

30. Marriage between people who are similar in age, SES, ethnicity, and the like, called _____ , is _____ (more/less) likely to succeed than marriage that is outside the group, called _____ . Similarity in leisure interests and _____ preferences, called _____ _____ , is particularly important to marital success.

31. A third factor affecting marriage is _____ _____ , the extent to which the partners perceive equality in the relationship. According to _____ theory, marriage is an arrangement in which each person contributes something useful to the other.

32. An estimated _____ percent of all adults in the United States spend part of adulthood in gay or lesbian partnerships. Homosexual couples _____ (have/do not have) the same relationship problems as heterosexual couples.

33. In the United States, almost one out of every _____ first marriages ends in divorce. This rate _____ (varies/ does not vary significantly) from country to country. Worldwide, divorce has _____ (increased/decreased/remained stable) over most of the past 50 years but has _____ recently.

34. Many developmentalists believe that spouses today expect _____ (more/less) from each other than spouses in the past did.

35. Most people find the initial impact of divorce to be quite _____ (negative/positive) and adjustment to divorce _____ (more/less) difficult than they expected.

State three reasons why this is so.

36. Another adjustment problem is that the ex-spouses' _____ _____ usually shrinks in the first year after divorce.

37. Newly divorced people are more prone to

_____

_____

_____ .

In most cases, such effects _____ . (do/do not) eventually dissipate with time.

38. Compared to others, single divorced adults are _____ (most/least) likely to be very happy with their lives.

Identify several factors that contribute to spouse abuse.

39. One form of spouse abuse,

_____ _____

_____ , entails outbursts of fighting, with both partners sometimes becoming involved.

40. The second type of abuse,

_____ _____ ,

occurs when one partner, almost always the _____ , uses a range of methods to punish and degrade the other. This form of abuse leads to the _____-_____ syndrome and _____ (becomes/does not usually become) more extreme with time.

Generativity (pp. 476–485)

41. The motivation to _____ is one of the strongest of human motives. The observable expression of this motive _____ (varies/does not vary) with culture, personality, gender, and cohort.

42. Even more important to workers than their paycheck is the opportunity that work provides to satisfy _____ needs by allowing them to:

a. _____

_____ .

b. _____

_____ .

c. _____

_____ .

d. _____

_____ .

43. Today, the employment scene is very different from the way it was before. One reason for this is the shift in developing nations from an economy based on _____ to one based on _____ , and in developed nations from an economy based on _____ to one based on _____ and

_____ .

44. Among the fastest-growing occupations in the United States are _____

_____

_____ .

45. In many of today's jobs, although the skills are quite _____ , they may be obsolete tomorrow. This means that people in their 20s should seek educational and vocational settings that foster a variety of general abilities such as

_____ .

46. Another reason for the variability in the job cycle is that workers today are more _____ . For example, in developed nations nearly _____ (how much?) the civilian labor force is female. _____ diversity in the work place is also much greater today than in the past.

47. In the happiest couples, _____ (one/neither/both) spouse(s) work(s) either very long hours or very few hours.

48. Many women and members of ethnic minorities continue to experience difficulty in breaking through the _____ _____ , an invisible barrier to career advancement.

State two implications of these trends for young adults just starting out in the work world.

49. Women who are simultaneously wife, mother, and employee_____ (inevitably/do not necessarily) experience the stress of multiple obligations called

_____ _____ .

In fact, among families where both spouses work

_____ _____

is more prevalent as two people share obligations.

50. Generally speaking, adults who balance marital, parental, and vocational roles _____ (are/are not) happier and more successful than those who function in only one or two of them.

51. Today, family _____—coordinating housework, child care, work schedules, and so on—typically requires a level of planning and mutual agreement that was unnecessary in earlier generations.

52. Following a divorce, the financial burden of child rearing usually falls more heavily on the _____parent, who is most often the _____.

53. Proportionately, about _____ of all North American adults will become stepparents, adoptive parents, or foster parents at some point in their lives.

54. Strong bonds between parent and child are particularly hard to create when a child has already formed _____ to other caregivers.

55. Because they are legally connected to their children for life, _____ (adoptive/step/foster) parents have an advantage in establishing bonds with their children.

56. Stepchildren, foster children, and adoptive children tend to leave home _____ (at the same age as/earlier than/later than) children living with one or both biological parents.

Testing Yourself

After you have completed the audio and text review questions, see how well you do on the following quiz. Correct answers, with text and audio references, may be found at the end of this chapter.

1. According to Erik Erikson, the first basic task of adulthood is to establish:
   a. a residence apart from parents.
   b. intimacy with others.
   c. generativity through work or parenthood.
   d. a career commitment.

2. Most social scientists who study adulthood emphasize that:
   a. intimacy and generativity take various forms throughout adulthood.
   b. adult lives are less orderly and predictable than stage models suggest.
   c. each culture has a somewhat different social clock.
   d. all of the above are true.

3. Which of the following was *not* identified as a gateway to attraction?
   a. physical attractiveness
   b. frequent exposure
   c. similarity of attitudes
   d. apparent availability

4. The social circles of ex-spouses usually _____ in the first year following a divorce.
   a. shrink
   b. grow larger
   c. become more fluid
   d. become less fluid

5. In the United States and other Western countries, the lower a person's socioeconomic status:
   a. the younger the age at which the social clock is "set" for many life events.
   b. the older the age at which the social clock is "set" for many life events.
   c. the more variable are the settings for the social clock.
   d. the less likely it is that divorce will occur.

6. According to Erikson, the failure to achieve intimacy during early adulthood is most likely to result in:
   a. generativity.
   b. stagnation.
   c. role diffusion.
   d. isolation.

7. Friendships are important for young adults because:
   a. friendship ties are voluntary.
   b. compared to earlier cohorts, they are less likely to be caring for older relatives.
   c. they are likely to postpone marriage.
   d. of all the above reasons.

8. Beginning with the lower-level needs, what is the correct order in Maslow's hierarchy?
   a. self-fulfillment, psychological, basic
   b. psychological, basic, self-fulfillment
   c. basic, psychological, self-fulfillment
   d. basic, self-fulfillment, psychological

9. According to Robert Sternberg, consummate love emerges:
   a. as a direct response to passion.
   b. as a direct response to physical intimacy.
   c. when commitment is added to passion and intimacy.
   d. during the early years of parenthood.

10. An arrangement in which two unrelated, unmarried adults of the opposite sex live together is called:
    a. cross-sex friendship.
    b. a passive-congenial pattern.
    c. cohabitation.
    d. affiliation.

11. Differences in religious customs or rituals are *most* likely in a:
    a. homogamous couple.
    b. heterogamous couple.
    c. cohabiting couple.
    d. very young married couple.

12. Who formulated the concept that major life transitions occur at approximately ages 20, 30, and 40, based on his study of a small group of men in the 1960s?
    a. Erik Erikson
    b. Daniel Levinson
    c. Abraham Maslow
    d. Robert Sternberg

13. Homogamy is to heterogamy as:
    a. marriage outside the group is to marriage within the group.
    b. marriage within the group is to marriage outside the group.
    c. companionate love is to passionate love.
    d. passionate love is to companionate love

14. Adults who successfully combine the roles of spouse, parent, and employee tend to report:
    a. less overall happiness than other adults.
    b. more overall happiness than other adults.
    c. regrets over parental roles.
    d. problems in career advancement.

15. Compared to adolescents who live with their biological parents, stepchildren, foster children, and adoptive children:
    a. leave home at an older age.
    b. leave home at a younger age.
    c. have fewer developmental problems.
    d. have the same developmental problems.

16. In the seventeenth century most marriages were ended _____ ; today most are ended _____ .
    a. by divorce; by the death of a spouse
    b. by the death of a spouse; by divorce
    c. before children were born; after children are born
    d. after children were born; before children are born

17. Compared to the nineteenth century, the number of stepfamilies today is:
    a. significantly greater.
    b. about the same.
    c. a little greater.
    d. significantly less.

18. According to experts, one common mistake made by many stepfamilies is to:
    a. try to become the same as nuclear families.
    b. allow their stepchildren to do anything they want.
    c. discipline their stepchildren too harshly.
    d. avoid establishing any "deep" relationships within the stepfamily.

19. Concerning children within stepfamilies, which of the following is true?
    a. Small children tend to form new loyalties only with difficulty.
    b. Small children tend to think in terms of absolutes such as, "You can only love one mom and one dad."
    c. Small children often feel resentful and hostile toward a stepparent.
    d. All of the above are true.

20. According to counselor Elaine Horigian, in the final stage of stepfamily living:
    a. family members "let go" of unrealistic expectations and realize that their stepfamily will never be the same as a nuclear family.
    b. each family member "bends over backward" trying to please other family members.
    c. family members become alienated to the extent that a sense of closeness is impossible.
    d. none of the above occurs; it is impossible to predict such stages.

21. The key difference between common couple violence and intimate terrorism is:
    a. the presence of mental illness in the violent partner in intimate terrorism.
    b. the violent control of one partner by the other in intimate terrorism.
    c. the presence of children in intimate terrorism.
    d. the cyclical nature of common couple violence.

22. The prime effect of the social clock is to make an individual aware of:
    a. his or her socioeconomic status.
    b. the diversity of psychosocial paths during early adulthood.
    c. the means of fulfilling affiliation and achievement needs.
    d. the "right" or "best" time for assuming adult roles.

23. Depending on the amount of stress they are under, women who simultaneously serve as mother, wife, and employee may experience:
    a. marital equity.
    b. a glass ceiling.
    c. role overload.
    d. social homogamy.

NAME _____   INSTRUCTOR _____

LESSON 19: GENOGRAMS

Exercise

As an exercise in studying the trends described in the audio program, and reflecting on your own life experiences, construct a **genogram** of your own, or another, family. A genogram is a map of several generations within a family, something like a family tree. By convention, in genograms males are represented by squares and females by circles. Marriage is indicated by a solid line drawn from circle to square, and divorce by a dashed line. Death is indicated by drawing an "X" through the circle or square. The genogram is expanded horizontally to include additional individuals within a given generation, and vertically to document the family history across several generations. Here, for example, is the beginning of a genogram representing the Beesley family, whose members were introduced in the audio program.

Jack   Penny   Lyn   Shelly

Heather

This genogram would be completed by adding Penny's and Lyn's brothers, sisters, parents, and grandparents.

Since the turn of the century, family relationships and the typical structure of family genograms have changed in several ways. For one thing, families with multigenerational living members are much more common. For another, the average size of nuclear families has declined and there are more single-parent and stepparent households. These changes are resulting in more complex genograms. As Lyn Beesley said of Heather's family tree, "It had a whole lot of branches on it!" Is the same going to be true of your genogram?

Here are the symbols to be used in constructing your genogram. It might be a good idea to make a rough draft before drawing the final version on the back of this sheet. Hand the completed genogram in to your instructor.

male   female   marriage   divorce   deceased   children

LESSON GUIDELINES

Audio Question Guidelines

1. **Stepfamilies** are much more complex than nuclear families for several reasons:

   When parents remarry, children become members of two households.

   Competition may exist within and among stepfamily relationships.

   There are more relationships—that is, extra in-laws, grandparents, and so on.

2. In the seventeenth century, stepfamilies were very common due to the deaths of spouses and a high rate of remarriage among widows and widowers. In the eighteenth and nineteenth centuries, the number of stepfamilies declined. In the middle of the twentieth century, as divorce rates began to soar and people continued to live longer than in the past, the number of stepfamilies began to rise again.

   Although it is not easy to count the number of stepfamily households, the rising trend is expected to continue.

3. Stage One (The "Honeymoon" Stage): For approximately six months after the remarriage, everyone "tries too hard" and avoids dealing with his or her true feelings of fear, resentment, and threat.

   Stage Two (The "Conflict" Stage): Negative feelings are now expressed. It's necessary for the natural parent to support the stepparent and give him or her credibility.

   Stage Three (The "Letting Go" Stage): The stepfamily begins to realize that it will never be the same as a nuclear family and lets go of some of the myths, ideals, and dreams it once held. This is a very rewarding stage because the stepfamily members realize that their relationships are deep and caring, even though they are different from those within a nuclear family.

4. The new stepfamily is often immediately faced with a set of very difficult problems involving deeply held feelings of loyalty. It takes a long time for children to develop new attachments. Stepparents often are disappointed that their relationships with stepchildren are not as close as they would like.

   Stepfamilies often attempt to re-create the exclusive, close-knit relationships of a nuclear family, which usually is not possible.

   The extra relationships within stepfamilies may create hostility and competition.

   Stepparents may feel alienated, awkward, and as if they are constantly "walking on eggs."

   With so many diverse relationships within a stepfamily, social etiquette is often difficult. Graduations and weddings can pose problems, for example. Issues of sexuality also are different than they are in nuclear families. Sexual feelings between husband and wife, between stepparents and stepchildren, and between unrelated youngsters suddenly brought together must all be dealt with.

5. Children may feel that they have "lost" a natural parent.

   Stepparents lose the sense of "being first" in their relationships with stepchildren.

   Stepparents may also experience a sense of loss of the dreams that accompany a first-time marriage.

   "Natural" parents feel a sense of loss of their former spouse.

Textbook Question Answers

1. affiliation and achievement (affection and instrumentality or interdependence and independence or communion and agency)

2. love; work

3. love; belonging; success; esteem

4. intimacy versus isolation; generativity versus stagnation

5. orderly; predictable

In the 1950s, men in their early 20s would finish their education, choose their occupation, marry, buy a house, and have children. Women would marry and have children.

6. do not take; social clock; the culturally set timetable that establishes when various events and endeavors are appropriate

7. socioeconomic status; younger

8. women; marry; childbearing

9. 18; 30; 30; 40

10. close friendship; romantic partnership

11. friends

Friends choose each other, often for the very qualities that make them good sources of emotional support. They are also a source of self-esteem.

12. **a.** Most young adults try to postpone the over-riding commitments of marriage and having children.

    b. Because today's elderly are healthier, few young adults must provide care for aging parents.

13. gateways to attraction

    a. physical attractiveness

    b. apparent availability

    b. absence of "exclusion criteria"

    b. frequent exposure

14. filters; excluded

15. are; shared activities; interests; intimate; emotional

Women talk more often about their intimate concerns and delve deeper into personal and family issues; men typically talk about external matters such as sports, politics, or work.

16. women; men

17. female

18. passion; intimacy; commitment; developmental progression

19. seven

20. personal intimacy; commitment

21. consummate

22. passion; intimacy; commitment

23. still common in many nations

24. cohabitation

25. does not; happy; healthy; financial status; stress

26. higher; 10; 50; 49

27. half

28. happier; healthier; richer

29. less; identity

30. homogamy; more; heterogamy; role; social homogamy

31. marital equity; social exchange

32. 2 to 5 percent; have

33. two; varies; increased; stabilized

34. more

35. negative; more

First, until the divorce, ex-spouses often are unaware of things that were going well. Second, even after divorce, emotional dependence between the former partners often is strong. Third, other people behave unpredictably and badly, creating new problems instead of providing needed social support.

36. social circle

37. loneliness, disequilibrium, promiscuous sexual behavior, and erratic patterns of eating, sleeping, working, and drug and alcohol use; do

38. least

Many factors contribute to spouse abuse, including social pressures that create stress, cultural values that condone violence, personality pathologies, and drug and alcohol addiction.

39. common couple violence

40. intimate terrorism; husband; battered-wife; becomes

41. achieve; varies

42. generativity

    a. develop and use their personal skills

    b. express their creative energy

    c. aid and advise coworkers

    d. contribute to the community

43. agriculture; industry; industry; information; service

44. those related to computers; others include physical or occupational therapist, human service worker, home health aide, medical assistant, fitness trainer, and special education teacher

45. specific; decision making, memory, cooperation, and problem solving

46. diverse; half; Ethnic

47. neither

48. glass ceiling

First, success at work today depends more than ever on the same human relations skills needed in successful friendships and marriages. Second, to be successful today workers must be able to adapt to the varied work environment.

49. do not necessarily; role overload; role buffering

50. are

51. logistics

52. custodial; mother

53. one-third

54. attachments

55. adoptive

56. earlier than

Answers to Testing Yourself

1. **b.** is the answer. (textbook, p. 460)

2. **d.** is the answer. (textbook, p. 462)

3. **c.** is the answer. (textbook, p. 465)

4. **a.** is the answer. (textbook, p. 474)

   c. & d. The fluidity of social circles following divorce was not discussed.

5. **a.** is the answer. (textbook, p. 463)

   d. Low SES is actually a risk factor for divorce.

6. **d.** is the answer. (textbook, p. 460)

   a. Generativity is a characteristic of the crisis following the intimacy crisis.

   b. Stagnation occurs when generativity needs are not met.

   c. Erikson's theory does not address this issue.

7. **d.** is the answer. (textbook, p. 465)

8. **c.** is the answer. (textbook, p. 460)

9. **c.** is the answer. (textbook, p. 468)

   d. Sternberg's theory is not concerned with the stages of parenthood.

10. **c.** is the answer. (textbook, p. 469)

11. **b.** is the answer. (textbook, p. 470)

    a. By definition, homogamous couples share values, background, and the like.

    c. & d. These may or may not be true, depending on the extent to which such a couple is homogamous.

12. **b.** is the answer. (textbook, pp. 461–462)

13. **b.** is the answer. (textbook, p. 470)

14. **b.** is the answer. (textbook, p. 481)

    c. Most parents report that they are pleased that they have had children.

15. **b.** is the answer. (textbook, p. 484)

c. & d. The text does not discuss variations in the incidence of developmental problems in the various family structures.

16. **b.** is the answer. Today, with higher divorce rates and longer life expectancy, marriages are ended more by divorce than by death. (audio program)

17. **a.** is the answer. Today, approximately one child in four will spend some time living with a stepparent before turning 17. (audio program)

18. **a.** is the answer. A stepparent can never replace a natural parent; to attempt to do so is, according to experts, disastrous. (audio program)

19. **d.** is the answer. For all of these reasons, stepparents are often disappointed that they cannot quickly develop close relationships with their stepchildren. (audio program; textbook, pp. 483–484)

20. **a.** is the answer. According to Horigian, this final stage of "letting go" is very rewarding. Once families are freed from the disappointment of lost dreams, the relationships within a family are released to grow in their own unique ways. (audio program)

21. **b.** is the answer. (textbook, p. 475)

22. **d.** is the answer. (textbook, p. 462)

23. **c.** is the answer. However, role overload may not always be experienced by women serving multiple functions. (textbook, p. 481)

    a. Just the opposite may be true. She may feel that she is shouldering the burden of responsibility.

    b. & d. These may be true but they have nothing to do with her feeling overloaded.

Middle Adulthood: Biosocial Development

AUDIO PROGRAM: Improving the Odds

ORIENTATION

How long do you think you will live? What are the odds that you will survive to be 100 years old? Is there anything you can do to improve these odds? An individual's **longevity** is limited by the biological clock, but the limit is flexible. Chapter 20 of *The Developing Person Through the Life Span,* 6/e, deals with biosocial development during the years from 40 to 60. The first section describes changes in appearance and in the functioning of the sense organs and vital body systems, noting the potential impact of these changes. This section also discusses the changes in the sexual-reproductive system that occur during middle adulthood. The next section discusses the latest ways in which variations in health are measured to reflect quality of living as well as traditional measures of illness and death rates. The third section discusses the health habits of middle-aged adults, focusing on smoking, drinking, gaining weight, and exercise. The chapter concludes with an exploration of variations in health related to ethnicity, pointing out that, overall, middle-aged persons are healthier today than in earlier cohorts.

In audio program 20, "Improving the Odds," we meet two middle-aged individuals concerned about the health of their changing bodies. As the program unfolds, Susan, 47, and Larry, 59, complete the **life-expectancy questionnaire** designed by psychologist Diana Woodruff-Pak. Although the test obviously cannot predict how long each person will live, it is a useful tool that identifies factors likely to extend or shorten that life. These factors focus on each person's **genetic history**, **personal health habits**, **socioeconomic status**, and **social** and **personality characteristics**. As Susan and Larry work through the questionnaire, it becomes clear that certain factors related to longevity, such as how long one's ancestors lived, are beyond the individual's control. But factors under one's control can add or subtract 20 years to/from a life. We wonder what the questionnaire predicts for Larry and Susan.

LESSON GOALS

By the end of this lesson you should be prepared to:

1. Describe the typical pattern of physical development that occurs during middle adulthood.

2. Describe age-related changes in the sexual-reproductive system and discuss their impact on sexual expression.

3. Differentiate four measures of health, and explain the concept of quality-adjusted life years.

4. Describe the relationship between health and certain lifestyle factors—smoking, alcohol use, gaining weight, and exercise.

5. Explain how variations in health are related to ethnicity.

Audio Assignment

Listen to the audio tape that accompanies Lesson 20: "Improving the Odds."

Write answers to the following questions. You may replay portions of the program if you need to refresh your memory. Answer guidelines may be found in the section at the end of this chapter.

1. What is the difference in life expectancy for men and women and why do researchers believe that this difference is a biological rather than a social phenomenon?

2. What is the relationship between an individual's predicted longevity and his or her genetic history?

3. In what ways do personal health habits predict longevity?

4. What is the relationship between an individual's predicted longevity and his or her socioeconomic status?

5. What is the relationship between an individual's predicted longevity and his or her social and personality characteristics?

6. What does it mean when there is a correlation between two variables?

7. Several limitations of the life-expectancy test were mentioned in the program. What are they?

Textbook Assignment

Read Chapter 20: "Middle Adulthood: Biosocial Development," pages 491–517 in *The Developing Person Through the Life Span*, 6/e, then work through the material that follows to review it. Complete the sentences and answer the questions. As you proceed, evaluate your performance for each section by consulting the answers on page 255. Do not continue with the next section until you understand each answer. If you need to, review or reread the appropriate section in the textbook before continuing.

Primary and Secondary Aging (pp. 491–498)

1. Age-related changes that are inevitable consequences of aging are called _____ _____ , while those that are the consequence of unhealthy behaviors are called

_____ _____ .

2. Secondary aging includes many _____ and _____ conditions, most of which _____ (can be slowed or reversed/cannot be altered) by a change in behavior or by medical interventions.

3. Some of the normal changes in appearance that occur during middle adulthood include

_____

_____

_____

4. Between ages 35 and 65, the lens of the eye becomes _____ _____ and the cornea becomes _____ .

5. As part of _____ aging, the rate of hearing loss is faster in _____ (women/men).

6. With normal aging, the ability to hear differences in _____ _____ declines faster than the ability to understand _____ .

7. Some losses in hearing during middle adulthood are the result of _____ and some are the consequence of _____ .

8. Speech-related hearing losses are first apparent for _____-(high/low) frequency sounds.

9. Systemic declines in the efficiency and the organ reserve of the _____ , _____ , and _____ _____ make middle-aged people _____ (more/less) vulnerable to chronic disease. Declines are also evident in the _____ system, resulting in an increased risk of _____ diseases such as _____ _____ and _____ .

10. Thanks to better _____ _____ and _____ _____ , the overall death rate before age _____ has declined dramatically throughout the _____ (entire/ developed) world. This is especially true for the two leading causes of death in this age group: _____ _____ and _____ . The overall health of middle-aged adults _____ (varies/does not vary) significantly from one nation to another.

11. At an average age of _____ , a woman reaches _____ , as ovulation and menstruation stop and the production of the hormones _____ , _____ , and _____ drops considerably.

12. All the various biological changes that extend from three years before to three years after cessation of the menstrual cycle are referred to as the _____ . The first symptom is typically shorter _____ ,

_____ followed by variations in the timing of her _____ . Symptoms such as hot flashes and flushes and cold sweats are caused by _____ _____ , that is, a temporary disruption in the body mechanisms that maintain body temperature.

13. Two other serious changes caused by reduced levels of _____ are loss of bone _____ , which can lead to the thin and brittle bones that accompany _____ , and an increase of arterial fat deposits that can set the stage for _____ _____ _____ .

14. The psychic consequences of menopause are _____ (variable/not variable). European and North American cultures' perceptions of this aspect of menopause _____ (have/have not) changed over time.

15. Over the past two or three decades, many women used _____ _____ _____ to reduce perimenopausal symptoms.

16. Long-term use of HRT beyond menopause has been shown to increase the risk of _____ and has no proven effects on _____ .

17. Physiologically, men _____ (do/do not) experience anything like menopause. Although the average levels of testosterone decline gradually, if at all, with age, they can dip if a man becomes _____ _____ or unusually worried.

Measuring Health (pp. 498–502)

18. Perhaps the most solid indicator of health of given age groups is the rate of _____ , or death. This rate is often _____-adjusted to take into account the higher death rate among the very old. By this

measure, the country with the lowest rate is

_____ , and the country with the

highest rate is _____ .

19. A more comprehensive measure of health is

_____ , defined as

_____ of all kinds.

20. To truly portray quality of life, we need to mea-

sure _____ , which refers to a per-

son's inability to perform basic activities, and

_____ , which refers to how healthy

and energetic a person feels.

21. In terms of quality of life, _____ is

probably the most important measure of health.

22. The concept of _____-

_____ _____ indicates

how many years of full vitality are lost as a result

of a particular disease or disability. The reciprocal

of this statistic is known as _____-

_____ _____

_____ .

23. The total reduction in vitality that is caused by a

disease-induced disability in a given population

is called the _____ _____

_____ .

Health Habits Through the Years (pp. 502–508)

24. Health improvements that are undertaken early

add more _____ than do treatments

begun after an illness has been recognized.

25. For most conditions and diseases, it is a person's

_____ _____ over the

years that have the greatest influence on delaying

and preventing physiological decline.

26. Cigarette-smoking is a known risk factor for most

serious diseases, including _____

_____ .

27. All smoking diseases are

_____- and _____-sen-

sitive. Although smoking rates have dropped in

North America, rates in most _____

nations and in _____ and

_____ _____ nations

have not. These statistics highlight the impor-

tance of _____ _____

in smoking.

28. Some studies find that adults who drink moder-

ately may live longer, possibly because alcohol

increases the blood's supply of

_____-_____

_____ , a protein that helps reduce

the amount of _____-

_____ _____ in the

body. Another possible explanation of the rela-

tionship between moderate drinking and longevi-

ty is that moderate drinking may reduce

_____ and aid_____ .

However, even moderate alcohol consumption

poses a heath risk if it is associated with

_____ or _____ .

List some of the health hazards of excessive alcohol

use.

29. Overweight, defined as

_____ , is

present in _____ (what percent?) of

middle-aged residents of the United States.

Obesity, defined as

_____ , is

a risk factor for _____ ,

_____ , and _____ ,

and a contributing factor for _____ ,

the most common disability for older adults.

30. Throughout much of the world, the percentage of

people who are overweight or obese is

_____ (less than/greater

than/about the same as) that of previous

generations.

31. Some experts believe that people of African,

_____ , or _____-

_____ ethnicity are _____

(harmed/unharmed) by a BMI of 25–30. Experts _____ (agree/do not agree) that a BMI over 30 is always harmful.

32. Between ages 20 and 50, a person's metabolism _____ (slows/increases) by about a third, which means that middle-aged people need to eat _____ (more/less) simply to maintain their weight.

33. Current explanations for the trends in overweight and obesity focus on _____ factors, on _____ , and on _____ .

34. The best way to lose weight is to _____ . People who are active _____ (do/do not) have lower rates of serious illness and death than inactive people. An additional advantage is enhanced _____ functioning due to improved circulation to the _____ .

List some of the health benefits of regular exercise.

Ethnic Variations in Health (pp. 509–516)

35. Individuals who are relatively well-educated, financially secure, and living in or near cities tend to live _____ (shorter/longer) lives and have _____ (more/ fewer) chronic illnesses or disabilities.

36. The reasons for regional differences in the health of Americans include variations in

_____

_____ .

37. Between the ages of 45 and 54, the chance of dying is twice as high for_____ , and only half as high for _____ , as it is for European Americans. In between are the mortality rates for _____ _____ and _____-

_____ . Self-reported health status, morbidity, and disability _____ (do/do not) follow the same ethnic patterns as does mortality.

38. In all minority groups, the illness and death rates among recent immigrants are _____ (higher/lower) than among long-time U.S. residents.

State several possible explanations for this difference.

39. In examining ethnic differences in health, developmentalists recognize that there _____ (are/are not) ethnic differences in genetic risks for certain illnesses.

40. The U.S. health care system works less well for people who are _____ _____ and for those who are _____ . Members of these groups are less likely than others to have _____ _____ or to seek _____ _____ . Another reason is that doctors, like all people, are subject to _____ , which influences the treatments they recommend for patients who are members of ethnic minority groups. A third reason is that the members of ethnic minorities are less likely to seek _____ care.

41. Compared to people in rich nations, those in poor nations _____ (experience/do not experience) higher rates of disease, injury, and death. Conditions such as lung and breast cancer, which once were more common among the rich than the poor, have been called _____

_____ _____ .

42. Socioeconomic status may help explain why the health of immigrants is generally _____ (better/worse) than that of native-born members of the same ethnic group. Immigrants often were

raised in families with relatively _____ (high/low) SES.

43. Among the health hazards that accompany the social context of poverty is more _____ , more _____ , and more _____ _____ of every kind.

44. Among African-American adult males, those of higher SES have _____ (higher/lower) rates of hypertension, likely caused by greater _____ _____ .

Testing Yourself

After you have completed the audio and text review questions, see how well you do on the following quiz. Correct answers, with text and audio references, may be found at the end of this chapter.

1. The life expectancy advantage that females have over males is:
   a. found in no species other than humans.
   b. probably a social rather than a biological effect.
   c. probably a biological rather than a social effect.
   d. only a recent historical development.

2. Individuals whose diets are rich in _____ tend to live the longest.
   a. vegetables, fruits, and simple foods
   b. meat, fish, and other high-protein foods
   c. saturated fats
   d. simple carbohydrates

3. The leading cause of mortality in both sexes is:
   a. lung cancer.   c. heart disease.
   b. accidents.   d. stroke.

4. At age 80 there are about twice as many women as men alive; this is probably due to the fact that:
   a. although males are born at a higher rate than are females, they are more susceptible to the hazards of life at every age.
   b. estrogen protects females against the heart disease that kills many males.
   c. testosterone makes males more susceptible to heart disease.
   d. all of the above are true.

5. The major influence on longevity is an individual's :
   a. personal health habits.
   b. socioeconomic status.
   c. genetic history.
   d. personality.

6. During the years from 40 to 60, the average adult:
   a. becomes proportionally slimmer.
   b. gains about 5 pounds per year.
   c. gains about 1 pound per year.
   d. is more likely to have pockets of fat settle on various parts of the body.

7. (Thinking Like a Scientist) Regarding health, the "tragedy of the commons" refers to the tendency of people to:
   a. seek their own immediate pleasure even when doing so harms the well-being of society.
   b. avoid confronting medical symptoms that might signify serious illness.
   c. passively accept medical treatment and fail to assume responsibility for their own health habits.
   d. do all of the above.

8. Age-related deficits in speech-related hearing are most noticeable for:
   a. high-frequency sounds.
   b. low-frequency sounds.
   c. mid-range-frequency sounds.
   d. rapid conversation.

9. Primary aging refers to age-related changes that are:
   a. the consequence of unhealthy behaviors.
   b. caused by society's failure to eliminate unhealthy conditions.
   c. inevitable.
   d. reversible if health habits improve.

10. Which of the following is an example of a secondary age-related loss?
   a. Genes on the sex chromosomes cause men's hearing to decline twice as fast as women's.
   b. Between the ages of 35 and 65, the lens of the eye becomes less elastic.
   c. As we grow older, the corneas of our eyes become flatter.
   d. Adults who have spent years working on loud machines develop specific hearing deficits.

11. At midlife, individuals who _____ tend to live longer and have fewer chronic illnesses or disabilities.
    a. are relatively well educated
    b. are financially secure
    c. live in or near cities
    d. are or do all of the above

12. The term that refers to diseases of all kinds is:
    a. mortality.
    b. morbidity.
    c. disability.
    d. vitality.

13. On average, women reach menopause at age:
    a. 39.
    b. 42.
    c. 46.
    d. 51.

14. In explaining ethnic variations in health and illness during middle age, _____ factors are more important than_____ factors.
    a. genetic; social and psychological
    b. social and psychological; genetic
    c. intrinsic; cultural
    d. cultural; extrinsic

15. The reduction in estrogen production during and after menopause increases the risk of:
    a. osteoporosis.
    b. coronary heart disease.
    c. both a. and b.
    d. none of the above.

16. Mortality is usually expressed as:
    a. the number of deaths each year per 1,000 individuals in a particular population.
    b. the total number of deaths per year in a given population.
    c. the average age of death among the members of a given population.
    d. the percentage of people of a given age who are still living.

17. The concept that indicates how many years of full physical, intellectual, and social health are lost to a particular physical disease or disability is:
    a. vitality.
    b. disability.
    c. morbidity.
    d. quality-adjusted life years.

18. The total reduction in vitality that is caused by a specific condition is called the:
    a. DALY.
    b. QALY.
    c. burden of disease.
    d. morbidity rate.

19. Which of the following is true of all smoking diseases?
    a. They are a natural result of smoking for ten years or more, whether or not the person eventually quit.
    b. They are related to dosage of nicotine taken in and to length of time the person has smoked.
    c. They are all incurable.
    d. They are all based on the psychological addiction to tobacco.

20. The first symptom of the climacteric is usually:
    a. shorter menstrual cycles.
    b. a drop in the production of progesterone.
    c. increased variation in the timing of ovulation.
    d. weight gain.

21. People are more vulnerable to disease during middle adulthood because:
    a. they exercise beyond their capacity.
    b. they tend to have poorer health habits.
    c. their vital body systems decline in efficiency.
    d. of all of the above reasons.

22. Which of the following was *not* suggested as an explanation for variations in health among recent immigrants and long-time U.S. residents?
    a. Hardier individuals tend to emigrate.
    b. Immigrants who are more assimilated tend to have healthier lifestyles.
    c. Recent immigrants tend to be more optimistic.
    d. Recent immigrants have stronger family support.

23. Which of the following is true of sexual expressiveness in middle age?
    a. Menopause impairs a woman's sexual relationship.
    b. Men's frequency of ejaculation increases until approximately age 55.
    c. Signs of arousal in a woman are as obvious as they were at age 20.
    d. The levels of sex hormones gradually diminish and responses slow down.

NAME _____   INSTRUCTOR _____

LESSON 20: HOW LONG WILL YOU LIVE?

Exercise

An individual's life span is determined by many factors, including genetic history, personal health habits, socioeconomic status, and personality. To see how these factors interact, complete the following life expectancy questionnaire for yourself (or for someone you know). The basic life expectancy for American males of all races today is 73.6 years; for females it is 79.4 years. Write this beginning number down; then, as you check through the list, add or subtract the appropriate number of years for each item.

Beginning Life Expectancy   _____

1. Longevity of grandparents
   Add 1 year for each grandparent living beyond age 80. Add one-half year for each grandparent surviving beyond the age of 70.   _____

2. Longevity of parents
   If your mother lived beyond the age of 80, add 4 years. Add 2 years if your father lived beyond 80.   _____

3. Cardiovascular disease among close relatives
   If any parent, grandparent, or sibling died from cardiovascular disease before age 50, subtract 4 years for each incidence. If any died from the above before the age of 60, subtract 2 years.   _____

4. Other heritable disease among close relatives
   If any parent, grandparent, or sibling died before the age of 60 from diabetes or peptic ulcer, subtract 3 years. If any died before 60 from stomach cancer, subtract 2 years. Women whose close female relatives have died before 60 from breast cancer should also subtract 2 years. Finally, if any close relatives have died before the age of 60 from any cause except accidents or homicide, subtract 1 year for each incidence. _____

5. Childbearing
   Women who cannot or do not plan to have children, and those over 40 who have never had children, should subtract one-half year. Women who have had over seven children, or plan to, should subtract 1 year.   _____

6. Mother's age at your birth
   Was your mother over the age of 35 or under the age of 18 when you were born? If so, subtract 1 year.   _____

7. Birth order
   Are you the first-born in your family? If so, add 1 year.   _____

8. Intelligence
   If you feel that you are superior in intelligence, add 2 years.   _____

9. Weight
   If you are more than 30 percent overweight, subtract 5 years.
   If you are more than 10 percent overweight, subtract 2 years.   _____

10. Dietary habits
    If you eat a lot of vegetables and fruits, and usually stop eating
    before feeling full, add 1 year. If you drink five or more cups of
    coffee per day, subtract one-half year.   _____

11. Smoking
    If you smoke two or more packs of cigarettes a day, subtract 12 years. If you smoke
    between one and two packs a day, subtract 7 years. If you smoke less than a pack a day,
    subtract 2 years.   _____

12. Drinking
    If you are a moderate drinker, add 3 years. If you are a light
    drinker, add 1.5 years. If you are a heavy drinker, subtract 8 years.   _____

13. Exercise
    If you exercise briskly at least three times a week, add 3 years.   _____

14. Sleep
    If you sleep more than 10 hours or less than 5 hours a night, subtract 2 years.

                                                                                          _____

15. Sexual activity
    If you enjoy sexual activity at least once a week, add 2 years.   _____

16. Regular physical examinations
    If you have an annual physical examination by your physician, add 2 years.

                                                                                          _____

17. Health status
    If you have a chronic illness at present, subtract 5 years.   _____

18. Years of education
    If you graduated from college, add 4 years. If you attended college
    but did not graduate, add 2 years. If you graduated from high school
    but did not attend college, add 1 year. If you have less than an
    eighth-grade education, subtract 2 years.   _____

19. Occupational level (former, if retired; spouse's, if you are not working)
    Professional, add 1.5 years; technicians, administrators, managers,
    and agricultural workers, add 1 year; semi-skilled workers should
    subtract one-half year; laborers should subtract 4 years.   _____

20. Family income
    If your family income is above average for your education and
    occupation, add 1 year. If it is below average for your education
    and occupation, subtract 1 year.

    _____

21. Activity on the job
    If your job involves a lot of physical activity, add 2 years. If your
    job requires that you sit all day, subtract 2 years.

    _____

22. Age and work
    If you are over the age of 60 and still on the job, add 2 years.
    If you are over the age of 65 and have not retired, add 4 years.

    _____

23. Rural vs. urban dwelling
    If you live in an urban area and have lived in or near the city for
    most of your life, subtract 1 year. If you have spent most of your
    life in a rural area, add 1 year.

    _____

24. Married vs. divorced
    If you are married and living with your spouse, add 1 year.
    Men: If you are separated or divorced and living alone,
    subtract 9 years (not alone: subtract 4 years). If you are widowed
    and living alone subtract 7 years (not alone: subtract 3 years).
    Women: If you are separated or divorced and living alone, subtract
    4 years. If you are widowed and living alone, subtract 3 years.
    If you are separated, divorced, or widowed and not living alone,
    subtract 2 years.

    _____

25. Single living status
    Unmarried women (living alone or with others) and unmarried men
    who live with family or friends should subtract 1 year for each
    unmarried decade past age 25. Unmarried men who live alone
    should subtract 2 years for each decade after 25.

    _____

26. Life changes
    If you are always changing things in your life—jobs, residences,
    friends—subtract 2 years.

    _____

27. Friendship
    If you have at least two close friends in whom you can confide
    almost all the details of your life, add 1 year.

    _____

28. Aggressive personality
    If you have an aggressive and sometimes hostile personality,
    subtract 2 years.

    _____

29. Flexible personality
    If you are a calm, easygoing, adaptable person, add 2 years.
    If you are rigid, dogmatic, and set in your ways, subtract 2 years.

    _____

30. Risk-taking personality
    If you take a lot of risks, including driving without seat belts, exceeding the speed limit, and taking any dare that is made, subtract 2 years. If you use seat belts regularly, drive infrequently, and generally avoid risks and dangerous parts of town, add 1 year.   _____

31. Depressive personality
    Have you been depressed, tense, worried, or guilty for more than a period of a year or two? If so, subtract 1 to 3 years depending upon how seriously you are affected by these feelings.   _____

32. Happy personality
    Are you basically happy and content, and have you had a lot of fun in life? If so, add 2 years.   _____

After you have completed the longevity questionnaire, fill in the information requested on the handout and return the response sheet to your instructor.

National Center for Health Statistics. 1999. *United States Department of Health and Human Services.*

1. By how many years did your predicted longevity change as a result of the factors listed below? For each factor, a negative change indicates a *decrease* in longevity; a positive change in years indicates an *increase* in predicted longevity.

   a. Genetic history. Subtract your beginning life expectancy from your total after item 8 (intelligence).

   Number of years by which predicted longevity changed (indicate plus or minus) _____

   b. Personal health habits. Subtract your total after item 17 (health status) from your total following item 8 (intelligence). _____

   Number of years by which predicted longevity changed _____

   c. Socioeconomic status. Subtract your total in years following item 22 (age and work) from your total following item 17 (health status).

   Number of years by which predicted longevity changed _____

   d. Social and personality characteristics. Subtract your total in years following item 32 (happy personality) from your total following item 22 (age and work). _____

   Number of years by which predicted longevity changed _____

2. By how many years did your predicted longevity change (increase or decrease from beginning life expectancy) as a result of factors that are under your direct control?

   Number of years by which predicted longevity changed

3. By how many years did your predicted longevity change (increase or decrease from beginning life expectancy) as a result of factors that you cannot control?

   Number of years by which predicted longevity changed

4. Did completing the questionnaire encourage you or your subject to make any changes in your personal habits or lifestyle? If so, what are those changes?

5. Which, if any, variables were you surprised to discover were related to life expectancy? Why did they surprise you?

6. a.   Are there variables that did not appear in the questionnaire that you would also expect to be related to longevity? Name them.

    b.   Which research methods might you use to determine whether such a relationship does, in fact, exist?

7. What are the strengths and limitations of the correlational method of research?

LESSON GUIDELINES

Audio Question Guidelines

1. In all species of animals in the wild, the female of the species lives longer. The fact that this is true of all species, including humans, suggests a biological rather than a social effect.

   For humans, women maintain this biological edge from the first instant of life to the very end. About 120 males are conceived for every 100 females, but the hazards of male development are so great that at birth the ratio is down to 106 males for every 100 females. At age 80 there are only 50 males for every 100 females alive.

   Women are probably protected from cardiovascular disease (the most common cause of death in the United States) by the hormone estrogen. Because of their higher testosterone levels, men may be at an increased risk for cardiovascular disease.

2. Genetic history has the major influence on an individual's **longevity**. In order of importance, the longevity of one's mother, father, and grandparents is correlated with one's own life expectancy.

3. In promoting longevity, the following personal health habits are important: maintaining an ideal and stable body weight; eating a balanced diet rich in fruits, vegetables, and simple foods, yet low in fat and sugar; not smoking; drinking alcohol in moderation; engaging in regular exercise; and having regular physical examinations.

4. The higher a person's socioeconomic status, the longer he or she is likely to live. Longevity tends to be greater in people who have had more education, those who work in professional or managerial (rather than unskilled) professions, and in those with above average income for their age and occupation.

   The lower average socioeconomic status of African-Americans in the United States may explain why their life expectancy is approximately 6 years less than that of persons of European descent. Persons with low socioeconomic status are more likely to live in conditions less conducive to the maintenance of good health.

5. Greater longevity is found more commonly among persons who are socially integrated than among those who are not.

   Especially among men, divorce, widowhood, being single, and being separated predict shorter life expectancy.

   Experiencing many changes in one's life is also associated with reduced life expectancy.

   Being a happy person generally and having at least two close friends predicts a longer life expectancy.

   Being an aggressive personality is associated with reduced life expectancy.

6. When two factors or variables are correlated, it means that changes in one are predictive of changes in the other. A correlation between two variables, however, does not imply that changes in one *cause* changes in the other: A third factor might influence the two variables, which, although linked in a correlational fashion, do not influence one another.

7. Because the life-expectancy test is an example of correlational, rather than experimental, research, no conclusions about what "causes" a person to have lengthened or reduced life expectancy can be drawn.

   The life-expectancy test relies on the subjective assessment and memory of the respondent. The test's validity and accuracy are, therefore, subject to question.

   There has been no longitudinal "follow-up" of individuals who have taken the test to see if the predictions were accurate.

Textbook Question Answers

1. primary aging; secondary aging
2. diseases; chronic; can be slowed or reversed
3. hair turns gray and thins; skin becomes drier and more wrinkled; middle-age spread occurs; pockets of fat settle on the upper arms, buttocks, and eyelids; back muscles, connecting tissues, and bones lose strength, causing some individuals to become shorter; many become noticeably overweight
4. less elastic; flatter
5. primary; men
6. pure tones; conversation
7. genes (or primary aging); ear damage (or secondary aging)
8. high
9. lungs; heart; digestive system; more; immune; autoimmune; rheumatoid arthritis; lupus
10. medical practices; health practices;70; developed; heart disease; cancer; varies
11. 51; menopause; estrogen; progesterone; testosterone

12. climacteric (or perimenopause); menstrual cycles; period; vasomotor instability

13. estrogen; calcium; osteoporosis; coronary heart disease

14. variable; have

15. hormone replacement therapy (HRT)

16. heart disease, stroke, and breast cancer; senility

17. do not; sexually inactive

18. mortality; age; Japan; Sierra Leone

19. morbidity; disease

20. disability; vitality

21. vitality

22. quality-adjusted life years (QALYs); disability-adjusted life years (DALYs)

23. burden of disease

24. QALYs

25. health habits

26. cancer of the lung, bladder, kidney, mouth, and stomach, heart disease, stroke, pneumonia, and emphysema

27. dose-; duration-; European; Asian; Latin American; social norms

28. HDL (high-density lipoprotein); LDL(low-density lipoprotein); tension; digestion; cigarette smoking; overeating

Heavy drinking is the main cause of cirrhosis of the liver; it also stresses the heart and stomach, destroys brain cells, hastens calcium loss, decreases fertility, and is a risk factor for many forms of cancer.

29. a BMI of 25 or higher; 65 percent; a BMI of 30 or higher; heart disease; diabetes; stroke; arthritis

30. greater than

31. Latino, Asian-American; unharmed; agree

32. slows; less

33. environmental; evolution; genes

34. exercise more; do; cognitive; brain

Regular aerobic exercise increases heart and lung capacity, lowers blood pressure, increases HDL in the blood, and enhances cognitive functioning. It also sometimes helps reduce depression and hostility.

35. longer; fewer

36. the quality of the environment and health care, as well as genetic, dietary, religious, socioeconomic, medical, and cultural patterns

37. African-Americans; Asian-Americans; Native Americans; Hispanic-Americans; do

38. lower

One reason is that people who emigrate tend to be hardier. Another is health habits, which tend to be healthier in those less assimilated, particularly with regard to alcohol use, exercise, and diet. Recent immigrants also tend to be more optimistic and have stronger family communication and support.

39. are

40. ethnic minorities; poor; health insurance; medical care; bias; preventive

41. experience; diseases of affluence

42. better; high

43. pollution; crowding; health hazards

44. higher; work stress

Answers to Testing Yourself

1. **c.** is the answer. In all species of animals studied, including the human, the female of the species lives longer than the male. (audio program)

2. **a.** is the answer. People who live the longest are not overly concerned with food, but tend to eat diets that emphasize vegetables, fruits, and simple foods. (audio program)

3. **c.** is the answer. (audio program)

4. **d.** is the answer. (audio program)

5. **c.** is the answer. Personality, health habits, and socioeconomic status are all important, but personal genetic history is the *major* influence on how long a person will live. (audio program)

6. **d.** is the answer. (textbook, p. 492)

   b. & c. Weight gain varies substantially from person to person.

7. **a.** is the answer. (textbook, p. 508)

8. **a.** is the answer. (textbook, p. 495)

9. **c.** is the answer. (textbook, p. 491)

10. **d.** is the answer. (textbook, p. 491)

    a., b., & c. Each of these is an example of a primary, age-related loss.

11. **d.** is the answer. (textbook, p. 509)

12. **b.** is the answer. (textbook, p. 498)

    a. This is the overall death rate.

    c. This refers to a person's inability to perform activities that most others can.

    d. This refers to how physically, intellectually, and socially healthy an individual feels.

13. **d.** is the answer. (textbook, p. 495)

14. **b.** is the answer. (textbook, p. 511)

    c. & d. Genes and culture *are* intrinsic and extrinsic factors, respectively.

15. c. is the answer. (textbook, p. 495)

16. a. is the answer. (textbook, p. 498)

17. d. is the answer. (textbook, p. 499)

a. Vitality is a measure of how healthy and energetic a person feels.

b. Disability measures only the inability to perform basic activities.

c. Morbidity refers only to the rate of disease.

18. c. is the answer. (textbook, p. 501)

a. DALYs are measures of the impact that disability has on quality of life.

b. QALYs indicate how many years of an individual's vitality are lost due to a particular disease or disability.

d. Morbidity refers to the rate of diseases of all kinds in a given population.

19. b. is the answer. (textbook, p. 503)

20. a. is the answer. (textbook, p. 495)

21. c. is the answer. (textbook, p. 493)

a. If anything, people exercise under their capacity.

b. In fact, the middle-aged often have better health habits.

22. b. is the answer. Recent immigrants, who are less assimilated, tend to have healthier lifestyles. (textbook, p. 511)

23. d. is the answer. (textbook, p. 495)

Middle Adulthood: Cognitive Development

AUDIO PROGRAM: What Makes an Expert?

ORIENTATION

For most of this century, psychologists were convinced that intelligence peaks during adolescence and then gradually declines throughout adulthood. Within the past 40 years, however, research has led to the opposite conclusion, that in some ways intelligence actually improves during adulthood. Audio program 21 explores how intelligence changes through the adult years and describes the methodology by which developmental psychologists study these changes.

Chapter 21 of *The Developing Person Through the Life Span*, 6/e, notes that researchers today believe that there are several kinds of intelligence, each of which may increase, decrease, or remain stable with age. This section includes a discussion of the debate over whether cognitive abilities inevitably decline during adulthood, or may possibly remain stable or even increase.

The next section focuses on the tendency of adults to select certain aspects of their lives to focus on as they age. In doing so, they optimize development in those areas and compensate for declines in others. Each person's cognitive development occurs in a unique context influenced by variations in genes, life experiences, and cohort effects.

A final section discusses the cognitive expertise that often comes with experience, pointing out the ways in which expert thinking differs from that of the novice. Expert thinking is more specialized, flexible, and intuitive and is guided by more and better problem-solving strategies.

The chapter concludes with a discussion of stress and ways of coping with stress. Although stress is everywhere, for humans, cognitive appraisal of a stressful event is critical in determining whether or not that event becomes a stressor.

The audio program, "What Makes an Expert?" states that as people grow older they get better and better at things that are important to them, while abilities that are not practiced decline. Focusing on the particular **expertise** of a musical savant and a professor of surgery, the program, like the text, explores the many ways in which experts are better than novices at what they do. They are more intuitive and flexible, use better problem-solving strategies, and often process information and perform automatically. During the program, commentary is provided by psychologist Neil Charness and professor of surgery George Zuidema.

As the program opens, we hear a piano sonata played by John LaFond. Although he has been blind since birth, suffers from severe epilepsy, is mentally retarded, and is nearly paralyzed on the right side of his body, LaFond has specialized very successfully in one domain: music.

LESSON GOALS

By the end of this lesson you should be prepared to:

1. Briefly trace the history of the controversy regarding adult intelligence, including the findings of cross-sectional and longitudinal research and how cross-sequential research compensates for their shortcomings.

2. Distinguish between fluid and crystallized intelligence, and explain how each is affected by age.

3. Outline the theories of intelligence put forth by Robert Sternberg and Howard Gardner.

4. Explain the concept of selective optimization with compensation, and describe how the cognitive processes of experts differ from those of novices.

5. Discuss the impact of stressors on development during middle adulthood and differentiate two forms of coping.

Audio Assignment

Listen to the audio tape that accompanies Lesson 21: "What Makes an Expert?"

Write answers to the following questions. You may replay portions of the program if you need to refresh your memory. Answer guidelines may be found in the Lesson Guidelines section at the end of this chapter.

1. Explain what the abilities of a middle-aged musical savant, a chess grand master, and a skilled physician indicate about the nature of intelligence.

2. Describe the ways in which thinking changes as a person develops expertise in a particular area.

3. Discuss whether experts in different fields of specialization have different peak years of achievement and productivity during the life span.

Textbook Assignment

Read Chapter 21: "Middle Adulthood: Cognitive Development," pages 519–541 in *The Developing Person Through the Life Span*, 6/e, then work through the material that follows to review it. Complete the sentences and answer the questions. As you proceed,

evaluate your performance for each section by consulting the answers on page 271. Do not continue with the next section until you understand each answer. If you need to, review or reread the appropriate section in the textbook before continuing.

What Is Intelligence? (pp. 519–530)

1. Historically, psychologists have thought of intelligence as _____ (a single entity/several distinct abilities).

2. A leading theoretician, _____, argued that there is such a thing as general intelligence, which he called _____.

3. For the first half of the twentieth century, psychologists were convinced that intelligence peaks during _____ and then gradually declines.

4. During the 1950s, Nancy Bayley and Melita Oden found that on several tests of concept mastery, the scores of gifted individuals _____ (increased/decreased/remained unchanged) between ages 20 and 50.

5. Follow-up research by Bayley demonstrated a general _____ (increase/decrease) in intellectual functioning from childhood through young adulthood. This developmental trend was true on _____, _____, and _____, key subtests on _____ _____ _____.

6. Bayley's study is an example of a _____ (cross-sectional/longitudinal) research design. Earlier studies relied on _____ (cross-sectional/longitudinal) research designs.

Briefly explain why cross-sectional research can sometimes yield a misleading picture of adult development.

7. Throughout the world, studies have shown a general trend toward _____ (increasing/decreasing) average IQ over successive generations. This trend is called the _____ _____ , and because of it, IQ tests are _____ every 15 years or so.

8. Cite three reasons that longitudinal findings may be misleading.

   a. _____

   b. _____

   c. _____

9. One of the first researchers to recognize the problems of cross-sectional and longitudinal studies of intelligence was _____ .

10. Schaie developed a new research technique combining cross-sectional and longitudinal approaches, called _____-_____ research.

Briefly explain this type of research design.

11. Using this design, Schaie found that on five _____ _____ _____ , most people improved throughout most of adulthood. The results of this research are known collectively as the _____ _____ _____ .

12. In the 1960s, researchers _____ and _____ differentiated two aspects of intelligence, which they called _____ and _____ intelligence.

13. As its name implies, _____ intelligence is flexible reasoning used to draw inferences and understand relations between concepts. This type of intelligence is also made up of basic mental abilities, including

_____ _____ ,
_____ _____ , and
_____ _____
_____ .

14. The accumulation of facts, information, and knowledge that comes with education and experience with a particular culture is referred to as _____ intelligence.

15. During adulthood, _____ intelligence declines markedly, along with related abilities such as _____ _____ and _____-_____ _____ . However, if a person's intelligence is simply measured by one _____ score, this decline is temporarily disguised by a(n) _____ (increase/decrease) in _____ intelligence.

16. The theorist who has proposed that intelligence is composed of three fundamental aspects is _____ . The _____ aspect consists of the mental processes that foster academic proficiency by making efficient learning, remembering, and thinking possible. This type of thinking is particularly valued at

_____

(what stage of life?).

17. The _____ aspect enables the person to be flexible and innovative when dealing with new situations. This type of thinking is always _____ rather than _____ , meaning that such thinkers frequently find _____ solutions to problems rather than relying on the one that has always been considered correct.

18. The _____ aspect concerns the ability to adapt to the contextual demands of a given situation. This type of thinking is particularly useful for managing the conflicting personalities in a _____ or _____ .

19. Practical intelligence _____ (is/is not) related to traditional intelligence as measured by IQ tests.

20. Schaie's research on adult changes in intelligence reveals an increase in cognitive abilities from age _____ until the late _____ , except for

_____ , which begins to shift slightly downward by age

_____ .

21. The researcher who believes that there are eight distinct intelligences is _____ .
Evidence from brain-damaged people _____ (supports/does not support) the multidimensional view of intelligence.

22. The value placed on different dimensions of intellectual ability _____ (varies/ does not vary) from culture to culture _____ (and/but not) from one stage of life to another.

Selective Gains and Losses (p. 530–540)

23. Researchers such as Paul and Margaret Baltes have found that people devise alternative strategies to compensate for age-related declines in ability. They call this _____

_____ _____

_____ .

24. Some developmentalists believe that as we age, we develop specialized competencies, or _____ , in activities that are important to us.

25. There are several differences between experts and novices. First, novices tend to rely more on _____ (formal/informal) procedures and rules to guide them, whereas experts rely more on their _____ and the immediate _____ to guide them. This makes the actions of experts more _____ and less _____ .

26. Second, many elements of expert performance become _____ , almost instinctive, which enables experts to process information more quickly and efficiently.

27. A third difference is that experts have more and better _____ for accomplishing a particular task.

28. A final difference is that experts are more _____ .

29. In developing their abilities, experts point to the importance of _____ , usually at least _____ (how long?) before their full potential is achieved. This highlights the importance of _____ in the development of expertise.

30. Research studies indicate that the benefits of expertise are quite _____ (general/specific) and that practice and specialization _____ (can/cannot) always overcome the effects of age.

31. Researchers distinguish stress, which is everywhere, from _____ , which are circumstances or events that damage a person's physical or psychological well-being. These circumstances contribute to a variety of adverse health conditions, including _____

_____ .

32. For humans, _____ _____ of an event is critical in determining whether or not that event becomes a stressor.

33. In _____-_____ coping, people try to cope with stress by tackling the problem directly. In _____-

_____ coping, people cope with stress by trying to change their emotions. Generally speaking, _____ (younger/older) adults are more likely to attack a problem and _____ (younger/ older) adults to accept it.

34. Many psychologists consider _____-

_____ coping to be the most effective in the long run.

Testing Yourself

After you have completed the audio and text review questions, see how well you do on the following quiz. Correct answers, with text and audio references, may be found at the end of this chapter.

1. Research on expertise indicates that during adulthood, intelligence:
   a. increases in most of the primary mental abilities.
   b. increases in specific areas of interest to the person.
   c. increases only in those areas associated with the individual's career.
   d. shows a uniform decline in all areas.

2. John LaFond, a musical savant, can easily reproduce a piano melody that he has heard for the first time. His ability to do so demonstrates expertise based on:
   a. superior short-term memory for individual notes.
   b. superior working memory for individual notes.
   c. superior ability to recognize and remember familiar musical patterns.
   d. compensation for retardation in other areas.

3. Which of the following is *not* characteristic of expertise, as described in the audio program?
   a. an intuitive approach to performance
   b. automatic cognitive processing
   c. a heightened ability to recognize familiar patterns *and* unusual cases
   d. superior intelligence and intellectual functioning

4. Compared to the peak years for achievement in mathematics, the peak years for achievement in history:
   a. tend to come at an earlier age.
   b. tend to come at a later age.
   c. tend to come at about the same age.
   d. cannot be predicted with any degree of accuracy.

5. Most of the evidence for an age-related decline in intelligence came from:
   a. cross-sectional research.
   b. longitudinal research.
   c. cross-sequential research.
   d. random sampling.

6. The major flaw in cross-sectional research is the virtual impossibility of:
   a. selecting subjects who are similar in every aspect except age.
   b. tracking all subjects over a number of years.
   c. finding volunteers with high IQs.
   d. testing concept mastery.

7. Because of the limitations of other research methods, K. Warner Schaie developed a new research design based on:
   a. observer-participant methods.
   b. in-depth questionnaires.
   c. personal interviews.
   d. both cross-sectional and longitudinal methods.

8. Why don't traditional intelligence tests reveal age-related declines in processing speed and short-term memory during adulthood?
   a. They measure only fluid intelligence.
   b. They measure only crystallized intelligence.
   c. They separate verbal and non-verbal IQ scores, obscuring these declines.
   d. They yield a single IQ score, allowing adulthood increases in crystallized intelligence to mask these declines.

9. Which of the following is most likely to *decrease* with age?
   a. vocabulary
   b. accumulated facts
   c. speed of thinking
   d. practical intelligence

10. The basic mental abilities that go into learning and understanding any subject have been classified as:
    a. crystallized intelligence.
    b. plastic intelligence.
    c. fluid intelligence.
    d. rote memory.

11. Some psychologists contend that intelligence consists of fluid intelligence, which _____ during adulthood, and crystallized intelligence, which

    _____ .
    a. remains stable; declines
    b. declines; remains stable
    c. increases; declines
    d. declines; increases

12. Charles Spearman argued for the existence of a single general intelligence factor, which he referred to as:
    a. *g*.
    b. practical intelligence.
    c. analytic intelligence.
    d. creative intelligence.

13. The Flynn effect refers to:
    a. the trend toward increasing average IQ.
    b. age-related declines in fluid intelligence.
    c. ethnic differences in average IQ scores.
    d. the impact of practice on expertise.

14. The shift from conscious, deliberate processing of information to a more unconscious, effortless performance requires:
    a. automatic responding.
    b. subliminal execution.
    c. plasticity.
    d. encoding.

15. Concerning expertise, which of the following is true?
    a. In performing tasks, experts tend to be more set in their ways, preferring to use strategies that have worked in the past.
    b. The reasoning of experts is usually more formal, disciplined, and stereotyped than that of the novice.
    c. In performing tasks, experts tend to be more flexible and to enjoy experimentation more than novices do.
    d. Experts often have difficulty adjusting to situations that are exceptions to the rule.

16. In general, problem-focused coping is to emotion-focused coping as:
    a. men are to women.
    b. women are to men.
    c. older adults are to younger adults.
    d. younger adults are to older adults.

17. Which of the following describes the results of Nancy Bayley's follow-up study of members of the Berkeley Growth Study?
    a. Most subjects reached a plateau in intellectual functioning at age 21.
    b. The typical person at age 36 improved on two of ten subtests of the Wechsler Adult Intelligence Scale: Picture Completion and Arithmetic.
    c. The typical person at age 36 was still improving on the most important subtests of the intelligence scale.

    d. No conclusions could be reached because the sample of subjects was not representative.

18. Which of the following is *not* one of the general conclusions of research about intellectual changes during adulthood?
    a. In general, most intellectual abilities increase or remain stable throughout early and middle adulthood until the 60s.
    b. Cohort differences have a powerful influence on intellectual differences in adulthood.
    c. Intellectual functioning is affected by educational background.
    d. Intelligence becomes less specialized with increasing age.

19. The psychologist who has proposed that intelligence is composed of analytic, creative, and practical aspects is:
    a. Charles Spearman.   c. Robert Sternberg.
    b. Howard Gardner.   d. K. Warner Schaie.

20. According to the text, the current view of intelligence recognizes all of the following characteristics *except*:
    a. multidimensionality.
    b. plasticity.
    c. interindividual variation.
    d. *g*.

21. Thinking that is more intuitive, flexible, specialized, and automatic is characteristic of:
    a. fluid intelligence.
    b. crystallized intelligence.
    c. expertise.
    d. plasticity.

22. For people, a critical factor in determining whether a situation or event becomes a stressor is:
    a. the person's age.
    b. the person's gender.
    c. the person's ethnicity.
    d. cognitive appraisal.

23. Cherie, who is upset after learning that a less-experienced coworker received the promotion she had been expecting, schedules a meeting with her boss to discuss her concerns. Cherie's strategy for coping with this stressor is an example of:
    a. problem-focused coping.
    b. emotion-focused coping.
    c. reaction formation.
    d. displacement.

LESSON 21 EXERCISE: CREATIVITY

One theme of this lesson is that contemporary psychologists take a broader view of intelligence than was the case in previous years. Experts recognize that earlier studies of intelligence failed to consider that generational differences, or **cohort effects**, may influence scores on standardized intelligence tests. Intelligence is now considered **multidimensional** and **multidirectional** in nature rather than being a single, fixed entity. One dimension of intelligence is the specialized knowledge that comes with the development of **expertise**. Another is creativity. The term "creativity" is used to describe the behavior of individuals who are able to find novel, and practical, solutions to problems.

How is creativity related to more traditional dimensions of intelligence? Research has shown that although a certain degree of intelligence is obviously necessary for creativity to be manifest, other factors, such as individual life experiences, are also important.

In attempting to study how creativity changes during adulthood, developmentalists have used several approaches. On the following page is a copy of the *Remote Associates Test* devised by Sarnoff and Mednick. This test is based on the idea that creativity reflects an ability to see relationships among ideas that are remote from one another. Several studies have reported that creative abilities tend to hold up well through middle adulthood, and may even extend into late adulthood. This is especially true for individuals who regularly engage in creative thinking, such as those whose professions require and call upon their creativity.

Arrange to administer the *Remote Associates Test* to two individuals, preferably a young adult or adolescent, and an older adult. If you wish to take the test yourself, do so first, and then test the other person. Two copies of the test are printed, one for each person to be tested. Instructions for the test are given on the test sheet. You will need to time the number of minutes it takes for you and/or your test-taker(s) to complete the test. Correct answers to the test are given at the end of this lesson following the Lesson Guidelines section. When you have finished the testing, answer the questions on page 269 and hand that page in to your instructor.

REMOTE ASSOCIATES TEST

Instructions: In this test you are presented with three words and asked to find a fourth word that is related to all three. Write this word in the space to the right.

For example, what word do you think is related to these three?

paint   doll   cat   _____

The answer in this case is "house": house paint, doll house and house cat.

1. call	pay	line	_____
2. end	burning	blue	_____
3. man	hot	sure	_____
4. stick	hair	ball	_____
5. blue	cake	cottage	_____
6. man	wheel	high	_____
7. motion	poke	down	_____
8. stool	powder	ball	_____
9. line	birthday	surprise	_____
10. wood	liquor	luck	_____
11. house	village	golf	_____
12. plan	show	walker	_____
13. key	wall	precious	_____
14. bell	iron	tender	_____
15. water	pen	soda	_____
16. base	snow	dance	_____
17. steady	cart	slow	_____
18. up	book	charge	_____
19. tin	writer	my	_____
20. leg	arm	person	_____
21. weight	pipe	pencil	_____
22. spin	tip	shape	_____
23. sharp	thumb	tie	_____
24. out	band	night	_____
25. cool	house	fat	_____
26. back	short	light	_____
27. man	order	air	_____
28. bath	up	gum	_____
29. ball	out	jack	_____
30. up	deep	rear	_____

Source: Gardner, T. (1980). *Exercises for general psychology* (pp. 115–116). New York: Macmillan.

REMOTE ASSOCIATES TEST

Instructions: In this test you are presented with three words and asked to find a fourth word that is related to all three. Write this word in the space to the right.

For example, what word do you think is related to these three?

paint   doll   cat   _____

The answer in this case is "house": house paint, doll house and house cat.

1. call   pay   line   _____
2. end   burning   blue   _____
3. man   hot   sure   _____
4. stick   hair   ball   _____
5. blue   cake   cottage   _____
6. man   wheel   high   _____
7. motion   poke   down   _____
8. stool   powder   ball   _____
9. line   birthday   surprise   _____
10. wood   liquor   luck   _____
11. house   village   golf   _____
12. plan   show   walker   _____
13. key   wall   precious   _____
14. bell   iron   tender   _____
15. water   pen   soda   _____
16. base   snow   dance   _____
17. steady   cart   slow   _____
18. up   book   charge   _____
19. tin   writer   my   _____
20. leg   arm   person   _____
21. weight   pipe   pencil   _____
22. spin   tip   shape   _____
23. sharp   thumb   tie   _____
24. out   band   night   _____
25. cool   house   fat   _____
26. back   short   light   _____
27. man   order   air   _____
28. bath   up   gum   _____
29. ball   out   jack   _____
30. up   deep   rear   _____

Source: Gardner, T. (1980). *Exercises for general psychology* (pp. 115–116). New York: Macmillan.

NAME _____   INSTRUCTOR _____

LESSON 21: CREATIVITY

Exercise

1. What were the ages of your test-takers?
   a. Younger person's age _____
   b. Older person's age _____

2. How long did it take your participants to take the Remote Associates Test?
   a. Younger person's time _____ minutes
   b. Older person's time _____ minutes

3. Of the 30 items on the Remote Associates Test, how many did your test-takers answer correctly?
   a. Younger person's total _____
   b. Older person's total _____

4. Do you consider that the Remote Associates Test is a valid test of creativity? of any kind of intelligence? Why or why not? What relationship (if any) would you expect to find between performance on a test of creativity and the test-taker's age? Why?

5. What (if any) cohort effects (historical events, education, etc.) do you believe would influence your performance (or that of someone in your cohort) on an instrument like the Remote Associates Test?

LESSON GUIDELINES

Audio Question Guidelines

1. LaFond's ability in music (compared to his severe general retardation) indicates that intelligence can be very narrowly specialized. LaFond's memory span for individual notes is not unusually high. Rather, as a result of spending thousands of hours at the piano, LaFond has developed an uncanny ability to recognize and remember familiar *patterns* of notes.

This superior pattern memory is similar to the "Grand Master intuition" seen in expert chess players. After many years of experience, chess masters have built up a large memory repertoire of chess patterns that helps them to play more intuitively, recognize instantly the structure of a situation, and determine its likely outcome.

Experienced physicians diagnose symptoms more quickly and spot rare cases as a result of recognizing familiar patterns.

In general, then, these abilities indicate not only the specialized nature of intelligence, but also the growth of **practical intelligence** with experience.

2. Relying more than novices on their accumulated experience, experts are more intuitive and less stereotyped in their problem-solving behaviors.

Many elements of expert performance become automatic and less tied to focused attention.

As **expertise** is acquired, certain skills and cognitive processes become more specialized.

Experts generally have more, and better, strategies for accomplishing particular tasks.

Experts tend to be more flexible in their work.

3. Most people tend to do their greatest work in the decade of their 30s. This varies from field to field, however.

In fields such as mathematics, the peak years of achievement tend to be a little earlier. This is because the individual needs fewer facts before he or she can go to work and be productive.

In fields such as history, which require the accumulation of a greater knowledge base, the peak years of achievement tend to be somewhat later.

Textbook Question Answers

1. a single entity
2. Charles Spearman; *g*
3. adolescence
4. increased
5. increase; vocabulary; comprehension; information; adult intelligence scales
6. longitudinal; cross-sectional

Cross-sectional research may be misleading because each age group has its own unique history of life experiences and because in each generation academic intelligence increases as a result of improved education.

7. increasing, Flynn effect; renormed
8. a. People who are retested several times may improve their performance simply as a result of practice.
   b. Because people may drop out of lengthy longitudinal studies, the remaining subjects may be a self-selected sample.
   c. Longitudinal research takes a long time.
9. Schaie
10. cross-sequential

In this approach, each time the original group of subjects is retested a new group is added and tested at each age interval.

11. primary mental abilities; Seattle Longitudinal Study
12. Cattell; Horn; fluid; crystallized
13. fluid; inductive reasoning; abstract thinking; speed of thinking
14. crystallized
15. fluid; processing speed; short-term memory; IQ; increase; crystallized
16. Robert Sternberg; analytic; the beginning of adulthood
17. creative; divergent; convergent; unusual
18. practical; family; organization
19. is not
20. 20; 50s; number ability; 40
21. Howard Gardner; supports
22. varies; and
23. selective optimization with compensation
24. expertise
25. formal; accumulated experience; context; intuitive; stereotypic
26. automatic
27. strategies
28. flexible (or creative)
29. practice; 10 years; motivation

30. specific; cannot

31. stressors; heart attacks, strokes, overeating, alcohol abuse, severe depression, anger

32. cognitive appraisal

33. problem-focused coping; emotion-focused coping; younger; older

34. problem-focused

Answers to Testing Yourself

1. **b.** is the answer. The widespread belief that intelligence inevitably declines during adulthood is based on a misconception of intelligence as a single, fixed entity rather than a multidimensional and multidirectional entity. (audio program; textbook, p. 536)

2. **c.** is the answer. Experts do not have "better" memory per se; the key to their expertise lies in how their knowledge and memories are organized. (audio program)

3. **d.** is the answer. There is no evidence that experts are more "intelligent" than nonexperts; moreover, the concept of intelligence as a single general ability is probably not valid. (audio program)

4. **b.** is the answer. Success in fields such as history is based partly on the accumulation of knowledge over a long period of time. (audio program)

5. **a.** is the answer. (textbook, p. 520)

   b. Although results from this type of research may also be misleading, longitudinal studies often demonstrate age-related *increases* in intelligence.

   c. Cross-sequential research is the technique devised by K. Warner Schaie that combines the strengths of the cross-sectional and longitudinal methods.

   d. Random sampling refers to the selection of subjects for a research study.

6. **a.** is the answer. (textbook, p. 520)

   b. This is a problem in longitudinal research.

   c. & d. Neither of these is particularly troublesome in cross-sectional research.

7. **d.** is the answer. (textbook, p. 522)

   a., b., & c. Cross-sequential research as described in this chapter is based on *objective* intelligence testing.

8. **d.** is the answer. (textbook, p. 524)

   a. & b. Traditional IQ tests measure both fluid and crystallized intelligence.

9. **c.** is the answer. (textbook, p. 524)

a., b., & d. These often increase with age.

10. **c.** is the answer. (textbook, p. 523)

    a. Crystallized intelligence is the accumulation of facts and knowledge that comes with education and experience.

    b. Although intelligence is characterized by plasticity, "plastic intelligence" is not discussed as a specific type of intelligence.

    d. Rote memory is memory that is based on the conscious repetition of to-be-remembered information.

11. **d.** is the answer. (textbook, pp. 523–524)

12. **a.** is the answer. (textbook, p. 519)

    b. Practical intelligence refers to the intellectual skills used in everyday problem solving.

    c. & d. These are two aspects of intelligence identified in Robert Sternberg's theory.

13. **a.** is the answer. (textbook, p. 521)

14. **a.** is the answer. (textbook, p. 533)

    b. This was not discussed in the chapter.

    c. Plasticity refers to the flexible nature of intelligence.

    d. Encoding refers to the placing of information into memory.

15. **c.** is the answer. (textbook, p. 534)

    a., b., & d. These are more typical of *novices* than experts.

16. **d.** is the answer. Younger adults are more likely to attack a problem; older adults are more likely to accept it, coping by changing their feelings about it. (textbook, p. 538)

    a. & b. Women and men do not differ in their tendencies toward emotion- or problem-focused coping.

17. **c.** is the answer. (textbook, p. 520)

    b. The text does not indicate that they improved on those tests.

    d. No such criticism was made of Bayley's study.

18. **d.** is the answer. In fact, intelligence often becomes *more specialized* with age. (textbook, p. 531)

19. **c.** is the answer. (textbook, p. 525)

    a. Charles Spearman proposed the existence of an underlying general intelligence, which he called *g*.

    b. Howard Gardner proposed that intelligence consists of eight autonomous abilities.

    d. K. Warner Schaie was one of the first researchers to recognize the potentially distorting cohort effects on cross-sectional research.

20. **d.** is the answer. This is Charles Spearman's term for his idea of a general intelligence, in which intelligence is a single entity. (textbook, p. 519)

a. Multidirectionality simply means that abilities follow different trajectories with age, as explained throughout the chapter.

c. Interindividual variation is a way of saying that each person is unique.

21. **c.** is the answer. (textbook, pp. 532–534)

22. **d.** is the answer. (textbook, p. 537)

a., b., & c. Research suggests that, for humans, cognitive appraisal of events is critical in determining whether they become stressors. Age, gender and ethnicity were not discussed as important variables in whether or not events are appraised as stressful

23. **a.** is the answer. (textbook, p. 538)

b. In this style of coping, people try to change their emotions.

c. & d. these are examples of psychological defenses.

Answers to the Remote Associates Test

1. phone   **2.** book   **3.** fire   **4.** pin   **5.** cheese
6. chair   **7.** slow   **8.** foot   **9.** party   **10.** hard
11. green   **12.** floor   **13.** stone   **14.** bar   **15.** fountain   **16.** ball   **17.** go   **18.** cover   **19.** type
20. chair   **21.** lead   **22.** top   **23.** tack   **24.** watch
25. cat   **26.** stop   **27.** mail   **28.** bubble   **29.** black
30. end

Middle Adulthood: Psychosocial Development

AUDIO PROGRAM: The Life Course of Work

ORIENTATION

Lesson 22 is concerned with **middle age**, a period when the reevaluation of career goals, shifts in one's family responsibilities, and a growing awareness of one's mortality often lead to turmoil and change. Chapter 22 of *The Developing Person Through the Life Span*, 6/e, first examines the question of whether there is stability of personality throughout adulthood, identifying five basic clusters of personality traits that remain fairly stable throughout adulthood. One personality trend that does occur during middle age, as gender roles become less rigid, is the tendency of both sexes to take on characteristics typically reserved for the opposite sex. The section also shows that although middle adulthood may have its share of pressures and stress, a crisis is not inevitable.

The second section explores changes in the marital relationship and relationships with relatives in middle adulthood. It also depicts the changing dynamics between middle-aged adults and their adult children and aging parents, describing the various demands of the younger and older generations.

The final section of the chapter examines the evolution of work in the individual's life during middle adulthood. As many women and men begin to balance their work lives with parenthood and other concerns, many engage in a scaling back of their effort in the workplace.

The program explores career development during middle age. Most of us define ourselves by the work we perform. But what happens when the basic structure of our job changes? or we change? At some point during middle age, most adults reach a plateau in their career development that prompts a reevaluation of career objectives.

In the program, the stories of Mary and Dan illustrate how the life course of work has changed. Mary, 48, returned to college when the youngest of her three children started high school. She has continued with graduate training in the hopes of beginning a new career. Sociologist Alice Rossi, who has done extensive research on the work and family lives of women, offers a historical perspective on women like Mary, who return to school and then to work after careers as mothers and homemakers.

Dan, 56, has practiced dentistry for 30 years. Although he would never think of quitting his profession, changes in the field have caused him to stop recommending it to others as a career. Professor of Business Stephen Lazarus, who has worked extensively with those threatened by occupational changes, discusses the impact of career crises on workers and offers advice to working adults of all ages.

As the program opens, we hear Professor Lazarus discussing the dramatic changes that have occurred in the life course of work.

LESSON GOALS

By the end of this lesson you should be prepared to:

1. Describe the Big Five clusters of personality traits, and discuss reasons for their relative stability during adulthood.

2. Explain the tendency toward gender-role convergence during middle adulthood, and discuss problems with the concept of the midlife crisis.

3. Discuss how and why marital relationships tend to change during middle adulthood.

4. Discuss the impact of divorce and remarriage during middle adulthood, including reasons for the high divorce rate among the remarried, and describe the dilemma faced by middle-aged women in the "marriage market."

5. Characterize the relationship between middle-aged adults, their siblings, and the older and younger generations.

6. Differentiate three patterns of grandparent–grandchild relationships, and discuss historical trends in their prevalence.

7. Describe how the balance among work, family, and self often shifts during middle adulthood.

Audio Assignment

Listen to the audio tape that accompanies Lesson 22: "The Life Course of Work."

Write answers to the following questions. You may replay portions of the program if you need to refresh your memory. Answer guidelines may be found in the Lesson Guidelines section at the end of this chapter.

1. What historical, economic, and demographic factors have led to the return of large numbers of married women to school and the labor force?

2. In what ways has the life course of work changed in recent generations?

3. What advice is offered in the program for those making occupational choices at ages 20, 40, and 60?

Textbook Assignment

Read Chapter 22: "Middle Adulthood: Psychosocial Development," pages 543–570 in *The Developing Person Through the Life Span*, 6/e, then work through the material that follows to review it. Complete the sentences and answer the questions. As you proceed, evaluate your performance for each section by consulting the answers on page 289. Do not continue with the next section until you understand each

answer. If you need to, review or reread the appropriate section in the textbook before continuing.

Personality Throughout Adulthood (pp. 543–549)

1. The major source of developmental continuity during adulthood is the stability of

   _____ .

2. List and briefly describe the Big Five personality factors.

   a. _____
      _____

   b. _____
      _____

   c. _____
      _____

   d. _____
      _____

   e. _____
      _____

3. Whether a person ranks high or low in each of the Big Five is determined by the interacting influences of _____ , _____ , early-_____ _____ , and the experiences and choices made at a younger age. By age _____ , the Big Five usually become quite stable. This stability results in large part from the fact that by this age most people have settled into an _____

   _____ .

4. Certain traits such as _____ toward others and _____ about oneself are influenced by friends and jobs and thus may change if the _____ changes.

5. Of the Big Five traits, _____ and _____ tend to increase slightly with age, while _____ and _____ tend to decrease. The most stable trait seems to be _____ .

6. The cumulative experiences of living a life often lead to greater _____ with age.

7. During middle age, gender roles _____ (loosen/become more rigid). Some researchers even believe that there is a _____ _____ of personality traits. There

may even be a _____

_____ , as women become more

_____ , while men become more

able to openly express _____ or

_____ .

8. One reason for gender-role shifts during middle age is that reduced levels of _____ _____ may free men and women to express previously suppressed traits. However, it is also possible that these biological changes are caused by _____ _____ .

9. The psychoanalyst who believed that everyone has both a masculine and feminine side is _____ . According to this theory, middle-aged adults begin to explore the

_____ _____

of their personality.

10. Longitudinal research suggests a _____ explanation for gender convergence in personality. The current cohort of middle-aged adults is _____ (more/less) marked in their convergence of sex roles because sex roles today are _____ (more/less) sharply defined than in the past.

11. The notion of a midlife crisis _____ (is/is not) accepted by most developmentalists as an inevitable event during middle age.

Family Relationships in Midlife (pp. 549–564)

12. Being the "generation in the middle," middle-aged adults are the _____ _____ of their families.

13. The group of people with whom we form relationships that guide us through life constitutes our _____ _____ .

14. For the majority of middle-aged adults, their most intimate relationship is with their _____ . For some, however, intimacy is achieved through _____ with a partner.

15. The belief that adults frequently experience role overload at midlife _____ (is/is not) borne out by research studies.

16. Throughout adulthood, the family relationship most closely linked to personal happiness, health, and companionship is _____ .

17. After the first decade or so, marital happiness tends to gradually _____ (increase/decrease). Spouse abuse is more common among _____ (younger/middle-aged) spouses than among _____ (younger/middle-aged) spouses.

List several possible reasons for this finding.

18. Divorce in middle adulthood is typically _____ (more/less) difficult than divorce in early adulthood.

19. Most divorced people remarry, on average, within _____ years of being divorced.

State several of the benefits that remarriage may bring to middle-aged adults.

20. Second marriages end in divorce _____ (more/less) often than first marriages.

21. Middle-aged _____ (women/men) are disadvantaged when it comes to finding a marriage partner for two reasons:

   a. _____

   b. _____

22. American families today are _____ (more/less) likely to consist of several generations living under the same roof. The role of family dynamics at midlife is sometimes ignored because the word _____ is often confused with _____ , the latter defined as _____

_____ .

23. Because of their role in maintaining the links between the generations, middle-aged adults become the _____ . This role tends to be filled most often by _____ (women/men).

24. The relationship between most middle-aged adults and their parents tends to _____ (improve/worsen) with time. One reason is that, as adult children mature, they develop a more _____ view of the relationship as a whole.

Briefly explain why this is especially true *today*.

25. Three generations of a family living under one roof is more common among _____- and _____- Americans.

26. Whether or not middle-aged adults and their parents live together depends mostly on _____ , which is the belief that _____ .

27. The "hourglass effect" describes the relationships between _____ , who often become _____ (closer/more distant) in the second half of life than they were in young adulthood.

28. Most middle-aged adults _____ (maintain/do not maintain) close relationships with their children.

29. In the United States, nearly _____ (what proportion?) of all middle-aged parents have at least one child still living with them. This is most likely to happen when the parents are _____ and the children are _____ .

30. More than two-thirds of Americans become a _____ during middle adulthood. Most react quite _____ (positively/negatively) to the occurrence of this event.

31. The grandparent–grandchild bond tends to be closer if the grandchild is relatively _____ , if the parent is the _____ , and if the grandparent is _____ .

32. Grandparent–grandchild relationships take one of three forms: _____ , _____ , or _____ . A century ago, most American grandparents adopted a _____ role. The _____ pattern, which was prevalent among grandparents for most of the twentieth century, is rare today among those who _____ .

33. Most contemporary grandparents seek the _____ role as they strive for the love and respect of their grandchildren while maintaining their own _____ .

34. Among native-born Americans, the involved pattern of grandparenting is found most often in _____ families.

State several reasons that this is so.

35. Grandparents who take over the work of raising their children's children are referred to as _____ _____ . This role is more common when parents are _____ _____ .

36. Grandparents are most likely to provide surrogate care for children who need _____ _____ , such as infants who are _____ - _____ or school-age boys who are _____ . If the relationship is the result of a legal decision that the parents were _____ or _____ , it becomes _____ _____ .

37. More than one in _____
(how many?) grandparents witnesses the divorce
of an adult child. As a result, the parents of the
_____ ex-spouse are often shut out
of their grandchildren's lives.

38. It was once popularly believed that the demands
placed on middle-aged adults by the younger
and older generations were so burdensome that
this group was referred to as the

_____ .

Generally speaking, this belief
_____ (has been/has not been)
supported by research.

Work in Middle Adulthood (pp. 564–569)

39. As people age, the _____ (intrin-
sic/extrinsic) rewards associated with working
tend to become more important than the
_____ (intrinsic/extrinsic) rewards.

40. Job security usually _____ (increas-
es/decreases) during middle adulthood.

41. The popular belief that men are more concerned
with their work than their family life
_____ (is/is not) supported by
research.

42. Both men and women report that being a good
_____ , a loving _____ ,
and a loyal _____ are more important than being a good _____ .

43. During _____ adulthood, the combined demands of the workplace and the individual's own aspirations for promotion often create

_____ .

44. In general, adults are physically and psychologically healthier if they have _____
(one primary role/multiple roles).

45. During the _____ stage of marriage,
women and men with children often engage in a
_____ _____ of their
employment effort in order to combine work and

_____ .

Briefly describe three different scaling-back strategies.

46. Mandatory retirement is _____
(legal/illegal) in most jobs and in most nations.
Workers who retire before age _____
tend to be poorer and sicker than their employed
age-mates.

47. (Changing Policy) Average salary and average
household income are highest in

_____ _____ .

48. (Changing Policy) Current fears about the retirement costs of the _____-
_____ generation have
_____ (reduced/increased) the
income of young adults, who pay proportionally
_____ (less/more) Social Security
than older workers. As a backlash, some have
called for _____ _____
in the form of equal contributions from each
generation.

Testing Yourself

After you have completed the audio and text review
questions, see how well you do on the following quiz.
Correct answers, with text and audio references, may
be found at the end of this chapter.

1. The return of large numbers of married women to
the labor force was largely provoked by:
   a. the civil rights movement of the 1950s and
   1960s.
   b. a shortage of unmarried women in the work
   force following World War II.
   c. efforts of lobbying groups such as the
   National Organization for Women.
   d. the increase in life expectancy during the past
   75 years.

2. Today, more than _____ of women with
preschool children are employed.
   a. one-fourth
   b. one-third
   c. one-half
   d. two-thirds

3. A recent national survey of men in their 50s and
60s found that _____ percent had changed
occupations at least once in their lives.
   a. 25
   b. 50
   c. 75
   d. 90

4. Which of the following pieces of advice was offered in the audio program to workers at various stages in their occupational careers?
   a. "Don't expect that your life will be divided into three neat segments corresponding to school, work, and retirement."
   b. "Don't expect that your family will fully understand or support you if you make too dramatic a career change during adulthood."
   c. "Baby boomers will find reduced career opportunities in the years to come, due to shrinking promotional opportunity, pressure from younger workers, and an unwillingness of older workers to retire."
   d. All of the above were offered as advice.

5. According to the experts heard in the audio program, for most professions:
   a. 40 is not too late to begin a new career.
   b. people who do not begin their career until middle age will not have sufficient time to make a significant contribution to their field.
   c. productivity increases directly with the number of years of experience a person has in the field.
   d. all of the above are true.

6. The most important factor in how a person adjusts to middle age is his or her:
   a. gender.
   b. developmental history.
   c. age.
   d. race.

7. The Big Five personality factors are:
   a. emotional stability, openness, introversion, sociability, locus of control.
   b. neuroticism, extroversion, openness, emotional stability, sensitivity.
   c. extroversion, agreeableness, conscientiousness, neuroticism, openness.
   d. neuroticism, gregariousness, extroversion, impulsiveness, openness.

8. Concerning the prevalence of midlife crises, which of the following statements has the *greatest* empirical support?
   a. Virtually all men, and most women, experience a midlife crisis.
   b. Virtually all men, and about 50 percent of women, experience a midlife crisis.
   c. Women are more likely to experience a midlife crisis than are men.
   d. Few contemporary developmentalists believe that the midlife crisis is a common experience.

9. Middle-age shifts in personality often reflect:
   a. increased agreeableness, conscientiousness, and generativity.
   b. rebellion against earlier life choices.
   c. the tightening of gender roles.
   d. all of the above.

10. During middle age, gender roles tend to:
    a. become more distinct.
    b. reflect patterns established during early adulthood.
    c. converge.
    d. be unpredictable.

11. Regarding the concept of the "sandwich generation," most developmentalists agree that:
    a. middle-aged adults often are burdened by being pressed on one side by adult children and on the other by aging parents.
    b. women are more likely than men to feel "sandwiched."
    c. men are more likely than women to feel "sandwiched."
    d. this concept is largely a myth.

12. Which of the following statements *best* describes the relationship of most middle-aged adults to their aging parents?
    a. The relationship tends to improve with time.
    b. During middle adulthood, the relationship tends to deteriorate.
    c. For women, but not men, the relationship tends to improve with time.
    d. The relationship usually remains as good or as bad as it was in the past.

13. In families, middle-aged adults tend to function as the _____ , celebrating family achievements, keeping the family together, and staying in touch with distant relatives.
    a. sandwich generation
    b. nuclear bond
    c. intergenerational gatekeepers
    d. kinkeepers

14. Which of the following is *not* one of the basic forms of grandparent–grandchild relationships?
    a. autonomous   c. companionate
    b. involved   d. remote

15. During middle adulthood, *scaling back* refers to the tendency of both men and women to:
    a. limit their involvement in activities that take away from their careers.
    b. deliberately put less than full effort into their work.
    c. pull away from their spouses as they reevaluate their life's accomplishments.
    d. explore the "shadow sides" of their personalities.

16. Most grandparents today strive to establish a(n) _____ relationship with their grandchildren.
    a. autonomous
    b. involved
    c. companionate
    d. remote

17. Concerning the degree of stability of personality traits, which of the following statements has the greatest research support?
    a. There is little evidence that personality traits remain stable during adulthood.
    b. In women, but less so in men, there is notable continuity in many personality characteristics.
    c. In men, but less so in women, there is notable continuity in many personality characteristics.
    d. In both men and women, there is notable continuity in many personality characteristics.

18. People who exhibit the personality dimension of _____ tend to be outgoing, active, and assertive.
    a. extroversion
    b. agreeableness
    c. conscientiousness
    d. neuroticism

19. According to Jung's theory of personality:
    a. as men and women get older, gender roles become more distinct.
    b. to some extent, everyone has both a masculine and a feminine side to his or her character.
    c. the recent blurring of gender roles is making adjustment to midlife more difficult for both men and women.
    d. gender roles are most distinct during childhood.

20. Which of the following personality traits was *not* identified in the text as tending to remain stable throughout adulthood?
    a. neuroticism
    b. introversion
    c. openness
    d. conscientiousness

21. An individual's "social convoy" is most likely to be made up of:
    a. older relatives.
    b. younger relatives.
    c. people of the same gender.
    d. members of the same generation.

22. Which of the following would be a good example of an ecological niche?
    a. an extrovert marries an introvert
    b. a conscientious person cohabits with someone who is disorganized
    c. a sculptor marries a canvas artist
    d. a workaholic marries a homebody

23. Which of the following is *not* true concerning marriage during middle adulthood?
    a. Divorce at this time is more difficult than divorce in early adulthood.
    b. Most middle-aged divorced adults remarry within five years.
    c. Remarriages break up more often than first marriages.
    d. Remarried people report higher average levels of happiness than people in first marriages.

LESSON 22 EXERCISE: THE UNISEX OF LATER LIFE

The Developing Person Through the Life Span, 6/e, notes that as people get older, both men and women tend to become more androgynous. According to personality theorist Carl Jung, every individual has both a masculine and feminine side of personality. During early adulthood, the side that conforms to social expectations is dominant. Then during **middle age**, men and women become more flexible and feel freer to explore the opposite side of their characters. The sharp gender-role distinctions of earlier adulthood break down and each sex moves closer to a middle ground between the traditional gender roles. Many women become more assertive and self-confident. Many men become more considerate, more nurturant, and less competitive as career goals become less important.

Traditional measures of masculinity and femininity are based on the assumption that these traits represent endpoints of a single bipolar dimension that considers the sexes as opposites. Recently, however, several researchers have developed a measure of androgyny based on a reconceptualization of masculinity and femininity as independent dimensions. This test of androgyny—the PRF ANDRO scale—contains separate sub-scales for femininity and masculinity, and is shown on the next page.

To help you to better understand the concept of androgyny, administer the test to two adults of the same sex but in different seasons of life. For example, you might test an adult in his or her 20s, and one in his or her 50s. You might wish to include yourself as one of the subjects. Alternatively, you might ask an older adult to complete the test "as you see yourself now," and "as you were during your early adulthood."

After you have collected your data, determine separate masculinity and femininity scores for each of your respondents by giving them 1 point on each subscale for each answer that agrees with those in the following key. Then complete the questions on page 295 and hand only that page in to your instructor.

Masculinity Key

2. T	12. T	31. T	47. T
3. F	15. F	33. T	48. F
4. T	17. T	34. F	50. T
6. F	25. T	35. F	52. T
7. T	26. T	38. F	54. F
8. T	27. T	40. F	
10. F	29. T	42. T	
11. T	30. T	46. F	

Femininity Key

1. T	20. T	37. T	53. T
5. F	21. T	39. T	55. T
9. F	22. F	41. T	56. F
13. T	23. T	43. T	
14. T	24. F	44. T	
16. F	28. F	45. T	
18. T	32. F	49. T	
19. F	36. T	51. F	

THE PRF ANDRO SCALE*

For each statement below write (T) True or (F) False to indicate whether the statement applies to you or to the person you are testing.

_____   **1.** I like to be with people who assume a protective attitude with me.

_____   **2.** I try to control others rather than permit them to control me.

_____   **3.** Surfboard riding would be dangerous for me.

_____   **4.** If I have a problem I like to work it out alone.

_____   **5.** I seldom go out of my way to do something just to make others happy.

_____   **6.** Adventures where I am on my own are a little frightening to me.

_____   **7.** I feel confident when directing the activities of others.

_____   **8.** I will keep working on a problem after others have given up.

_____   **9.** I would not like to be married to a protective person.

_____   **10.** I usually try to share my problems with someone who can help me.

_____   **11.** I don't care if my clothes are unstylish, as long as I like them.

_____   **12.** When I see a new invention, I attempt to find out how it works.

_____   **13.** People like to tell me their troubles because they know I will do everything I can to help them.

_____   **14.** Sometimes I let people push me around so they can feel important.

_____   **15.** I am only very rarely in a position where I feel a need to actively argue for a point of view I hold.

_____   **16.** I dislike people who are always asking me for advice.

_____   **17.** I seek out positions of authority.

_____   **18.** I believe in giving my friends lots of help and advice.

_____   **19.** I get little satisfaction from serving others.

_____   **20.** I make certain that I speak softly when I am in a public place.

_____   **21.** I am usually the first to offer a helping hand when it is needed.

_____   **22.** When I see someone I know from a distance I don't go out of my way to say "Hello."

_____   **23.** I would prefer to care for a sick child myself rather than hire a nurse.

_____   **24.** I prefer not being dependent on anyone for assistance.

_____   **25.** When I am with someone else, I do most of the decision-making.

_____   **26.** I don't mind being conspicuous.

_____   **27.** I would never pass up something that sounded like fun just because it was a little hazardous.

_____   **28.** I get a kick out of seeing someone I dislike appear foolish in front of others.

*Source: Berzins, J., Welling, M.A., & Wetter, R.E. (1978). A new measure of psychological androgyny based on the Personality Research Form. *Journal of Consulting and Clinical Psychology, 46,* 126, 138. Reprinted with permission.

_____ 29. When someone opposes me on an issue, I usually find myself taking an even stronger stand than I did at first.

_____ 30. When two persons are arguing, I often settle the argument for them.

_____ 31. I will not go out of my way to behave in an approved way.

_____ 32. I am quite independent of the people I know.

_____ 33. If I were in politics, I would probably be seen as one of the forceful leaders of my party.

_____ 34. I prefer a quiet, secure life to an adventurous one.

_____ 35. I prefer to face my problems by myself.

_____ 36. I try to get others to notice the way I dress.

_____ 37. When I see someone who looks confused, I usually ask if I can be of any assistance.

_____ 38. It is unrealistic for me to insist on becoming the best in my field of work all of the time.

_____ 39. The good opinion of one's friends is one of the chief rewards for living a good life.

_____ 40. If I get tired while playing a game, I generally stop playing.

_____ 41. When I see a baby, I often ask to hold him.

_____ 42. I am quite good at keeping others in line.

_____ 43. I think it would be best to marry someone who is more mature and less dependent than I.

_____ 44. I don't want to be away from my family too much.

_____ 45. Once in a while I enjoy acting as if I were tipsy.

_____ 46. I feel incapable of handling many situations.

_____ 47. I delight in feeling unattached.

_____ 48. I would make a poor judge because I dislike telling others what to do.

_____ 49. Seeing an old or helpless person makes me feel that I would like to take care of him.

_____ 50. I usually make decisions without consulting others.

_____ 51. It doesn't affect me one way or another to see a child being spanked.

_____ 52. My goal is to do at least a little bit more than anyone else has done before.

_____ 53. To love and be loved is of greatest importance to me.

_____ 54. I avoid some hobbies and sports because of their dangerous nature.

_____ 55. One of the things that spurs me on to do my best is the realization that I will be praised for my work.

_____ 56. People's tears tend to irritate me more than arouse my sympathy.

THE PRF ANDRO SCALE*

For each statement below write (T) True or (F) False to indicate whether the statement applies to you or to the person you are testing.

_____ 1. I like to be with people who assume a protective attitude with me.

_____ 2. I try to control others rather than permit them to control me.

_____ 3. Surfboard riding would be dangerous for me.

_____ 4. If I have a problem I like to work it out alone.

_____ 5. I seldom go out of my way to do something just to make others happy.

_____ 6. Adventures where I am on my own are a little frightening to me.

_____ 7. I feel confident when directing the activities of others.

_____ 8. I will keep working on a problem after others have given up.

_____ 9. I would not like to be married to a protective person.

_____ 10. I usually try to share my problems with someone who can help me.

_____ 11. I don't care if my clothes are unstylish, as long as I like them.

_____ 12. When I see a new invention, I attempt to find out how it works.

_____ 13. People like to tell me their troubles because they know I will do everything I can to help them.

_____ 14. Sometimes I let people push me around so they can feel important.

_____ 15. I am only very rarely in a position where I feel a need to actively argue for a point of view I hold.

_____ 16. I dislike people who are always asking me for advice.

_____ 17. I seek out positions of authority.

_____ 18. I believe in giving my friends lots of help and advice.

_____ 19. I get little satisfaction from serving others.

_____ 20. I make certain that I speak softly when I am in a public place.

_____ 21. I am usually the first to offer a helping hand when it is needed.

_____ 22. When I see someone I know from a distance I don't go out of my way to say "Hello."

_____ 23. I would prefer to care for a sick child myself rather than hire someone to nurse him or her.

_____ 24. I prefer not being dependent on anyone for assistance.

_____ 25. When I am with someone else, I do most of the decision-making.

_____ 26. I don't mind being conspicuous.

_____ 27. I would never pass up something that sounded like fun just because it was a little hazardous.

_____ 28. I get a kick out of seeing someone I dislike appear foolish in front of others.

*Source: Berzins, J., Welling, M.A., & Wetter, R.E. (1978). A new measure of psychological androgyny based on the Personality Research Form. _Journal of Consulting and Clinical Psychology, 46,_ 126, 138. Reprinted with permission.

_____ 29. When someone opposes me on an issue, I usually find myself taking an even stronger stand than I did at first.

_____ 30. When two persons are arguing, I often settle the argument for them.

_____ 31. I will not go out of my way to behave in an approved way.

_____ 32. I am quite independent of the people I know.

_____ 33. If I were in politics, I would probably be seen as one of the forceful leaders of my party.

_____ 34. I prefer a quiet, secure life to an adventurous one.

_____ 35. I prefer to face my problems by myself.

_____ 36. I try to get others to notice the way I dress.

_____ 37. When I see someone who looks confused, I usually ask if I can be of any assistance.

_____ 38. It is unrealistic for me to insist on becoming the best in my field of work all of the time.

_____ 39. The good opinion of one's friends is one of the chief rewards for living a good life.

_____ 40. If I get tired while playing a game, I generally stop playing.

_____ 41. When I see a baby, I often ask to hold him or her.

_____ 42. I am quite good at keeping others in line.

_____ 43. I like to be with people who are less dependent than I.

_____ 44. I don't want to be away from my family too much.

_____ 45. Once in a while I enjoy acting as if I were tipsy.

_____ 46. I feel incapable of handling many situations.

_____ 47. I delight in feeling unattached.

_____ 48. I would make a poor judge because I dislike telling others what to do.

_____ 49. Seeing a helpless person makes me feel that I would like to take care of him or her.

_____ 50. I usually make decisions without consulting others.

_____ 51. It doesn't affect me one way or another to see a child being spanked.

_____ 52. My goal is to do at least a little bit more than anyone else has done before.

_____ 53. To love and be loved is of greatest importance to me.

_____ 54. I avoid some hobbies and sports because of their dangerous nature.

_____ 55. One of the things that spurs me on to do my best is the realization that I will be praised for my work.

_____ 56. People's tears tend to irritate me more than arouse my sympathy.

NAME _____   INSTRUCTOR   _____

LESSON 22: THE UNISEX OF LATER LIFE

Exercise

1. List the ages of your questionnaire respondents and their scores on the masculinity and femininity subscales.

	Age	Sex	Masculinity Score	Femininity Score
Respondent 1:	_____	_____	_____	_____
Respondent 2:	_____	_____	_____	_____

2. Do your respondents' masculinity and femininity scores support the viewpoint that both men and women tend to become more androgynous as they get older? If not, what possible explanation might there be for the discrepancy?

3. What are some of the masculine and feminine characteristics identified in the two subscales of the "PRF ANDRO" questionnaire? To what extent do you consider that these characteristics reflect only temporary settings of the social clock? That is, would these characteristics of masculine and feminine behavior hold true at other times in history?

4. Do you consider that the "PRF ANDRO" scale is a valid test of androgyny, masculinity, and/or femininity? Explain your response.

LESSON GUIDELINES

Audio Question Guidelines

1. Until World War II, female employment was largely restricted to young unmarried women. After their marriage or the birth of a child, most women withdrew from the labor force.

   After the war, in the early 1950s, there were approximately four million fewer unmarried women than before the war. Since jobs tended to be gender stratified, employers had no alternative but to begin hiring married women to fill jobs previously held by unmarried women.

   The emergence of continuing education programs for older students occurred in the 1960s.

   These changes have resulted in a resetting of the social clock, such that with each passing decade, the woman returning to the work force is younger because she has been absent from the labor force for a shorter period of time.

   Today, more than half of women with preschool children are employed.

2. One major change is that more and more women today are either returning to the work force or have never left it, despite establishing families and becoming mothers.

   Another change is that the "one job for life" rule no longer holds. In fact, the odds of staying in one occupation for life are getting slimmer all the time. One national survey found that 90 percent of men in their late 50s and 60s had changed occupations at least once in their lives.

   These changes have led some experts to recommend thinking of work as we do our lives—in terms of seasons.

3. Experts recommend that those just beginning a career spend time talking to people who are actually in that occupation to find out what the job is really like.

   Another recommendation is that young people no longer count on a "linear experience" of being educated in their early 20s, working until 65, and then retiring. Rather, experiences should occur in parallel, as people periodically break away from work in order to refresh themselves in school or acquire new skills.

   Experts warn those at **midlife**—the "outriders of the baby boom generation"—that shrinking promotional opportunity, pressure from the younger generation, and an unwillingness of those who are older to retire may result in fewer career opportunities in the years ahead.

For those nearing retirement without any previous commitment to leisure, experts warn that retirement may become a dull, boring trap. Their advice is for middle-aged people to start thinking about part-time work, hobbies, or other ways of maintaining identifiable and satisfying pursuits.

Textbook Question Answers

1. personality
2. a. extroversion: outgoing, assertive
   b. agreeableness: kind, helpful
   c. conscientiousness: organized, conforming
   d. neuroticism: anxious, moody
   e. openness: imaginative, curious
3. genes; culture; childhood experiences; 30; do; ecological niche
4. warmth; confidence; context
5. agreeableness; conscientiousness; openness; neuroticism; extroversion
6. generativity
7. loosen; gender convergence; gender crossover; assertive; tenderness; sadness
8. sex hormones; life changes
9. Carl Jung; shadow side
10. historical; less; less
11. is not
12. cohort bridges
13. social convoy
14. spouse; cohabitation
15. is not
16. marriage
17. increase; younger; middle-aged

Families at this stage typically have greater financial security and have met the goal of raising a family. In addition, disputes over equity in domestic work and other issues of parenting generally subside. A third reason is that many couples have more time for each other.

18. more
19. five

Divorced women typically become financially more secure, and divorced men typically become healthier and more social once they have a new partner. For men, bonds with a new wife's custodial children or a new baby replace strained relationships with children from the previous marriage.

20. more
21. women

a. Middle-aged men tend to marry younger women.

b. Men die at younger ages.

22. less; family; household; people who eat and sleep together in the same dwelling

23. kinkeepers; women

24. improve; balanced

Most of today's elderly are healthy, active, and independent, giving them and their grown children a measure of freedom and privacy that enhances the relationship between them.

25. Hispanic; Asian

26. familism; family members should be close and supportive of one another

27. siblings; closer

28. maintain

29. half; in good health; financially needed, perhaps because they are unemployed or single parents

30. grandparent; positively

31. young; first sibling to have children; neither too young nor too old

32. remote; involved; companionate; remote; involved; were born in the United States

33. companionate; independence (autonomy)

34. minority

Many immigrant and minority families:

- do not trust the majority culture to transmit their cultural values, language, and customs.

- have grandparents who are not well positioned in the labor market, and can afford to be caregivers

- have parents who are poor, and therefore forced to rely on free care provided by grandparents

35. surrogate parents; poor, young, unemployed, drug- or alcohol-addicted, single, or newly divorced

36. intensive involvement; drug-affected; rebellious; abusive; neglectful; kinship care

37. three; noncustodial

38. sandwich generation, has not been

39. intrinsic; extrinsic

40. increases

41. is not

42. parent; spouse; friend; worker

43. early; workaholics

44. multiple roles

45. establishment; scaling back; parenthood

One spouse may choose to work part time. Or, both partners may work full time, one at a "job" to earn money and the other at a lower-paying "career." In another scaling-back strategy, the partners take turns pursuing work and domestic and child care.

46. illegal; 60

47. middle adulthood

48. baby-boom; reduced; more; generational equity

Answers to Testing Yourself

1. **b.** is the answer. This shortage caused employers to begin hiring married women. (audio program)

2. **c.** is the answer. (audio program)

3. **d.** is the answer. The odds of staying in one occupation for life are getting slimmer all the time. (audio program)

4. **d.** is the answer. (audio program)

5. **a.** is the answer. Many experts consider that the freshness a 40-year-old brings to a new career may compensate for a limited number of years he or she has in which to contribute to the profession. (audio program)

6. **b.** is the answer. (textbook, p. 548)

7. **c.** is the answer. (textbook, p. 544)

8. **d.** is the answer. (textbook, p. 548)

   a. & b. Recent studies have shown that the prevalence of the midlife crisis has been greatly exaggerated.

   c. The text does not suggest a gender difference in terms of the midlife crisis.

9. **a.** is the answer. (textbook, p. 545)

   b. This answer reflects the notion of a midlife crisis—a much rarer event than is popularly believed.

   c. Gender roles tend to loosen in middle adulthood.

10. **c.** is the answer. (textbook, p. 546)

    a. Gender roles become *less* distinct during middle adulthood.

    b. Gender roles often are most distinct during early adulthood, after which they tend to loosen.

    d. Although there *is* diversity from individual to individual, gender-role shifts during middle adulthood are nevertheless predictable.

11. **d.** is the answer. (textbook, p. 562)

    b. & c. Women are no more likely than men to feel burdened by the younger and older generations.

12. **a.** is the answer. (textbook, p. 554)

    c. The relationship improves for both men and women.

d. Because most of today's elderly are healthy, active, and independent, this gives them and their grown children a measure of freedom and privacy that enhances the relationship between them.

13. d. is the answer. (textbook, p. 553)

a. This was a term used to describe middle-aged women *and* men, who are pressured by the needs of both the younger and older generations.

b. & c. These terms are not used in the text.

14. a. is the answer. (textbook, p. 558)

15. b. is the answer. (textbook, p. 566)

16. c. is the answer. (textbook, p. 558)

a. This is not one of the basic patterns of grandparenting.

b. This pattern was common for most of the twentieth century.

d. This pattern was common in the nineteenth century.

17. d. is the answer. (textbook, p. 545)

18. a. is the answer. (textbook, p. 544)

b. This is the tendency to be kind and helpful.

c. This is the tendency to be organized, deliberate, and conforming.

d. This is the tendency to be anxious, moody, and self-punishing.

19. b. is the answer. (textbook, p. 547)

a. Jung's theory states just the opposite.

c. If anything, the loosening of gender roles would make adjustment easier.

d. According to Jung, gender roles are most distinct during adolescence and early adulthood, when pressures to attract the other sex and the "parental imperative" are highest.

20. b. is the answer. (textbook, p. 545)

21. d. is the answer. (textbook, p. 549)

22. c. is the answer. (textbook, p. 544)

23. d. is the answer. (textbook, p. 552)

Late Adulthood: Biosocial Development

AUDIO PROGRAM: Opening the Biological Clock

ORIENTATION

Lesson 23 of *Seasons of Life* is about the biosocial changes that occur during late adulthood. Chapter 23 of *The Developing Person Through the Life Span*, 6/e, covers biosocial development during late adulthood, discussing the myths and reality of this final stage of the life span. In a society such as ours, which glorifies youth, there is a tendency to exaggerate the physical decline brought on by aging. In fact, the changes that occur during the later years are largely a continuation of those that began earlier in adulthood, and the vast majority of the elderly consider themselves to be in good health.

Several theories have been advanced to explain the aging process. The most useful of these focus on our genetic makeup and cellular malfunctions, which includes declining immune function. However, environment and lifestyle factors also play a role, as is apparent from studies of those who live a long life.

Is the physical decline that occurs during an individual's 60s, 70s, or 80s an inevitable product of the **biological clock**? In the audio program, "Opening the Biological Clock," Dr. Robert Butler and biologist Richard Adelman point out that many physical changes of late adulthood that once were attributed to aging may be caused by disease, variation in social context, and other factors that are not intrinsic to aging itself.

Another issue addressed in the program and text is why aging, and ultimately death, occur. Since 1900 over 25 years have been added to the **average life expectancy** of the average newborn, largely as a result of better health practices and the elimination of certain childhood diseases, accidents, and other events that led to an early death. Although the number of years a newborn can look forward to has increased, the **maximum life span**—the biological limit of life—remains fixed at about 100 to 120 years of age.

As science continues to unravel the mysteries of the biological clock, a number of fascinating questions are raised for future research. Why do we die? Can our life span be increased? Is there a master gene that programs when the hour of death will come? What effect will added years of life have on intellectual potential? on the family? on society? What is surprising is the reaction of old people themselves to the prospect of living for 130 to 140 years.

LESSON GOALS

By the end of this lesson you should be prepared to:

1. Define ageism, and identify two reasons for changing views about old age.

2. Distinguish among three categories of the aged, and explain the current state of the dependency ratio.

3. Give a realistic description of the physical changes that are due to aging itself and those that are a result of such external factors as social context and disease.

4. Outline the wear-and-tear and genetic aging theories, and explain senescence from an epigenetic perspective.

5. Discuss the cellular aging theory, and explain what the Hayflick limit is and how it supports the idea of a genetic clock.

Audio Assignment

Listen to the audio tape that accompanies Lesson 23: "Opening the Biological Clock."

Write answers to the following questions. You may replay portions of the program if you need to refresh your memory. Answer guidelines may be found in the Lesson Guidelines section at the end of this chapter.

1. Define and differentiate biological clock, life span, and life expectancy. What (if any) changes have occurred in each of these during the past century?

   biological clock

   life span

   life expectancy

2. Explain the "watch in the water" metaphor introduced in the audio program. If the biological clock is the watch, what in the water influences its operation and has an impact on older bodies?

3. (Audio Program and text) How did the age-related incidence rates of acute and chronic disease change during the last 50 or 60 years? In what ways do these changes complicate efforts to isolate the causes of physical changes associated with aging?

4. Discuss why researchers are "rewriting the book on aging and sexuality," by addressing the following questions.

   a. What causes the changes in sexual response that occur with age?

   b. What is the impact of social context on sexuality? How did the policy decision to segregate older men and women living in nursing homes lead to an erroneous conclusion regarding the biology of aging and sexuality?

5. Identify three physical features of growing old that are probably intrinsic to the process of aging.

6. Explain the concept of programmed death at the cellular level. What research evidence supports the idea of a genetically based limit to the life of a cell, and the possibility of resetting this limit?

Textbook Assignment

Read Chapter 23: "Late Adulthood: Biosocial Development," pages 575–603 in *The Developing Person Through the Life Span*, 6/e, then work through the material that follows to review it. Complete the sentences and answer the questions. As you proceed, evaluate your performance for each section by consulting the answers on page 303. Do not continue with the next section until you understand each answer. If you need to, review or reread the appropriate section in the textbook before continuing.

Prejudice and Prediction (pp. 576–582)

1. The prejudice that people tend to feel about older people is called _____ .

2. The cultural bias that labels older people as infirm and ill _____ (is/is not) weakening.

3. The multidisciplinary study of aging is called _____ . The traditional medical specialty devoted to aging is _____ . Most doctors in this field see patients who are _____ , which leads them to consider aging as an _____ .

4. In the past, when populations were sorted according to age, the resulting picture was a(n) _____ , with the youngest and _____ (smallest/ largest) group at the bottom and the oldest and _____ (smallest/largest) group at the top.

   List two reasons for this picture.

   a. _____
      _____

   b. _____
      _____

5. Today, because of _____ _____ and increased _____ , the shape of the population is becoming closer to a(n) _____ .

6. The fastest-growing segment of the population is people age _____ and older.

7. The shape of the demographic pyramid _____ (varies/is the same) throughout the world. _____ .

8. The ratio of self-sufficient, productive adults to dependent children and elderly adults is called the _____ _____ . Because of the declining _____ rate and the small size of the cohort just entering _____ _____ , this ratio is _____ (lower/higher) than it has been for a century.

9. There is an inverse ratio between birth rates and _____ . Most people over age 65 _____ (are/are not) "dependent."

10. Approximately _____ percent of the elderly live in nursing homes.

11. Older adults who are healthy, relatively well off financially, and integrated into the lives of their families and society are classified as _____-_____ .

12. Older adults who suffer physical, mental, or social deficits are classified as _____-_____ . The _____-_____ are dependent on others for almost everything; they are _____ (the majority/a small minority) of those over age 65. Age _____ (is/is not) an accurate predictor of dependency. For this reason, some gerontologists prefer to use the terms _____ aging, _____ aging, and _____ aging.

13. Researchers have been able to extend the life of some animal species by reducing their _____ .

14. Vitamin and mineral needs _____ (increase/decrease) with age. However, calorie requirements _____ (increase/decrease) by about _____ percent from those of early and middle adulthood. During late adulthood, a diet that is _____ and healthy is even more important than earlier.

Primary Aging in Late Adulthood (pp. 583–592)

15. Developmentalists distinguish between the irreversible changes that occur with time, called

    _____ _____ ,

    and _____ _____ ,

    which refers to changes caused by particular

    _____ or _____ . This

    latter category of age-related changes

    _____ (is/is not) inevitable with the

    passage of time.

16. An increasingly important factor in late adulthood is _____ .

17. As people age, the skin becomes

    _____ , _____ , and

    _____ (more/less) elastic, which

    produces wrinkling and makes blood vessels and

    pockets of fat more visible. Dark patches of skin

    known as "_____

    _____ " also become visible. Many

    men experience the genetic condition called

    _____ _____

    _____ .

18. Most older people are _____

    than they were in early adulthood, because their

    _____ have settled closer together.

19. With age, body fat tends to collect more in the

    _____ and _____

    _____ than in the arms, legs, and

    upper face.

20. Body weight is often _____

    (higher/lower) in late adulthood, particularly in

    _____ (men/women), who have

    more _____ and less body

    _____ than the other sex.

21. The leading cause of death from injury after age

    60 are _____ . How well a person is

    able to move his or her _____

    _____ is one of the best predictors

    of vitality in old age.

22. For many of the healthy elderly, the most troubling part of aging is _____

    _____ .

23. More than _____ percent of those

    older than 80 have one of the three major eye diseases of the elderly. The first of these,

    _____ , involves a thickening of the

    _____ of the eye. The second,

    _____ , involves the

    _____ of the eyeball because of a

    buildup of _____ within the eye.

    The disease _____

    _____ _____

    involves deterioration of the _____ .

24. The leading cause of legal blindness among the

    elderly is _____

    _____ _____ .

25. Age-related hearing loss, or _____ ,

    affects about _____ percent of those

    aged 65 and older. Some elderly persons experience a buzzing or ringing in the ears called

    _____ . The hard-of-hearing are

    often mistakenly thought to be _____

    or _____ _____ , and

    are more subject to _____ and

    _____ .

26. Many people function well with sensory impairment, for three reasons: _____ ,

    _____ _____ , and

    _____ .

27. Sometimes younger adults automatically lapse

    into _____ when they talk to older

    adults.

    Describe this form of speech.

28. During late adulthood, all the major body systems become _____ and less

    _____ . As a result, serious diseases

    such as _____ _____

_____ , _____ ,

_____ _____

_____ _____ , and

most forms of _____ are much more
common in late adulthood.

29. Whether a person becomes ill also depends than
on past _____ _____
and current _____ .

30. Older people take _____
(less/more) time to recover from illnesses and are
_____ (less/more) likely to die of
them.

31. A frequent sleep complaint among older adults is
_____ , which is often treated by
prescription _____ drugs.

Explain why this medical intervention may be particularly harmful in late adulthood.

32. Frequent waking during the night becomes more
common during late adulthood because the
decrease in the brain's _____
_____ with advancing age means
sleep is not as deep and _____ are
not as long.

33. Many gerontologists now recommend
_____ rather than pharmacological
solutions to treat insomnia in the elderly.

34. A goal of many researchers is a limiting of the
time any person spends ill, that is, a(n)

_____ _____

_____ .

Theories of Aging (pp. 593–599)

35. The oldest theory of aging is the

_____-_____-

_____ theory, which compares the
human body to a(n) _____ . Overall,

this analogy _____ (is a good
one/doesn't hold up).

State three facts that support the wear-and-tear
theory.

36. Some theorists believe that, rather than being a
mistake, aging is incorporated into the
_____ plans of all species.

37. The oldest age to which members of a species can
live, called the _____
_____ , which
in humans is approximately _____
years, is quite different from _____
_____ ,which is
defined as _____
_____ .

38. Life expectancy varies according to

_____ , _____ ,

and _____ factors that affect frequency of _____ in childhood, adolescence, or middle age. In the United States
today, average life expectancy at birth was about
_____ for men and
_____ for women.

39. In ancient times, average life expectancy was only
about _____ years, due to the fact
that _____ .
In 1900, in developed nations, the average life
expectancy was about age _____ .
This increase was due largely to better
_____ _____ mea-
sures, including _____ ,
_____ , and _____ .

Briefly state one possible explanation for primary
aging according to epigenetic theory.

40. The leading causes of death in early adulthood are _____ (genetic/nongenetic) events. Among the genetic diseases that evolutionary process would have no reason to select against are _____ _____ .

41. Another theory of aging suggests that some occurrence in the _____ themselves, such as the accumulation of accidents that occur during _____ , causes aging. According to this theory, toxic environmental agents and the normal process of _____ repair result in _____ that damage the instructions for creating new cells.

42. Another aspect of the cellular theory of aging is that metabolic processes can cause electrons to separate from their atoms, resulting in atoms called _____ that scramble DNA molecules or produce errors in cell maintenance and repair.

43. Free radical damage may be slowed by certain _____ that nullify the effects of free radicals. These include vitamins _____ , _____ , and _____ , and the mineral _____ .

44. When human cells are allowed to replicate outside the body, the cells stop replicating at a certain point, referred to as the _____ _____ . Cells from people with diseases characterized by accelerated aging replicate _____ (more/fewer) times before dying.

45. According to this theory, DNA acts as a genetic _____ , switching on genes that promote aging at a genetically predetermined age. Support for this theory comes from several diseases that involve premature signs of aging and early death, including _____ _____ and the rare disease _____ .

46. The "attack" cells of the immune system include the _____ from the bone marrow, which create _____ that attack invading _____ and _____ , and the _____ from the _____ gland, which produce substances that attack any kind of infected cells.

47. Over the course of adulthood the power, production, and efficiency of T and B cells _____ (increases/decreases/ remains constant).

48. Additional support for the immune theory of aging comes from research on AIDS, or _____ _____ _____ _____ , which is caused by_____ , or _____ _____ _____ .

49. Individuals with stronger immune systems tend to live _____ (longer/shorter) lives than their contemporaries. This has led some researchers to conclude that the _____ of the immune system is *the* cause of aging.

50. Females tend to have _____ (weaker/stronger) immune systems than males, as well as _____ (smaller/ larger) thymus glands. However, as a result, women are more vulnerable to _____ diseases such as rheumatoid arthritis.

The Centenarians (pp. 599–602)

51. The places famous for long-lived people are in _____ , _____ regions where pollution is minimized. Furthermore, in these places, tradition ensures that the elderly are _____ and play an important social role. Because of the absence of _____ _____ , some researchers believe the people in these regions are lying about their true age.

List four characteristics shared by long-lived people in these regions.

a. _____

b. _____

c. _____

d. _____

Testing Yourself

After you have completed the audio and text review questions, see how well you do on the following quiz. Correct answers, with text and audio references, may be found at the end of this chapter.

1. Which of the following best expresses the concept of the biological clock?
   a. a gene that scientists have discovered that determines life expectancy
   b. a gene that determines life span
   c. a metaphor for the body's many ways of timing its physical development
   d. the time frame in which human evolution takes place

2. What is the most probable explanation for the increase in life expectancy that has occurred since 1900?
   a. The biological clock has been reset as a natural result of the evolution of the human species.
   b. Cultural, rather than biological, evolution has occurred, in the form of increased knowledge leading to the control of disease.
   c. A decrease in chronic disease has occurred in older people.
   d. The rate of accidents in older people has decreased.

3. Why do researchers find it difficult to determine the physical effects of aging per se?
   a. The biological clock is sensitive to social context.
   b. It is difficult to differentiate the effects of disease from those of aging.
   c. The range of individual differences in behavior increases in older people.
   d. Researchers find it difficult for all of the above reasons.

4. What, if any, changes occurred in maximum life span and average life expectancy during the twentieth century?
   a. Life span has increased by 25 years; life expectancy has not changed.
   b. Life span remains the same; life expectancy has increased.
   c. Both life span and life expectancy have increased.
   d. There have been no changes in life span or life expectancy.

5. "Programmed death" refers to the fact that when normal human or animal cells are grown under artificial laboratory conditions:
   a. the cells from species with longer life spans survive longer than cells from species with shorter life spans.
   b. the cells from young individuals survive longer than those from older individuals.
   c. cells will reproduce a finite number of times and then die.
   d. all of the above occur.

6. Ageism is:
   a. the study of aging and the aged.
   b. prejudice or discrimination against older people.
   c. the genetic disease that causes children to age prematurely.
   d. the view of aging that the body and its parts deteriorate with use.

7. The U.S. demographic pyramid is becoming a square because of:
   a. increasing birth rates and life spans.
   b. decreasing birth rates and life spans.
   c. decreasing birth rates and increasing life spans.
   d. rapid population growth.

8. Primary aging refers to the:
   a. changes that are caused by illness.
   b. changes that can be reversed or prevented.
   c. irreversible changes that occur with time.
   d. changes that are caused by poor health habits.

9. Geriatrics is the:
   a. medical specialty devoted to aging.
   b. study of secondary aging.
   c. multidisciplinary study of old age.
   d. study of optimal aging.

10. Which disease involves the hardening of the eyeball due to the buildup of fluid?
    a. cataracts
    b. glaucoma
    c. senile macular degeneration
    d. myopia

11. As a result of the slowdown and loss of efficiency in the body's major systems, which of the following is more common in late adulthood?
    a. coronary heart disease
    b. strokes
    c. most forms of cancer
    d. All of the above are equally common.

12. A direct result of damage to cellular DNA is:
    a. errors in the reproduction of cells.
    b. an increase in the formation of free radicals.
    c. decreased efficiency of the immune system.
    d. the occurrence of a disease called progeria.

13. Which theory explains aging as due in part to mutations in the cell structure?
    a. wear and tear
    b. immune system deficiency
    c. cellular accidents
    d. genetic clock

14. According to the cellular aging theory of a genetic clock, aging:
    a. is actually directed by the genes.
    b. occurs as a result of damage to the genes.
    c. occurs as a result of hormonal abnormalities.
    d. can be reversed through environmental changes.

15. Laboratory research on the reproduction of cells cultured from humans and animals has found that:
    a. cell division cannot occur outside the organism.
    b. the number of cell divisions was the same regardless of the species of the donor.
    c. the number of cell divisions was different depending on the age of the donor.
    d. under the ideal conditions of the laboratory, cell division can continue indefinitely.

16. Presbycusis refers to age-related:
    a. hearing losses.
    b. decreases in ability of the eyes to focus on distant objects.
    c. changes in metabolism.
    d. changes in brain activity during sleep.

17. Highly unstable atoms that have unpaired electrons and cause damage to other molecules in body cells are called:
    a. B cells.
    b. T cells.
    c. free radicals.
    d. both a. and b.

18. In triggering our first maturational changes and then the aging process, our genetic makeup is in effect acting as a(n):
    a. immune system.
    b. secondary ager.
    c. demographic pyramid.
    d. genetic clock.

19. Age-related changes in the immune system include all of the following except:
    a. shrinkage of the thymus gland.
    b. loss of T cells.
    c. reduced efficiency in repairing damage from B cells.
    d. reduced efficiency of antibodies.

20. Women are more likely than men to:
    a. have stronger immune systems.
    b. have smaller thymus glands.
    c. be immune to autoimmune diseases such as rheumatoid arthritis.
    d. have all of the above traits.

21. Changes in appearance during late adulthood include all of the following except a:
    a. slight reduction in height.
    b. significant increase in weight.
    c. redistribution of body fat.
    d. marked wrinkling of the skin.

22. Regarding the body's self-healing processes, which of the following is not true?
    a. The hormone estrogen may offer women some protection against heart disease.
    b. Given a healthy lifestyle, cellular errors accumulate slowly, causing little harm.
    c. Aging makes cellular repair mechanisms less efficient.
    d. Women who postpone childbirth have less efficient cellular repair mechanisms.

23. In studies of three regions of the world known for the longevity of their inhabitants, the long-lived showed all of the following characteristics except:
    a. their diets were moderate.
    b. they were spared from doing any kind of work.
    c. they interacted frequently with family members, friends, and neighbors.
    d. they engaged in some form of exercise on a daily basis.

LESSON 23: AGEISM

Exercise

A central theme of this lesson is that most people's perceptions of aging are inaccurate and reflect **ageist** stereotypes of biosocial development in late adulthood. As pointed out by experts in the program, these stereotypes stem from our preoccupation with physical decline that is more the result of disease than it is of aging.

Sociologist Bernice Neugarten has drawn a distinction between the **young-old**—the majority of the elderly who are, for the most part, healthy and vigorous—and the **old-old**—those who suffer major physical, mental, or social losses. The text indicates the ironic fact that many professionals who work with the elderly, including those who specialize in **gerontology**, have inadvertently fostered ageism by focusing on the difficulties and declines of the old-old, and by studying the aged residents of nursing homes, who are often infirm.

Think of two elderly adults whom you know, one who fits Neugarten's description of the young-old and one who fits her description of the old-old. These individuals may be relatives, friends, or even public personalities you have read about. Write a paragraph about each person, briefly describing his or her health, personality, and lifestyle, and explain why you have classified him or her as young-old or old-old. Also indicate the extent to which each person fits, or does not fit, the usual stereotypes of the older adult. Finally, speculate as to why each person developed as he or she did. What losses, for example, might the old-old person have experienced? Hand the completed exercise in to your instructor.

Description of "young-old" individual

Description of "old-old" individual

LESSON GUIDELINES

Audio Question Guidelines

1. The **biological clock** is a metaphor for the body's way of timing its physical development.

   Life span refers to the biological limit of life.

   Life expectancy refers to the number of years a typical newborn can expect to live, allowing for the hazards of his or her particular historical time.

   Although life expectancy has increased by 25 years since 1900, the biological clock (and therefore life span) has not changed. Then and now we are timed genetically to have a **maximum life span** of between 100 and 120 years.

2. In investigating the biosocial effects of aging, it is important to remember that aging, or the operation of the biological clock (or watch), occurs in a specific historical context in which social, biological, and other types of influences (the water) interact with those of aging itself.

   Chronic disease, for example, produces many physical changes (e.g., in balance) that once were thought to be intrinsic to the process of aging.

   Social context manifests itself in many behaviors, including sexual response, hormone levels, and even neural connections in the brain.

3. **Acute diseases**, such as influenza or the common cold, occur frequently in early life but diminish with age. They have nearly been eliminated as causes of death among older persons in the United States.

   Chronic diseases, such as cancer and heart disease, are uncommon in the young but increase in incidence with age.

   Chronic diseases themselves often produce behavioral changes that are difficult to isolate from the effects of aging per se because the diseases are much more common in older persons. As stated in the program, "You can't say the cause is aging unless you're sure it's not disease."

4. **a.** Sexual response does slow down with age, but the cause may be chronic disease rather than aging. Changes in the physiology of circulation and the nervous system, possibly brought on by disease, may account for this slowing down, rather than themselves being an inevitable result of aging. These changes may therefore be correctable through the use of certain medications or surgery.

   b. It was once accepted as fact that the level of the male hormone testosterone declines with age. Dr. Robert Butler has discovered that this "fact" came from studies of older men living separately from women in institutions. When these studies have been repeated in recent years, either in community-dwelling men or in institutionalized men who are socialized with women, not only do testosterone levels fail to diminish, but sexual capability is shown not to be lost in normal, healthy elderly men. Thus, social context has a significant effect on a person's sexuality.

5. Three physical features that appear intrinsic to the process of aging are a slowing down of behavior (e.g., reflexes, cognitive functioning), an increased variation in behavior, and the longer lives of women.

6. Biologists are convinced that components of our bodies are genetically programmed to die. Biologist Leonard Hayflick discovered that when normal human cells are grown in the laboratory, they will reproduce a finite number of times and then die.

   Cells from older individuals do not survive as long as cells from younger individuals.

   Cells from longer-lived animal species survive longer than cells from species with shorter life spans.

   Introducing genetic material from cells that are nearly dead into younger cells will cause premature death.

   This evidence suggests that at the level of the cell there is some mechanism that is counting and that prescribes the moment of death for the cell.

   Biologists have also found that infecting cells with certain viruses will cause them to divide infinitely, in effect resetting the biological clock so that the cell will not die. Biologists are also acquiring the ability to remove, add, and modify genes—techniques that might affect the biological clock.

Textbook Question Answers

1. ageism
2. is
3. gerontology; geriatrics; ill; illness
4. pyramid; largest; smallest
   a. Each generation of young adults gave birth to more than enough children to replace themselves.
   b. A sizable number of each cohort died before advancing to the next higher section of the pyramid.
5. fewer births; survival; square

6. 100

7. varies

8. dependency ratio; birth; late adulthood; higher

9. longevity; are not

10. 5

11. young-old

12. old-old; oldest-old; a small minority; is not; optimal; usual; impaired

13. diet

14. increase; decrease; 10; varied

15. primary aging; secondary aging; conditions; illnesses; is not

16. how people cope with primary aging

17. dryer; thinner; less; age spots; male pattern baldness

18. shorter; vertebrae

19. torso; lower face

20. lower; men; muscle; fat

21. falls; lower body

22. isolation from other people

23. 40; cataracts; lens; glaucoma; hardening; fluid; senile macular degeneration; retina

24. senile macular degeneration

25. presbycusis; 40; tinnitis; retarded; mentally ill; depression; demoralization

26. technology; specialist care; determination

27. elderspeak

Like babytalk, elderspeak uses simple and short sentences, exaggerated emphasis, slower talk, higher pitch, and repetition.

28. slower; efficient; coronary heart disease, strokes, chronic obstructive pulmonary disease; cancer

29. health habits; exercise

30. more; more

31. insomnia; narcotic

Prescription doses are often too strong for an older person, causing confusion, depression, or impaired cognition.

32. electrical activity; dreams

33. cognitive

34. compression of morbidity

35. wear-and-tear; machine; doesn't hold up

Women who have never been pregnant tend to live longer than other women. People who are overweight tend to sicken and die at younger ages. One breakthrough of modern medical technology is replacement of worn-out body parts.

36. genetic

37. maximum life span; 120; average life expectancy; the number of years the average newborn of a particular species is likely to live

38. historical; cultural; socioeconomic; death; 74; 80

39. 20; so many babies died; 50; public health; sanitation, immunizations, and antibiotics

One explanation is that since reproduction is essential for the survival of our species, it was genetically important for deaths to occur either very early in life or after childbearing and child rearing.

40. nongenetic; Parkinson's disease, Huntington's disease, Alzheimer's disease, type II diabetes, coronary heart disease, and osteoporosis

41. cells; cell reproduction; DNA; mutations

42. oxygen free radicals

43. antioxidants; A; C; E; selenium

44. Hayflick limit; fewer

45. clock; Down syndrome; progeria

46. B cells; antibodies; bacteria; viruses; T cells; thymus

47. decreases

48. acquired immune deficiency syndrome; HIV; human immunodeficiency virus

49. longer; decline

50. stronger; larger; autoimmune

51. rural; mountainous; respected; verifiable birth or marriage records

   a. Diet is moderate, consisting mostly of fresh vegetables.

   b. Work continues throughout life.

   c. Families and community are important.

   d. Exercise and relaxation are part of the daily routine.

Answers to Testing Yourself

1. **c.** is the answer. Although a number of actual mechanisms have been proposed, the "biological clock" is only a metaphor for these mechanisms. (audio program)

2. **b.** is the answer. Life span has not increased, therefore "a" is incorrect. The incidence rates of chronic diseases and accidents in older people have not decreased, therefore "c" and "d" are also incorrect. (audio program)

3. **d.** is the answer. (audio program)

4. **b.** is the answer. Life expectancy, but not life span, has increased. (audio program; textbook, p. 594)

5. **d.** is the answer. Programmed death is exemplified by all of these. (audio program; textbook, p. 597

6. **b.** is the answer. (textbook, p. 577)

   a. This is gerontology.

   c. This is progeria.

   d. This is the wear-and-tear theory.

7. **c.** is the answer. (textbook, p. 579)

8. **c.** is the answer. (textbook, p. 583)

   a., b., & d. These are examples of secondary aging.

9. **a.** is the answer. (textbook, p. 577)

10. **b.** is the answer. (textbook, p. 585)

    a. Cataracts are caused by a thickening of the lens.

    c. This disease involves deterioration of the retina.

    d. Myopia, which was not discussed in this chapter, is nearsightedness.

11. **d.** is the answer. (textbook, p. 589)

12. **a.** is the answer. (textbook, p. 596)

    b. In fact, free radicals damage DNA, rather than vice versa.

    c. The immune system compensates for, but is not directly affected by, damage to cellular DNA.

    d. This genetic disease occurs too infrequently to be considered a *direct* result of damage to cellular DNA.

13. **c.** is the answer. (textbook, p. 596)

14. **a.** is the answer. (textbook, p. 597)

    b. & c. According to the cellular aging theory of a genetic clock, time, rather than genetic damage or hormonal abnormalities, regulates the aging process.

    d. The cellular aging theory of a genetic clock makes no provision for environmental alteration of the genetic mechanisms of aging.

15. **c.** is the answer. (textbook, p. 597)

16. **a.** is the answer. (textbook, p. 586)

17. **c.** is the answer. (textbook, p. 597)

    a. & b. These are the "attack" cells of the immune system.

18. **d.** is the answer. (textbook, p. 597)

    a. This is the body's system for defending itself against bacteria and other "invaders."

    b. Secondary aging is caused not only by genes but also by health habits and other influences.

    c. This is a metaphor for the distribution of age groups, with the largest and youngest group at the bottom, and the smallest and oldest group at the top.

19. **c.** is the answer. B cells create antibodies that *repair* rather than damage cells. (textbook, p. 597)

20. **a.** is the answer. (textbook, p. 598)

    b. & c. Women have *larger* thymus glands than men. They are also *more* susceptible to autoimmune diseases.

21. **b.** is the answer. Weight often decreases during late adulthood. (textbook, pp. 583–584)

22. **d.** is the answer. The text does not discuss the impact of age of childbearing on a woman's cell repair mechanisms. However, it does note that women who have never been pregnant may *extend* life. (textbook, p. 593)

23. **b.** is the answer. In fact, just the opposite is true. (textbook, pp. 600–601)

Late Adulthood: Cognitive Development

AUDIO PROGRAM: The Trees and the Forest

ORIENTATION

Each season of life has its own way of thinking. Lesson 24 centers on thinking during late adulthood. Chapter 24 of *The Developing Person Through the Life Span*, 6/e, describes the changes in cognitive functioning associated with late adulthood. The first section reviews the parts of the information-processing system, providing experimental evidence that suggests declines in both the control processes and the retrieval strategies of older adults.

The second section describes neurological and other reasons for this decline. Nonetheless, real-life conditions provide older adults with ample opportunity to compensate for the pattern of decline observed in the laboratory. It appears that, for most people, cognitive functioning in daily life remains essentially unimpaired.

The main reason for reduced cognitive functioning during late adulthood is dementia, the subject of the third section. This pathological loss of intellectual ability can be caused by a variety of diseases and circumstances; risk factors, treatment, and prognosis differ accordingly.

The final section of the chapter makes it clear that cognitive changes during late adulthood are by no means restricted to declines in intellectual functioning. For many individuals, late adulthood is a time of great aesthetic, creative, philosophical, and spiritual growth.

Audio program 24, "The Trees and the Forest," points out that many of the fears of adults as they approach old age are exaggerated. **Alzheimer's disease**, for example, is not nearly as common as public anxiety would suggest. For most people today, late adulthood brings neither a loss nor a disease of memory, but a change of memory. Conscious memory for the short term (**primary memory**) and memory for the very long term (**tertiary memory**) change very lit-

tle with age. What does decline with age appears to be memory for the immediate term—the kind of memory researchers refer to as **secondary memory**. But, as the audio program and the text point out, even this loss may be more the result of disuse and poor strategies of memorization than aging per se. When older persons are taught better strategies, they often are able to use them effectively.

In this program, psychologist K. Warner Schaie discusses the cognitive changes that are likely to come with each decade after 60. Marion Perlmutter, another psychologist, reflects on **wisdom**, which may be the special gift of this season.

LESSON GOALS

By the end of this lesson you should be prepared to:

1. Discuss cognitive changes in information processing in old age.

2. Explain why different measures of cognition may be needed to assess thinking in older and younger adults.

3. Suggest several reasons, other than the aging process itself, that might contribute to age-related declines in cognitive functioning.

4. Summarize the causes and effects of the different dementias.

5. Discuss the potential for new cognitive development, cognitive growth, and wisdom during late adulthood.

Audio Assignment

Listen to the audio tape that accompanies Lesson 24: "The Trees and the Forest."

Write answers to the following questions. You may replay portions of the program if you need to

refresh your memory. Answer guidelines may be found in the Lesson Guidelines section at the end of this chapter.

1. Discuss how the focus of the study of intelligence in older persons has changed in recent years.

2. Describe each of the following memory stages and whether the function of each stage normally changes as an individual ages.

    a. primary memory

    b. secondary memory

    c. tertiary memory

3. Discuss whether the decline in secondary memory is intrinsic to older age or is the result of deficiencies in strategies of encoding and retrieval.

4. Describe the normal changes in intellectual functioning that occur in most persons during their 60s, 70s, and 80s.

5. Discuss the concept of wisdom as introduced in the audio program. What kinds of wisdom may come in later life?

Textbook Assignment

Read Chapter 24: "Late Adulthood: Cognitive Development," pages 605–631 in *The Developing Person Through the Life Span,* 6/e, then work through the material that follows to review it. Complete the sentences and answer the questions. As you proceed, evaluate your performance for each section by consulting the answers on page 319. Do not continue with the next section until you understand each answer. If you need to, review or reread the appropriate section in the textbook before continuing.

Changes in Information Processing (pp. 605–611)

1. In Schaie's longitudinal study, beginning at about age _____ , older adults began to show significant declines on the five "primary mental abilities": _____

    _____ , _____

    _____ , _____

    _____ , _____

    _____ , and _____

    _____ .

2. Researchers agree, however, that there are significant _____ (differences/similarities) in intellectual ability in later life.

3. The _____ _____

    stores incoming sensory information for a split second after it is received. Research suggests that age _____ (has no impact on/causes small declines in) the sensitivity and power of the sensory register.

4. Age-related changes in the sensory register _____ (can/cannot) easily be compensated for.

5. In order for sensory information to be registered, it must cross the _____ _____ . Due to sensory-system declines, some older people _____ (can/cannot) register certain information.

6. One study found that _____ accounted for nearly one-third of the variance in cognitive scores for older adults.

7. Some experts believe that the simplest way to predict how much an older person has aged intellectually may be to measure _____ , _____ , or _____ .

8. Once information is perceived, it must be placed in _____ _____ .

9. Of all the aspects of information processing, _____ _____ is the component that shows the most substantial declines with age.

10. Working memory has two interrelated functions: to temporarily _____ information and then to _____ it.

11. Older adults are particularly likely to experience difficulty when they are asked to remember several items of information while _____ them in complex ways. This is especially true if the new information is mixed with material that is _____ .

12. The difficulty older adults have in multitasking is called the _____-_____ _____ .

13. The _____ _____ consists of the storehouse of information held in _____-_____ memory. This storehouse is far from perfect, because _____ _____ and _____ _____ allow

most material to be forgotten, never reaching this part of memory. And those memories that do are still subject to _____ .

14. Long-term memory for _____ remains unimpaired over the decades, and may even increase at least until age _____ . Also unimpaired are specific areas of _____ . Events that are _____ in nature and based on _____ rather than factual details are also remembered better.

15. A common memory error is _____ _____ , not remembering who or what was the source of a specific piece of information.

16. One way of investigating long-term memory and aging has been to make _____-_____ comparisons of people's memories of public events or facts. Another has been to probe memory of _____ learning.

17. Overall, how much of their knowledge base is available to older adults seems to depend less on _____ and more on _____ _____ .

18. Research on memory reveals that the particulars of the _____ _____ are crucial in how well elderly people perform.

19. The _____ _____ of the information-processing system function in an executive role and include _____ mechanisms, _____ strategies, _____ _____ , and _____ _____ .

20. Older adults are more likely to rely on prior _____ , general _____ , and _____ _____ _____ . Use of _____ strategies also worsens with age.

21. A significant part of the explanation for memory difficulties in the aged may be inadequate

_____ _____ .

22. Memory takes two forms: _____ memory is "automatic" memory involving

_____ , _____

responses, _____ procedures, and the _____ . This type of memory is _____ (more/less) vulnerable to age-related deficits than is _____ memory. This latter type of memory involves

_____ , _____ ,

_____ , and the like, most of which was _____ (consciously/unconsciously) learned.

23. As people get older, differences in implicit and explicit memory might be reflected in their remembering how to _____ a particular task but not being as able to _____ its actions.

24. Some decline in control processes may also be the result of _____ , or refusing to change familiar strategies, rather than a direct result of aging.

Reasons for Age-Related Changes (pp. 611–617)

25. Declines in cognitive functioning may be caused by _____ _____ ,

_____ _____ , or

_____ .

26. Neural-cell loss probably _____ (is/is not) the main factor behind age-related declines in cognitive functioning.

27. One universal change is a _____ in brain processes This can be traced to reduced production of _____ , including

_____ , _____ ,

_____ , and _____ . It is also due to reductions in the volume of

_____ _____ , the speed of the _____ , and the pace of activation of various parts of the cortex.

28. According to some experts, the slowing of brain processes means that thinking becomes

_____ , _____ , and

_____ with advancing age. Using memory tricks and reminders, however, older adults often are able to _____ for slower processing and _____

_____ .

29. (Thinking Like a Scientist) Two noninvasive neuroimaging techniques that allow researchers to see the dynamic workings of the brain are

_____ and _____

scans. These techniques involve neuroimaging that is _____ , that is, in living brains.

30. (Thinking Like a Scientist) Neuroscience has demonstrated that the brain has _____ (one or two/many) language areas. Imaging studies have also shown that _____ and _____ can be formed in adulthood, that intellectual ability _____ (correlates/does not correlate) with brain size, that attention-deficit disorder may be caused by an immature _____

_____ , and that people use their brains differently as they age.

31. (Thinking Like a Scientist) Older brains sometimes show more brain activity, perhaps because their brains compensate for intellectual slowdown by _____ .
Another possible explanation is that the brain "_____ " and no longer uses a different region for each function.

32. The overall slowdown of cognitive abilities that often occurs in the days or months before death is called _____ _____ .

33. Declines in cognitive functioning may also be associated with systemic conditions that affect the brain and other organs such as

_____ , _____ ,

_____ , and

_____ .

Several factors contribute to these diseases, including _____

_____ .

34. Declines in cognitive functioning may also be associated with ageism, including disparaging _____ .

35. Older adults may _____ (overestimate/underestimate) their memory skills when they were younger; consequently, they tend to _____ (overestimate/underestimate) their current memory losses. As a result of this misperception, older adults may lose _____ in their memory.

36. The impact of ageist stereotypes on cognitive functioning is revealed in a study in which the memory gap between old and young _____ (deaf/hearing) _____ (Chinese/American) students was twice as great as that for _____ (deaf/hearing) _____ (Chinese/American) students and five times as great as that for _____ .

37. Laboratory tests of memory may put older persons at a disadvantage because they generally use _____ material, which reduces motivation in older adults.

38. Most older adults _____ (do/do not) consider memory problems a significant handicap in daily life.

Dementia (pp. 618–625)

39. Although pathological loss of intellectual ability in elderly people is often referred to as _____ , a more precise term for this loss is _____ , which is defined as _____ .

40. Traditionally, when dementia occurred before age _____ , it was called _____ _____ ; when it occurred after this age, it was called _____ _____ . This age-based distinction is arbitrary, however,

because the same _____ may occur at any age.

41. Dementia, which can be caused by more than 70 diseases and circumstances, is characterized by _____ _____ and _____ . Dementia lasts a long time; that is, it is _____ .

42. The most common form of dementia is _____ _____ . This disorder is characterized by abnormalities in the _____ _____ , called _____ and _____ , that destroy normal brain functioning.

43. Plaques are formed _____ (inside/outside) the brain cells from a protein called _____ ; tangles are masses of protein found _____ (inside/outside) the cells. Plaques and tangles usually begin in the _____ of the brain.

44. Physiologically, the brain damage that accompanies this disease _____ (does/does not) vary with the age of the victim.

45. With age, Alzheimer's disease becomes _____ (more/no more/less) common, affecting about one in every _____ adults over age 65 and about 1 in every _____ over age 85.

46. About _____ (what proportion?) of the population inherits the gene _____ , which increases the risk of Alzheimer's disease. The protective _____ allele of the same gene may dissipate the _____ that cause the formation of plaques.

47. When Alzheimer's disease appears in _____ (middle/late) adulthood, which is quite _____ (common/rare), it usually progresses _____ (less/more) quickly, reaching the last phase within _____ years. In such cases, the disease is caused by one of several _____ abnormalities.

48. The first stage of Alzheimer's disease is marked by _____ about recent events. Most people _____ (recognize/do not recognize) that they have a memory problem during this stage, which is often indistinguishable from the normal decline in _____ memory.

49. In the second stage, there are noticeable deficits in the person's _____ and _____-_____ . Changes in _____ are common in this stage. The third stage begins when memory loss becomes dangerous and _____ because the person can no longer manage _____ _____ _____ . People in the fourth stage require _____-_____ _____ . In the fifth stage, people no longer_____ and do not respond with any action or emotion at all. In general, death comes _____ (how many years?) after stage one.

50. The second major type of dementia is _____ _____ . This condition occurs because a temporary obstruction of the _____ _____ , called a(n) _____ , prevents a sufficient supply of blood from reaching the brain. This causes destruction of brain tissue, commonly called a(n) _____ .

51. The underlying cause of VaD or MID is systemic _____ , which is common in people who have problems with their _____ systems, including those with _____ _____ , _____ , tingling or _____ in their extremities, and _____ . Measures to improve circulation, such as _____ , or to control hypertension and diabetes through _____ and _____ , can help to prevent or control the progress of VaD.

52. Unlike the person with Alzheimer's disease, the person with VaD shows a _____ (gradual/sudden) drop in intellectual functioning. The prognosis for a person with VaD is generally quite _____ (good/poor).

53. Another category of dementias, called _____ _____ , originates in brain areas that do not directly involve thinking and memory. These dementias, which cause a progressive loss of _____ control, include _____ disease, _____ disease, and _____ _____ .

54. The best known of these dementias is _____ _____ , which produces muscle tremors or rigidity. This disease is related to the degeneration of neurons that produce the neurotransmitter _____ .

55. Many AIDS and syphilis patients develop a brain _____ that causes dementia.

56. Chronic alcoholism can lead to _____ syndrome, the chief symptom of which is severely impaired _____-_____ _____ .

57. Oftentimes, the elderly are thought to be suffering from brain disease when, in fact, their symptoms are a sign of _____ dementia caused by some other factor such as _____ , _____ , _____ , _____ , _____ , _____ , or other _____ _____ .

58. The most common cause of reversible dementia is _____ . Symptoms of dementia can result from drug _____ that occur when a person is taking several different medications. This problem is made worse by the fact that many of the drugs prescribed to older adults can, by themselves, slow down _____ _____ .

59. In general, psychological illnesses such as schizophrenia are _____ (more/less) common in the elderly than in younger adults. Approximately _____ percent of the

elderly who are diagnosed as demented are actually experiencing psychological illness.

60. At some time during their later years, _____ (many/a small percentage of) older adults experience symptoms of depression. Generally speaking, depression _____ (is/is not) very treatable in late adulthood.

61. One consequence of untreated depression among the elderly is that the rate of _____ is higher for those over age _____ than for any other group.

New Cognitive Development in Later Life
(pp. 625–630)

62. According to Erik Erikson, older adults are more interested in _____

_____

than younger adults and, as the "social witnesses" to life, are more aware of the _____ of the generations.

63. According to Abraham Maslow, older adults are more likely to achieve _____ .

64. Many people become more appreciative of _____ and _____ _____ as they get older.

65. Many people also become more _____ and _____ than when they were younger.

66. One form of this attempt to put life into perspective is called the _____ _____ , in which the older person connects his or her own life with the future.

67. One of the most positive attributes commonly associated with older people is _____ , which Baltes defines as expert knowledge in the _____ _____ of life.

Testing Yourself

After you have completed the audio and text review questions, see how well you do on the following quiz. Correct answers, with text and audio references, may be found at the end of this chapter.

1. The longest-lasting kind of memory is called:
   a. primary memory.
   b. secondary memory.
   c. tertiary memory.
   d. sensory register.

2. The two basic functions of working memory are:
   a. storage that enables conscious use and processing of information.
   b. temporary storage and processing of sensory stimuli.
   c. automatic memories and retrieval of learned memories.
   d. permanent storage and retrieval of information.

3. New cognitive development in late adulthood is characterized by Professor Perlmutter as:
   a. dementia.   c. wisdom.
   b. tertiary memory.   d. encoding.

4. Which type of material would most likely *not* be lost from the memory of a person in his or her 70s?
   a. the names of former business associates
   b. phone numbers of favorite shops
   c. early experiences with the family
   d. dates of appointments

5. The information-processing component that is concerned with the temporary storage of incoming sensory information is:
   a. working memory.   c. the knowledge base.
   b. long-term memory. d. the sensory register.

6. (Thinking Like a Scientist) Neuroimaging studies have demonstrated each of the following *except*
   a. the human brain has dozens of areas that are activated when language is used.
   b. intellectual ability does not correlate with brain size.
   c. people use their brains differently as they age.
   d. most people, most of the time, only use about 10 percent of their brain capacity.

7. Laboratory studies of memory in late adulthood often fail to take into account the effects of:
   a. the knowledge base of older adults.
   b. the testing process itself.
   c. the explicit memory that is central to the functioning of older adults.
   d. the ability of older adults to rely on their long-term memories.

8. Memory for skills is called:
   a. explicit memory.
   b. declarative memory.
   c. episodic memory.
   d. implicit memory.

9. Strategies to retain and retrieve information in the knowledge base are part of which basic component of information processing?
   a. sensory register
   b. working memory
   c. control processes
   d. explicit memory

10. The plaques and tangles that accompany Alzheimer's disease usually begin in the:
    a. temporal lobe.
    b. frontal lobe.
    c. hippocampus.
    d. cerebral cortex.

11. Secondary aging factors that may explain some declines in cognitive functioning include:
    a. fewer opportunities for learning in old age.
    b. disparaging self-perceptions of cognitive abilities.
    c. difficulty with traditional methods of measuring cognitive functioning.
    d. all of the above.

12. When using working memory, older adults have particular difficulty:
    a. holding several items of information in memory while analyzing them in complex ways.
    b. picking up faint sounds.
    c. processing blurry images.
    d. recalling the meaning of rarely used vocabulary.

13. The most common cause of reversible dementia is:
    a. a temporary obstruction of the blood vessels.
    b. genetic mutation.
    c. overmedication.
    d. depression.

14. Dementia refers to:
    a. pathological loss of intellectual functioning.
    b. the increasing forgetfulness that sometimes accompanies the aging process.
    c. abnormal behavior associated with mental illness and with advanced stages of alcoholism.
    d. a genetic disorder that doesn't become overtly manifested until late adulthood.

15. Which of the following diseases does *not* belong with the others?
    a. Huntington's disease
    b. Parkinson's disease
    c. multiple sclerosis
    d. multi-infarct dementia

16. Alzheimer's disease is characterized by:
    a. a proliferation of plaques and tangles in the cerebral cortex.
    b. a destruction of brain tissue as a result of strokes.
    c. rigidity and tremor of the muscles.
    d. an excess of fluid pressing on the brain.

17. Multi-infarct dementia and Alzheimer's disease differ in their progression in that:
    a. multi-infarct dementia never progresses beyond the first stage.
    b. multi-infarct dementia is marked by sudden drops and temporary improvements, whereas decline in Alzheimer's disease is steady.
    c. multi-infarct dementia leads to rapid deterioration and death, whereas Alzheimer's disease may progress over a period of years.
    d. the progression of Alzheimer's disease may be halted or slowed, whereas the progression of multi-infarct dementia is irreversible.

18. Medication has been associated with symptoms of dementia in the elderly for all of the following reasons *except*:
    a. standard drug dosages are often too strong for the elderly.
    b. the elderly tend to become psychologically dependent upon drugs.
    c. drugs sometimes have the side effect of slowing mental processes.
    d. the intermixing of drugs can sometimes have detrimental effects on cognitive functioning.

19. The primary purpose of the life review is to:
    a. enhance one's spirituality.
    b. produce an autobiography.
    c. give advice to younger generations.
    d. put one's life into perspective.

20. Conscious memory for words, data, and concepts is called _____ memory.

    a. sensory
    b. implicit
    c. explicit
    d. knowledge base

21. On balance, it can be concluded that positive cognitive development during late adulthood:

    a. occurs only for a small minority of individuals.
    b. leads to thought processes that are more appropriate to the final stage of life.
    c. makes older adults far less pragmatic than younger adults.
    d. is impossible in view of increasing deficits in cognitive functioning.

22. A key factor underlying the older adult's cognitive developments in the realms of aesthetics, philosophy, and spiritualism may be:

    a. the realization that one's life is drawing to a close.
    b. the despair associated with a sense of isolation from the community.
    c. the need to leave one's mark on history.
    d. a growing indifference to the outside world.

23. Marisa's presentation on "Reversing the Age-Related Slowdown in Thinking" includes all of the following points *except*:

    a. regular exercise.
    b. avoiding the use of anti-inflammatory drugs.
    c. cognitive stimulation.
    d. consumption of antioxidants.

LESSON 24 EXERCISE: PERSONAL WISDOM IN OLDER ADULTS

One theme of Lesson 24 is that each season of life has its own way of thinking and its own gift of knowledge. Both the text and audio program note that despite the cognitive declines of late adulthood, positive changes occur as well, as the elderly develop new interests, new patterns of thought, and what Professor Marion Perlmutter and others have referred to as **personal wisdom**. Many older adults become more responsive to nature, more appreciative of the arts, more philosophical, and more spiritual. To examine cognitive development in later life, ask an older adult whom you know well to complete the following Life/Values/Goals questionnaire. If you are an older adult, complete the questionnaire yourself. You, or the person you ask to complete the questionnaire, should answer the question from two life-cycle perspectives: as you (or your subject) felt during early or middle adulthood, and as you (or your subject) feel now, during late adulthood. Then answer the questions on page 327 and hand only that page into your instructor.

Source: Bugen, Larry A. (1979). *Death and dying: Theory, research, practice*. Dubuque, IA: Wm. C. Brown, p. 457.

LIFE/VALUES/GOALS QUESTIONNAIRE

As you see your life now, try to answer the following questions.

1. What three things would your friends say about you and your life if you died today?

2. Given the likelihood that you will not die today, and have some time left to change some things in your life, what three things would you most like to have said about you and your life?

3. If someone were to witness a week of your life, what assumptions would that person make about your values, that is, what matters most to you?

4. What values do you hold that are not evident from the way you live your daily life?

5. What three goals are important to you as you plan your life?

LIFE/VALUES/GOALS QUESTIONNAIRE

Try to answer the following questions as you might have answered them when you were a younger adult.

1. What three things would your friends say about you and your life if you died today?

2. Given the likelihood that you will not die today, and have some time left to change some things in your life, what three things would you most like to have said about you and your life?

3. If someone were to witness a week of your life, what assumptions would that person make about your values, that is, what matters most to you?

4. What values do you hold that are not evident from the way you live your daily life?

5. What three goals are important to you as you plan your life?

NAME _____ INSTRUCTOR _____

LESSON 24: PERSONAL WISDOM IN OLDER ADULTS

Exercise

Based on your responses to the Life/Values/Goals questionnaire, or those of your subject, answer the following questions.

1. Do your responses, or those of your subject, indicate a shift in life values, or goals, from early adulthood to later adulthood? What kind of shift?

2. Has the relationship between the way your subject lives life and his or her personal values changed during late adulthood? In what ways?

3. Would you say that the answers to the Life/Values/Goals questionnaire show evidence of a philosophical turn in thinking, or of the emergence of a special personal wisdom, during late adulthood? Why or why not?

LESSON GUIDELINES

Audio Question Guidelines

1. At one time the study of intelligence in old age was a study of what was believed to be the inevitable loss of function.

   Today researchers realize that each time of life has its own way of thinking, its own gift of knowledge that compensates for other losses.

   For the first time in history, as more people reach their 60s, 70s, and 80s, researchers are testing older persons in an effort to understand how thinking changes as people age.

2. a. **Primary memory** refers to memory that lasts for a minute or two. It is used to keep information in a person's conscious mind. Primary memory changes very little with age.

   b. **Secondary memory** refers to the storage of long-term memories that we are not consciously aware of. Secondary memory often becomes less reliable with age.

   c. **Tertiary memory** refers to memory for things over the long, long term, often involving experiences from early life. Tertiary memory does not decline with age, perhaps because we go over these distinctive memories time and time again.

3. Older persons do not automatically use the best strategies to put information into secondary memory (encoding). This may simply be a result of disuse of such strategies following retirement.

   Older persons can successfully use more efficient encoding and retrieval strategies when they are taught how.

   Examples of encoding and retrieval strategies include the use of imagery, context cues, the formation of rhymes and acronyms (e.g., "H-O-M-E-S," to retrieve the names of the five Great Lakes: Huron, Ontario, Michigan, Erie, Superior).

4. Using a **sequential research** program, in which the same group of people are periodically tested and retested (longitudinal research), and a new sample is added at each testing (cross-sectional research), Professor Schaie has studied people in their 60s, 70s, and 80s.

   The intellectual functioning of people in their 60s is not significantly different from that of people in their 50s.

   Beginning in the decade of the 60s, when most people are entering retirement, the saying "Use it or lose it" becomes an accurate description of intellectual change. There is often a loss of the selective skills once used in work but no longer needed after a person has retired.

   Sometime in the 70s many people experience an acceleration of *physical* decline. As a consequence, they restrict their environment and exposure to new and interesting things, which may accelerate *mental* decline.

   Among persons in their 80s there are wide individual differences in intellectual functioning, but as a rule, there are some losses in performance as compared to the 60s and 70s.

5. Professor Perlmutter believes that many older adults possess a form of **personal wisdom** that is characterized by:

   a. a greater sensitivity to perspective in life, and knowing what is important, and what is not.

   b. a more global and less self-centered view.

   c. a better integration of emotion and cognition.

   d. knowing what to remember and what to forget.

   e. knowing how to compensate for some of the cognitive losses that accompany age.

Textbook Question Answers

1. 60; verbal meaning; spatial orientation; inductive reasoning; number ability; word fluency

2. differences

3. sensory memory (or register); causes small declines in

4. can

5. sensory threshold; cannot

6. sensory impairment

7. vision; hearing; smell

8. working memory

9. working memory

10. store; process

11. analyzing; distracting

12. dual-task deficit

13. knowledge base; long-term; selective attention; selective memory; alteration

14. vocabulary; 80; expertise; happy; emotions

15. source amnesia

16. cross-sectional; high school

17. how long ago information was learned; how well it was learned

18. testing process
19. control processes; storage; retrieval; selective attention; logical analysis
20. knowledge; principles; rules of thumb; retrieval
21. control processes
22. implicit; habits; emotional; routine; senses; less; explicit; words; data; concepts; consciously
23. perform; describe
24. resistance
25. primary aging; secondary aging; ageism
26. is not
27. slowdown; neurotransmitters; dopamine; glutamate; acetylcholine; serotonin; neural fluid; cerebral blood flow
28. slower; simpler; shallower; compensate; sensory deficits
29. PET; fMRI; in vivo
30. many; neurons; dendrites; does not correlate; prefrontal cortex
31. recruiting extra brain areas; dedifferentiates
32. terminal decline
33. hypertension; diabetes; arteriosclerosis; and diseases affecting the lungs; poor eating habits, smoking, and lack of exercise
34. stereotypes
35. overestimate; overestimate; confidence
36. hearing; American; deaf; American; Chinese
37. meaningless
38. do not
38. senility; dementia; severely impaired judgment, memory, or problem-solving ability
40. 60; presenile dementia; senile dementia (or senile psychosis); symptoms
41. mental confusion; forgetfulness; chronic
42. Alzheimer's disease; cerebral cortex; plaques; tangles
43. outside; B-amyloid; inside; hippocampus
44. does not
45. more; 100; 5
46. one-fifth; apoE4; apoE2; proteins
47. middle; rare; more; three to five; genetic
48. absentmindedness; recognize; explicit
49. concentration; short-term memory; personality; debilitating; basic daily needs; full-time care; talk; 10 to 15
50. vascular dementia or multi-infarct dementia; blood vessels; infarct; stroke (or ministroke)

51. arteriosclerosis; circulatory; heart disease, hypertension, numbness, diabetes; regular exercise; diet; drugs
52. sudden; poor
53. subcortical dementias; motor; Parkinson's; Huntington's; multiple sclerosis
54. Parkinson's disease; dopamine
55. infection
56. Korsakoff's; short-term memory
57. reversible; medication; inadequate nutrition; alcohol abuse; depression; mental illness
58. overmedication; interactions; mental processes
59. less; 10
60. many; is
61. suicide; 60
62. arts, children, and the whole of human experience; interdependence
63. self-actualization
64. nature; aesthetic experiences
65. reflective; philosophical
66. life review
67. wisdom; fundamental pragmatics

Answers to Testing Yourself

1. **c.** is the answer. Tertiary memory is memory for the long, long term. It includes our very first memories of life. (audio program)

2. **a.** is the answer. (audio program; textbook, p. 607)

    b. These are the functions of the sensory register.

    c. This refers to long-term memory's processing of implicit and explicit memories, respectively.

    d. This is the function of long-term memory.

3. **c.** is the answer. Perlmutter is just beginning research into wisdom, the ability to "see the trees rather than the forest." (audio program)

4. **c.** is the answer. Early, meaningful life experiences seem to last forever. (audio program)

5. **d.** is the answer. (textbook, p. 606)

    a. Working memory deals with mental, rather than sensory, activity.

    b. & c. Long-term memory, which is a subcomponent of the knowledge base, includes information that is stored for several minutes to several years.

6. **d.** is the answer. (textbook, pp. 611–612)

7. **b.** is the answer. (textbook, p. 616)

8. **d.** is the answer. (textbook, p. 610)

a. & b. Explicit memory is memory of facts and experiences, which is why it is often called declarative memory.

c. This type of memory, which is a type of explicit memory, was not discussed.

9. **c.** is the answer. (textbook, p. 609)

10. **d.** is the answer. (textbook, p. 618)

11. **d.** is the answer. (textbook, pp. 614–615)

12. **a.** is the answer. (texxtbook, p. 607)

b. & c. These may be true, but they involve sensory memory rather than working memory.

d. Memory for vocabulary, which generally is very good throughout adulthood, involves long-term memory.

13. **c.** is the answer. (textbook, p. 622)

14. **a.** is the answer. (textbook, p. 618)

15. **d.** is the answer. Each of the other answers is an example of subcortical dementia. (textbook, p. 621)

16. **a.** is the answer. (textbook, p. 618)

b. This describes multi-infarct dementia.

c. This describes Parkinson's disease.

d. This was not given in the text as a cause of dementia.

17. **b.** is the answer. (textbook, p. 621)

a. Because multiple infarcts typically occur, the disease *is* progressive in nature.

c. The text does not suggest that MID necessarily leads to quick death.

d. At present, Alzheimer's disease is untreatable.

18. **b.** is the answer. (textbook, pp. 622–623)

19. **d.** is the answer. (textbook, p. 626)

20. **c.** is the answer. (textbook, p. 610)

a. Sensory memory, or the sensory register, stores incoming sensory information for only a split second.

b. This is unconscious, automatic memory for skills.

c. Explicit memory *is* only one part of the knowledge base. Another part—implicit memory—is unconscious memory for skills.

21. **b.** is the answer. (textbook, pp. 625–627)

a. & d. Positive cognitive development is *typical* of older adults.

c. Pragmatism is one characteristic of wisdom, an attribute commonly associated with older people.

22. **a.** is the answer. (textbook, p. 626)

b. & c. Although these may be true of some older adults, they are not necessarily a *key* factor in cognitive development during late adulthood.

d. In fact, older adults are typically *more* concerned with the whole of human experience.

23. **b.** is the answer. In fact, *use* of anti-inflammatory drugs may help sustain cognitive functioning in old age. (textbook, p. 614)

Late Adulthood: Psychosocial Development

AUDIO PROGRAM: Three Grandparents

ORIENTATION

As noted in Chapter 25 of *The Developing Person Through the Life Span*, 6/e, there is great variation in development after age 65. Certain psychosocial changes are common during this stage of the life span —retirement, the death of a spouse, and failing health —yet people respond to these experiences in vastly different ways.

Individual experiences may help to explain the fact that theories of psychosocial aging, discussed in the first section of the chapter, are often diametrically opposed. The second section of the chapter focuses on the challenges to generativity that accompany late adulthood, such as finding new sources of achievement once derived from work. In the third section, the importance of marriage, friends, neighbors, and family in providing social support is discussed, as are the different experiences of married and single older adults. The final section focuses on the frail elderly— the minority of older adults, often poor and/or ill, who require extensive care.

In audio program 25, "Three Grandparents," we meet three very different grandparents whose stories address three questions: What is the right age to become a grandparent? How has the dramatic rise in divorce rates affected grandparents? What are the effects of this century's great increase in length of life on the experience of being a grandparent?

Most people become grandparents during their 40s or 50s. Developmentalist Linda Burton has found that **on-time** grandparents are happier and better prepared than those who have the role of grandparent thrust on them early, in their 20s or 30s.

Sociologist Andrew Cherlin notes that in the wake of divorces grandparental ties are normally weakened on the father's side and strengthened on the mother's side. He points out that increased longevity means that many grandparents can now expect to spend half their lives with their grandchildren and that many will become great-grandparents. Although grandparenthood has changed, it still remains a central role in the family structure.

As the program opens, we hear the voices of three grandparents, each beginning his or her own unique story.

LESSON GOALS

By the end of this lesson you should be prepared to:

1. Discuss the psychosocial development of older persons from a variety of theoretical perspectives.

2. Discuss the impact of retirement on the individual, and identify several alternative sources of achievement during late adulthood.

3. Describe the components of the social convoy, and explain this convoy's increasing importance during late adulthood.

4. Explain how being a grandparent has changed during the past century, and discuss the relationships between the generations as it exists today.

5. Describe the frail elderly, explain why their number is growing, and identify various factors that may protect the elderly from frailty.

Audio Assignment

Listen to the audio tape that accompanies Lesson 25: "Three Grandparents."

Write answers to the following questions. You may replay portions of the program if you need to refresh your memory. Answer guidelines may be found in the Lesson Guidelines section at the end of this chapter.

1. Discuss the impact of being an "on-time" or "off-time" grandparent.

2. Discuss how grandparents are affected by the divorce of their children. What effect does divorce usually have on grandparental ties on the mother's side? on the father's side?

3. Describe the three phases of grandparenting. How does the grandparent's relationship to the grandchildren change during these phases?

4. Contrast the typical role of today's grandparent with that of grandparents at the turn of the century.

5. Discuss the typical role of today's grandparent in the family. How is this role likely to change in the future?

Textbook Assignment

Read Chapter 25: "Late Adulthood: Psychosocial Development," pages 633–666 in *The Developing Person Through the Life Span*, 6/e, then work through the material that follows to review it. Complete the sentences and answer the questions. As you proceed, evaluate your performance for each section by consulting the answers on page 333. Do not continue with the next section until you understand each answer. If you need to, review or reread the appropriate section in the textbook before continuing.

Theories of Late Adulthood (pp. 634–644)

1. Theories of psychosocial development in late adulthood include _____ theories, _____ theories, and _____ theories.

2. _____ theories emphasize the active part that individuals play in their own psychosocial development. As one such theorist, _____ , described it, people attempt to _____ .

3. The most comprehensive theory is that of _____ , who called life's final crisis _____ versus _____ .

4. Another version of self theory suggests that the search for _____ is lifelong. This idea originates in Erikson's crisis of _____ versus _____ .

5. Partly as a result of changes in _____ , _____ , and _____ , maintaining identity during late adulthood is particularly challenging. In the strategy _____ _____ , new experiences are incorporated unchanged. This strategy involves _____ reality in order to maintain self-esteem.

6. The opposite strategy is _____ _____ , in which people adapt to new experiences by changing their self-concept. This process can be painful, since it may cause people to doubt their _____ and _____ , leading to what Erikson called _____ .

7. Paul Baltes emphasizes _____ _____ _____ , which is the idea that individuals set their own _____ , assess their own _____ , and then figure out how to accomplish what they want to achieve despite the _____ and _____ of later life.

8. People who have a strong sense of _____ believe that they can master any situation life presents, including aging. Research studies demonstrate that there is a negative correlation between this belief and feelings of _____ , _____ , and _____ . Studies also reveal that women tend to feel more effective at _____ _____ ; men tend to feel more effective at _____ _____ .

9. Self theories have recently received strong support from research in the field of _____ _____ , which has shown that various life events seem to be at least as much affected by _____ as by life circumstances. Studies of twins have found that genetic influences often _____ (weaken/become more apparent) later in life. Behavioral geneticists _____ (often/sometimes/never) claim that any aspect of the self is entirely genetic.

10. Theorists who emphasize _____ maintain that _____ forces limit individual _____ and direct life at every stage. One form of this theory focuses on _____ _____ , reflecting how industrialized nations segregate the oldest generation.

11. According to _____ theory, in old age the individual and society mutually withdraw from each other. This theory is _____ (controversial among/almost universally accepted by) gerontologists.

12. The opposite idea is expressed in _____ theory, which holds that older adults remain socially active. According to this theory, if older adults do disengage, they do so _____ (willingly/unwillingly).

13. The dominant view is that the more _____ the elderly play, the greater their _____ _____ and the longer their lives.

14. The most recent view of age stratification is that disengagement theory and activity theory are too _____ . According to this view, older adults become more _____ in their social contacts.

15. Two other categories of stratification that are especially important in late adulthood are _____ and _____ . Another stratification theory, which draws attention to the values underlying the gender divisions promoted by society, is _____ theory. According to this theory, _____ policies and _____ values make later life particularly burdensome for women.

16. Currently in the United States, women make up nearly _____ (what proportion?) of the population over age 65 and 70 percent of the elderly who are _____ .

17. According to the _____ _____ theory, race is a _____ _____ , and racism and racial discrimination shape the experiences and attitudes of both racial _____ and racial _____ .

18. Some theorists believe that stratification theory unfairly stigmatizes _____ and _____ groups. They point out that compared to European-Americans, elderly _____ - and _____ - Americans are more often nurtured by _____ families. As a result of this _____ , fewer are put in nursing homes. Similarly, elderly women are less likely than elderly men to be _____ and _____ because they tend to be _____ and _____ .

19. An important concept in age stratification theory is that _____ shifts often change the meaning of gender and ethnicity.

20. To better understand stratification theory, a _____ perspective is needed. In

many nations, age stratification is not apparent, and how people are treated depends more on factors such as their _____ ,

_____ _____ , and

_____ _____

_____ .

21. According to _____ theory, each person's life is an active, changing, self-propelled process occurring within ever-changing _____ contexts.

22. According to _____ theory, people experience the changes of late adulthood in much the same way they did earlier in life. Thus, the so-called _____ _____ personality traits are maintained throughout old age.

23. The dynamic viewpoint stresses that the entire _____ _____ works toward _____ , even as elements of _____ _____ change.

24. Self theories echo _____ theories in the importance they place on childhood _____ and _____ .
Social stratification theories apply many concepts from _____ theory. And the stress on dynamic change is an extension of _____ theory.

Keeping Active (pp. 644–649)

25. Many of the elderly use the time they once spent earning a living to pursue _____ interests.

26. The eagerness of the elderly to pursue educational interests is exemplified by the rapid growth of _____ , a program in which older people live on college campuses and take special classes.

27. Compared to younger adults, older adults are _____ (more/less) likely to feel a strong obligation to serve their community.

28. About 40 percent of the elderly in the United States are involved in structured _____ , often through _____ , _____ , or _____ .

29. Many elderly people also provide regular _____ _____ to an elderly relative or _____ _____ , also usually for relatives.

30. Religious faith _____ (increases/ remains stable/decreases) as people. Religious institutions are particularly important to older Americans who feel _____ _____ .

31. By many measures, the elderly are more _____ active than any other age group. Compared to younger people, the elderly are more likely to _____ _____ .

Although the political activism of the older generation causes some younger adults to voice concerns regarding _____ _____ , the idea that the elderly are narrowly focused on their self-interest is unfair.

32. The major United States organization affecting the elderly is the _____ .

33. Many older adults stay busy by maintaining their _____ and _____ . This reflects the desire of most elderly people to _____ (relocate when they retire/age in place). One result of this is that many of the elderly live _____ .

34. Rather than moving, many elderly people prefer to remain in the neighborhoods in which they raised their children, thus creating

_____ _____

retirement communities.

The Social Convoy (pp. 649–656)

35. The phrase _____ _____ highlights the fact that the life course is traveled in the company of others.

36. Elderly Americans who are married tend to be _____ , _____ , and _____ than those who never married or who are divorced or widowed.

37. The best predictor of the nature of a marriage in its later stages is _____ _____ .

Give two possible reasons that marriages may improve with time.

38. Poor health generally has a _____ (major/minor) impact on the marital relationship.

39. There are four times as many _____ (widows/widowers) as _____ (widows/widowers), due to choices that were made during _____ _____ .

40. The death of a mate usually means not only the loss of a close friend and lover but also a lower _____ , less _____ , a(n) _____ social circle, and disrupted _____ _____ .

41. In general, living without a spouse is somewhat easier for _____ (widows/ widowers).

State several reasons for this being so.

42. A study of loneliness found that adults without partners _____ (were/were not) lonelier than adults with partners and that divorced or widowed adults _____ (were/were not) lonelier than never-married adults. The loneliest of all were _____ _____ . The least lonely were _____ _____ .

43. Only about _____ percent of those currently over age 65 in the United States have never married.

44. Older people's satisfaction with life is more strongly correlated to contact with _____ than to contact with younger members of their own family.

45. Compared to men, women tend to have _____ (larger/smaller) social circles, including _____ and a close _____ (male/female) friend who is not related.

46. Because more people are living longer, more older people are part of _____ families than at any time in history. Sometimes, this takes the form of a _____ family, in which there are more _____ than in the past but with only a few members in each generation.

47. Today, when one generation needs help, assistance typically flows from the _____ (younger/older) generation to their _____ (parents/children) instead of vice versa.

48. While intergenerational relationships are clearly important to both generations, they also are likely to include _____ and _____ . The _____– _____ relationship is an example of this.

The Frail Elderly (pp. 656–665)

49. Elderly people who are physically infirm, very ill, or cognitively impaired are called the _____ _____ .

50. The crucial sign of frailty is an inability to perform the _____ _____ , which comprise five tasks: _____ , _____ , _____ , _____ , and _____ _____ .

51. Actions that require some intellectual competence and forethought are classified as _____ _____ .

These include such things as _____ _____ .

52. The number of frail elderly is _____ (increasing/decreasing). One reason for this trend is that _____ _____ . A second reason is that medical care now _____ _____ . A third is that health care emphasizes _____ _____ more than _____ _____ . The result has been an increasing _____ (morbidity/ mortality) rate, even as _____ (morbidity/mortality) rates fall. A final reason is that adequate nutrition, safe housing, and other preventive measures often don't reach those who _____ _____ .

53. One of the best defenses against frailty is an active drive for _____ and _____ . These measures are better predictors of future frailty than is _____ or _____ .The dynamic perspective also reminds us that some people enter late adulthood with protective _____ in place. These include _____ .

54. (Changing Policy) Many elderly persons never become frail because of four protective factors: _____ , _____ _____ , _____ _____ , and _____ _____ .

55. In caring for the frail elderly, cultures such as that of _____(which country?) stress the obligation of children to their parents, rather than of the elderly caring for each another, as in the _____ _____ .

State three reasons that caregivers may feel unfairly burdened and resentful.

a. _____ _____

b. _____ _____

c. _____ _____

56. An especially helpful form of caregiver support is _____ , in which a professional caregiver takes over to give the family caregiver a break.

57. The frail elderly are particularly vulnerable to _____ _____ . Most cases of elder maltreatment _____ (involve/do not involve) family members.

58. Many older Americans and their relatives feel that _____ _____ should be avoided at all costs.

Testing Yourself

After you have completed the audio and text review questions, see how well you do on the following quiz. Correct answers, with text and audio references, may be found at the end of this chapter.

1. Most people become grandparents during their _____ or _____ . Since the beginning of this century, the average age has _____ .
  a. 40s; 50s; increased   **c.** 40s; 50s; not changed
  b. 50s; 60s; increased   **d.** 50s; 60s; not changed

2. Which of the following is true of women who become grandmothers during their 20s and 30s?
  a. Because of inexperience, they usually do not do as good a job as women who become grandmothers later.
  b. They often are not as happy with their roles as are "on-time" grandmothers.
  c. Later, when the grandchildren are grown, they are more likely to reject the role of great-grandparent.
  d. All of the above are true.

3. Concerning the effects of divorce on grandparents, which of the following most often occurs?
  a. Grandparental ties weaken on the father's side and strengthen on the mother's side.
  b. Grandparental ties strengthen on the father's side and weaken on the mother's side.
  c. Grandparental ties strengthen on both the father's side and the mother's side.
  d. Grandparental ties weaken on both the father's side and the mother's side.

4. How does the great-grandparent/great-grand-child relationship usually differ from the grand-parent/grandchild relationship?
   a. It is often closer because the great-grandchildren tend to be more spoiled.
   b. It is usually more distant as a result of the additional layer of family in between.
   c. It is about the same as that between grandparent and grandchild.
   d. It is often much more argumentative since the generational gap between them reflects very different cultural values.

5. Sociologist Andrew Cherlin suggests that grandparents are in the difficult position of having to balance two different desires with respect to their role in the family:
   a. the desire to maintain equally close relationships with their children and their grandchildren.
   b. to make sure the grandchildren are brought up "in the right way" and yet do so without insulting their children by questioning their competence as parents.
   c. to feel secure that they will be cared for in their old age and yet not be a burden to their children or grandchildren.
   d. the desire to be autonomous and yet retain an important role in the family.

6. According to disengagement theory, during late adulthood people tend to:
   a. become less role-centered and more passive.
   b. have regrets about how they have lived their lives.
   c. become involved in a range of new activities.
   d. exaggerate lifelong personality traits.

7. (Changing Policy) Regarding generational equity, which of the following is implicit in a life-span perspective?
   a. The current distribution of benefits is particularly imbalanced for racial minorities.
   b. The outlay of public funds for health care is weighted toward preventive medicine in childhood and adolescence.
   c. As a group, the elderly are wealthier than any other age group.
   d. Each age and cohort has its own particular and legitimate economic needs that other generations might fail to appreciate.

8. Elderhostel is:
   a. a special type of nursing home in which the patients are given control over their activities.
   b. a theory of psychosocial development advocating that the elderly can help each other.
   c. an agency that allows older people of the opposite sex to live together unencumbered by marriage vows.
   d. a program in which older people live on college campuses and take special classes.

9. Longitudinal studies of monozygotic and dizygotic twins have recently found evidence that:
   a. genetic influences weaken as life experiences accumulate.
   b. strongly supports disengagement theory.
   c. some traits seem even more apparent in late adulthood than earlier.
   d. all of the above are true.

10. A former pilot, Eileen has always been proud of her 20/20 vision. Although to the younger members of her family it is obvious that her vision is beginning to fail, Eileen denies that she is having any difficulty and claims that she could still fly an airplane if she wanted to. An identity theorist would probably say that Eileen's distortion of reality is an example of:
    a. identity assimilation.
    b. identity accommodation.
    c. selective optimization.
    d. disengagement.

11. Because women tend to be caregivers, they are:
    a. more likely than men to be depressed.
    b. more likely than men to be lonely.
    c. more likely than men to be depressed and lonely.
    d. less likely than men to be lonely or depressed.

12. The idea that individuals set their own goals, assess their abilities, and figure out how to accomplish what they want to achieve during late adulthood is referred to as:
    a. disengagement.
    b. selective optimization with compensation.
    c. dynamic development.
    d. age stratification.

13. After retirement, the elderly are likely to:
    a. pursue educational interests.
    b. become politically involved.
    c. do volunteer work because they feel a particular commitment to their community.
    d. do any of the above.

14. Which of the following theories does *not* belong with the others?
    a. disengagement theory
    b. feminist theory
    c. critical race theory
    d. continuity theory

15. Which of the following is most true of the relationship between the generations today?
    a. Because parents and children often live at a distance from each other, they are not close.
    b. Older adults prefer not to interfere in their children's lives.
    c. Younger adults are eager to live their own lives and do not want to care for their parents.
    d. The generations tend to see and help each other frequently.

16. On average, older widows:
    a. live about 10 years after their husband dies.
    b. almost always seek another husband.
    c. find it more difficult than widowers to live without a spouse.
    d. experience all of the above.

17. In general, during late adulthood the *fewest* problems are experienced by individuals who:
    a. are married.
    b. have always been single.
    c. have long been divorced.
    d. are widowed.

18. Which of the following is true of adjustment to the death of a spouse?
    a. It is easier for men in all respects.
    b. It is initially easier for men but over the long term it is easier for women.
    c. It is emotionally easier for women but financially easier for men.
    d. It is determined primarily by individual personality traits, and therefore shows very few sex differences.

19. According to dynamic theories:
    a. self-integrity is maintained throughout life.
    b. adults make choices and interpret reality in such a way as to express themselves as fully as possible.

    c. people organize themselves according to their particular characteristics and circumstances.
    d. each person's life is largely a self-propelled process, occurring within ever-changing social contexts.

20. Which of the following most accurately expresses the most recent view of developmentalists regarding stratification by age?
    a. Aging makes a person's social sphere increasingly narrow.
    b. Disengagement is always the result of ageism.
    c. Most older adults become more selective in their social contacts.
    d. Older adults need even more social activity to be happy than they did earlier in life.

21. Developmentalists fear that because younger African-Americans are less dependent on family and church, they may experience greater social isolation in late adulthood than did earlier generations. If this does in fact occur, it would most directly:
    a. provide support for disengagement theory.
    b. be an example of how a cohort shift can change the meaning of ethnicity.
    c. illustrate the process of selective optimization with compensation.
    d. support activity theory.

22. Which of the following would *not* be included as an instrumental activity of daily life?
    a. grocery shopping   c. making phone calls
    b. paying bills   d. taking a walk

23. Which of the following is *not* a major factor contributing to an increase in the number of frail elderly?
    a. an increase in average life expectancy
    b. a research focus on acute, rather than chronic, illnesses
    c. inadequate expenditures on social services
    d. a lack of facilities in many areas to care for the elderly

NAME _____   INSTRUCTOR _____

LESSON 25: GRANDPARENTS

Exercise

A number of issues pertaining to grandparents are raised in the text and audio program. These include the changing role of grandparents due to increased life expectancy, greater geographical mobility of offspring, greater financial independence, rising divorce rates, and the trend toward egalitarian relationships with grandchildren.

To help you apply the information in this lesson to your own life, reflect on the changing role of grandparents by writing brief answers to the questions that follow, then hand the completed exercise in to your instructor.

1. Describe your relationship with one of your grandparents. Was (is) it close and loving? How frequently did (do) you see him or her? To what extent did he or she participate in your upbringing?

2. In what ways is (was) your relationship to your grandparents different from that between your parents and *their* grandparents?

3. If you are a grandparent, in what ways does your role as grandparent differ from that of your grandparents? If you are not a grandparent, but hope to be one some day, how would you *like* your role as grandparent to differ from that of your grandparents?

4. The text notes that styles of grandparenting vary by gender, age at which one becomes a grandparent, and ethnic group, for example. If you would care to, describe how any of these factors have influenced your own relationships as a grandchild or grandparent.

LESSON GUIDELINES

Audio Question Guidelines

1. Developmentalist Linda Burton has found that grandmothers who assumed the role early (in their 20s or 30s) were not as happy with their new role as were **on-time** grandmothers (those who became grandmothers in their 40s or 50s). The early transition to grandmotherhood seemed to throw their life course out of synchronization. According to Burton, their rejection of the grandmother role amounts to their putting up a "speed bump" in their developmental cycle, saying in effect, "Stop, you're trying to push me into a middle-age stage of development."

On-time grandmothers were much happier with their transition to the grandmother role because it came at a time in their lives when they expected it and when they were prepared for it.

2. The 1960s and 1970s saw a dramatic rise in divorce rates. Today one of every two marriages is likely to end in divorce. It is therefore not surprising that divorce is having a tremendous impact on grandparents, often weakening their ties to their grandchildren.

Sociologist Andrew Cherlin has found that whether a daughter or son is getting the divorce often makes a big difference. In most cases of divorce, mothers keep custody of the children. For a grandparent, that means that if a daughter is getting divorced, the grandparent is likely to have a closer relationship with the grandchildren because he or she is more likely to be called on to help. If a son is getting divorced, it often is more difficult for the grandparent to maintain a relationship with the grandchildren.

3. Phase one of grandparenting begins with the birth of the grandchild. This phase is the best, according to most grandparents. Sociologist Cherlin has found that grandparental ties and emotional investment are highest during this phase.

Phase two occurs during the grandchild's adolescence. During this phase the grandchild needs to establish independence from his or her parents and grandparents. The relationship between grandparents and grandchild becomes more distant.

Phase three begins when the grandchild becomes an adult. During this phase the relationship often again becomes close. In many cases the usual roles of grandparent and grandchild start to be reversed: it is the grandchild who is likely to provide more in the way of support to his or her elderly grandparent.

4. In this century grandparenthood has become a much lengthier period of life and more distinct from the period of parenthood.

Because of the increase in life expectancy, most people can now spend an entire career—perhaps even half their lives—as grandparents.

Increased longevity has made great-grandparenting much more common today than it was at the turn of the century.

Unlike grandparents, great-grandparents almost never become involved in a "hands-on" way with their great-grandchildren. This may be due to the fact that there are too many layers of family (parents and grandparents) insulating them from their great-grandchildren. In addition, most great-grandparents are fairly elderly and, although they love their great-grandchildren, they are not as interested in, or capable of, helping out as they were with their grandchildren.

5. Although grandparents today range in age from their 20s on up, and come in infinite varieties, grandparents share several common features.

For one, they are a kind of family insurance policy, standing in the background ready to help out in the case of a family crisis, such as parental illness, divorce, or unemployment.

A second common feature is the norm of noninterference. Grandparents are supposed to leave parenting to the parents; as a result, they must balance two very different desires: retaining their own autonomy, while maintaining a strong role in the family.

Andrew Cherlin believes that grandparents' role as symbols of family continuity and love may actually increase in the future: as family size declines there are fewer grandchildren for grandparents to spend time with, giving the average grandparent more resources and more time to devote to a grandchild.

Textbook Question Answers

1. self; stratification; dynamic
2. Self; Abraham Maslow; self-actualize
3. Erik Erikson; integrity; despair
4. identity; identity; role confusion
5. appearance; health; employment; identity assimilation; distorting
6. identity accommodation; values; beliefs; despair

7. selective optimization with compensation; goals; abilities; limitations; declines

8. self-efficacy; fear, loneliness, distress; selecting and maintaining friendships and at deepening their spiritual lives; managing money and getting things done

9. behavioral genetics; genes; become more apparent; never

10. stratification; social; choice; age stratification

11. disengagement; controversial among

12. activity; unwillingly

13. roles; life satisfaction

14. extreme; selective

15. gender; ethnicity; feminist; social; cultural

16. 60; poor

17. critical race; social construct; minorities; majorities

18. women; minority; African; Hispanic; multigenerational; familism; lonely; depressed; caregivers; kinkeepers

19. cohort

20. multicultural; personality; family connections; ability to work

21. dynamic; social

22. continuity; Big Five

23. social system; continuity; individual lives

24. psychoanalytic; self-concept; identity; sociocultural; epigenetic

25. educational

26. Elderhostel

27. more

28. volunteering; churches; hospitals; schools

29. personal care; child care

30. increases; alienated from society

31. politically; vote in elections and lobby for their interests; generational equity

32. AARP (formerly the American Association of Retired Persons)

33. home; yard; age in place; alone

34. naturally occurring

35. social convoy

36. healthier; wealthier; happier

37. its nature early on

One reason may be traced to the effects of their children, who were a prime source of conflict when they were younger but are now a source of pleasure. Another is that all the shared contextual factors tend to change both partners in similar ways, bringing them closer together in personality, perspectives, and values.

38. minor

39. widows; widowers; young adulthood

40. income; status; broken; daily routines

41. widows

One reason is that elderly women often expect to outlive their husbands and have anticipated this event. Another is that in most communities widows can get help from support groups. A third is that many elderly men were dependent on their wives to perform the basic tasks of daily living.

42. were; were; men currently without a partner who had lost two or more wives through death or divorce within the past few years; wives still in their first marriage

43. 4

44. friends

45. larger; relatives; female

46. multigenerational; beanpole; generations

47. older; children

48. tension; conflict; mother–daughter

49. frail elderly

50. activities of daily life (ADLs); eating; bathing; toileting; dressing; transferring from a bed to a chair

51. instrumental activities of daily life (IADLs); shopping, paying bills, driving a car, taking medications, and keeping appointments

52. increasing; more people are reaching old age; prolongs life; death postponement; life enhancement; morbidity; mortality; need them the most

53. autonomy; control; income; health; buffers; family members and friends, past education and continued educational opportunity, pensions, good health habits

54. attitude; social network; physical setting; financial resources

55. Korea; United States

a. If one relative is doing the caregiving, other family members tend to feel relief rather than an obligation to help.

b. Care receivers and caregivers often disagree about the nature and extent of care that is needed.

c. Services designed for caregivers are difficult to obtain from social agencies.

56. respite care

57. elder abuse; involve

58. nursing homes

Answers to Testing Yourself

1. **c.** is the answer. Most people become grandparents during their 40s or 50s. This figure has not changed significantly during the past century. (audio program)

2. **b.** is the answer. (audio program)

3. **a.** is the answer. Grandparental ties usually strengthen on the mother's side following divorce. This is due to the fact that in most cases of divorce the mother retains custody of the children. (audio program)

4. **b.** is the answer. Great-grandparental ties are usually weaker than grandparental ties. (audio program)

5. **d.** is the answer. (audio program)

6. **a.** is the answer. (textbook, p. 638)

   b. This answer depicts a person struggling with Erikson's crisis of integrity versus despair.

   c. This answer describes activity theory.

   d. Disengagement theory does not address this issue.

7. **d.** is the answer. (textbook, pp. 647–648)

   a. Some people believe this, but it is not advocated by life-span developmentalists.

   b. Just the opposite is true.

   c. Although some of the elderly are among the richest, most are in the middle-income bracket.

8. **d.** is the answer. (textbook, p. 645)

9. **c.** is the answer. (textbook, p. 637)

   a. Such studies have found that genetic influences do not weaken with age.

   b. This research provides support for self theories rather than disengagement theory.

10. **a.** is the answer. (textbook, p. 636)

    b. Accommodating people adapt to new experiences (such as failing vision) by changing their self-concept.

    c. People who selectively optimize are more realistic in assessing their abilities than Eileen evidently is.

    d. There is no sign that Eileen is disengaging, or withdrawing from her social relationships.

11. **d.** is the answer. (textbook, p. 640)

12. **b.** is the answer. (textbook, p. 636)

    a. This is the idea that the elderly withdraw from society as they get older.

    c. This is the theory that each person's life is a self-propelled process occurring within ever-changing social contexts.

    d. According to this theory, the oldest generation is segregated from the rest of society.

13. **d.** is the answer. Contrary to earlier views that retirement was not a happy time, researchers now know that the elderly are generally happy and productive, spending their time in various activities. (textbook, pp. 645–647)

14. **d.** is the answer. Each of the other theories can be categorized as a stratification theory. (ptextbook, p. 643)

15. **d.** is the answer. (textbook, pp. 654–655)

16. **a.** is the answer. (textbook, p. 651)

    b. & c. In fact, just the opposite is true.

17. **a.** is the answer. (textbook, p. 649)

18. **c.** is the answer. (textbook, p. 652)

19. **d.** is the answer. (textbook, p. 643)

    a. This expresses continuity theory.

    b. This expresses self theory.

    c. This expresses stratification theory.

20. **c.** is the answer. (textbook, p. 639)

    a. This is the central idea behind disengagement theory.

    b., & d. These ideas are expressions of activity theory.

21. **b.** is the answer. (textbook, p. 643)

    a. & d. This finding does not bear directly on either theory of late adulthood.

    c. Selective optimization is an example of *successful* coping with the losses of late adulthood, which would seem to run counter to feelings of social isolation.

22. **d.** is the answer. (textbook, p. 656)

23. **c.** is the answer. Many nations spend substantial money on services for the elderly. (textbook, p. 657)

    a. As more people reach old age, the absolute numbers of frail individuals will increase.

    b. Such research neglects the study of diseases that are nonfatal, yet disabling.

    d. Services are relatively scarce in rural areas, where a large number of elderly people reside.

Death and Dying

ORIENTATION

The final lesson of *Seasons of Life* is concerned with death and dying. Depending on a person's age, experiences, beliefs, and historical and cultural context, death can have many different meanings. The Epilogue of *The Developing Person Through the Life Span*, 6/e, begins by focusing on how dying patients and their families plan for death and with the controversial issue of whether and when we should hasten the death of a loved one. The section also discusses hospice and other forms of palliative care designed to help the terminally ill patient to die "a good death."

The next section explores the reactions that death prompts, noting that perceptions of death vary markedly according to their historical and cultural context. Although the concept of an unvarying sequence of stages among the dying is not universally accepted, the pioneering work of Elisabeth Kübler-Ross was instrumental in revealing the emotional gamut experienced by terminally ill patients and the importance of honest communication.

The final section deals with changing expressions of bereavement and how people surviving the death of a loved one can be aided in the process of recovery.

Audio program 26, "Of Seasons and Survivors," examines how the ending of one person's life affects the continuing stories of the family members who survive. Through the stories of two very different deaths, the listener discovers that losing a loved one "in season," at the end of a long life, has a very different impact from losing a loved one "out of season," in the prime of life. Expert commentary is provided by psychologist Camille Wortman, who has studied the grieving process extensively.

As the program opens, we hear the voice of a father describing the tragic death of his 30-year-old son.

LESSON GOALS

By the end of this lesson you should be prepared to:

1. Explain the concept of palliative care, focusing on the advantages and disadvantages of hospices.

2. Discuss the steps that patients, family members, and medical personnel can take to plan for a swift, pain-free, and dignified death.

3. Identify Kübler-Ross's stages of dying, and discuss these stages in light of more recent research.

4. Describe cultural and religious variations in how death is viewed and changes in the mourning process.

5. Contrast the impact of an "in-season" death and an "out-of-season" death on surviving family members.

Audio Assignment

Listen to the audio tape that accompanies Lesson 26: "Of Seasons and Survivors."

Write your answers to the following questions. You may replay portions of the program if you need to refresh your memory. Answer guidelines may be found in the Lesson Guidelines section at the end of this chapter.

1. Identify two misunderstandings the general public has about the grieving process.

2. Describe two ways in which well-intentioned persons are often not helpful to those who are grieving.

3. Explain how people *can* be helpful to those who have lost a loved one and identify another factor that facilitates the recovery process.

4. Contrast the impact of "in-season" and "out-of-season" deaths on surviving family members.

3. A major factor in our understanding of the psychological needs of the dying was the pioneering work of _____ .

4. In recent years, physicians have become _____ (more/less) accepting of death, especially when the _____ _____ is gone.

5. The institution called the _____ provides care to terminally ill patients. The first modern institution of this type was opened in London by _____ .

6. Insurance companies typically will not pay for hospice care unless the person is expected to die within _____ (how many?) months.

7. Most hospices _____ (will/will not) serve children.

State several criticisms of hospice care.

Textbook Assignment

Read the Epilogue: "Death and Dying," pages Ep-1–Ep-16 in *The Developing Person Through the Life Span*, 6/e, then work through the material that follows to review it. Complete the sentences and answer the questions. As you proceed, evaluate your performance for each section by consulting the answers on page 345. Do not continue with the next section until you understand each answer. If you need to, review or reread the appropriate section in the textbook before continuing.

1. Customs and rituals related to dying, death, and bereavement function to bring

_____ , _____ , and

then _____ . Some developmentalists are concerned about the cultural loss of these rituals due to increasing _____ .

Deciding How to Die (pp. Ep-1–Ep-7)

2. Over most of human history, dying was accepted as a _____ . By the end of the twentieth century, however, death became less of an _____ event.

8. Medical care that is designed not to treat an illness but to relieve pain and suffering is called

_____ _____ .

9. The least tolerable physical symptom of fatal illness is _____ . Physicians once worried about causing _____ if pain relievers such as _____ were given too freely, but they increasingly realize that pain destroys _____ and _____ faster than almost any infection. Pain medication for dying patients may have the _____ _____ of reducing pain while _____ _____ .

10. All competent individuals _____ (have the legal right/do not necessarily have the legal right) to control decisions related to life-prolonging treatments, including _____ _____ , in which a seriously ill

person is allowed to die naturally, and
_____ _____ , in
which someone intentionally acts to terminate the
life of a suffering person. Usually, if a patient
prefers to die naturally, the order_____
is placed on that person's hospital chart.

11. Some people make a _____
_____ to indicate what medical
intervention they want if they become incapable
of expressing those wishes. To avoid complications, each person should also designate a

_____ _____

_____ , someone who can make
decisions for them if needed.

12. Proxies _____ (do/do not) guaran-
tee a problem-free death. One problem is that
_____ members may disagree with
the proxy; another is that proxy directives may be
_____ by hospital staff.

13. Active euthanasia is _____
(legal/illegal) in most parts of the world. In

_____-_____

_____ , a doctor provides the means
for someone to end his or her own life. In

_____ _____ , a
patient asks someone else to cause his or her
death.

14. In the United States, the state of _____
has allowed physician-assisted suicide since 1998
but under very strict guidelines. Since that time,
concerns that physician-assisted suicide might be
used more often with minorities, the poor, and
the disabled _____ (have/have not)
been proven to be well-founded.

Preparing for Death (pp. Ep-7–Ep-12)

15. The study of death is called _____ .

16. Kübler-Ross's research led her to propose that the
dying go through _____ (how
many?) emotional stages. In order, the stages of
dying are _____ , _____ ,
_____ , _____ , and
_____ .

17. Other researchers typically _____
(have/have not) found the same five stages of
dying occurring in sequence.

18. A "good death" is one that is _____ ,
_____ , and _____ and
that occurs at _____ , surrounded by
_____ . Because of modern medical
techniques, a swift and peaceful death is
_____ (more/less) difficult to ensure
today than in the past.

19. Through the study of death we have learned that
perceptions of death are _____
(variable/the same) in all cultures.

20. In most _____ traditions, elders
take on an important new status through death.

21. In many _____ nations, death
affirms religious faith and caring for the dying is
a holy reminder of mortality.

22. Among Buddhists, disease and death are
inevitable sufferings, which may bring
_____ . Among _____ ,
helping the dying to relinquish their ties to this
world and prepare for the next is considered an
obligation for the immediate family.

23. Preparations for death are not emphasized in the
_____ tradition because hope for
_____ should never be
extinguished.

24. Many _____ believe that death is
the beginning of eternity in _____
or _____ ; thus, they welcome or
fear it.

25. Two themes that emerge in religious and cultural
variations of death practices are

a. _____

b. _____

Coping with Bereavement (pp. Ep-12–Ep-16)

26. The sense of loss following a death is called
_____ . An individual's emotional
response to this sense of loss is called
_____ .

27. The ceremonies and behaviors that comprise the public response to a death are called _____ . These ceremonies are designed by _____ to channel _____ toward _____ of life.

28. A crucial factor in mourning is people's search for _____ in death. This is typically more difficult for deaths that are _____ or _____ .

29. In recent times, mourning has become more _____ , less _____ , and less _____ . Younger generations are likely to prefer _____ _____ , while older generations prefer _____ _____ . One result of these trends is that those who have lost a loved one are more likely to experience _____ _____ and _____ _____ than in the past.

30. The practice of excluding unmarried partners, ex-spouses, and other people from mourning may create "_____ _____ ."

31. List two steps that others can follow to help a bereaved person.

    a. _____

    b. _____

32. One thing that may be more harmful than helpful to a bereaved person is _____ _____ .

33. A frequent theme of those who work with the bereaved is the value of a(n) _____ _____ .

Testing Yourself

After you have completed the audio and text review questions, see how well you do on the following quiz. Correct answers, with text and audio references, may be found at the end of this chapter.

1. In her research with grieving families, Professor Wortman has found that:
    a. most people lose their attachment to the lost loved one within a year of the death.
    b. people often remain attached to a lost loved one for many years.
    c. people who remain attached to a lost loved one need professional counseling.
    d. women are better than men at adjusting to the loss of a loved one.

2. Which of the following statements would probably be the *most* helpful to a grieving person?
    a. "It must have been his or her time to die."
    b. "Why don't you get out more and get back into the swing of things?"
    c. "It must have been God's will that he or she was taken from you."
    d. "If you need someone to talk to, call me at any time."

3. Professor Wortman found that the single *most* helpful element in a person's recovery from the loss of a loved one was:
    a. the person getting back to his or her normal routine.
    b. the person's religious faith.
    c. having an understanding relative.
    d. having a friend who has experienced a similar loss.

4. Which of the following is true concerning the timing of death?
    a. Today, death is more likely than ever to come in any season of life.
    b. Today, death is more likely to come at the end of a long life.
    c. The timing of death has not changed significantly over the course of human history.
    d. Death is less predictable today than ever before.

5. In helping a person cope with the loss of a loved one, it is *not* a good idea to:
    a. rush the person through his or her grief.
    b. provide a philosophical perspective on death.
    c. encourage the person to forget and get on with life.
    d. do any of the above.

6. Passive euthanasia is most accurately described as:
   a. care designed to relieve pain and suffering.
   b. a situation in which treatment relieves pain while at the same time hastening death.
   c. a situation in which a person is allowed to die naturally.
   d. a situation in which someone takes action to bring about another person's death.

7. Medical advances have meant that death today is more often:
   a. far less painful for the dying individual.
   b. emotionally far less painful for the bereaved.
   c. a solitary, lengthy, and painful experience.
   d. predictable, and therefore a less traumatic experience.

8. Kübler-Ross's stages of dying are, in order:
   a. anger, denial, bargaining, depression, acceptance.
   b. depression, anger, denial, bargaining, acceptance.
   c. denial, anger, bargaining, depression, acceptance.
   d. bargaining, denial, anger, acceptance, depression.

9. A health care proxy is most accurately described as a(n):
   a document that indicates what medical intervention an individual wants if he or she becomes incapable of expressing those wishes.
   b. person chosen by another person to make medical decisions if the second person becomes unable to do so.
   c. situation in which, at a patient's request, someone else ends his or her life.
   d. indication on a patient's chart not to use heroic life-saving measures.

10. Most adults hope that they will die:
    a. with little pain.
    b. with dignity.
    c. swiftly.
    d. in all of the above ways.

11. Living wills are an attempt to:
    a. make sure that passive euthanasia will not be used in individual cases.
    b. specify the extent of medical treatment desired in the event of terminal illness.
    c. specify conditions for the use of active euthanasia.
    d. ensure that death will occur at home rather than in a hospital.

12. *Hospice* is best defined as:
    a. a document that indicates what kind of medical intervention a terminally ill person wants.
    b. mercifully allowing a person to die by not doing something that might extend life.
    c. an alternative to hospital care for the terminally ill.
    d. providing a person with the means to end his or her life.

13. Palliative care refers to:
    a. heroic measures to save a life.
    b. conservative medical care to treat an illness.
    c. efforts to relieve pain and suffering.
    d. allowing a terminally ill patient to die naturally.

14. A situation in which, at a patient's request, another person acts to terminate his or her life is called:
    a. involuntary euthanasia.
    b. voluntary euthanasia.
    c. a physician-assisted suicide.
    d. DNR.

15. Which of the following is a normal response in the bereavement process?
    a. experiencing powerful emotions
    b. culturally diverse emotions
    c. a lengthy period of grief
    d. All of the above are normal responses.

16. A double effect in medicine refers to a situation in which:
    a. the effects of one drug on a patient interact with those of another drug.
    b. medication relieves pain and has a secondary effect of hastening death.
    c. family members disagree with a terminally ill patient's proxy.
    d. medical personnel ignore the wishes of a terminally ill patient and his or her proxy.

17. Criticisms made against hospices include all of the following *except*:
    a. the number of patients served is limited.
    b. in some cases a life is being ended that might have been prolonged.
    c. burnout and the rapid growth of hospices might limit the number of competent hospice workers.
    d. the patient is needlessly isolated from family and friends.

18. Younger generations tend to prefer _____ and older generations tend to prefer _____ .
    a. burial after a traditional funeral; burial after a traditional funeral
    b. a small memorial service after cremation; a small memorial service after cremation
    c. burial after a traditional funeral; a small memorial service after cremation
    d. a small memorial service after cremation; burial after a traditional funeral

19. Ritual is to emotion as:
    a. grief is to mourning.
    b. mourning is to grief.
    c. affirmation is to loss.
    d. loss is to affirmation.

20. Healing after the death of a loved one is most difficult when:
    a. the death is a long, protracted one.
    b. the bereaved is not allowed to mourn in the way or she wishes.
    c. a period of grief has already elapsed.
    d. there are no other mourners.

NAME _____   INSTRUCTOR _____

LESSON 26: COPING WITH DEATH AND DYING

Exercise

A central theme of this lesson is that death has many meanings, depending on a person's age, experience, beliefs, and his or her historical and cultural context. A number of issues are discussed, including our culture's tendency to institutionalize and deny death, the decline of "good deaths" as medical technology has provided new ways of prolonging life, developmental shifts in the way people view death, **euthanasia, assisted suicide**, and the pros and cons of the **hospice** as an alternative to hospitals for those who are dying.

To stimulate your thinking about these issues, complete the following questions. If you would like to ask these questions of someone other than yourself, feel free to do so. If you need more space for the answers, you may use additional sheets of paper. Hand the completed exercise in to your instructor.

1. What kind of ceremony or mourning ritual would you like to have when you die? What are your reasons for that choice?

2. What would you want to do if you had just six months to live?

3. A very close friend is in the hospital with a terminal illness, but no one has told her anything about the illness and the doctors are cheerily reassuring her she is going to get better. Your friend asks you if she is dying. What would you say?

4. How would you explain the death of a grandparent to a 7-year-old child? (Be aware of a 7-year-old's understanding of death.)

5. Your 40-year-old friend has recently been widowed. List three things you should *not* say or do to her, and explain why.

6. Knowing that you have a terminal illness, would you prefer to be kept alive by artificial means for as long as possible or to be allowed to die in a hospice?

LESSON GUIDELINES

Audio Question Guidelines

1. In her research on the process of grieving, Professor Camille Wortman has found that the general public has many misconceptions about grief. One is the belief that those who are bereaved are eventually able to break their attachment to the lost loved one. In reality, it is very common for the bereaved to remain attached to the loved one for a long time.

   Another misunderstanding is that after a year or two those who have lost a loved one will recover and get back to their normal routine. Professor Wortman has found that the vast majority of people who have lost a loved one experience permanent changes in their lives as a result.

2. Well-intentioned people often attempt to relate to people who are grieving in ways that are not helpful. For example, it is usually not helpful to provide a philosophical perspective on the event, such as the comment, "Well, it was her time to die."

   In addition, it is not helpful to try to hurry people through their grief by encouraging them to "get back into the swing of things."

3. Professor Wortman suggests that bereaved persons are comforted by social support, such as a friend who listens, sympathizes, and does not ignore the real pain and complicated emotions that accompany **mourning**.

   Those who would comfort the bereaved should also realize that bereavement is likely to be a demanding process that may last for months or even years.

   Professor Wortman found that recovery from the loss of a loved one was facilitated by some form of religious faith.

4. Every life, short or long, leaves a legacy and lasting effect on surviving family members. The impact of losing a loved one in the prime of his or her life is different from that of losing a loved one at the end of a long life. The sudden death of a person who is not "supposed" to die, such as the young man in the audio program, is usually the most difficult to bear. Surviving members of the family are often tormented by conflicting emotions of guilt, denial, anger, and sorrow.

   Death is somewhat easier to cope with when it is expected. Losing someone unexpectedly does not allow family members to come together with the dying person and share their affection for one another. Having time to anticipate and prepare for the death does not necessarily reduce the pain of loss, but it can reduce the conflicting emotions associated with it.

Textbook Question Answers

1. acceptance; hope; reaffirmation; globalization
2. part of life; everyday
3. Elisabeth Kübler-Ross
4. more; quality of life
5. hospice; Cecily Saunders
6. six
7. will not

   The fact that hospice patients must be diagnosed as terminally ill and give up all hope of recovery severely limits the number of participants. Patients and their families must accept this diagnosis, agreeing that life or a cure is virtually impossible. Also, hospice care is expensive and therefore not available to everyone. Finally, hospices were typically designed to meet the needs of adults with terminal cancer, not for older patients with combinations of illnesses that are not necessarily fatal.

8. palliative care
9. pain; addiction; morphine; health; vitality; double effect; speeding up death
10. have the legal right; passive euthanasia; active euthanasia; DNR (do not resuscitate)
11. living will; health care proxy
12. do not; family; ignored
13. illegal; physician-assisted suicide; voluntary euthanasia
14. Oregon; have not
15. thanatology
16. five; denial; anger; bargaining; depression; acceptance
17. have not
18. swift; painless; dignified; home; friends and family; more
19. variable
20. African
21. Muslim
22. enlightenment; Hindus
23. Jewish; life
24. Christians; heaven; hell
25. **a.** Religious and spiritual concerns often reemerge at death.

    b. Returning to one's roots is common for dying people.

26. bereavement; grief

27. mourning; cultures; grief; reaffirmation

28. meaning; unexpected; violent

29. private; emotional; religious; small memorial services after cremation; burial after a traditional funeral; social isolation; physical illness

30. disenfranchised grief

31. **a.** Be aware that powerful, complicated, and culturally diverse emotions are likely.

   b. Understand that bereavement is often a lengthy process.

32. expecting certain reactions from that person

33. intimate, caring relationship

Answers to Testing Yourself

1. **b.** is the answer. It is a common misconception that the bereaved are eventually able to break their attachments to loved ones who have died. (audio program)

2. **d.** is the answer. Professor Wortman's research has consistently found that the social support of a friend who is available to listen is an important aspect of the recovery process. (audio program)

3. **b.** is the answer. Having "c" an understanding relative and/or "d" a friend who has experienced a similar loss are/is also helpful to recovery, but religious faith seems to be the most beneficial of all. (audio program)

4. **b.** is the answer. Death is more likely to come "in season" today as a result of improved health practices and control of disease. (audio program)

5. **d.** is the answer. Altering the natural process of grieving by "a" rushing it, "b" attempting to rationalize it, or "c" denying it can have a crippling effect on the bereaved. (audio program)

6. **c.** is the answer. (textbook, p. Ep-4)

   a. This describes palliative care.

   b. This is the "double effect" that sometimes occur with morphine and other opiate drugs.

   d. This is active euthanasia.

7. **c.** is the answer. (textbook, p. Ep-8)

8. **c.** is the answer. (textbook, p. Ep-7)

9. **b.** is the answer. (textbook, p. Ep-4)

   a. This is a living will.

   c. This is voluntary euthanasia.

   d. This refers to "DNR."

10. **d.** is the answer. (textbook, p. Ep-8)

11. **b.** is the answer. (textbook, p. Ep-4)

12. **c.** is the answer. (textbook, p. Ep-2)

   a. This is a living will.

   b. & d. These are forms of euthanasia.

13. **c.** is the answer. (textbook, p. Ep-3)

14. **b.** is the answer. (textbook, p. Ep-5)

   a. There is no such thing as involuntary euthanasia.

   c. In this situation, a doctor provides the means for a *patient* to end his or her own life.

   d. DNR, or *do not resuscitate*, refers to a situation in which medical personnel allow a terminally ill person who has experienced severe pain to die naturally.

15. **d.** is the answer. (textbook, pp. Ep12–Ep-13)

16. **b.** is the answer. (textbook, p. Ep-3)

17. **d.** is the answer. A central feature of hospices is that the dying are *not* isolated from loved ones, as they might be in a hospital. (textbook, p. Ep-2)

18. **d.** is the answer. (textbook, p. Ep-14)

19. **b.** is the answer. Mourning refers to the ceremonies and rituals that a religion or culture prescribes for bereaved people, and grief refers to an individual's emotional response to bereavement. (textbook, p. Ep-12)

20. **b.** is the answer. (textbook, p. Ep-14)

   a. & c. In such situations, death is expected and generally easier to bear.

   d. This issue was not discussed.

The Television Term Project

The five television programs of *Seasons of Life*, hosted by David Hartman, present the stories of people at all stages of life. The programs may be viewed any time during the semester and perhaps more than once. After you watch each one, respond to the questions designated. These questions will help you integrate the television programs with other aspects of the course.

If possible, watch the television programs with other people—students in the course, family, or friends. Feel free to discuss the questions with them. Then write your own answers.

In some cases you will have to choose between questions for "younger" and "older" students. No matter what your age, pick the question better suited to you. Once you have answered all twenty-five questions, send the entire set of answers to your instructor.

PROGRAM ONE: INFANCY AND EARLY CHILDHOOD
(Conception to Age 6)

Program One follows the biological, social, and psychological clocks through the first six years of life. It explores the development of attachment, autonomy, gender identity, autobiographical memory, and the sense of self. In addition, it addresses the controversial issues of day care and expert "advice" on how to raise children. The program also discusses the dramatic changes that have occurred in the seasons of life, and introduces some of the families and experts who will appear throughout the series.

STORIES

- The Kennedy family of Butler, Pennsylvania, takes great pride in the 50 years and four generations they have worked the family dairy farm. At the head of the family are Martha, 72, and Francis, 69. Grandson Jeffrey and his wife Janice, both 22, have just become the proud parents of the newest Kennedy, Justin, whose birth brings back memories for each member of the family. Martha and Francis remember the birth of Jim, Justin's grandfather, and ponder how different the world will be for Justin as he grows up. Jim and wife Rita, both 45, wonder if Jeffrey and Janice are too young to be having a baby. Says Rita, "When I see people today with babies, I think, 'Oh boy! Are they young!' But we were at that stage one time too. I have to remember that."

- A day-care center in Pittsburgh is the setting for several vignettes about the effects of multiple caregivers on children. One such child is 5-week-old Grant Templin, whose mother Diane is returning to her full-time job. "It's very difficult for me as a new mother to leave such a little baby," she worries, "even though I know I'm leaving him in very competent hands."

- Meredith Wilson, at age 2, is racing into early childhood, the period when toddlers begin to establish independence and develop a sense of self. As Meredith struggles to draw a line—sometimes a battle line—between herself and others, mother Patty sighs, "It's hard to keep up with her." But keep up with her she does, for each time Meredith claims her independence she also wants to return to Mom and reestablish the bond of basic trust that was the legacy of her infancy.

- Gilberto Agosto, at age 3, is old enough to have his own cubbyhole at the day-care center he attends in East Harlem, New York. Although he and his friends are only beginning to understand the differences between boys and girls, already they prefer to play with others of the same sex. One of the things Gilberto shares with boys his own age is a biological tendency to be more aggressive than girls.

- James McManus, at age 4, not only knows that he's a boy and acts like one, but he also is forming autobiographical memories that will both shape and reflect his self-identity. When he's an adult, perhaps his first memory of life will be of running faster than the wind as he plays a game of ghost with his mother.

- At an art class in Boston, children eagerly paint pictures depicting themselves, their families, and important events, such as the loss of a pet. According to art educator Nancy Smith, a child's drawings are "the roots of it all—the first emergings of a great enormous tree" that is the child's sense of self.

- It's the first day of school for 6-year-old Jamillah Johnson, who lives with her grandmother in the Boston suburb of Roxbury, Massachusetts. At the end of early childhood, Jamillah is about to take a big step into the world of teachers, classmates, and formal education. Walking to the school, Jamillah's grandmother offers her granddaughter some loving admonitions.

   Now answer questions 1–4, pages 353–354.

PROGRAM TWO: CHILDHOOD AND ADOLESCENCE (Ages 6–20)

Program Two presents the stories of nine young people who spell out different versions of growth and development during a sometimes tumultuous season. The biological clock slows growth in childhood, giving humans a latent period in which to learn the skills and information critical to their culture. According to the social clock, this is the time to go to school, to work at acquiring a sense of industry, and to develop feelings of being useful and competent. At the close of childhood, the biological clock again ticks loudly, bringing on adolescence and what probably is the most challenging and complicated season of life. By the time they reach early adulthood, adolescents have formed a fragile sense of who they are and have taken up authorship of their life stories.

STORIES

- Six-year-old Jamillah Johnson carries a pink backpack and a serious expression to her first day at kindergarten in her neighborhood elementary school. Her grandmother is holding her hand now, but schoolteachers are about to exert a very significant influence on her cognitive and social development. In class the teacher reminds Jamillah and her classmates: "Raise your hand. Stand straight. Stand still and quiet. Stand right behind the person in front of you." On the playground Jamillah makes overtures to a potential

friend. Her grandmother's words to her ring true: "You're going to be on your own. Everything you learn now is important to you."

- Nine-year-old Karl Haglund learns to love his handicapped brother Gerry. Describing her sons' sometimes argumentative relationship, the boys' mother comments, "We tried to explain to Karl that at times he has to be more understanding of Gerry's special needs. That can be frustrating for a nine-year-old to understand. Yet, when push comes to shove, Karl wants to be where Gerry is." Karl has a reading problem, but is nevertheless developing a sense of industry.

- Eleven-year-old Jason Kennedy does his part on the family farm—raising calves, doing chores, and working in the field. "Our kids are not smart 'street-wise' like kids in town," says his father Jim, "but you tell a farm kid to do anything and he'll give it a shot." Jason loves to show animals. Though he has lost his share of competitions, he revels in first-place ribbons and his father's pride.

- Twelve-year-old Candy Reed finds her way amid the social stresses of junior high school. Her grandfather, who helps his single-parent daughter raise Candy, says fondly, "She wants to feel she's a big girl, but we don't feel she's quite big enough yet." Her mother worries that some day discipline may alienate her daughter. "You can't be too permissive," she says, "you can't always just be a teenager's friend."

- Fifteen-year-old Kim Henderson must be responsible for her 18-month-old Angela at the same time she works to finish high school herself. Although her mother and sister care for the toddler during the day, Kim's after-school time is spent with her daughter. Kim is trying hard to be the best mom she can be—a blend of her own mother and grandmother—but she wants her daughter's experiences to be different from her own. "I hope Angela doesn't turn out like me," she says, "I don't want her to have a baby the same time I did. It could ruin her life."

- Seventeen-year-old Nuket Curran may be the most rebellious of the program's protagonists. Through her choices of music, clothing, and hair, she tries to distance herself from the crowd in her urban Pittsburgh high school. A talented artist, she has filled an autobiographical canvas with starkly drawn symbols of her emotions. Despite her rebelliousness, Nuket has some sound advice for adults, reminding them that, "Being a teenager is not easy. We're growing up and should be allowed to make stupid mistakes from time to time—to a point!"

- Eighteen-year-old Michael Shelton clashes with his stepfather over the family car. Unrepentant about his speeding, he jokes that his next investment will be a radar detector. Michael, who is about to enter a college program in commercial art, discusses his complex feelings about his biological parents and stepparents. Michael wants the girls he dates to be good looking. Although his dating habits have been tempered by the threat of AIDS, "Nobody in his right mind would go with a girl only for her personality and mind," he says.

- Eighteen-year-old Trey Edmundson gets ready for the senior prom. Although his mother died when he was 12, he has had a loving aunt and uncle looking out for him. "Thank God we went through that period quickly," says his uncle, Reverend Charles Stith, of Trey's adolescence. "At times," Trey admits, "teens want to be treated as adults; other times they want to do things kids would do."

- Seventeen-year-old Heather Robinson finds time to give love and attention to young children and an elderly woman. She volunteers at the local library, reading stories to preschoolers. And for three years she has enjoyed a very special relationship with Ida Rhine, an elderly, blind, retired musician she calls her advisor, confessor, and confidante. Soon Heather will be going away to college, where she has been accepted into a prestigious writing program. What has helped her, she says, "is just knowing that I've actually done something for somebody and not always feeling like there's so much out there that's wrong and that there's nothing I can do."

Now answer questions 5–8, pages 355–356.

PROGRAM THREE: EARLY ADULTHOOD (Ages 20–40)

Program Three of *Seasons of Life* explores development during early adulthood by telling the stories of young people at different ages and of different statuses. As children and teenagers, we impatiently await the "rites of passage" that officially signal our entry into this season. But for young adults today, the vast array of lifestyle choices may be intimidating as well as exciting. The social clock ticks very loudly for people in their 20s and makes enormous demands all at once. The messages are urgent: Get a job. Find a mate. Start a family. In early adulthood we form a dream of the future and try to make that dream a reality.

STORIES

- It's an important day in the life of Justin Miller, age 21. On the threshold of early adulthood, he prepares to graduate from Carnegie-Mellon University with a degree in artistic design and hopes for a promising career. "My biggest fear is that I won't be successful," he worries. "You can easily get stagnant in some place and not move anywhere. That would be the worst that could happen to me." Like many college graduates today, Justin is putting his personal life on hold until his career is successfully launched. Still, he admits to thinking a lot about having a family, especially at the end of the day when he returns to his empty apartment.

- May-Ling Agosto's life, at age 21, has never been easy. Raised by her mother in New York City's Spanish Harlem, May-Ling married at 15 and now has a 3-year-old son. She is separated from her husband. "We're very strong pigheaded women in our family," she smiles. "If a husband is not going to do anything for you, what do you need him for?" May-Ling has fought her way back from cocaine addiction and looks ahead with excitement. She is training as a computer technician and has just moved into a one-bedroom, subsidized apartment in the Bronx after a three-year wait. "Now it's just up to me," she vows.

- Anthony and Julianne Cugini, 28 and 23, belonged to the same Catholic church all their lives before they met at a youth organization event. Religion and family are strong supports for them. The Cuginis have been married one year and have a baby girl. "My dreams aren't far-fetched at all," Julianne says. "I want to have a marriage that works." Her husband agrees, "I'm as happy as I've ever been in my life," he confides.

- Donna Radocaj, 31, feels her dreams have been shattered. Divorce has left her struggling to cope with her two small children; in contrast to her comfortable married life, she now suffers through days with "no food and no money." Resolve and bitterness come together for Donna at this point in her life: "I thought by now I'd have my house in the country," she reflects. "I'm settling for second best."

- Phillip and Patti Wilson, both 30, were married 9 years before their daughter Meredith was born. They admit that marriage and parenting have revamped earlier dreams. "When I was 20," Patti says, "I never thought I'd be in Pennsylvania. I never thought I'd be married. I *never* thought I'd have kids." Phillip confesses that he had a TV image of what a husband was. "When the husbands came home the wives were relaxed." Despite the fact that their marriage has had its ups and downs, Patti speaks poetically about their baby: "I feel like I found something that I had before, but I just didn't know it. Like a new room in the house. You've passed the door so many times, but you never bothered to open it. Then I opened it, and it's the best room in the house."

- Thirty-one-year-old Bronwyn Reed was an unwed mother at 19. Now she supports her daughter Candy with a job she enjoys, but is not committed to. She is a physical therapist at a local hospital. "I don't have a career I can be proud of," she says in disappointment, "but when you have a job you don't want to do, you have to seek fulfillment in other ways." For Bronwyn that is music; she is an accomplished vocalist. Bronwyn feels ambiguous about her status as a single mother. "Sometimes I'm glad I'm not married," she says, "and sometimes I'd give an arm and a leg to have somebody else to talk to."

- Free-lance writer David Nimmons and union organizer David Fleischer are an openly gay couple in their early 30s. Like many adults his age, Nimmons was ready to settle down when he and Fleischer met. "People I know who are in couples are really working at something that seems like a good and valiant challenge," he says. "How lucky I am to have found this, because it fits so well for me."

- The idea that she may never marry and have children is a painful one for Christine Osborne, 39. While she is a very successful Chicago ad executive, personally she longs for a family. "I feel very envious of people who not only have happy marriages, but who have children," she says. Ruefully she notes her grandmother's dying words to her: "You're too picky." "It hasn't happened," she shrugs, tears in her eyes. "Now what?"

- Deborah and Charles Stith, both in their late thirties, would seem to have it all. He is an ordained Methodist minister in Boston. She is a physician and the State Commissioner of Public Health. They have two small children Charles calls "major events," and Deborah jokes about wanting seven more. Yet they too admit to struggling. They also raised Deborah's now-teen-age nephew after her sister died. "There are many points

along the way we could have gotten divorced," Deborah acknowledges. "I'm not going anywhere," says Charles. "I picked the best I'm capable of picking."

Now answer questions 9–12, pages 357–358.

PROGRAM FOUR: MIDDLE ADULTHOOD (Ages 40–60)

Program Four explores development during the fifth and sixth decades of life. Gray hair, wrinkles, and reading glasses are signals from the biological clock that life is half over—that there is more "time lived" than "time left." This is the season in which the biological and social clocks fade in importance and the psychological clock ticks more loudly. For those who have reached positions of expertise and power, middle age will be a time of personal and social command. For others who have experienced great losses—that of a child, of a spouse, or of a job—it will demand new directions. It is a season that ushers in androgyny: Women find new strength and men become more nurturing. Caring for others—what Erikson called generativity—is also emblematic of the middle years, as both sexes provide help to their extended families and the larger "human family," and begin to create a legacy for those who will come after them.

STORIES

- Former Cleveland Browns quarterback Brian Sipe faces the "precipice" of middle age at 37—after a lifetime of sports. "We all wish we were kids a little longer than we were," he says, "but I'll always be proud of what I did." Sipe is anxious to redirect his future. He thinks he might like to be an architect. And although he misses the regimen of professional sports, he's ready to take a next step. "There's nothing stopping me," he declares.

- Born January 1, 1946, Kathleen Wilkins was America's first official "baby boomer" and is now the first of her cohort to reach middle age. Recently separated from her husband, Kathleen has returned to college to study for an MBA while continuing her career in restaurant management. Not afraid of growing older, she says, "At 40, as a 'boomer,' I have more to offer than a 22-year-old. I can bring not only an expertise that I went back and studied for, I can bring life experiences."

- Daniel Cheever, 44, is the president of Wheelock College in Boston. At one time he considered leaving the field of education, but after 10 years as a public school superintendent, "I decided I had paid my dues in one field and that's where I would reap my reward." Cheever and his wife Abby both have professional careers, and Cheever has done most family chores since Abby entered law school more than 10 years ago. Both he and Abby look forward to the challenge of their life together now that their children will be in college.

- Jim Kennedy, 45, is celebrating his 25th wedding anniversary on the family dairy farm Jim's father mortgaged to him two decades ago. Although he and wife Rita once considered going out of business and can remember struggling to find 24 cents to buy a loaf of bread, today they sell 1.25 million pounds of milk a year. Jim has accumulated enough acreage to be able to offer any or all of his five children part of the family business. "The money isn't in farming," he says, "but it's a darned good life."

- The good life is gone for Matt Nort, 52, who lost his job at a Pittsburgh steel mill some time ago. Nort, who does not have a high school education, gets by on part-time work and hopes for a chance. "The dream is gone, probably gone forever," he worries. As he struggles to reconnect his life, he confronts many new feelings, including depression, bewilderment, and even thoughts of suicide. Yet Nort has strong faith, and a loving family. "It's just you and me against the world," his wife says, smiling at him.

- Kris Rosenberg, 55, fought her way back from a crippling bout with polio, a divorce, and perhaps most important, a devastating loss of self-esteem. Today she directs "Returning Women," a training program for older women who want to reenter the work force. "I can be real to them," she explains, noting that she was once as frightened and tentative as her students. Kris and her husband have reunited since her comeback, but they maintain separate lives, checking accounts, and rooms in the house. Having, in effect, turned her losses into gains, Kris notes, "For the first time I feel like an individual person."

- Harriet Lyons, 59, climbed out of despair and totally reconstructed her life after losing everything, including family mementos, when she lost her job. Eventually she found work with the Bank of Boston, and is setting goals for herself once again. Lyons raises her granddaughter Jamillah because her daughter, Jamillah's mother, is addicted to drugs. Despite this sadness, she is excited about the friendships she is strengthening

with her six children and grandchildren, noting, "I guess in a lot of ways I'm coming to where I wanted to be in the first place. I feel good about myself. I've got a lot to offer."

- Dave and Ruth Rylander, 57 and 53, have lived a parent's nightmare. Their daughter Lynn died of leukemia when she was 19. As a result of their love for her and their own longing for meaning in their lives, both Rylanders have taken up careers in social service. Ruth runs peace movement activities for the Presbyterian church and Dave is the director of a local food bank. "I think she'd like what I'm doing today," Dave says. "She was the kind of young woman who cared about people." Ruth speaks eloquently about their lives today: "We've seen tragedies, joys. We have done our apprenticeship. Sometimes I am more cautious, but in many ways I'm less cautious. After all, what do I have to be afraid of?"

Now answer questions 13–16, pages 359–360.

PROGRAM FIVE: LATE ADULTHOOD (Ages 60+)

Late adulthood is a season of great diversity. It is the season upon which the twentieth century, with World Wars I and II, the Great Depression, and a 25-year increase in life expectancy, has had its most telling impact. Late adulthood is one kind of season if you have your health and financial resources; it is quite another if you don't. Some older adults extend the activities of middle age into their 70s. Others take advantage of their newly found leisure to change their lives completely. As the biological clock eventually runs down and the end of life comes into view, individuals work to achieve a sense of integrity. Now the lifelong suspense leaves their story, and they see how it will end. And they wonder: Was it a good story? Was it true to who I was? And are there a few last things I might do to give my life a better ending?

STORIES

- Harry Crimi, 61, has operated the family butcher shop in south Philadelphia for as long as he has been married—40 years. His wife Antoinette, 60, was born in the house they live in now, and her 93-year-old father is still with her. "He deserves the honor and glory of dying at home," she says. Harry and Antoinette dote on their family. Their children and grandchildren visit often. "You don't have time to cater to your children," Harry explains, "but you make time for your grandchildren." Where did the time go? "When you're 20 or 30," Harry shakes his head, "you don't imagine being 61 years old. But now that I'm 61, I wonder where all the years went."

- In Detroit, Tom and Vivian Russell, 61 and 60, are buying a new home in retirement. He has worked 40 years for the post office; she has been a social worker. Tom grew up in an African-American family in the segregated South where he remembers life as a constant struggle. Vivian was also raised in a poor family, one of nine children. They are a remarkably giving couple. Tom meets in Christian fellowship with inmates of a Federal penitentiary and Vivian is training as a hospice volunteer. As Tom says, "I hope we can continue to help people, continue to show our warmness, continue to do it together."

- Seventy-four-year-old Lyman Spitzer will leave an important scientific legacy. NASA will soon put into space a telescope designed by the astronomer/ physicist. Spitzer remains fascinated with knowledge and continues the vigorous physical activities he has enjoyed all his life, not the least of which is mountain climbing. "No one has reproached me for being overly rash at my age," he contends. Spitzer has been married 51 years to Doreen Spitzer, who heads the American School in Greece. After all he and his wife have studied and experienced, life is still a fascinating puzzle. "I can well imagine," Spitzer says, "long after we know all that we need to know about the universe, we may still be trying to understand the nature of life."

- Milton Band, 78, and wife wife Rowena, enjoy the "good life" at a retirement center in Holiday Springs, Florida, where the relaxed atmosphere has afforded them a new intimacy in their marriage. "I feel like I'm 16 years old," Rowena says. "It's a wonderful, unbelievable thing (retirement), all of it, like a dream." Milton, who left his law career nine years ago, celebrates time to himself and an escape from the rat race.

- Francis Kennedy, 70, jokes about a few aches and pains and a forgetful moment or two, but he is still active on the family farm, baling hay and milking cows. "You could sit down, and I could sit down, and we could really cry the blues with each other. That wouldn't do any good," he claims. "We've got to get going. Tomorrow's another day. Be ready for it."

- Ellen Hanes is not as fortunate as her peers in good health. She is one of the frail elderly who requires constant care, and she lives in a private nursing home in Flushing, New York. Thirty-five percent of all sick elderly Americans will spend their life savings in a nursing home before they die. "If I had known I would be like this, I would have made more arrangements for myself. The doctors put me here," she says.

- Miriam Cheifetz lost her husband a year ago. When she found her loneliness unbearable, she moved to a group home in Chicago where she feels more comfortable. The women in the home share facilities, chores, and the stories of their lives. Miriam treasures memories of her husband and frequent visits from her affectionate family: "There's a thread that goes through your whole life, and when you see some of that in your children, you feel that your life was not in vain."

- "I hope I don't lose my upper plate when I blow," is Minna Citron's comment as she blows out the candles on her 90th birthday cake. After a long, unconventional life (her ex-husband once said, "Why can't you be like other people and just stay put?"), Citron enjoys her position as "curator of a career"—her own, as a prominent artist. Mobbed by friends at her birthday party, she is in high spirits: "I love my friends. . . I want to go on enjoying life if I can."

- George Nakashima, 84, chose a life of contemplation and art. Although he began work as a railroad gandy dancer in the Northwest, a career in architecture and design eventually took him to Paris, India, and Japan. During World War II, Nakashima, his wife, and 6-week-old daughter were forced into a detention camp set up by the U.S. government. There he began to train under a fine Japanese carpenter, schooled in the traditional manner. Nakashima came to love working with wood and developed a spiritual affinity for nature. Today he and his son and daughter painstakingly fashion works of art. "I take great pride in being able to take living things that will die, and give them a second life. It is a great feeling to be a part of nature, and to be a part of life itself," he says.

Now answer questions 17–25, pages 361–367.

NAME _____   INSTRUCTOR_____

The Television Term Project

Return pages 353–367 to your instructor.

1. Imagine that you had been born at a different point in history—for example, 100 years ago, or in your parents' generation. Select one setting of the social clock (one "age norm") that was different back then. How might your development have been altered had you lived at that time?

2. Give an example of how the biological, social, and psychological clocks each exert their influence in the first few years of life.

3. What important developments occur during the first year of life? What do the experts say and what is your own personal view?

4. **Younger students** (or those who are not parents): Of all the changes that occur between birth and age 6, which is the most remarkable to you? Why? Do you believe that someone's personality is well set by the time he or she goes to school?

Older students (or parents): Did any of the episodes or experts in this first program provide insight into the development of your own child or children? Explain.

5. Did any of the stories provide insight into your own childhood or adolescence or those of your children? What did you learn about yourself or your children?

6. Which qualities and experiences of the people in the program would you hope to see in any children you might have? Why? Which qualities and experiences would you prefer not to see?

7. What experiences of childhood and adolescence were *not* portrayed in this program? Which of these should have been included?

8. What are some of the losses that occur during childhood and adolescence? What new potentials emerge during this stage of life? In what ways do these losses and gains relate to developmental events specific to childhood?

9. Did any of the stories provide insight into yourself as you are now or when you were a young adult? What did you learn about yourself?

10. **Younger students:** Which qualities and experiences of the people depicted in the program would you like to have during your own early adulthood? Why? Which would you like to avoid?

   Older students: What experiences of early adulthood were *not* portrayed in this program? Which of these should have been included?

11. What are some of the losses that occur during early adulthood? What new potentials emerge?

12. Based on your own experiences, and/or those of the people in the program, in what ways are the events of early adulthood a reflection of the developmental legacies of earlier stages of life? How might the experiences of early adulthood influence later life?

13. **Younger students:** Did any of these stories provide insight into your parents' lives and experiences? Why or why not? Do you see them differently in any way as a result? Explain.

   Older students: Did any of these stories provide insight into your own middle adulthood? Why or why not? Did you learn anything about yourself? Explain.

14. **Younger students:** Which qualities and experiences of these people would you like to have in your middle years? Why? Which would you like to avoid?

   Older students: What experiences of middle adulthood were *not* portrayed in this program? Which of these should have been included?

15. What are some of the losses that occur during middle adulthood? What are the potential gains of this stage?

16. Based on your own experiences and/or those of the people in the program, in what ways are the events of middle adulthood related to the earlier stages of life? How do the events of middle adulthood influence later life?

17. Did any of the stories provide insight into yourself, your parents, or your grandparents? Do you see yourself or your relatives differently as a result?

18. **Younger students:** Which qualities and experiences of the people in the program would you like to have in your later years? Why? Which would you like to avoid?

    Older students: What experiences of late adulthood were *not* portrayed in this program? Which of these should have been included?

19. What are some of the losses that occur during late adulthood? What are the potential gains of this season?

20. Based on your own experiences and/or those of the people in the program, in what ways do the events of late adulthood build on what happened in earlier seasons of life? Can you predict how a life will turn out from the way it began?

SUMMING UP

Your answers to the following questions should draw on the content of the entire *Seasons of Life* series, as well as your own life experiences.

21. Draw a family tree of the Kennedys, including only those members who appear in the television programs. Briefly identify each member of the family tree and describe at least one memorable characteristic about each person.

22. For each of the seasons of life—infancy, childhood, adolescence, early adulthood, middle adulthood, and late adulthood—think of someone in your family or from among your acquaintances. Does each of these people share similarities with one (or more) of the people in the series? Briefly describe similarities (and differences) below.

Infancy

Childhood

Adolescence

Early Adulthood

Middle Adulthood

Late Adulthood

23. Using bar graphs on the lines below, indicate how loudly the biological, social, and psychological clocks are "ticking" during each stage of life. During which stages is each clock most influential? The relative control exerted by the three developmental clocks should be indicated by the height of the bar—the greater the control, the higher the bar. Be sure to label each bar with a B, S, or P. In the example below, during early adulthood the social clock is ticking the loudest, followed by the biological clock, and then the psychological clock.

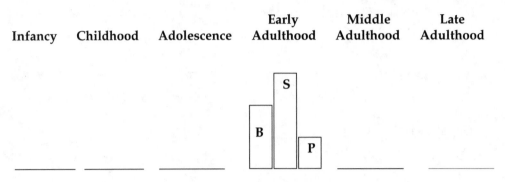

Infancy   Childhood   Adolescence   **Early Adulthood**   **Middle Adulthood**   **Late Adulthood**

Comment on the pattern you see across the life span.

24. One theme of the *Seasons of Life* series is that lives become more diverse as people age. Do you find this increasing diversity to be true, based on your own life experiences? Why or why not? What are some of the reasons life's paths tend to "fan out" as people grow older?

25. Another theme of *Seasons of Life* concerns how the life story evolves as we get older. For each stage—infancy, childhood, adolescence, early adulthood, middle adulthood, and late adulthood—state briefly how well-formed the life story is likely to be and what issues it is likely to address.

Infancy

Childhood

Adolescence

Early Adulthood

Middle Adulthood

Late Adulthood